First World War
and Army of Occupation
War Diary
France, Belgium and Germany

56 DIVISION
Headquarters, Branches and Services
General Staff
1 January 1918 - 30 April 1919

WO95/2935

The Naval & Military Press Ltd
www.nmarchive.com
Published in association with The National Archives

Published by

The Naval & Military Press Ltd

Unit 10 Ridgewood Industrial Park,

Uckfield, East Sussex,

TN22 5QE England

Tel: +44 (0) 1825 749494

www.naval-military-press.com

www.nmarchive.com

This diary has been reprinted in facsimile from the original. Any imperfections are inevitably reproduced and the quality may fall short of modern type and cartographic standards.

© **Crown Copyright**
Images reproduced by permission of The National Archives, London, England, 2015.

Contents

Document type	Place/Title	Date From	Date To
Miscellaneous	A The National Archives		
Heading	56th Division General Staff Jan 1918-May 1919		
Heading	War Diary of General Staff 56th Division From 1st January 1918 To 31st January 1918 Vol 24		
Operation(al) Order(s)	56th Division Order No. 148	03/01/1918	03/01/1918
Miscellaneous	56th Division G.3/810.	07/01/1918	07/01/1918
Miscellaneous	Strategical Move And Reinforcement Schemes, Reserve Division XIII Corps.	07/01/1918	07/01/1918
Miscellaneous	Movement Of 56th Division By Strategical Trains	07/01/1918	07/01/1918
Miscellaneous	Issued With Reference To 56th Division Order No. 148	07/01/1918	07/01/1918
Miscellaneous	Table "D" 1		
Miscellaneous	Table "B" 2		
Miscellaneous	Table "D" 2		
Miscellaneous	Scheme 'B' For the Move of Reserve Division, XIII Corps, by road to Maroeuil-Ecoivres & ACQ areas.	07/01/1918	07/01/1918
Miscellaneous	March Table To Accompany Scheme 'B'		
Miscellaneous	Scheme 'C'	08/01/1918	08/01/1918
Miscellaneous	Scheme "C" Move Of 56th Division By Tactical Trains From Reserve Area To Ecurie	07/01/1918	07/01/1918
Miscellaneous	Composition Of Omnibus Train		
Miscellaneous	Table "B" To Accompany Scheme "C"		
Miscellaneous	56th Division G.3/832	10/01/1918	10/01/1918
Operation(al) Order(s)	56th Division Order No. 147	31/01/1917	31/01/1917
Miscellaneous	Table Of Moves To Accompany 56th Division Order No. 147		
Heading	War Diary Of General Staff 56th Division From 1st February 1918 To 28th February 1918 Vol 25		
War Diary	Villers Chatel	01/02/1918	12/02/1918
War Diary	Victory Camp	12/02/1918	28/02/1918
Miscellaneous	Location Table At 6 A. M.	01/02/1918	01/02/1918
Operation(al) Order(s)	56th Division Order No. 149	03/02/1918	03/02/1918
Miscellaneous	March Table To Accompany 56th Division Order No 149		
Miscellaneous	To Accompany 56th Division Order No. 149	04/02/1918	04/02/1918
Operation(al) Order(s)	56th Division Order No. 149	05/02/1918	05/02/1918
Operation(al) Order(s)	56th Division Order No. 150	06/02/1918	06/02/1918
Map	Maroeuil		
War Diary	Victory Camp Roclincourt	01/01/1918	06/01/1918
War Diary			
War Diary	Villers Chatel	14/01/1918	31/01/1918
Miscellaneous	Location Table		
Heading	War Diary General Staff 56th Division March 1918		
Miscellaneous	Report on the Operations of 56th Division in the Vicinity of Oppy & Gavrelle, 28th & 29th March, 1918	04/04/1918	04/04/1918
Miscellaneous	Appendix XXVI Orders & Instructions issued during the Operations, 28th March, 1918.	28/03/1918	28/03/1918
Miscellaneous	A Form Messages And Signals		
Miscellaneous	Appendix XXVI Orders & Instructions issued during the Operations, 29th March, 1918.	29/03/1918	29/03/1918
Miscellaneous	Priority (sd) B. Pakenham Lt. Col.		

Operation(al) Order(s)	56th Division Order No. 157	29/03/1918	29/03/1918
Operation(al) Order(s)	56th Division Order No. 158	29/03/1918	29/03/1918
Miscellaneous	Location Table To Accompany 56th Div. Order No. 158	29/03/1918	29/03/1918
Map	Maroeuil		
Miscellaneous	App XXX		
War Diary	Victory Camp	01/03/1918	30/03/1918
War Diary	ACQ	30/03/1918	31/03/1918
Miscellaneous	Appendices I To XXX		
Miscellaneous	56th Div Location Table	01/03/1918	01/03/1918
Miscellaneous	XIII Corps-Right Division Re-Organisation on A 2 Brigade Front.	19/03/1918	19/03/1918
Operation(al) Order(s)	59th (London) Division Order No. 151	20/03/1918	20/03/1918
Miscellaneous	Table Of Reliefs To Accompany 56th Division Order No. 151		
Miscellaneous	Addendum No. 1 To 56th (London) Division Order No. 151	21/03/1918	21/03/1918
Miscellaneous	A Form Messages And Signals		
Operation(al) Order(s)	56th Division Warning Order No. 152	22/03/1918	22/03/1918
Miscellaneous	A Form Messages And Signals		
Miscellaneous	167th Infantry Brigade	22/03/1918	22/03/1918
Miscellaneous	O.C. 56th Div. Signals "Q" XIII Corps (for Information)	23/03/1918	23/03/1918
Miscellaneous	Appendix VII 56th Division No. G.3/136	23/03/1918	23/03/1918
Miscellaneous	A Form Messages And Signals		
Operation(al) Order(s)	56th Division Order No. 153	24/03/1918	24/03/1918
Miscellaneous	A Form Messages And Signals		
Miscellaneous	Appendix XIV	25/03/1918	25/03/1918
Miscellaneous	A Form Messages And Signals		
Miscellaneous	Appendix XVII 56th Division G.3/146	25/03/1918	25/03/1918
Miscellaneous	A Form Messages And Signals Appendix XVIII		
Operation(al) Order(s)	56th Division Order No. 154	26/03/1918	26/03/1918
Operation(al) Order(s)	56th Division Warning Order No. 155	27/03/1918	27/03/1918
Operation(al) Order(s)	56th Division Order No. 156	27/03/1918	27/03/1918
Miscellaneous	A Form Messages And Signals Appendix XXII		
Miscellaneous	Appendix XXV		
Miscellaneous	Appendix XXVI Orders & Instructions Issued During The Operations 28th March 1918		
Miscellaneous	Appendix XXVII Orders & Instructions Issued During The Operations 29th March 1918		
Miscellaneous	A Form Messages And Signals App. XXVIII		
Miscellaneous	Appendix XXIX 56th Div. No. G.3/206	30/03/1918	30/03/1918
Miscellaneous	Appendix XXX Map Shewing Boundaries & H.Qs. 56th Division	28/03/1918	28/03/1918
Miscellaneous	168th Inf. Bde. G.93	15/11/1918	15/11/1918
Miscellaneous	Report On The Operations Of 56th Division In The Vicinity Of Oppy & Gavrelle 28th & 29th March, 1918.	04/04/1918	04/04/1918
Heading	War Diary General Staff 56th Division April 1918		
War Diary	ACQ	01/04/1918	07/04/1918
War Diary	Warlus	08/04/1918	30/04/1918
Miscellaneous	56th Division Location Table	01/04/1918	01/04/1918
Map	Boundaries & Headquarters 56th Div		
Miscellaneous	167th Infantry Brigade	02/04/1918	02/04/1918
Miscellaneous	56th Division No. G.3/210	01/04/1918	01/04/1918
Miscellaneous	56th Division "G"	01/04/1918	01/04/1918
Miscellaneous	First Army No.1 1882 (S)	30/03/1918	30/03/1918

Miscellaneous	Appendix II 56th Division G. 3/215	01/04/1918	01/04/1918
Miscellaneous	Appendix III 56th Division No. G.3/217	01/04/1918	01/04/1918
Miscellaneous	Appendix IV 56th Division No. G.3/207.	01/04/1918	01/04/1918
Miscellaneous	A Form Messages And Signals Appendix V		
Miscellaneous	Appendix VI "A" Form Messages And Signals		
Operation(al) Order(s)	56th Division Order No. 159	06/04/1918	06/04/1918
Miscellaneous	March Table To Accompany 56th Division Order No. 159	06/04/1918	06/04/1918
Operation(al) Order(s)	56th Division Order No. 160	06/04/1918	06/04/1918
Miscellaneous	March Table To Accompany 56th Division Order No. 160		
Operation(al) Order(s)	56th Division Order No. 161	11/04/1918	11/04/1918
Operation(al) Order(s)	56th Division Order No. 162	17/04/1918	17/04/1918
Operation(al) Order(s)	56th Division Warning Order No. 163	19/04/1918	19/04/1918
Operation(al) Order(s)	56th Division Order No. 164	22/04/1918	22/04/1918
Operation(al) Order(s)	56th Division Order No. 166	29/04/1918	29/04/1918
Operation(al) Order(s)	56th Division Order No. 165	26/04/1918	26/04/1918
Heading	War Diary Of General Staff 56th Division From 1st May 1918 To 31st May 1918 Vol 28		
War Diary	Warlus	01/05/1918	31/05/1918
Miscellaneous	56th Division Location Table	01/05/1918	01/05/1918
Operation(al) Order(s)	56th Division Order No. 167	01/05/1918	01/05/1918
Operation(al) Order(s)	56th Division Order No. 168	02/05/1918	02/05/1918
Operation(al) Order(s)	56th Division Order No. 169	08/05/1918	08/05/1918
Operation(al) Order(s)	56th Division Order No. 170	18/05/1918	18/05/1918
Operation(al) Order(s)	56th Division Order No. 171	27/05/1918	27/05/1918
Miscellaneous	56th Division Tactical Progress Report No. 52 From 6 am 28th May to 6 am 29th May 1918	29/05/1918	29/05/1918
Heading	War Diary Of General Staff 56th Division. From 1st June 1918 To 30th June 1918 Vol 29		
War Diary	Warlus	01/06/1918	30/06/1918
Miscellaneous	56th Division Location Table	01/06/1918	01/06/1918
Operation(al) Order(s)	56th Division Order No. 172	05/06/1918	05/06/1918
Operation(al) Order(s)	56th Division Order No. 173	11/06/1918	11/06/1918
Miscellaneous	Amendment To 56th Division Order No. 173	12/06/1918	12/06/1918
Miscellaneous	56th Division Instructions No. 1 For Forthcoming Operation By 168th Infantry Brigade	13/06/1918	13/06/1918
Operation(al) Order(s)	56th Division Order No. 174	13/06/1918	13/06/1918
Operation(al) Order(s)	56th Division Order No. 175	15/06/1918	15/06/1918
Operation(al) Order(s)	56th Division Order No. 176	19/06/1918	19/06/1918
Operation(al) Order(s)	56th Division Order No. 177	23/06/1918	23/06/1918
Operation(al) Order(s)	56th Division Order No. 178	27/06/1918	27/06/1918
Miscellaneous	A Form Messages And Signals		
Heading	War Diary Of General Staff 56th Division From July 1st 1918 To July 31st 1918 Vol 30		
War Diary	Warlus	01/07/1918	14/07/1918
War Diary	Roellecourt	15/07/1918	18/07/1918
War Diary	Villers Chatel	19/07/1918	31/07/1918
Miscellaneous	56th Division Location Table at 6 p.m.		
Operation(al) Order(s)	56th Division Order No. 179	01/07/1918	01/07/1918
Operation(al) Order(s)	56th Division Warning Order No. 180	07/07/1918	07/07/1918
Miscellaneous	March Table To Accompany 56th Division Warning Order No. 180		
Operation(al) Order(s)	56th Division Order No. 181	09/07/1918	09/07/1918
Miscellaneous	March Table To Accompany 56th Division Order No. 181		

Miscellaneous	Amendment No. 3 To 56th Division Order No. 181	12/07/1918	12/07/1918
Miscellaneous	A Form Messages And Signals	15/07/1918	15/07/1918
Miscellaneous	A Form Messages And Signals	11/07/1918	11/07/1918
Miscellaneous	Amendment No. 4 To 56th Division Order No. 181	14/07/1918	14/07/1918
Miscellaneous	Amended March Table To Accompany 56th Division Order No. 181		
Operation(al) Order(s)	56th Division Order No. 182	13/07/1918	13/07/1918
Miscellaneous	56th Division Scheme for Moves Whilst in G.H.Q. Reserve	15/07/1918	15/07/1918
Miscellaneous	Embussing Table Reference 1/40000 Map, Sheet 36. B.		
Miscellaneous	Amendment No. 1 To 56th Division Order No. 181	10/07/1918	10/07/1918
Operation(al) Order(s)	56th Division Warning Order No. 183	15/07/1918	15/07/1918
Operation(al) Order(s)	56th Division Order No. 184	17/07/1918	17/07/1918
Miscellaneous	March Table To Accompany 56th Division Order No. 184	18/07/1918	18/07/1918
Operation(al) Order(s)	56th Division Order No. 185	19/07/1918	19/07/1918
Operation(al) Order(s)	56th Division Order No. 186	29/07/1918	29/07/1918
Miscellaneous	Table "A" To Accompany 56th Division Order No. 186	30/07/1918	30/07/1918
Miscellaneous	In Continuation Of 56th Division Order No. 186 Of 29th Inst.	29/07/1918	29/07/1918
Operation(al) Order(s)	56th Division Order No. 187	30/07/1918	30/07/1918
Miscellaneous	Table B. To Accompany 56th Division Order No. 187		
Heading	WO95/2935		
Heading	War Diary General Staff 56th Division August-1918 Vol 31		
War Diary	Villers Chatel	01/08/1918	01/08/1918
War Diary	Warlus	02/08/1918	18/08/1918
War Diary	Le Cauroy	19/08/1918	21/08/1918
Miscellaneous	Report On Operations In VI And XVII Corps		
Miscellaneous	Operations In XVII Corps Operations On 25th August 1918	05/09/1918	05/09/1918
Miscellaneous	56th Division Location Table	01/08/1918	01/08/1918
Operation(al) Order(s)	56th Division Order No. 188	07/08/1918	07/08/1918
Operation(al) Order(s)	56th Division Warning Order No. 189	14/08/1918	14/08/1918
Miscellaneous	Appendix 'A'		
Operation(al) Order(s)	56th Division Order No. 190	15/08/1918	15/08/1918
Miscellaneous	Reference 56th Div. Order No. 190	16/08/1918	16/08/1918
Operation(al) Order(s)	56th Division Order No. 191	19/08/1918	19/08/1918
Map	British Trenches In Red.		
Miscellaneous	Amendment No. 1 To 56th Division Order No. 191	19/08/1918	19/08/1918
Miscellaneous	March Table To Accompany 56th Div, Order No. 192		
Operation(al) Order(s)	56th Division Order No. 192	21/08/1918	21/08/1918
Map	Map		
Operation(al) Order(s)	56th Division Order No. 193	22/08/1918	22/08/1918
Miscellaneous	Addendum No. 1 To 56th Division Order No. 193	22/08/1918	22/08/1918
Miscellaneous	Signal Instructions To Accompany 56th Division Order No. 193	22/08/1918	22/08/1918
Miscellaneous	Urgent Operations Priority	24/08/1918	24/08/1918
Miscellaneous	A Form Messages And Signals	26/08/1918	26/08/1918
Miscellaneous	A Form Messages And Signals	28/08/1918	28/08/1918
Miscellaneous	Messages And Signals	23/08/1918	23/08/1918
Operation(al) Order(s)	56th Division Order No. 195	30/08/1918	30/08/1918
Operation(al) Order(s)	56th Division Order No. 196	31/08/1918	31/08/1918
War Diary	Boileux St. Marc.	01/09/1918	08/09/1918
War Diary	Les Fosses Farm.	09/09/1918	25/09/1918
War Diary	Villers Cagnicourt	26/09/1918	30/09/1918

Miscellaneous	56th Division No. G.A. 145	06/10/1918	06/10/1918
Miscellaneous	Operations Carried Out By 56th Division during Period 27th-29th Sept. Inclusive.	04/10/1918	04/10/1918
Miscellaneous	A Form Messages And Signals	30/09/1918	30/09/1918
Miscellaneous	56th Division Location Table	01/09/1918	01/09/1918
Operation(al) Order(s)	56th Division Warning Order No. 197	04/09/1918	04/09/1918
Operation(al) Order(s)	56th Division Order No. 198	04/09/1918	04/09/1918
Operation(al) Order(s)	56th Division Warning Order No. 199	05/09/1918	05/09/1918
Operation(al) Order(s)	56th Division Order No. 200	05/09/1918	05/09/1918
Miscellaneous	Table "A" To Accompany 56th Division Order No. 200		
Miscellaneous	A Form Messages And Signals	05/09/1918	05/09/1918
Miscellaneous	Amendment No. 1 To 56th Division Order No. 200	06/09/1918	06/09/1918
Operation(al) Order(s)	56th Division Order No. 201	11/09/1918	11/09/1918
Operation(al) Order(s)	56th Division Defence Orders No. 1	11/09/1918	11/09/1918
Map	Defensive Lines 56th Div.		
Miscellaneous	In the case of a hostile attack being foreseen, the order "Man Battle Stations" Will be Sent out from Divisional H.Q., on receipt of Which-		
Miscellaneous	56th Division Provisional Defence Scheme	22/09/1918	22/09/1918
Operation(al) Order(s)	56th Division Order No. 204	18/09/1918	18/09/1918
Operation(al) Order(s)	56th Division Warning Order No. 202	16/09/1918	16/09/1918
Miscellaneous	A Form Messages And Signals	16/09/1918	16/09/1918
Operation(al) Order(s)	56th Division Order No. 203	17/09/1918	17/09/1918
Map	Map A		
Operation(al) Order(s)	56th Division Order No. 205	24/09/1918	24/09/1918
Operation(al) Order(s)	56th Division Order No. 206	24/09/1918	24/09/1918
Operation(al) Order(s)	56th Division Order No. 207	25/09/1918	25/09/1918
Miscellaneous	Addendum To 56th Division Order No. 207	25/09/1918	25/09/1918
Miscellaneous	Instructions No. 1 To Accompany 56th Division Orders Nos. 205,206,207.	25/09/1918	25/09/1918
Miscellaneous	Operations Carried Out By 56th Division During Poriod 27th-29th Sept. Inclusive	04/10/1918	04/10/1918
Miscellaneous	Amendment No. 1 To 56th Division Order No. 206	26/09/1918	26/09/1918
Operation(al) Order(s)	56th Division Order No. 208	29/09/1918	29/09/1918
Map	To Accompany 56th Div. Operation Order No. 205		
Map	Map		
War Diary	Villers Les Cagnicourt	01/10/1918	11/10/1918
War Diary	Villers Cagnicourt	12/10/1918	15/10/1918
War Diary	Etrun	16/10/1918	30/10/1918
War Diary	Basseville	31/10/1918	31/10/1918
Miscellaneous	56th Division Location Table	01/10/1918	01/10/1918
Operation(al) Order(s)	56th Division Order No. 209	01/10/1918	01/10/1918
Miscellaneous	A Form Messages And Signals	02/10/1918	02/10/1918
Operation(al) Order(s)	56th Division Order No. 210	04/10/1918	04/10/1918
Miscellaneous	Amendment No. 3 To 56th Division Order No. 211	11/10/1918	11/10/1918
Miscellaneous	Amendment No. 2 To 56th Division Order No. 211	09/10/1918	09/10/1918
Miscellaneous	Amendment No. 1 To 56th Division Order No. 211	05/10/1918	05/10/1918
Operation(al) Order(s)	56th Division Order No. 211	05/10/1918	05/10/1918
Miscellaneous	A Form Messages And Signals	07/10/1918	07/10/1918
Operation(al) Order(s)	56th Division Order No. 212	06/10/1918	06/10/1918
Operation(al) Order(s)	56th Division Order No. 213	09/10/1918	09/10/1918
Operation(al) Order(s)	56th Division Order No. 214	09/10/1918	09/10/1918
Operation(al) Order(s)	56th Division Warning Order No. 215	12/10/1918	12/10/1918
Operation(al) Order(s)	56th Division Order No. 216	13/10/1918	13/10/1918
Operation(al) Order(s)	56th Division Order No. 217	13/10/1918	13/10/1918

Miscellaneous	March Table To Accompany 56th Division Order No. 217		
Operation(al) Order(s)	56th Division Order No. 218	30/10/1918	30/10/1918
Miscellaneous	March Table For Move By Road Issued With 56th Division Order No. 218		
Miscellaneous	Operations carried out by 56th Division between October 10th-October 16th Whilst Under the Command of the Canadian Corps		
Miscellaneous	Report On A Surprise Attack On Aubigny-Au-Bac 13th October 1918	15/10/1918	15/10/1918
Miscellaneous	Report On Operation Aubigny AU Bac 13 Oct 1918		
Miscellaneous	Canadian Corps. G.M. 77/3	26/12/1918	26/12/1918
Miscellaneous	Report On A Surprise Attack On Aubigny-Au-Bac 13th October 1918	15/10/1918	15/10/1918
Miscellaneous	Appendix NA Headquarters 56th Division	01/10/1918	01/10/1918
Heading	56th Division General Staff War Diary For November 1918		
Miscellaneous	56th Div		
War Diary	Basseville	01/11/1918	01/11/1918
War Diary	Monchaux	02/11/1918	04/11/1918
War Diary	Saultain	05/11/1918	07/11/1918
War Diary	Sebourg	08/11/1918	08/11/1918
War Diary	Fay Le Franc	09/11/1918	27/11/1918
War Diary	Harveng	28/11/1918	30/11/1918
Miscellaneous	56th Division Location Table	01/11/1918	01/11/1918
Miscellaneous	Amendment to 56th Division G.A. 191 (Addendum to 56th Div. Order No. 220)	02/11/1918	02/11/1918
Miscellaneous	Addendum To 56th Division Order No. 220	02/11/1918	02/11/1918
Operation(al) Order(s)	56th Division Order No. 220	02/11/1918	02/11/1918
Operation(al) Order(s)	56th Division Order No. 221	03/11/1918	03/11/1918
Operation(al) Order(s)	56th Division Order No. 222	05/11/1918	05/11/1918
Operation(al) Order(s)	56th Division Order No. 223	06/11/1918	06/11/1918
Map	Map		
Miscellaneous	56th Division G. 3/499	16/10/1918	16/10/1918
Miscellaneous	H.Q. 56th Division	15/10/1918	15/10/1918
Map	Map		
Miscellaneous	A Form Messages And Signals	04/10/1918	04/10/1918
Miscellaneous	A Form Messages And Signals	05/10/1918	05/10/1918
Miscellaneous	A Form Messages And Signals	07/10/1918	07/10/1918
Map	Map		
Operation(al) Order(s)	56th Division Order No. 224	24/11/1918	24/11/1918
Miscellaneous	March Table To Accompany 56th Division Order No. 224		
Miscellaneous	56th Division No. G.A. 299	26/11/1918	26/11/1918
Miscellaneous	Order 224 56th Division G. 3/528	06/11/1918	06/11/1918
Heading	War Diary General Staff 56th Division December 1918 Vol 35		
War Diary	Harvengt	01/12/1918	28/12/1918
Miscellaneous	56th Division Location Table	01/12/1918	01/12/1918
Heading	Headquarters, 56th Division General Staff War Diary January 1919 Vol 36		
War Diary	Harvengt	01/01/1919	25/01/1919
Miscellaneous	56th Division Location Table		
Heading	General Staff 56th Division War Diary February 1919 Vol 37		
War Diary	Harvengt	25/02/1919	25/02/1919

Heading	56th Division General Staff War Diary March 1919 Vol 38		
War Diary	Harvengt	01/03/1919	28/03/1919
War Diary	Jemappes	29/03/1919	31/03/1919
Miscellaneous	56 Division Location Table		
War Diary	Jemappes Belgium	01/04/1919	30/04/1919
Miscellaneous	G.O.C. British Troops In France & Flanders. (Records Section)	17/05/1919	17/05/1919
War Diary		00/05/1919	00/05/1919

D ALMOND.

Piece reference WO 95/2935

Headquarters Branches and Services: General Staff

Context

- **WO** Records created or inherited by the War Office, Armed Forces, Judge Advocate General, and related bodies
  - **Division within WO** Records of the Armed Forces from commands, headquarters, regiments and corps
    - **WO 95** War Office: First World War and Army of Occupation War Diaries
      - PART I: FRANCE, BELGIUM AND GERMANY
        - 56 DIVISION

Record Summary

Scope and content	Headquarters Branches and Services: General Staff
Covering dates	1918 Jan. - 1919 May
Held by	The National Archives, Kew
Legal status	Public Record(s)

FEBRUARY 1918 MISSING

THE FOLDERS FOR
JANUARY 1918
SEPTEMBER 1918
OCTOBER 1918
ARE EITHER
BADLY DAMAGED
OR MISSING

56TH DIVISION

GENERAL STAFF

JAN 1918–MAY 1919

56TH DIVISION

SECRET

WAR DIARY

OF

GENERAL STAFF

56th DIVISION.

FROM 1st JANUARY 1918

TO 31st JANUARY 1918.

-----------oOo-----------

SECRET.   Copy No. 29

56th DIVISION ORDER No. 148.

3rd January 1918.

In continuation of 56th Division Order No. 147. -

1. 56th Divisional Artillery will be relieved by 62nd Divisional Artillery in the Line under arrangements to be made between C.R.As. 62nd and 56th Divisions.
    Relief to be completed by 9 a.m. January 16th.

2. From 12 noon, 8th January, 56th Division, will be in G.H.Q. reserve, and will be held in readiness to entrain from AUBIGNY, SAVY, TINCQUES at 48 hours notice. Orders regarding this will be issued later.

3. From 12 noon, 8th January, until the Artillery relief is complete, the personnel of the 62nd Divisional Artillery will be held in readiness to relieve personnel of 56th Divisional Artillery at short notice. In the event of such a relief being ordered guns will be exchanged in situ and all arrangements made so as to permit of 56th Divisional Artillery moving complete with the Division.

4. Pioneer battalion, less 1 Company, will move to BAILLEUL-aux-CORNAILLES on 9th January.

5. 193rd (Div.) Machine Gun Coy. will on relief move to CAMBIGNEUL.

6. ACKNOWLEDGE.

F. B. Hurndall Major
for
Lieut-Colonel,
General Staff.

Issued at 8.0 a.m.

Copy No.		Copy No.	
1.	167th Infantry Brigade.	17.	56th Div. Supply Column.
2.	168th Infantry Brigade.	18.	56th Div. Amm. Sub Park.
3.	169th Infantry Brigade.	19.	A.D.C.
4.	1/5th Cheshire Regt.	20.	Camp Commandant.
5.	C.R.A.	21.	French Mission.
6.	C.R.E.	22.	XIII Corps "G".
7.	193rd (Div.) M.G.Coy.	23.	XIII Corps "Q".
8.	D.M.G.O.	24.	15th Division.
9.	56th Div. Signal Coy.	25.	31st Division.
10.	56th Div. Gas Officer.	26.	Guards Division.
11.	A.D.M.S.	27.	176th Tunnelling Coy.R.E.
12.	"Q"	28.	62nd Division.
13.	A.P.M.	29.)	War Diary.
14.	D.A.D.O.S.	30.)	
15.	D.A.D.V.S.	31.	File.
16.	56th Div. Train.		

War Diary Copies. B2

SECRET.   56th Division G.3/P10.

167th Infantry Brigade.   56th Div. Supply Column.
168th Infantry Brigade.   56th Div. Amm. Sub Park.
169th Infantry Brigade.   A.D.C.
1/5th Cheshire Regt.   Camp Commandant.
C.R.A.   French Mission.
C.R.E.   XIII Corps "G"
193rd (Div.) M.G.Coy.   XIII Corps "Q"
D.M.G.O.   15th Division.
56th Div. Signal Coy.   31st Division.
56th Div. Gas Officer.   Guards Division.
A.D.M.S.   176th Tunnelling Coy. R.E.
"Q"   62nd Division.
A.P.M.   War Diary
D.A.D.O.S.   File.
D.A.D.V.S.
56th Div. Train.

ADDENDA to 56th DIVISION ORDERS Nos. 147 and 148.

1. On relief of 56th Division by 62nd Division, the C.R.A., 62nd Division will command the Artillery covering the Right Divisional Sector.

2. Personnel of 62nd Division Heavy and Medium Trench Mortars will relieve personnel of 56th Division Heavy and Medium Trench Mortars in the line on January 8th.
    Details of relief to be arranged between C.R.A's concerned.

3. 56th Divisional Artillery will be relieved in the line by the 62nd Divisional Artillery on January 16th. Guns will be taken over 'in situ'.
    Details of relief will be arranged between C.R.A's 56th and 62nd Divisions.

4. ACKNOWLEDGE.

B. Pakenham
Lieut-Colonel,
General Staff, 56th Division.

7.1.18.

War Diary B3

SECRET. 56th Division No. G.3/808.

STRATEGICAL MOVE AND REINFORCEMENT SCHEMES,

RESERVE DIVISION, XIII CORPS.

1. Whilst the Division is in rest, it will be in G.H.Q. Reserve.
Should a hostile attack develop, however, on the front of XIII Corps, it may be required to move at short notice either into close reserve or to reinforce the Divisions in the line.

2. The Moves for which the Division has to be prepared are as follows :-

   (A) Strategic Move out of the Corps area - it will be continually ready to entrain at 48 hours notice at TINCQUES, SAVY and AUBIGNY.

   (B) Move by march route to the MAROEUIL - ECOIVRES - ACQ area.

   (C) Move by tactical trains - entraining at AUBIGNY and detraining at ECURIE.

3. The above-mentioned moves will be described as Scheme 'A', Scheme 'B' and Scheme 'C'.

4. Orders, which will become operative only on receipt of a telegram ordering the particular move, are issued herewith in the case of Scheme 'A'. Orders for Schemes 'B' and 'C' will follow as soon as ready.
Orders will be prepared by all concerned and kept ready for immediate issue, copies of such orders being sent to the next higher formation.

5. Precautions will be taken in every unit to guard against delay in the delivery to a responsible person of the telegram or orders mentioned in para. 4, e.g., at night; during the absence of a unit from its billets; during training &c.

B. Pakenham
Lieut-Colonel.
General Staff.

7: 1: 1918.

Copies to :-
167th Infantry Brigade.
168th Infantry Brigade.
169th Infantry Brigade.
1/5th Cheshire Regt.
C.R.A.
C.R.E.
193rd (Div.) M.G. Coy.
56th Div. M.G. Officer.
56th Div. Signal Coy.
56th Div. Gas Officer.
A.D.M.S.
"Q"
A.P.M.
D.A.D.O.S.
D.A.D.V.S.
56th Div. Train.
56th Div. Supply Col.
56th Div. Amm. Sub-Park.
A.D.C.
Camp Commandant.
French Mission.
XIII Corps "G".
XIII Corps "Q".
War Diary
File.

War Diary B4

SECRET.　　　　　　　　　　　　　　　　　　56th Division No. G.3/807.

SCHEME A.

Movement of 56th Division by Strategical Trains.

1. Herewith copy of arrangements for entrainment and detrainment for 56th Division in case a move is ordered whilst it is in G.H.Q. Reserve.

2. This scheme will become operative on receipt of a telegram from Divisional Headquarters worded as follows :-

> "Move AAA Scheme 'A' AAA Time of first train AAA SAVY _____ AAA AUBIGNY _____ AAA TINQUES _____ AAA Acknowledge.

3. Acknowledge.

B. Pakenham
Lieut-Colonel.
General Staff,
56th Division.

7: 1: 1918.

Copies to :-
167th Infantry Brigade.
168th Infantry Brigade.
169th Infantry Brigade.
1/5th Cheshire Regt.
C.R.A.
C.R.E.
193rd (Div.) M.G. Coy.
56th Div. M.G. Officer.
56th Div. Signal Coy.
56th Div. Gas Officer.
A.D.M.S.
"Q".
A.P.M.
D.A.D.O.S.
D.A.D.V.S.
56th Div. Train.
56th Div. Supply Col.
56th Div. Amm. Sub-Park.
A.D.C.
Camp Commandant.
French Mission.
XIII Corps "G".
XIII Corps "Q".
War Diary.
File.

S C H E M E   "A". A.Q.S. 482

Arrangements for the Entrainment and Detrainment of the 56th Division in case a move by rail is ordered whilst in G.H.Q. Reserve.

Issued with reference to 56th Division Order No. 148.

1. STATIONS OF ENTRAINMENT.

Units will entrain at stations as under, under the orders of the Brigadier Generals Commanding Brigade Groups and Divisional Artillery and of Divl. H.Q. in the case of Units of Divl. Troops not affiliated (to Inf. Bdes.)

At SAVY
167th Brigade Group.
Divisional Train Headquarters.
193rd Machine Gun Coy.
247th (Div.) Employment Coy.
Mobile Veterinary Section.
280th Bde. R.F.A. (less "D" Bty) and portion of DAC

At TINQUES
168th Bde. Group.
1/5th (E. of C.) Bn. Cheshire Regt.
Headquarters D.A.C. No. 1 Coy. Divisional Train.
Divisional Artillery Headquarters.
D/280th Battery R.F.A.
Heavy and Medium T.M. Batteries.

At AUBIGNY
169th Brigade Group.
Divisional Headquarters.
Divisional R.E. Headquarters.
Headquarters and No. 1 Section Divl. Signal Coy.
281st Bde. R.F.A. and portion of D.A.C.

2. Times of entrainment

The order of entrainment is shown in Table "D". Trains from each station will leave at 3 hour intervals.

All Transport will arrive at Stations of Entrainment 3 hours and personnel 1½ hours before the time of departure of the train in which they are to travel.

3. LOADING PARTY.

Each Infantry Brigade will detail a Company from their last train load as a loading party for all trains, except those conveying units of Divisional Artillery, which leave their respective entraining stations. These Companies, with their cookers and rations, will report to the R.T.O., at the entraining station 4 hours before the first train is due to leave. They will travel by the last train of their Brigade Group.

4. UNLOADING PARTY.

Similarly each Infantry Brigade will detail a Company from their first train load as unloading party for all trains arriving at their respective detraining stations, except those conveying Units of Divisional Artillery. They will report to the R.T.O., immediately on arrival at the station of detrainment. They will be rationed by their own unit and will rejoin their unit after the last train of their Brigade Group has been unloaded.

5. Divisional Artillery will make their own arrangements for loading and unloading parties. 1 Company of 5th Cheshire Regt. travelling with part of the SAA Section D.A.C., will assist in loading and unloading that train.

6. FIELD COMPANIES.
   Each Field Coy. R.E., will detail 1 Officer and 60 O.R., to assist the permanent loading and unloading parties at Stations of Entrainment and Detrainment in dealing with their own transport. These parties will report to the Officers referred to in para. 7, 3 hours before the departure of the trains by which the Field Coys. travel, and to the Officers referred to in para. 8 on arrival.

7. ENTRAINMENT OFFICERS.
   Each Infantry Brigade will detail two Officers, not below the rank of Captain, to report to the R.T.O., of their respective entraining station 4 hours before the first train is due to leave, to assist him in the general supervision of the entrainment of the Division (less Artillery). The Officers will work in 2 reliefs and will travel by the last train of their Brigade Group. The C.R.A. will make corresponding arrangements for Officers to assist in the entrainment of (the Divl. Arty.

8. DETRAINMENT OFFICERS.
   Similarly each Infantry Brigade will detail 2 Officers to proceed by the first train, and report for the same purpose to the R.T.O., at the Station of Detrainment. Similar arrangements will be made by the C.R.A. for supervising the detraining of the Divisional Artillery.

9. O.C., Signal Coy. will detail a Motor Cyclist orderly for duty at each station of entrainment and detrainment. They will report to the Officers mentioned in paras 7 and 8.

10. A.D.M.S., will detail an Ambulance Car to be on duty at AUBIGNY Station during the period of the entrainment; and another Car to be on duty at a detraining station, which will be notified later, during the period of detrainment.

11. ENTRAINMENT AND DETRAINMENT OFFICERS.
    While Entrainment and Detrainment Officers are on duty they should wear the blue Brigade armband as a distinguishing badge.

12. DIVISIONAL STAFF.
    An Officer from Division Headquarters will visit stations of entrainment and detrainment at frequent intervals.

13. POLICE.
    For the Control of Traffic on the road approaches to each of the Entraining Stations the A.P.M., will detail 6 policemen to report to the Officers referred to in para. 7, four hours before the first train is due to leave. These policemen will travel by the last train and will rejoin Div. H.Q. from the station of detrainment.
    For the Control of Traffic on the roads leading from each of the detraining stations the A.P.M. will also detail 6 policemen to proceed by the first train from each station with orders to report to the Officers referred to in para. 8 on arrival. On completion of detrainment these policemen will rejoin Div. H.Q. The A.P.M. will provide the necessary Rations for those 36 policemen.

14. BAGGAGE and SUPPLY WAGONS.
    Baggage and Supply Wagons will entrain with the Units for which they are carrying.
    Baggage Wagons will join Units on receipt of orders to entrain.
    Supply Wagons will join Units before they entrain, as arranged in para 18.

15. **ENTRAINMENT.**
   (a) A Senior Officer from each Unit must be sent to report to the R.T.O. at Stations of Entrainment to receive detailed instructions, in sufficient time to permit of them being made known to all concerned before the arrival of the Unit at the Station.
   (b) Units must provide a horse holder for each horse, also drag ropes for use as breast lines in the trucks. The Railway Authorities provide lashings for vehicles.
   (c) No fused bombs or grenades are to be carried on any train.
   (d) No lights will be lit in any train after dark. The fires of cookers will be drawn before entrainment.

16. **MOTOR CARS etc.**
   All Motor Cars, Motor Ambulances and Motor Cycles will proceed by road on the days on which the Units to which they belong entrain.

17. **SURPLUS BAGGAGE.**
   In the event of lorries being available for moving surplus baggage arrangements will be notified at the time.
   If lorries are not available surplus baggage will be dumped by Units at the Divisional Dump, BETHONSART, directly orders are received to entrain.
   O.C. Divl. Employment Company will hold a guard of 1 N.C.O. and 2 men with 7 days rations ready to take over this dump on its formation.
   Units in the 31st and 62nd Divl. Area will dump their surplus baggage at their Q.M. Stores and leave a guard of 1 N.C.O. and 2 men with 7 days rations.

18. **SUPPLIES.**
   Rations for consumption on the day of entrainment will be delivered in the normal manner, early on the day of entrainment minus 1.
   Rations for consumption on the day of entrainment plus 1 will be sent to Units by Supply Wagon early on the day of entrainment minus 1, and the loaded Supply Wagons will proceed to, and remain with, Units until the completion of the move.
   Rations for consumption on the day of entrainment plus 2, will be delivered as follows:-
   (i) For Units entraining before 12 noon, by Supply Column at Refilling Points in the new area, thence by Supply Wagon on day of entrainment, plus 1.

   (ii) For Units entraining after 12 noon, by Supply Column lorries direct to Entraining Stations, where they should be taken over by representatives of Units by 12 Noon on the day of Entrainment, and loaded by Units direct into their Railway Trains and not into Supply Wagons. Although in reality for consumption on day of entrainment plus 2, these rations should be consumed on day of entrainment plus 1, and the supplies already loaded on the supply wagons for consumption on day of entrainment plus 1 should be consumed on the day of entrainment plus 2.

Lieut.-Colonel,
A.A.& Q.M.G., 56th Division.

7th January, 1918.

TABLE "D" 1.

AUBIGNY.	SAVY.	TINQUES.	SERIAL NUMBER.	Date.	Time of departure.
1			(5630, 5631a, 5635, 5636, (5637		
	1		(5610, 5611a, 5615, 5616, (5617.		
		1	5620, 5621a, 5625, 5626, 5627.		
2			5631.		
	2		5611.		
		2	5621.		
3			5632.		
	3		5612.		
		3	5622.		
4			5633.		
	4		5613.		
		4	5623, 5604b.		
5			5634.		
	5		5614.		
		5	5624, 5604c.		
6			5601, 5605, 5603.		
	6		5607, 5608, 5609, 5675, 5690.		
		6	5604.		
7			5632a, 5678, 5683.		
	7		5612a, 5681, 5676.		
		7	5622a, 5677, 5682.		
8			5633a, 5634a, 5688.		
	8		5613a, 5614a, 5686.		
		8	5623a, 5624a, 5687.		
9			5651, 5672a.		
	9		5641, 5671a,		
		9	5602, 5670, 5675a.		
10			5650, 5672.		
	10		5640, 5671.		
		10	5673a, 5691, 5692, 5693, 5694.		
11			5652, 5672b.		
	11		5642, 5671b.		
		11	5673b, 5604a.		
12			5653, 5672c.		
	12		5643, 5671c.		
		12	5644, 5671d.		
13			5654, 5672d.		

In the event of the Division entraining less Artillery, Hdqrs. Divl. Arty. (5602) will entrain with Divl. Hdqrs. (5601) and Hdqrs. Divl. Engineers (5603) will travel by the 6th train from SAVY in addition to those already allotted to that train.

The Company of the 5th Cheshires (5604a) will travel by the second train from TINQUES in addition to 5621.

TABLE "D" 2.

		Serial No.	Description.
Entraining Station.	AUBIGNY	5601	Divl. H.Q.
	TINQUES	5602	H.Q. Divl. R.A.
	AUBIGNY	5603	" " R.E. (5604c.
		5604	1/5th Cheshires less 5604a, 5604b,
	TINQUES	5604a	1 Coy. 1 Cooker & team 1/5th Ches.
		5604b	2 G.S.W. & teams, 1/5th Cheshires.
		5604c	2 " " " "
	AUBIGNY	5605	H.Q. & No. 1 Sec. Divl. Signals.
	AUBIGNY	5606	----
		5607	247 Employment Coy. (& 5609).
	SAVY	5608	193 M.G.Coy.
		5609	247 Employment Coy. (& 5607).

167th Inf. Bde. Group.	5610	Bde. H.Q.
	5611	"A" Bn.(VILLERS BRULIN) less 11a.
Entraining Station -	5611a	1 Coy., 1 cooker & team "A" Bn.
	5612	"B" Bn. (TINQUES) less 12a.
SAVY.	5612a	1 Coy., 1 cooker & team "B" Bn.
	5613	"C" Bn. (CHELERS) less 13a.
	5613a	1 Coy., 1 cooker & team "C" Bn.
	5614	"D" Bn. (AUBREY CAMP) less 14a.
	5614a	1 Coy. 1 cooker & team "D" Bn.
	5615	Bde. Signal Sec.
	5616	Bde. M.G.C.
	5617	Bde. T.M.B.
	5676	No. 2 Coy. Divl. Train.
	5681	416 Fld. Coy. R.E.
	5686	2/1st London Fld. Ambce.

168th Inf. Bde. Group.	5620	Bde. H.Q.
	5621	"A" Bn.(MONCHY-BRETON) less 21a.
Entraining Station -	5621a	1 Coy. 1 cooker & team "A" Bn.
	5622	"B" Bn. (MAGNICOURT) less 22a.
TINQUES.	5622a	1 Coy. 1 cooker & team "B" Bn.
	5623	"C" Bn. (LA THIEULOYE) less 23a.
	5623a	1 Coy. 1 Cooker & team "C" Bn.
	5624	"D" Bn.(STEWART CAMP) less 24a.
	5624a	1 Coy. 1 cooker & team "D" Bn.
	5625	Bde. Signal Section.
	5626	Bde. M.G.C.
	5627	Bde. T.M.B.
	5677	No. 3 Coy. Divl. Train.
	5682	512th Fld. Coy. R.E.
	5687	2/2nd London Fld. Ambce.

169th Inf. Bde. Group.	5630	Bde. H.Q.
	5631	"A" Bn.(CAUCOURT) less 31a.
Entraining Station -	5631a	1 Coy. 1 cooker & team, "A" Bn.
	5632	"B" Bn. (FREVILLERS) less 32a.
AUBIGNY.	5632a	1 Coy. 1 cooker & team "B" Bn.
ø	5633	"D" Bn.(CAMBLIGNEUL) less 33a.
	5633a	1 Coy. 1 cooker & team "D" Bn.
	5634	"C" Bn. (TRAFALGAR CAMP) less 34a.
	5634a	1 Coy. 1 cooker & team "C" Bn.
	5635	Bde. Signal Section.
	5636	Bde. M.G.C.
	5637	Bde. T.M.B.
	5678	No. 4 Coy. Divl. Train.
	5683	513th Fld. Coy. R.E.
	5688	2/3rd London Fld. Ambce.

ø "D" Bn. is in the Red Line until 10th inst.

TABLE "D".

UNIT		Serial No.	Description
280th (London) Brigade, R.F.A.		5640	Bde. Headquarters.
		5641	93rd Battery.
		5642	"A" "
Entraining Station SAVY		5643	"C" "
" TINQUES		5644	"D" "
281st (London) Brigade R.F.A.		5650	Bde. Headquarters.
		5651	109th Battery.
Entraining Station AUBIGNY.		5652	"A" "
		5653	"B" "
		5654	"D" "
DIVL. AMMN. COL.	(Entraining Stn.		
	" TINQUES.	5670	H.Q. Divisional Ammn. Column.
		5671	No. 1 Sec. less 5671a,5671b,5671c,5671d.
	" SAVY.	5671a	1 G.S. Wgn & 4 Lmbd Ammn Wgns & Teams of
		5671b	- do - (5671.
		5671c	- do -
	" TINQUES.	5671d	- do -
		5672	No. 2 Sec. less 5672a,5672b,5672c,5672d.
		5672a	1 G.S. Wgn. 4 Lmbd Ammn Wgns & Teams of
	" AUBIGNY.	5672b	- do - (5672.
		5672c	- do -
		5672d	- do -
	" TINQUES.	5673a	½ S.A.A. Section D.A.C.
		5673b	- do -
DIVISIONAL TRAIN.	" SAVY.	5675	H.Q. Divisional Train.
	TINQUES.	5675a	No.1 Company.
	SAVY.	5676	No. 2 Company.
	TINQUES.	5677	No. 3 "
	AUBIGNY.	5678	No. 4 "
DIVISIONAL ENGINEERS.	" SAVY.	5681	416th (Edinburgh) Field Coy. R.E.
	TINQUES.	5682	512th (London) " "
	AUBIGNY.	5683	513th (") " "
MEDICAL UNITS.	" SAVY.	5686	2/1st London Field Ambulance.
	TINQUES.	5687	2/2nd "
	AUBIGNY.	5688	2/3rd "
VETERINARY UNIT.	" SAVY.	5690	1/1st London Mobile Veterinary Sec.
TRENCH MORTAR BATTERIES.	" TINQUES.	5691	"V" Trench Mortar Bty. (Heavy).
		5692	"X" " " (Medium).
		5693	"Y" " " (").
		5694	"Z" " " (").

War Diary B

56th Division No. G.3/811.

SECRET.
Copy No. 24

SCHEME 'B'
for the move of Reserve Division, XIII Corps, by road
to MAROEUIL - ECOIVRES & ACQ areas.

1. The Division (less Artillery) is to be prepared to move at short notice by march route to the ECOIVRES - MAROEUIL and ACQ areas.

2. The moves will be carried out in accordance with the March Table attached.

3. This Scheme will become operative only on receipt of a telegram from Divisional Headquarters worded as follows :-

   "MOVE AAA SCHEME 'B' AAA ZERO HOUR _____ AAA ACKNOWLEDGE"

   Zero hour will be the hour from which all moves will be calculated.

4. Orders for move of Artillery will be issued by G.O.C., R.A., XIII Corps.

5. ACKNOWLEDGE.

B Pakenham
Lieut-Colonel.
General Staff.

7: 1: 1918.

Issued to :-

Copy No.	
1	167th Infantry Brigade.
2	168th Infantry Brigade.
3	169th Infantry Brigade.
4	1/5th Cheshire Regt.
5	C.R.A.
6	C.R.E.
7	193rd (Div.) M.G. Coy.
8	56th Div. M.G. Officer.
9	56th Div. Signal Coy.
10	56th Div. Gas Officer.
11	A.D.M.S.
12	"Q"
13	A.P.M.
14	D.A.D.O.S.
15	D.A.D.V.S.
16	56th Div. Train.
17	56th Div. Supply Col.
18	56th Div. Amm. Sub-Park.
19	A.D.C.
20	Camp Commandant.
21	French Mission.
22	XIII Corps "G".
23	XIII Corps "Q".
24/5	War Diary.
26	File.

Ref. LENS Sheet, 1/100.000

MARCH TABLE TO ACCOMPANY SCHEME 'B'.

56th Divn. No.G.3/811.

Serial No.	Time	Unit	From	To	Instructions
1	Zero plus 3 hours	169 Inf.Bde.Group (less Supply Secn. of Train).	FREVILLERS Area.	MAROEUIL Area.	Route CAMBLIGNEUL - GAMBLAIN L'ABBE - LE PENDU, Cross Roads ½ mile S.E. of B in MIN.de BRAY.
2	Zero plus 3 hours	167 Inf.Bde.Group (less Supply Secn. of Train).	CHELERS Area.	ECOIVRES Area.	Route SAVY - CAPELLE FERMONT - ACQ. Tail of the column to be clear of SAVY Cross-roads by Zero plus 6 hours 30 minutes. 1/5 Cheshire Rgt. (Pioneers) to march with 167 Inf.Bde.Group as far as SAVY whence HAUTE-AVESNE,ROUEZ to ANZIN the
3	To be arranged by 168th Inf. Bde.	168 Inf.Bde.Group (less Supply Secn. of Train).	MONCHY-BRETON Area.	ACQ Area.	Route - Any roads North of VILLERS BRULIN - CHELERS - MONCHY-BRETON Road inclusive - SAVY - CAPELLE FERMONT. NOT to enter SAVY or CAMBLIGNEUL before Zero plus 6 hours 30 minutes.
4	"	Divnl. H.Q. H.Q., R.E.	VILLERS CHATEL Area.	CEMETERY Headquarters MAROEUIL.	As in Serial No. 1. NOT to enter CAMBLIGNEUL before Zero plus 5 hours.
5	"	193 (Div.) M.G. Coy.	Remains at CAMBLIGNEUL.		
6	Zero plus 7 hours	Mobile Vet.Sec.	TINCQUES.	CAMBLIGNEUL.	No restrictions.

P.T.O.

MARCH TABLE TO ACCOMPANY SCHEME 'B', continued:

Serial No.	Time	Unit	From	To	Instructions.
7		Div. Train. H.Q. No. 1 Coy.Train.	SAVY	ST. AUBIN.	Route. HAUTE AVESNES - Cross-roads at E of HALTE. No time restrictions.

NOTES :- Following distances to be maintained on the March :-
       Between Battalions   500 yards
       "   Companies   100 yards
       "   Unit and its transport 100 yards

If transport is Brigaded,
     between each Bn. transport .. 100 yards

Supply Sections of Train will, after collecting supplies, follow the same route as their respective Brigades, but will not pass CAMBLIGNEUL before Zero plus 5½ hours, or SAVY before Zero plus 9 hours.

TABLE OF BILLETS IN AREAS.
****

	MAROEUIL Area.	ECOIVRES Area.	ACQ Area.
Brigade H.Q. :	LOUEZ.	MT. ST ELOY.	ACQ.
'A' Battalion	MAROEUIL.	YORK CAMP, ECOIVRES.	ACQ.
'B' Battalion	MAROEUIL.	VILLAGE CAMP, ECOIVRES.	ACQ.
'C' Battalion	ST. AUBIN.	BRAY	PREVIN CAPELLE
'D' Battalion	ST. CATHERINE.	LANCASTER CAMP, MT. ST. ELOY.	CAMBLIGNEUL.
M.G.C. & T.M.B.	ANZIN.	DURHAM CAMP.	CAPELLE FERMONT.
Field Coy.R.E.	ST. AUBIN.	BRAY	AGNIERES (Y of AUBIGNY).
Field Ambulance } Company Train }		To be arranged by "Q", 56th Division.	
1/5th Cheshire Regt. (Pioneers).	ANZIN.		

SECRET.   Copy No. 24

SCHEME 'C'.   56th Division No. G.3/315

1. Scheme 'C' issued herewith contains instructions for the move of the 56th Division from the Reserve Area to ECURIE by Tactical Trains.

2. The following Tables are attached :-

   Table 'A' - For move by Tactical Trains.
   Table 'B' - For move of Transport (less that convoyed on Omnibus Trains).

3. The Scheme will come into force only on receipt of a telegram from Divisional Headquarters worded as follows :-

   "MOVE AAA SCHEME 'C' AAA TRAINS DEPART AS UNDER AAA AUBIGNY FIRST TRAIN _____ SECOND TRAIN _____ AAA SAVY FIRST TRAIN _____ SECOND TRAIN _____ THIRD TRAIN _____ AAA TINCQUES FIRST TRAIN _____ SECOND TRAIN _____ AAA ZERO HOUR WILL BE _____ AAA ACKNOWLEDGE.

4. Zero hour will be the hour from which all moves of transport by road will be calculated.

5. Orders for moves of Artillery will be issued by G.O.C. R.A., XIII Corps.

6. ACKNOWLEDGE.

                                            Lieut-Colonel.
                                            General Staff.

8. 1. 1918.

Issued to :-   Copy No.
               1   167th Infantry Brigade.
               2   168th Infantry Brigade.
               3   169th Infantry Brigade.
               4   1/5th Cheshire Regt.
               5   C.R.A.
               6   C.R.E.
               7   193rd (Div.) M.G. Coy.
               8   56th Div. M.G. Officer.
               9   56th Div. Signal Coy.
               10   56th Div. Gas Officer.
               11   A.D.M.S.
               12   "Q".
               13   A.P.M.
               14   D.A.D.O.S.
               15   D.A.D.V.S.
               16   56th Div. Train.
               17   56th Div. Supply Col.
               18   56th Div. Amm. Sub-Park.
               19   A.D.C.
               20   Camp Commandant.
               21   French Mission.
               22   XIII Corps "G".
               23   XIII Corps "Q".
               24/5   War Diary.
               26   File.

Table "A"

AQS/482.

SCHEME "C".

Move of 56th Division by Tactical Trains from Reserve Area to ECURIE.

1. **ENTRAINING STATIONS.**

   Units will entrain as follows, under the orders of Brigade Group Commanders and C.R.A., and of Divl. H.Q. in the case of Units of Divl. Troops not affiliated to Infantry Brigades.

   AUBIGNY.

   First Train. Personnel only. 169th Inf. Bde. less M.G.C. and T.M.B.
   Second Train. (Omnibus). Part transport of 169th Inf. Bde. only.
   (See Appendix Y).

   SAVY.

   First Train. Personnel only. 167th Inf. Bde. less M.G.C. & T.M.B.
   Second Train. " " 167, 168, 169 T.M.B. (with handcarts).
   193 M.G.C., 5th Cheshires, 416 Field Coy.R.E., 2/2nd and 2/3rd London Fld. Ambces.
   Divl. H.Q.
   H.Q. Divl. Engineers.
   H.Q. and No. 1 Sec. Divl. Signal Coy -
   X.Y.Z. and V.T.M. Batts.

   Third Train. (Omnibus). Part Transport of 167th Inf. Bde. only.
   (See Appendix Y)

   TINQUES.

   First Train. (Personnel only) 168th Inf.Bde.less M.G.C.,T.M.B.
   Second Train (Omnibus) Part Transpt. 168 Bde. only.(See Appendix Y)

   DETRAINING STATION - ECURIE.

2. **ENTRAINMENT & DETRAINMENT.**

   167th, 168th and 169th Bde. Group Commanders will each detail Officers to supervise the entrainment at SAVY, TINQUES, and AUBIGNY respectively. The detrainment at ECURIE will be supervised under Divisional arrangements.

3. **BAGGAGE.**

   All surplus baggage and stores will be placed in Unit dumps under a guard of 2 men for each Dump. This guard will be told off and 7 days rations held ready for them directly Units arrive in the Reserve Area. The position of Unit dumps will be reported to Div H.Q. directly a Unit has reconnoitred its billeting area. At least one blanket per man must be carried on the baggage wagons.

4. **NUCLEUS PERSONNEL.**

   The personnel mentioned in SS.135, Sect. XXX, will not proceed with their Units, but will concentrate at TINQUES after the departure of the last tactical train, and will there come under command of the Senior Officer. They will include a proportion of cooks and be provided by their Units with a sufficient number of Camp kettles; also rations for the following day if these are in possession of the Unit. Further orders regarding the move from TINQUES to PERNES will be sent from Divl. H.Q. to the Senior Officer of the Party, c/o. Town Major, TINQUES.

7th January, 1918.

Lc Lieut.-Colonel,
A.A.& Q.M.G., 56th Div.

APPENDIX "Y".

COMPOSITION OF OMNIBUS TRAIN.

UNIT.	Personnel. Offrs.	O.R.	Horses.	G.S. Limbered.	2 wheeled carts.
Riding Horses & Transport of Bde. H.Q.	-	14	9	1	-
" " Signal Section.	-	14	9	1	1
L.G. Detachment-Transport 4 L. G.S. Wagons per Battn.	-	32	32	16	-
Pack animals, 6 per Battn.	-	24	24	-	-
Medical Personnel and 1 Maltese Cart per Battn.	4	8	4	-	4
One Motorcart. per Battn	-	16	8	-	4
M.G. Company, and 2 L. G.S. Wagons per section.	10	200	34	8	1
Riders. 5 per Battn. 7 M.G.C.	-	28	27	-	-
	14	336	147	26	10

62 Axles.

£ Finds loading and unloading party of 100 men.

TABLE "B" to accompany SCHEME "C"

Reference LENS SHEET 1/100,000

Serial No.	Time.	Unit.	From	To	Instructions.
1.	Zero.	Transport of 169th Inf. Bde. Group & 193rd M.G.Coy.	FREVILLERS AREA.	Cross Roads on ARRAS SOUCHEZ Road 1½ miles NNE of ST. NICOLAS.	CAMBLIGNEUL - CAMBLAIN L'ABBE - LE PENDU - Cross Roads ANZIN.
2.	Zero plus 30 mins.	Transport of 167th Inf. Bde. Group, 1/5th Cheshires (Pioneers) & Mobile Veterinary Section.	CHELERS AREA.		SAVY - HAUTE, AVESNES - LOUEZ - ST. ALBIN.
3.	Zero plus 30 mins.	Transport of 168th Inf. Bde. Group.	MONCHY BRETON Area		As in Serial 1.
4.	Zero plus 2 hours.	Div. H.Q.	VILLERS CHATEL		As in Serial 1.
5.	Zero plus 3 hours.	Div. Train H.Q. & No. 1 Coy. Train.	SAVY		As in Serial 2.

Note. "Q" will arrange for an Officer to meet Transport at Arrival Point and direct it to Transport Lines or area allotted.
100 yds. distance to be maintained between each Battalion Transport.

War Diary Copies B4

SECRET. 56th Division G.3/832.

167th Infantry Brigade.	D.A.D.O.S.
168th Infantry Brigade.	D.A.D.V.S.
169th Infantry Brigade.	56th Div. Train.
1/5th Cheshire Regiment.	56th Div. Supply Column.
C.R.A.	56th Div. Amm. Sub Park.
C.R.E.	A.D.C.
193rd (Div.) M.G.Coy.	Camp Commandant.
56th Div. M.G.Officer.	French Mission.
56th Div. Signal Coy.	XIII Corps "G"
56th Div. Gas Officer.	XIII Corps "Q"
A.D.M.S.	War Diary.
"Q"	File.
A.P.M.	

AMENDMENT No. 1 to 56th DIVISION G.3/815 - SCHEME 'C'.

Table 'B' column 5
should read -
1¼ miles <u>NNW</u> of <u>ST.</u> in <u>ST. NICOLAS</u> <u>NOT</u> NNE.

H.Q. 56th Divn.
10.1.18.

F. B. Stundall Major
for Lieut-Colonel,
General Staff.

SECRET.   Copy No. 29

56th DIVISION ORDER No. 147.

31st Jan. 1917.

1. The 56th Division (less Artillery) will be relieved in the line by the 62nd Division (less Artillery).   Order regarding Artillery Reliefs will be issued later.

2. (a). The 167th and 168th Infantry Brigades will be relieved in the line by 185th and 187th Infantry Brigades respectively on 8th and 8th January, 1918.
(b) Reliefs of M.G.Coys. will be carried out 24 hours after the Infantry Reliefs in the Line.
(c) Details of above reliefs including Relief of men now attached to 176th Tunnelling Coy. R.E. will be arranged between Brigadiers concerned.
(d) Completion of above reliefs will be reported to Div. H.Q.

3. (a) 512th, 513th and 416th Field Coys. R.E. will be relieved by 460th, 461st and 457th Field Coys. R.E. under arrangements to be made between C.R.E. 53th and 62nd Divisions.
(b) On relief 512th and 513th Field Coy. will take over work and location of 460th and 461st Field Coys. R.E. under C.E. XIII Corps.
(c) Relief of Pioneer Battalion will be arranged between C.R.E. 56th Div. and C.R.E. 62nd Div.

4. Relief of Medical Units will be arranged between A.Ds.M.S. 56th and 62nd Division.

5. Relief of Divisional M.G.Coy. will be arranged between D.M.G.Os. 56th and 62nd Divisions.

6. (a). Command of Brigade fronts will pass to B.G&C. relieving Brigades on completion of the Infantry relief.
(b) Command of Divisional front will pass to G.O.C. 62nd Divn. at 11 a.m. 9th January.

7. On completion of reliefs, Brigade Groups will be located as follows :-
    167th Infantry Brigade Group   CHELERS Area.
    168th Infantry Brigade Group   MONCHY-BRETON Area.
    169th Infantry Brigade Group. FREVILLERS Area.

8. (a) Moves in connection with the Infantry reliefs will take place in accordance with the attached Table.

(b) Field Ambulances, Companies of Divisional Train, and 416th Field Coy. R.E. will move to their respective Brigade Group Areas.
(c) Moves of Pioneer Battalion and Div. M.G.Coy. will be notified later.

9. During the progress of relief Units of 185th, 186th and 187th Infantry Brigades located in 56th Divnl. Area will come under the tactical control of 56th Division. Units of 56th Div. in 62nd Div. area will come under 62nd Div.

10. C.R.E., 56th Division, will hand over to C.R.E. 62nd Division details of all work in progress, and will take over from C.R.E. 62nd Division details of all work under C.E. XIII Corps.

11. Relief of working parties under XIII Corps will take place as follows :-
    8th January   1 Bn. 169th Infantry Brigade will take over work and location of 1 Bn. 187th Infantry Brigade (under 31st Divn.).

/7th January.

P.T.O.

- 2 -

      7th January.   1 Bn. 168th Infantry Brigade will take over work and location of 1 Bn. 185th Infantry Brigade.

      9th January.   1 Bn. and 4 Officers and 190 O.R. 167th Infantry Brigade will take over work and location of 1 Bn. and 194 all ranks 186th Infantry Brigade.

     10th January.   1 Bn. 186th Infantry Brigade will take over work and location of 1 Bn. 169th Infantry Brigade.

12.   56th Div. H.Q. will close at VICTORY CAMP at 11 a.m. 9th January and open at VILLERS CHATEL same hour.

13.   ACKNOWLEDGE.

                                     F. B. Hurndall.
                                      Major
                             for Lieut-Colonel,
                                  General Staff.

Issued at 8.0 am

Copy No. 1. 167th Infantry Brigade.
        2. 168th Infantry Brigade.
        3. 169th Infantry Brigade.
        4. 1/5th Cheshire Regt.
        5. C.R.A.
        6. C.R.E.
        7. 193rd (Div.) M.G.Coy.
        8. D.M.G.O.
        9. 56th Div. Signal Coy.
      10. 56th Div. Gas Officer.
      11. A.D.M.S.
      12. "Q"
      13. A.P.M.
      14. D.A.D.O.S.
      15. D.A.D.V.S.
      16. 56th Div. Train.
      17. 56th Div. Supply Column.
      18. 56th Div. Amm. Sub Park.
      19. A.D.C.
      20. Camp Commandant.
      21. French Mission.
      22. XIII Corps "G".
      23. XIII Corps "Q".
      24. 15th Division.
      25. 31st Division.
      26. Guards Division.
      27. 176th Tunnelling Coy. R.E.
      28. 62nd Division.
      29.) War Diary.
      30.)
      31. File.

TABLE OF MOVES TO ACCOMPANY 56th DIVISION ORDER No. 147.
MAROEUIL Area includes MAROEUIL, ST.AUBIN, ANZIN, LOUEZ.

Date.	Div.	Unit.	From.	To.	Instructions.
5th Jan.	62nd	187th Bde. (less 1 bn.)	FREVILLERS Area.	MAROEUIL Area.	By busses to be arranged by 56th Div. "Q".
"	56th	169th Bde. (less 2 bns.)	MAROEUIL Area.	FREVILLERS Area.	Train for relief to be arranged by 56th Div. "Q". Not to enter Camp before noon.
6th Jan.	62nd	187th Bde. (less 1 Bn.)	MAROEUIL Area.	LINE.	
"	56th	1 Bn. 187th Bde.	TRAFALGAR CAMP Area.	LINE.	
"	"	168th Bde. 1 Bn. 169th Bde.	MAROEUIL Area.	MAROEUIL Area. TRAFALGAR CAMP Area.	Not to enter Camp before noon.
7th Jan.	62nd	185th Bde. (less 1 Bn.)	MONCHY-BRETON Area.	MAROEUIL Area.	
"	62nd 56th	1 Bn. 185th Bde. 168th Bde. (less 1 Bn.)	STEWARTS CAMP, A.29.b.1.7. MAROEUIL AREA.	MAROEUIL Area. MONCHY-BRETON Area.	To be clear of Camp by noon. By busses to be arranged by 56th Div. "Q". Not to enter Camp before noon.
"	56th	1 Bn. 168th Bde.	MAROEUIL Area.	STEWARTS CAMP A.29.b.1.7.	
8th Jan.	62rd 56th	185th Bde. 167th Bde.	MAROEUIL Area. LINE.	LINE. MAROEUIL Area.	Train for relief to be arranged by 56th Div. "Q".
9th Jan.	62nd	186th Bde. (less 1½ bns.)	CHELERS Area.	MAROEUIL	
"	62nd	1½ Bns. 186th Bde.	AUBREY and Tunnelling Coys. dugouts.	MAROEUIL Area.	To be clear of AUBREY CAMP by 12 noon. By busses to be arranged by 56th Div. "Q".
"	56th	167th Bde. (less 1½ Bns.)	MAROEUIL Area	CHELERS Area.	
"	56th	1½ Bns. 167th Bde.	MAROEUIL Area.	AUBREY CAMP and Tunnelling Coys. dugouts.	Not to enter AUBREY CAMP before noon.
10th Jan.	56th	1 Bn. 169th Bde.	RED LINE	FREVILLERS AREA.	By busses. Place of embussment to be arranged by 56th Div. "Q".

SECRET.

Vol 25

WAR DIARY

OF

GENERAL STAFF

56th DIVISION.

FROM 1st FEBRUARY 1918.
TO 28th FEBRUARY 1918.

------------oOo------------

WAR DIARY
or
INTELLIGENCE SUMMARY.

(Erase heading not required.)

56th Division, General Staff.

February, 1918. Army Form C. 2118.

Instructions regarding War Diaries and Intelligence Summaries are contained in F.S. Regs., Part II. and the Staff Manual respectively. Title pages will be prepared in manuscript.

Place	Date	Hour	Summary of Events and Information	Remarks and references to Appendices
VILLERS – CHATEL.	1918 Feb. 1st.		Reliefs carried out of Bns. in 167th, 168 & 169th Infantry Brigades working forward under C.E. XIII Corps.	APP. A.
	2nd.		G.O.C. attended Tactical Scheme of 169th Infantry Brigade during morning and demonstration of M.G. barrages and L.T.M. firing during afternoon.	
			G.S.O.I visited 62nd Division to arrange details of relief.	
	3rd.		Divisional Staff ride held. Attended by G.O.C., G.S.O.I, G.S.O.II, illustrating measures to be adopted for counter-attack in the event of an enemy break through on the right Divnl. front of XIII Corps. Held in actual ground.	
	4th	8 pm.	Operation Order No. 149 re relief of 62nd Division by 56th Division issued.	APP. B.
	5th		Amendment No. 1 to 56th Division Order No. 149 of 3rd February issued.	" B.
			Addendum No. 2 to 56th Division Order No. 149 of 3rd February issued. G.S.O. I visited 62nd Division to discuss details of reorganisation of Divisional Sector into a 3 Brigade front.	" B.
	6th.	8 am.	Operation Order No. 150 re reorganisation of Divisional Sector into a 3 Brigade front issued.	APP. B
	7th.		169th Infantry Brigade moved to MAROEUIL Area with H.Q. at ST.AUBIN. Weather wet.	APP. A.
	8th.		Units of 169th Infantry Brigade relieved units of 186th Infantry Brigade in the right section of 62nd Divisional front, the 5th and 16th London Regiments going into the front line. Relief took place after dark.	APP. A.
			Major-General DUDGEON, C.B. reassumed command of 56th Division on his return from short leave in England.	
	9th	9.30 a.m.	Command of Right Section of 62nd Division passed to B.G.C. 169th Infantry Brigade.	APP. A.
			168th Infantry Brigade moved into the MAROEUIL Area.	
	10th		168th Infantry Brigade relieved the 185th Infantry Brigade in the Left Section of 62nd Divisional front. Command passed at 10 p.m.	APP. A.
	11th		G.O.C. 56th Division took over Command of the Divisional front from G.O.C. 62nd Division at 11 a.m.	
			167th Infantry Brigade moved into Divisional Reserve in MAROEUIL Area.	APP. A.
			Slight hostile shelling of our Reserve Lines and GAVRELLE, otherwise the enemy was quiet. Weather boisterous. Visibility good at intervals.	
	12th.		Quiet day. Slight hostile shelling of MILL POST during the morning. 167th Infantry Brigade took over a portion of the Divisional front from 169th Infantry Brigade. The Divisional Sector is now held by 169th Inf. Bde. on the right, 167th Inf. Bde. in the Centre, and 168th Inf. Bde. on the Left, each with one battalion in the line, one in support and one	APP. A.

Army Form C. 2118.

WAR DIARY
or
INTELLIGENCE SUMMARY.

(Erase heading not required.)

Instructions regarding War Diaries and Intelligence Summaries are contained in F. S. Regs., Part II. and the Staff Manual respectively. Title pages will be prepared in manuscript.

Place	Date	Hour	Summary of Events and Information	Remarks and references to Appendices
VICTORY CAMP.	1918. Feb. 12th.		Quiet day. Weather wet and visibility poor. 169th Inf. Bde. carried out an inter-battalion relief.	APP. A.
	14th.		Quiet day. One of our snipers hit a German and 4 German stretcher bearers went out under a red flag and took him in. Enemy fired a few gas shells on to Right Brigade area. 168th Infantry Brigade carried out an inter-battalion relief.	APP. A.
	15th.		Visibility still poor. Enemy fired a few shells into GAVRELLE. G.O.C. & G.S.O.I attended a Conference at XIII Corps H.Q.	APP. A.
	16th.		Weather cold and clear. Hostile artillery shelled our battery positions at MAISON DE LA COTE with 5.9" and 4.2" very persistently. Our heavies including a 12" gun shelled enemy battery positions behind CREST WOOD. 167th Infantry Brigade carried out an inter-battalion relief.	APP. A.
	17th.		Hostile Artillery again shelled our battery position at MAISON DE LA COTE. Aircraft active on both sides.	APP. A.
	18th.		169th Infantry Brigade carried out an inter-battalion relief. During the preceding night a strong hostile patrol approached MILL POST but were driven off by Lewis Gun and rifle fire after throwing one egg bomb. Hostile artillery quiet except for a few gas shells near GAVRELLE. 168th Infantry Brigade carried out an inter-battalion relief.	APP. A.
	19th.		Weather cold and frosty making the trenches more passable. At 9 p.m. the enemy shelled MILL POST rather heavily in conjunction with a raid on the Division on our left, but no infantry action followed. Weather fine & cold.	
	20th.		Early this morning at 4.45 a.m. one of our patrols consisting of 5 O.R. was visiting GAVRELLE POST when they were challenged by a party of Germans. They charged but were driven off leaving 1 wounded man in the enemy's hands. The enemy was estimated to be 12 strong. Situation quiet. Slight shelling on both sides. 167th Infantry Brigade carried out an inter-battalion relief.	APP. A.
	21st		Situation normal. Enemy shelled our battery positions in vicinity of railway cutting (B.26 central) and Centre Bde. H.Q. very persistently throughout the day. 169th Inf. Bde. carried out an inter-battalion relief.	APP. A.
	22nd		Quiet day. 168th Infantry Brigade carried out an inter-battalion relief.	

Army Form C. 2118.

WAR DIARY
or
INTELLIGENCE SUMMARY.

(Erase heading not required.)

Instructions regarding War Diaries and Intelligence Summaries are contained in F. S. Regs., Part II. and the Staff Manual respectively. Title pages will be prepared in manuscript.

Place	Date	Hour	Summary of Events and Information	Remarks and references to Appendices
VICTORY CAMP.	Feb. 23rd.		The Commander-in-Chief visited Div. H.Q. and was received by the G.O.C. and heads of Staff Branches. Quiet day, except for hostile shelling of our battery positions in vicinity of MAISON DE LA COTE.	WM
	24th		Quiet day. Desultory sniping by both artilleries.	
	25th		167th Infantry Brigade carried out an inter-battalion relief. Visibility very good. Our artillery carried out a destructive shoot on enemy's batteries in FRESNES. Situation quiet in forward areas.	APP. A. WM
	26th		G.S.O. II returned from a month's leave in England. Quiet in forward areas. Considerable hostile shelling of our battery positions round the RAILWAY CUTTING and 167th Infantry Brigade H.Q. Weather clear and visibility good.	WM WM
	27th		Situation normal. Hostile artillery shelled BAILLEUL. Weather clear and cool, rain at night.	WM
	28th		168th & 169th Infantry Brigades carried out inter-battalion reliefs. Usual shelling of BAILLEUL. Our patrols were active during the night. 169th Infantry Brigade carried out an inter-battalion relief.	APP. A. APP. A.

5th March, 1918.

[signature]
Major-General,
Commanding 56th Division.

February 1918.   LOCATION TABLE at 6 a.m.   APPENDIX 'A'

	1st	2nd	3rd	4th	5th	6th	7th	8th	9th	10th	11th	12th	13th	14th	15th
Div. H.Q.	VILLERS-CHATEL										VICTORY CAMP, G.3.d.7.3.				
167th Inf.Bde. H.Q.	CHELERS										ST.AUBIN		B.27.a.4.8.		
1st Lond. Rgt.	TINQUES										MAROEUIL		LINE (C)		
3rd "	CHELERS										MAROEUIL SUPPORT				
7th Middx. "	AUBREY CAMP										WAKEFIELD CAMP (Res.)				
8th "															
168th Inf.Bde. H.Q.	ORLENCOURT							ST.AUBIN B.20.d.1.5.				RICLINCOURT (Bt.)			
4th Lond. Rgt.	MAGNICOURT							MAROEUIL LINE (L)							
12th "	STEWARTS CAMP							RICLINGHEM (W)				SUPPORT			
13th "	MONCHY-BRETON							MAROEUIL SUPPORT				LINE (L)			
14th "															
169th Inf.Bde. H.Q.	FREVILLERS						ST.AUBIN		MAISON BLANCHE, H.1.d.3.8.						
2nd Lond. Rgt.	TRAFALGAR CAMP CAUCOURT							ROUNDHAY CAMP (A.6.)				LINE (R)			
5th "	"						MAROEUIL LINE (L)								
9th "	"						ST.AUBIN LINE (R)				ST.AUBIN (Res.)				
16th "	FREVILLERS											SUPPORT			
Div. Arty. H.Q.	BERLES										VICTORY CAMP				
280 Bde.	BETHENCOURT														
281 "	LA TARGETTE														
Pioneers 1/5th CHESHIRE RGT.	BAILLEUL AUX-CORNAILLES									ST.CATHERINES					
193rd M.G. Coy.	CAMBLIGNEUL							ST.CATHERINES							

APPENDIX 'A'

February 1918. — LOCATION TABLE at 6 a.m.

	16th 17th 18th	19th 20th 21st	22nd 23rd 24th	25th 26th 27th 28th
Div. H.Q.	VICTORY CAMP, C.3.b.7.3.			
167th Inf.Bde. H.Q.	B.24.a.4.8.			
1st Lond. Rgt.	WAKEFIELD CAMP	SUPPORT	LINE	RESERVE
2nd "	LINE(C)	RESERVE	SUPPORT	LINE
7th Midx.				
8th "	B.24.a.6.4.(SUPPORT)	LINE	RESERVE	SUPPORT
168th Inf.Bde. H.Q.	B.20.b.5.			
4th Lond. Rgt.	ROCLINCOURT W.(Res)–B.21.b.6.4(Sup)	LINE	RESERVE	
13th "	B.21.a.6.9 Sup	RUCLINCOURT W.(Res)	RESERVE	
14th "	LINE(L)		SUPPORT	
169th Inf.Bde. H.Q.	MAISON BLANCHE, H.14.3.8.			
2nd Lond. Rgt.	LINE(R)	MONDHAM(Sup)	RESERVE	LINE
5th "	ST.AUBIN(Res) LINE(R)	RESERVE	SUPPORT	RESERVE
8th "		SUPPORT	LINE	
16th "	MONDHAM(Sup)–ST.AUBIN(Res)	LINE		SUPPORT
Div. Arty. H.Q.	VICTORY CAMP			
280 Bde.	H.16.8.0.			
281 "	B.21.a.05.25			
Pioneers – 1/5 Cheshire Regt	ST.CATHERINES			
193rd M.G.Coy.	ST.CATHERINES			

SECRET.   War Diary   Appendix B   Copy No. 28

56th DIVISION ORDER No. 149.   3rd February 1918.

1.   56th Division will relieve 62nd Division in the Right Divisional Sector XIII Corps between 8th & 11th inst., the relief to be completed by 6 a.m. February 11th.

2.   56th Division will pass from G.H.Q. Reserve at 12 noon 9th February.

3.   Moves in connection with the relief are given in the attached Table of Moves.

4.   Artillery reliefs will be completed by February 17th.

5.   Details of relief will be arranged between respective Infantry Brigadiers, C.R.A's., C.R.E's., A.Ds.M.S. & D.M.G.O's.

6.   The personnel of 56th Divisional Artillery will be held in readiness from 12 noon 9th February until the completion of the Artillery reliefs to relieve the personnel of 62nd Divisional Artillery at short notice.
    Guns will be taken over "in situ".

7.   Details of reliefs of Working Parties are given in Table "E"

8.   Command of Brigade Sections will pass at 9.30 a.m. following night of relief.

9.   Command of the Divisional Sector will pass at 11 a.m. 11th February at which hour Div. H.Q. will close at VILLERS CHATEL and open at VICTORY CAMP.

10. Field Ambulances & Train Cos. will move under the orders of A.D.M.S. & O.C. Train respectively.

11. ACKNOWLEDGE.

B Pakenham
Lieut-Colonel,
General Staff.

Issued at   8 p.m.

Copy No. 1. 167th Infantry Brigade.
       2. 168th Infantry Brigade.
       3. 169th Infantry Brigade.
       4. 1/5th Cheshire Regt.
       5. G.R.A.
       6. C.R.E.
       7. 193rd Div. M.G.Coy.
       8. 56th Div. M.G.Officer.
       9. 56th Div. Signal Coy.
      10. 56th Div. Gas Officer.
      11. A.D.M.S.
      12. "Q"
      13. A.P.M.
      14. D.A.D.O.S.
      15. D.A.D.V.S.
      16. 56th Div. Train.
      17. 56th Div. Supply Column.
      18. No. 56 Amm. Sub. Park.
      19. A.D.C.
      20. Camp Commandant.
      21. Div. Wing O. M. & R.C.
      22. 56th Div. Employment Coy.
      23. French Mission.
      24. XIII Corps.
      25. 62nd Division.
      26. 31st Division.
      27. Guards Division.
      28.) War Diary.
      29.)
      30. File.
      31. 170th Tunnelling Coy.
      32. 185th Tunnelling Coy.
      33. XIII Corps "Q"

P.T.O.

MARCH TABLE TO ACCOMPANY 56th DIVISION ORDER No. 149.

TABLE A.

Serial No.	Date. Feby.	Unit.	From.	To.	Remarks.
1.	6th	169th Bde. M.G.Coy.	LA COMTE.	ANZIN.	To relieve 186th/M.G.Coy. on (7/8th. Dismounted personnel by lorries, transport by road. & T. & B
2.	7th	169th Inf. Bde. (less 1 Battalion).	FREVILLERS Area.	MAROEUIL Area.	Battalion at CAUCOURT/to march. Remainder dismounted personnel by rail. Transport by road.
3.	7th	187th Inf. Bde. (less 2 Battalions).	MAROEUIL Area.	FREVILLERS AREA.	
4.	8th	168th & 193rd M.G.Coys.	Present areas.	168th Coy. ANZIN. 193rd " St. CATHERINES	Dismounted personnel of 168th Coy. by rail. Remainder and transport by road. Bde. To relieve 185th & 62nd Div. M.G.Coy. on 9th/10th.
5.	8th/9th.	169th Inf. Bde.	MAROEUIL Area & TRAFALGAR CAMP.	Right Section.	In relief of 185th Inf. Bde. By Light Railway.
6.	8th/9th.	186th Inf. Bde.	Right Section.	MAROEUIL Area.	
7.	9th	168th Inf. Bde. (less 1 Battalion)	MONCHY-BRETON Area.	MAROEUIL Area.	Dismounted personnel by rail. Transport by road.
8.	9th	186th Inf. Bde. (less 1 Battalion)	MAROEUIL Area.	MONCHY-BRETON Area.	
9.	10th/11th	168th Inf. Bde.	MAROEUIL Area.	Left Section.	In relief of 185th Inf. Bde. By light railway.
10.	10th/11th	185th Inf. Bde.	Left Section.	MAROEUIL Area.	
11.	11th	185th Inf. Bde.(less 1 Bn)	MAROEUIL Area.	Res.Div.Area.	

T A B L E A (Cont'd).

MARCH TABLE TO ACCOMPANY 56th DIVISION ORDER No. 149.

Serial no.	Date. Feby.	Unit.	From.	To	Remarks.
12.	11th	167th Inf. Bde.	CHELERS Area.	MAROEUIL Area.	As in Serial No. 7.
13.	12th	1 Bn. 167th Inf. Bde.	MAROEUIL Area.	RED LINE.	By Light Railway.

NOTE:- Details of moves by rail or lorry will be notified by "Q" 56th Division.

P.T.O.

TABLE "B"

To accompany 8th Division Order No. 149.

Reliefs of Working Parties, etc.

1. **Reliefs of parties working with Tunnellers.**
   (a)   200 men of 62nd Division working with 176th Tunnelling Coy. on RED Line will be relieved by a party of similar strength consisting of 67 men detailed from each Infantry Brigade (plus a proper proportion of officers and N.C.Os.)
   (b)   Party will proceed by rail to ARRAS on 7th Feb. where they will be met by a guide of 176th Tunnelling Coy.
         Details of train will be issued by "Q".
         300 (working strength) men of 56th Division working under 176th and 185th Tunnelling Cos. on Corps dugout scheme will be relieved at 12 noon, 8th Feb., by 187th Inf. Bde. and proceed to WINNIPEG Camp (ECOIVRES), coming under the orders of 168th Inf. Bde. on arrival of latter in HAROEUIL Area on 9th Feb. "Q" will arrange train.

2. **Reliefs of Pioneer Coys.**
   (i)   Coy. at Corps H.Q. will be relieved on morning 8th Feb. by 187th Inf. Bde. and will then relieve 100 men of 62nd Division working under C.E. on BROWN Line, and quartered in dugouts about BAILLEUL. "Q" to arrange train or lorries.
   (ii)   1 Coy. in B.19.d. remains.
   (iii) 1 Coy. at ST. CATHERINE'S moves on 10th instant to B.19.d. to replace Pioneer Coy. of 31st Division.
   (iv)   1 Coy. at ST. CATHERINE'S remains.
   (v)   Bn. H.Q. moves to ST. CATHERINE'S on 10th inst.

3. **Reliefs of Battalions working under C.E., XIII Corps.**
   (a)   Battalion 189th Inf. Bde. in TRAFALGAR CAMP will not be required for work from 7th Feb., and will come under the orders of B.G.C., 169th Inf. Bde. on arrival of latter in HAROEUIL Area.
   (b)   Battalion 168th Inf. Bde. in STEWART CAMP, will be relieved by 1 Battalion 186th Inf. Bde. at 3 p.m. 10th instant.
   (c)   1 Battalion 167th Inf. Bde. at AUBREY CAMP will be relieved by 1 Battalion 185th Inf. Bde. It will clear AUBREY CAMP at 5 p.m. 10th Feb., and march to ST. AUBIN, and will come under the command of B.G.C. 167th Inf. Bde. on arrival of latter in HAROEUIL Area on 11th inst.

4. **Relief of Battalion, 62nd Division, working in RED LINE.**
      1 Battalion 167th Inf. Bde. will relieve 1 Battalion, 187th Inf. Bde. in RED LINE, on 12th Feb. - relief to be complete by 12 noon. Light railway arrangements to be communicated by "Q".

War Diary Appendix B

56th Divn. No. G.3/884.

AMENDMENT No. 1 to 56th DIVISION ORDER No. 149
of 3rd February, 1918.

1. Reference para. 1 (a) of Table "B" -
   Delete in 4th line "officers and"

2. Reference para. 1 (a) of Table "B" each Brigade will detail one officer who will conduct their respective Brigade parties to 176th Tunnelling Company and will, on completion of that duty return to their units.

C. W. Haydon Capt.
for Lieut-Colonel,
General Staff, 56th Division.

4th February, 1918.

Copy to all recipients of Order.

S E C R E T

56th Division No. G.3/889

Copy No. 24

Addendum No. 2 to
56th Division Order No.149.

1. All Units of 56th Divn. on arrival in the forward area (including MAROEUIL area) will come under the tactical command of the G.O.C. 62nd Division, until the command of the Sector is handed over, and will report their arrival by wire to H.Q. 62nd Division.
   Similarly Units of 62nd Division remaining in the forward area after the command of the Sector is handed over, will come under the tactical command of G.O.C., 56th Division.

2. On relief, the code names used by 62nd Division will be taken over by this Division; list of code names taken over will be forwarded to this Office by 12 noon, 12th instant.

3. All maps, air-photos and defence schemes will be taken over by relieving Units.

4. ACKNOWLEDGE.

5th February, 1918.

C.W. Haydon loyl.
for. Lieut-Colonel,
General Staff, 56th Division.

Copy to all recipients of Order No. 149.

SECRET   Copy No. 29

56th DIVISION ORDER No. 150.

6th February, 1918

1. On completion of the relief of 62nd Division by 56th Division, the Divisional Sector will be reorganized and will be held by 3 Brigades in the line.

2. 167th Infantry Brigade will take over the centre Brigade front from 169th Infantry Brigade, the relief being carried out on the night 12th/13th February.
   Brigade H.Q. will be at B.27.a.4.6. (Railway cutting)

3. The rear (Brigade Reserve) Battalions of each Infantry Brigade will be accommodated as follows:-

   Right Brigade - ST. AUBIN
   Centre Brigade - WAKEFIELD CAMP.
   Left Brigade   - ROCLINCOURT W. Camp.

4. All details of relief will be arranged between Brigadiers concerned.

5. Maps showing the Brigade boundaries, H.Qrs., general distribution of troops, etc. are issued herewith to Infantry Brigadiers, C.R.A., C.R.E. and D.M.G.O. only.

6. Maps, air-photos and Battalion Defence Scheme of the new Centre Section will be taken over on relief.

7. ACKNOWLEDGE.

                                    C.W. Haydon Capt.
                                    for Lieut-Colonel,
                                    General Staff, 56th Division.

Issued at 8 a.m.

Copy No. 1. 167th Infantry Brigade.   Copy No. 17. 56th Div. Supply Col.
        2. 168th Infantry Brigade.   18. No.56 Am. Sub Park.
        3. 169th Infantry Brigade.   19. A.D.C.
        4. 1/5th Cheshire Regt.   20. Camp Commandant.
        5. C.R.A.   21. Div.Wing, C.M.& R.C.
        6. C.R.E.   22. 56th Div. Employ. Coy.
        7. 193rd Div. M.G.Coy.   23. French Mission.
        8. 56th Div. M.G.Officer.   24. XIII Corps.
        9. 56th Div. Signal Coy.   25. 62nd Division.
       10. 56th Div. Gas Officer.   26. 31st Division.
       11. A.D.M.S.   27. Guards Division.
       12. "Q"   28.) War Diary.
       13. A.P.M.   29.)
       14. D.A.D.O.S.   30. File.
       15. D.A.D.V.S.   31. 176th Tunnelling Coy.
       16. 56th Div. Train.   32. 185th Tunnelling Coy.
                                               33. XIII Corps "Q"

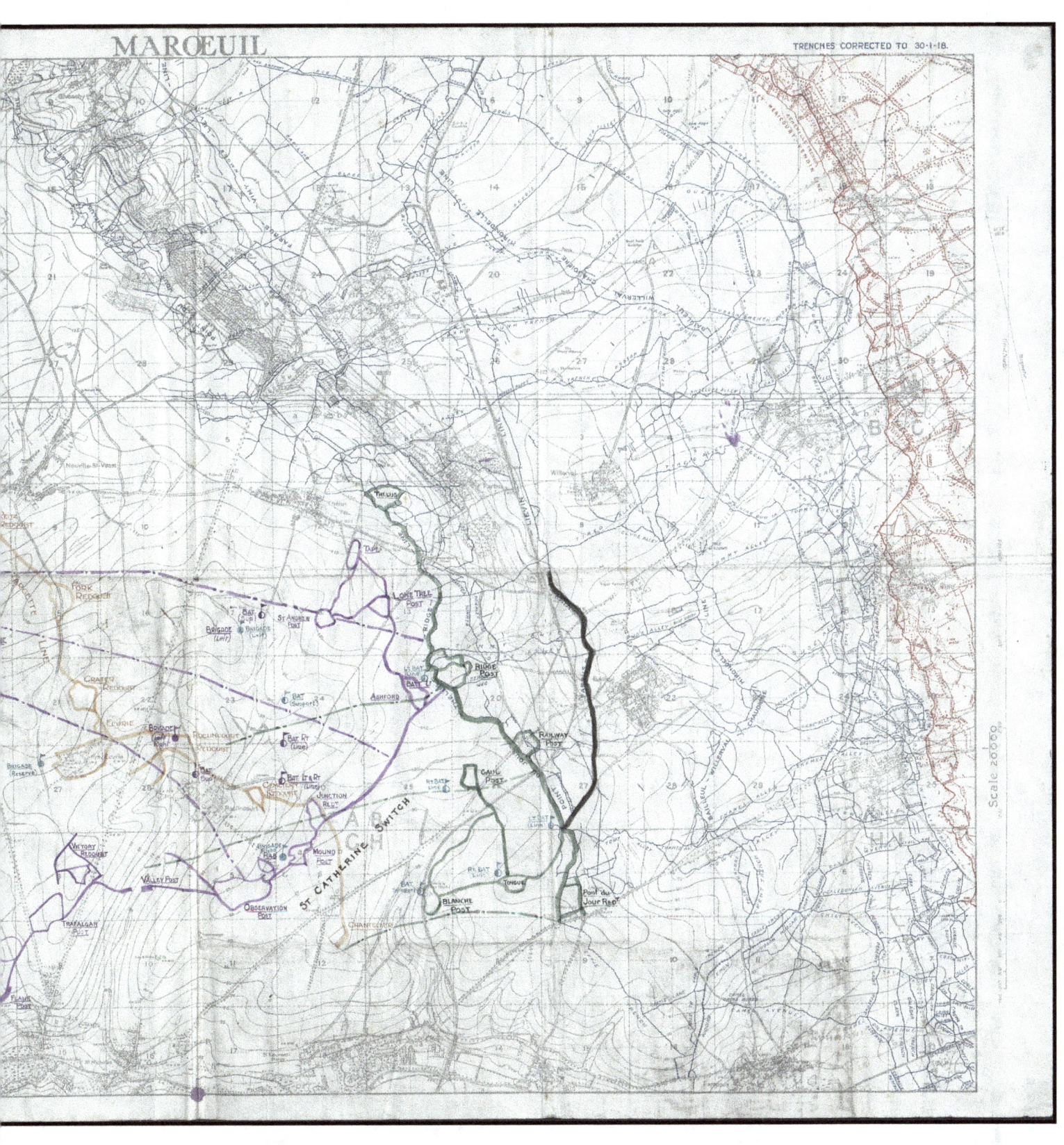

56th Division, WAR DIARY Army Form C. 2118.
General Staff.   or   January, 1918.
            INTELLIGENCE SUMMARY.
              (Erase heading not required.)

Instructions regarding War Diaries and Intelligence
Summaries are contained in F.S. Regs., Part II.
and the Staff Manual respectively. Title pages
will be prepared in manuscript.

Place	Date Jan.	Hour	Summary of Events and Information	Remarks and references to Appendices
VICTORY CAMP. ROCLINCOURT.	1st.		Hostile Artillery active on our back areas and battery positions near BAILLEUL. At 11.30 p.m. a small hostile patrol of 5 men penetrated our wire and rushed a sentry post in OPPY POST. They knocked down one sentry but the other promptly attacked them with the bayonet and put them to flight although wounded in three places by revolver bullets. Visibility poor owing to frost and snow. 169th Inf. Bde. carried out an inter-battalion relief.	APP. A.
	2nd.		Situation quiet. Enemy fired a few gas shells into GAVRELLE during the afternoon. Visibility very bad owing to mist. Slight thaw. XIII Corps Order No. 116 received for relief of 56th Division by 62nd Division - relief to be complete by 9th inst.	APP. A.
	3rd.		Quiet day except for hostile shelling of area round left Brigade H.Q. 168th Infantry Brigade relieved 169th Inf. Bde. in the right section., 169th Bde. going into Divnl. Reserve in the MAROEUIL Area. 167th Inf. Bde. carried out inter-battlion reliefs. Weather very cold again. Visibility fair. 56th Div. Order No. 148 for relief of Divnl. Artillery issued. Capt. HAYDON - G.S.O. III went to England on short leave.	APP. A. APP. B(1).
	4th.		Situation quiet. Slight hostile shelling of BAILLEUL. Weather frosty and poor visibility. Lt.Col. PAKENHAM, D.S.O., G.S.O.I. rejoined from leave. XIII Corps 850/243 (G.A.) of 4.1.18 received ordering 56th Divn. into G.H.Q. Reserve and to be under 48 hours notice to entrain.	
	5th		Enemy artillery and T.Ms. more active. Our position in front of OPPY receiving special attention. Our Stokes Mortars retaliated and blew up a hostile dump. Weather cold - visibility poor. 169th Inf. Bde. (Div. Reserve) was relieved by the 187th Inf. Bde. 62nd Division and moved into billets in the PREVILLERS AREA with Bde. H.Q. at PREVILLERS. 187th Inf. Bde. came under the command of G.O.C. 56th Division.	APP. A.
	6th		Situation normal. Aircraft on both sides active. One hostile machine driven down and forced to land near IZEL by one of our patrol scouts. The 187th Inf. Bde. relieved the 168th Inf. Bde. in the right section. 168th Inf. Bde. moved	

Army Form C. 2118.

WAR DIARY
or
INTELLIGENCE SUMMARY.
(Erase heading not required.)

Instructions regarding War Diaries and Intelligence Summaries are contained in F.S. Regs., Part II. and the Staff Manual respectively. Title pages will be prepared in manuscript.

Place	Date	Hour	Summary of Events and Information	Remarks and references to Appendices
VILLERS-CHATEL.	14th.		Heavy fall of snow interfering with training. G.O.C. visited 167th Inf. Bde.	
	15th.		Relief of 56th Div. Artillery by 62nd Div. Artillery commenced. Heavy rain and thaw.	
	16th.		Artillery Relief completed. The three battalions working in forward areas relieved by three other battalions of this Division. Weather stormy.	APP. A.
	17th.		Nothing to report. Weather very wet.	
	18th.		G.O.C., G.S.O. I and G.S.O. II attended 168th Brigade Platoon Competition. 416th Field Coy. R.E. moved in to Forward Area to ECURIE WOOD.	
	19th.		Nothing to report. G.S.O. III rejoined from leave.	
	20th.		Divisional Conference attended by G.O.C. Brigadiers and Divisional "G" Staff on the question of Training held at Div. H.Q.	
	21st.		G.O.C. inspected Div. Artillery at BERLES. G.S.O. I & G.S.O. II judged for 168th Inf. Bde. Platoon Competition.	
	22nd.		G.O.C. held a Conference of Brigadiers on the question of reorganisation of battalions.	
	23rd.		G.O.C. proceeded to ENGLAND on short leave. Brig-Genl. G.H.B.FREETH, C.M.G., D.S.O. assumed command of the Division.	
	24th.		G.S.O. II proceeded to England on short leave. The Three Battalions working in the forward area relieved by three other battalions of this Division.	
	25th.		Nothing to report. Weather fine and warm.	
	26th.		Divisional Platoon Competition won by 1/3rd London Regiment. G.O.C. and "G" Staff attended.	
	27th.		Nothing to report. Weather fine and warm.	

Army Form C. 2118.

WAR DIARY
or
INTELLIGENCE SUMMARY.

(Erase heading not required)

Place	Date	Hour	Summary of Events and Information	Remarks and references to Appendices
VILLERS-CHATEL.	28th		XIII Corps Platoon Competition, G.O.C. and "G" Staff attended.	
	29th		Nothing to report.	
	30th		1/3rd London Regiment, 1/9th London Regiment, 1/12th London Regiment split up and passed out of 56th Division in accordance with instructions for reorganising Divisions on 9 Bns. basis.	
	31st		G.S.O. I visited H.Qrs. XIII Corps in connection of relief of 62nd Division by 56th Division.	

B.W.Haydon Capt
for Brigadier-General,
Commanding 56th Division.

Appx A

January – LOCATION TABLE at 6 p.m. – 1918

	1	2	3	4	5	6	7	8	9	10	11	12	13	14	15
Div. H.Q.	Victory Camp		Roclincourt						Villers Châtel						
167th Inf.Bde. H.Q.	B.21.a.7.8							Louez	Chelers						
1st Lond. Rgt.	Roclincourt W.	B.24.a.65.95 (R)				Maroeuil	Monchy-Breton	Maroeuil	Villers Brulin						
3rd "	B.24.a.65.95 (L)	Roclincourt W (Res)				St Aubin	St Aubin Stuart's Camp	St Aubin	Aubrey Camp						
7th Midx.	B.1.c.8.7 (L)	B.2.a.1.5 (Sup)				Maroeuil	Maroeuil Magnicourt	Ottawa	Chelers						
8th "	B.2.a.1.5 (3)	B.1.c.8.7 (L)				Ottawa	Ottawa la Thieuloye	Maroeuil	Tinques						
M.G. Coy						Anzin	Bajus	Anzin	Tinquette						
						"	Bajus								
168th Inf.Bde. H.Q.	Louez		H.1.d.3.6.			Louez	Orlencourt								
4th Lond. Rgt.	St Aubin	St Aubin	B.30.a.6.1. (R)		Frevillers	Maroeuil	Monchy-Breton								
12th "	Maroeuil	Maroeuil	Wakefield Camp			St Aubin	Stuart's Camp								
13th "	Wakefield Camp	B.30.a.95.95. (L)	B.30.a.95.95. (L)			Maroeuil	Magnicourt								
14th "	Maroeuil	Roundhay Camp (Sup)				Ottawa	la Thieuloye								
M.G. Coy						Anzin	Bajus								
T.M.B.						"	Bajus								
169th Inf.Bde. H.Q.	H.1.d.3.6.		St Aubin		Frevillers		Trafalgar Camp			Le Cauroy Cambligneul					
2nd Lond. Rgt.	Roundhay Camp	St Aubin	St Aubin		Frevillers	Trafalgar Camp									
5th "	B.30.a.85.95 (L)	Maroeuil	Maroeuil												
9th "	Red Line				Caucourt										
16th "	B.30.a.6.1. (R)	Maroeuil	Maroeuil		La Comte (Cambligneul)										
M.G. Coy		Anzin	Anzin												
T.M.B.		Anzin	Anzin												
Div. Arty. H.Q.	Victory Camp	Victory Camp							Bailleul-aux-Cornailles						
280 Bde.	H.1.8.0.														
281 "	B.21.c.0.0.								Cambligneul						
Pioneers 1/5 Cheshire Rt	St Catherines														
193 M.G. Coy															

Appx A

56 Division — LOCATION TABLE at 6 p.m.

January 1918	16	17	18	19	20	21	22	23	24	25	26	27	28	29	30	31
Div. H.Q.	Villers-Châtel															
167th Inf.Bde. H.Q.	Chelers															
1st Lod. Rgt.	Aubrey Camp															
3rd "	Villers Brulin															
7th Midx.	Chelers															
8th "	Tinques				Tinques											
168th Inf.Bde. H.Q.	Orlencourt								Aubrey Camp							
4th Lond. Rgt.	Monchy Breton															
12th "	La Thieuloye								Stewarts Camp							
13th "	Magnicourt															
14th "	Stewarts Camp								Monchy-Breton							
169th Inf.Bde. H.Q.	Frevillers															
2nd Lond. Rgt.	Frevillers								Caucourt							
5th "	Trafalgar Camp															
9th "	Cambligneul								Trafalgar Camp							
16th "	Caucourt															
Div. Arty. H.Q.	Berles															
280 Bde.	Berles															
281 "	La Targette															
Pioneers.	Bailleul aux Cornailles															
193 M.G. Coy	Cambligneul															

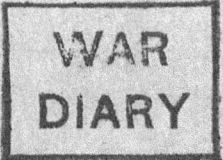

G E N E R A L   S T A F F

5 6 t h   D I V I S I O N

M A R C H

1 9 1 8

Attached:-

Report on Operations 28th
& 29th March.

Appendices I to XXX.

Appendix XXV.   Report on the Operations of 56th
                Division in the vicinity of OPPY
                & GAVRELLE, 28th & 29th March, 1918.

Appendix XXVI. Orders & Instructions issued during
                the Operations, 28th March, 1918.

Appendix XXVII. Orders & Instructions issued during
                the Operations, 29th March, 1918.

Appendix XXX.   Map shewing Boundaries & H.Qs. 56th
                Division, 6 a.m. 28.3.18.

SECRET.   56th Division No.G.3/222.

REPORT ON THE OPERATIONS of 56th DIVISION in the vicinity of OPPY & GAVRELLE, 28th & 29th March, 1918.

Reference Map MAROEUIL 1/20,000.

On 12th March information was received that an offensive by the enemy on a large front, which might include the VIMY Ridge, was imminent.

From this date Brigades in the line were ordered to be extremely alert and the whole Division stood to arms at 5 a.m. each morning.

Counter offensive shoots by the Artillery were carried out almost daily, especially at night and just prior to dawn, so as to disorganize any possibly assembly of troops for attack.

On 21st March the enemy offensive South of the R.SCARPE commenced and by 27th he was in occupation of the Village of MONCHY, which commanded the ground on the North of that river.

During this time it became apparent that the enemy would endeavour to envelop ARRAS, and to capture the VIMY Ridge from the South, and much work was done in improving the defensive switches facing South.

Night 27th/28th March.

On the night 27/28th March the Division was ordered to extend its left flank and relieve the troops of the 3rd Canadian Division for a distance of approximately 1500 yards. This entailed an extension of the front of the Right (169th) Infantry Brigade to include BRADFORD & BIRD POSTS, and the taking over by the Left (168th) Infantry Brigade of TOMMY & ARLEUX POSTS.

The dispositions of the two Brigades in the line were then -

169th Infantry Brigade.

Right Battn.   1/16th London Regiment (Queens Westminsters) holding
                                                    TOWY POST.
Left Battn.   5th London Regt. (London Rifle Brigade) holding
                                   MILL, BRADFORD & BIRD POSTS.

In BAILLEUL - WILLERVAL Line - 2nd Bn. London Regiment.
In FARBUS Line   - 1 Coy. 1/5th Cheshire Regt.
                                              (Pioneers).
In Brigade Reserve   - 2 Cos. 1st London Regt. (attached
                                    from 167th Infantry Brigade).
                                Detachment of 176th Tunnelling Coy.
                                R.E. (in POINT DU JOUR Redoubt).

168th Infantry Brigade.

Right Battn.   4th London Regt. - holding BEATTY, WOOD & OPPY Posts.
Left Battn.   1/13th London Regt. (Kensingtons) - holding TOMMY &
                                                    ARLEUX Posts.

In BAILLEUL - WILLERVAL Line - 1/14th London Regt. (London Scottish)
In CHESTER Post (B.15.d.)   - 2 Platoons 1/5th Cheshire Regt.
                                              (Pioneers).
In POINT DU JOUR Line & BRIERLEY HILL - 2 Cos. 1st London Regt.
                                (attached from 167th London Bde.)
                                and 1½ Cos. 1/5th Cheshire Regt.

In Divisional Reserve   - 167th Inf.Bde. (less 1 Bn.) and
                                3 Field Coys. R.E.

The above extension was ordered under XIII Corps Order No. 122, which laid down that the BAILLEUL - WILLERVAL Line was to be held as our front line, and our old front line system to be considered as an outpost line.

This was subsequently cancelled by XIII Corps Order No. 123, which ordered our front line system to be held as such in order to conform to the 4th Division on our right (XVII Corps).

/At

- 2 -

At 8.45 p.m. however, as a result of verbal orders from XIII Corps, this was modified as regards ARLEUX Post, in order to conform to the defensive line of the 3rd Canadian Division on our Left, and the troops holding this were ordered, if heavily attacked, to withdraw fighting to the ARLEUX LOOP SOUTH, switching back from TOMMY POST.

The reliefs resultant on this redistribution had not been completed at 3 a.m. when a heavy hostile bombardment opened.

At that hour the L.R.B. (169th Bde.) had not taken over BAILLEUL EAST Post, and one Company of the 1st Canadian Mounted Rifles had not been relieved from SUGAR POST. This latter Company remained in SUGAR POST throughout the battle, being placed by the courtesy of the B.G.C. 8th Canadian Infantry Brigade under the orders of 168th Infantry Brigade.

Commencement of the Battle.

At 3 a.m. the enemy opened a heavy bombardment consisting of heavy gas shelling of our rear lines of defence and Headquarters, followed later by H.E. on the BAILLEUL - WILLERVAL Line and FARBUS Line.

At about 5.0 a.m. a very heavy artillery and Trench Mortar bombardment was opened on our front line system and forward posts, which continued until about 7 a.m.

At 5.35 a.m. the S.O.S. was sent by Power Buzzer from TOWY Post but no infantry attack developed then.

Owing to the continuous enemy shelling there seemed to be no doubt that an attack was imminent, and, therefore, at about 6.15 a.m. H.Q. & 1 Bn. of 167th Infantry Brigade were sent forward to the neighbourhood of CHANTECLER together with all the Reserve Machine Guns of the Division.

At 6.40 a.m. counter preparation was ordered to be carried out by Heavy & Field Artillery.

At about 7.5 a.m. the S.O.S. Signal was again sent up from TOWY POST, and was almost immediately followed by the S.O.S. along the whole line up to and including OPPY Post. The remaining battalion of the 167th Infantry Brigade was ordered forward to the vicinity of CHANTECLER.

The enemy attack.

Under cover of a creeping barrage the enemy's infantry moved forward apparently about 7.5 a.m.

The Heavy T.M. & Artillery bombardment had obliterated the bulk of the forward posts from our Southern Boundary to OPPY POST (inclusive). With the exception of TOWY POST and of WOOD POST, in which the dispositions had been changed a day or two previously, the garrisons were apparently wiped out. There was only one survivor of the garrison of MILL POST, who reported that when he left the trenches were almost blotted out, and that the entrances to the large dug-out had already been smothered.

The garrisons of TOWY and WOOD Posts put up a gallant fight.

In the neighbourhood of GAVRELLE the enemy appears to have got into a pocket formed by TOWY and WATER Posts and by NAVAL Trench, and in this pocket he was exposed to the indirect fire of 14 machine guns, which were designed to bring S.O.S. fire on this area.

WOOD POST held out for about an hour, inflicting heavy casualties.

The garrison of TOWY POST made a stand in the Support Trench.

By 7.30 a.m. the enemy was attacking heavily in front, had passed over the Support Trench on either flank and was bombing up towards the Post from TOWY ALLEY in rear.

As it was manifest that there would soon be a shortage of bombs, the garrison after a stiff and splendid resistance, in which they were reduced to 2 Officers & 25 O.R., succeeded in

/fighting

fighting their way back down TOWY Trench and through the enemy back into the NAVAL Line. Meanwhile on the left of the 169th Bde. Section the enemy swarmed over our forward posts and was soon pressing through gaps in the wire and down old C.Ts. into the NAVAL - MARINE Line.

Very soon after the attack had begun the L.R.B. Headquarters personnel under Lieut-Colonel HUSEY, D.S.O. M.C. found themselves repelling a massive onset delivered in 3 successive moves on MARINE Trench.

The wire in front of this line, which had recently been thickened, caused the enemy considerable discomfiture and great losses were caused to him by rifle, Lewis Gun and Machine Gun fire, but such were his numbers that this party was soon outflanked from the North.

The B.G.C. 169th Inf. Bde. therefore ordered Lieut-Colonel HUSEY to fight his way to the junction of THAMES ALLEY and MARINE Trench and to withdraw slowly down THAMES ALLEY to the BAILLEUL - WILLERVAL Line, and by 10.30 a.m. the remains of his Battalion, numbering 4 Officers and 64 O.R. had taken up a position in the BAILLEUL - WILLERVAL Line.

Up to now the Q.W.R. under Lieut-Colonel GLASIER, D.S.O. on the right of 169th Inf. Bde. had been able to hold on to NAVAL Trench from their Southern boundary up to the GAVRELLE Road, and as long as the enemy were being held on the flanks by the L.R.B. and the Lancashire Fusiliers of the 4th Division, they were able successfully to ward off the enemy, inflicting great casualties on him.

Increasing pressure on both flanks soon rendered this position untenable and the enemy, who had been kept well in check, gradually surrounded the remainder of the garrison, and worked round to the right rear. Meanwhile information had been received that ORANGE HILL (S. of the SCARPE) had fallen.

The Corps Commander visited Divisional H.Q. and as a result of his verbal orders a wire was sent out at 10.30 a.m. ordering the withdrawal of 169th Inf. Bde. to the BAILLEUL - WILLERVAL Line, which was to be held at all costs.

1 Battalion of 167th Inf. Bde. was placed under the orders of 169th Inf. Bde. and 6 M.Gs. were sent forward to POINT DU JOUR to strengthen the right flank and our junction with 4th Division. 2 Field Coys. R.E. were also ordered up to strengthen the right flank by holding TONGUE and BLANCHE Posts. These orders were also telephoned to 169th Inf. Bde. and the withdrawal was carried out by the Q.W.R., who fought their way slowly back.

As regards the 168th Inf. Bde. the 4th London Regt. had been putting up a gallant defence on the MARQUIS Line. The Reserve Coy. had been moved forward from BOW Trench at 8.3 a.m. to counter-attack the enemy who had penetrated MARQUIS Trench. Heavy fighting occurred in DUKE Street and the BN. H.Q. there was lost and regained.

At 10.50 a.m. the Brigade was ordered to be prepared to withdraw from our front line system in conjunction with the 3rd CANADIAN DIVISION.

By 11.30 a.m. the position was critical, both flanks of the Battalion being turned, while some of the enemy were even in OUSE ALLEY, the only trench open for a withdrawal.

The remnants of the garrison therefore commenced their withdrawal over the open under the cover of the Reserve Company, which manned the OUSE ALLEY Switch.

At 11.40 a.m., in consequence of orders received from the Corps, an order was sent to 168th Inf. Bde. to withdraw the remainder of its troops (Kensington Regt.) from TOMMY and ARLEUX Posts, in conjunction with 3rd Canadian Div. who similarly received orders to withdraw in co-operation with the Brigade to the BAILLEUL - WILLERVAL Line.

After the withdrawal of 4th London Regt. the enemy made a strong bombing attack on the block in OUSE ALLEY near BOW TRENCH which was, however, effectively stopped by a Lewis Gun covering the block.

/Meanwhile

Meanwhile, as early as 7.30 a.m., while the 4th London Regt. were still fighting in the front system, enemy bombing parties had broken through on their right by TYNE and N. TYNE ALLEYS, captured the two machine guns in position about 100 yds. East of BAILLEUL EAST Post and attacked the post which was held by the London Scottish.

A counter-attack was promptly organized, the enemy was driven back 150 yds. the machine gun crews released from their dugout, and a new block formed in advance of their position.

Repeated attacks were made on this block, but assisted by the fire of Stokes and 6" Newton Mortars these were all repulsed, as also several attacks made over the open astride of the BAILLEUL - GAVRELLE Road.

During the whole morning the situation of the 4th Division on our right was very obscure, the Division being reported to have lost touch with its own Brigades, while the lateral line between 169th Inf. Bde. and 12th Inf. Bde. was also cut. At about noon, however, we were in touch in the BAILLEUL - WILLERVAL Line and later definite touch was also obtained in the POINT DU JOUR - THELUS Line and in the Switch from TOWY ALLEY to MISSOURI Trench.

Up to about 2 p.m. tentative attacks were made by various groups of the enemy on the BAILLEUL - WILLERVAL Line: the enemy method of advance appears to have been to throw their rifles forward into the nearest shell-hole, to hold up their hands in surrender, and then drop down alongside their rifles.

At 2 p.m. another severe bombardment broke out all along the BAILLEUL - WILLERVAL Line, and it was evident that the wire was being cut. During this period low flying enemy planes caused much trouble to the garrison.

At 5 p.m. a heavy attack developed on BAILLEUL EAST POST, which was however repulsed by concentrated artillery and small-arm fire.

By 6 p.m. the situation had become more or less quiet and arrangements were made for the relief of 169th Inf. Bde. by 167th Inf. Bde. when the situation permitted. This relief was eventually carried out, one Battalion of 8th Canadian Inf. Bde. (5th C.M.R.) being sent by the Corps to man and be responsible for the line POINT DU JOUR - Railway in B.27.a.

29th March.

During the night 28th/29th the R.E. were employed on blocking and filling in C.T's in front of the new front line and patrolling was actively carried out, the 13th London Regt. (Kensington Regt.) penetrating into ARLEUX LOOP SOUTH - KENT Road and the junction of TOMMY and BARON.

During the morning our patrols on the left were as active, and dominated those of the enemy, driving him right back to RAILWAY Trench, and even salved ammunition and equipment from the dugouts there.

In fact, on our left the enemy was slow to realize that a withdrawal had been made and it was not until about 3 p.m. that he established a post in the Gun pits about B.5.d.2.5.

On the remainder of the front there was much hostile movement during the whole day and many reports were received of his massing, while a prisoner we captured stated that the attack was to be renewed.

Later it became evident that the enemy was relieving the troops who had attacked.

Night 29th/30th.

On the night 29th/30th the Division (less Artillery) was relieved by 4th Canadian Division, the relief being completed by about 5 a.m.

Casualties.   The total casualties in the action were:-

	Officers.	Other Ranks
Killed	11	135
Wounded	19	405
Missing	25	893
Total	55	1433

General

The Division received the congratulations of the Corps and Army Commanders on its defence, and the G.O.C. on 30th March had the honour of being received by H.M. the King, who was pleased to express his appreciation of its behaviour.

NOTES.

Artillery (i) The frontage of the Division (about 5,000 yds.) was covered by 45 18-pdr. and 12 4.5" Hows. (including 9 18-pdr. of 3rd Canadian Division covering the front taken over on the night 27th/28th March.)

From 3 a.m. to 7.15 a.m. our artillery fired heavily on the enemy's front system, special concentrations being put down, in co-operation with the Heavy Artillery, on lines of organized shell-holes, considered at the time to be T.M. emplacements.

From 6.45 a.m. "counter-preparation" was put into effect and at 7.15 a.m. the S.O.S. barrage was put down.

From then until the withdrawal to the BAILLEUL - WILLERVAL Line was complete, barrage lines were adjusted with Brigade Commanders in accordance with the situation.

During the afternoon many excellent targets were presented, but owing to the limited number of guns, only a few could be taken off the barrage at one time to deal with them.

This was particularly unfortunate, as masses of Infantry, transport and batteries in the open were visible in all directions.

All battery positions were heavily shelled throughout the day and 12 18-pdrs. were destroyed or put out of action by shell fire.

Two 18-pdrs., forming an enfilade section near ARLEUX, obtained many targets with direct observation, until our infantry were ordered to withdraw.

The detachments then damaged the guns, removed dial sights and breechblocks, set the dugouts on fire and retired in accordance with orders.

During the night 28th/29th the artillery were withdrawn, gun by gun, to a range of 3600 yds. from our new front line. Allowing for the 14 guns put out of action, the average expenditure of ammunition was 750 rds. per gun and 650 rounds per Howitzer.

The Heavy Artillery did invaluable work in breaking up enemy masses and in counter battery work, and were assisted by 40 infantry.

/Our Defensive Wire.

Our Defensive Wire.

Much extra wire had been put out in the 6 weeks the Division had been in the line.

There were 3 belts of double apron wire on the NAVAL - MARINE Line. This stood the bombardment well and the enemy was seen to be greatly impeded by it.

Observation.

For the first couple of hours the battle field was covered by smoke.

When this cleared excellent observation was obtained from the Ridge, and it was largely due to this that every effort to advance was frustrated. At one time hostile batteries came into action in the open near BRADFORD POST and just West of the NAVAL - MARINE Line, but were promptly destroyed.

Communications.

The Corps buried cable system was invaluable and communication was maintained to forward battalions until they had to leave their H.Q. As the withdrawal proceeded, wires were cut.

Supply of Ammunition, etc.

The system of keeping all Reserve Ammunition in deep dugouts proved thoroughly sound, as otherwise large quantities would have been destroyed or buried.

There was no shortage of S.A.A. or bombs during the action.

Bearing of the enemy.

It was widely remarked that the enemy approached in a slow dazed manner. This may have been due to the great weight carried and that he was searching for gaps in our wire.

With one exception, where he was reported to have fired rifle grenades from the hip, the enemy infantry did not use their rifles.

They were reported, however, to have sent out light M.Gs. in front.

The clearest description of the enemy's formation is given by the 16th London Regiment (Q.W.R.) who report that he was in about 6 lines, almost shoulder to shoulder.

Enemy Losses.

All reports agree that the enemy losses were extremely heavy, and that they might have been even more heavier were it possible to get more time for individual training of men to get full value out of their weapons.

Machine Guns.

A captured German Officer of 152 Inf. Regt. stated that one of the main causes of the failure of the attack was the intensity of the M.G. barrage, which caused heavy casualties. Numerous targets were obtained for direct fire. Machine Guns were attacked in several instances by low flying aeroplanes, one being knocked out by a bomb, while others were destroyed by Artillery with aeroplane observation.

The total casualties in machine guns were 12, of which only 2 were lost to the enemy, the remainder being destroyed.

A.Dudgeon.
Major-General,
Commanding 56th Division

4th April, 1918.

Distribution :-
XIII Corps	D.M.G.Bn.
167th Infantry Brigade.	"Q"
168th Infantry Brigade.	G.O.C.
169th Infantry Brigade.	G.S.O.I.
C.R.A.	G.S.O.II.
C.R.E.	War Diary.
176 Tun Co RE	

A P P E N D I X   X X V I.

Orders & Instructions issued during the Operations,
28th March, 1918.

"A" Form.
MESSAGES AND SIGNALS.

Army Form C. 2121.
(In pads of 100.)

This message is on a/c of:
APP.XXVI.
~~APP.XXXV~~

TO: G.O.C. 56th Divn.

Sender's Number: G.308
Day of Month: 28
AAA

Will you please convey to the troops under your command my great appreciation of the splendid fight put up by them today against greatly superior numbers AAA They must look on today's action however as being a preliminary to a possible further attack in the morning AAA In no case must any portion of the RED LINE be given up AAA Addsd G.O.C. 56th Divn. reptd G.O.C. R.A.

From: 13th Corps
Time: 10.25 p.m.

(Z)

"A" Form.
MESSAGES AND SIGNALS.

Army Form C. 2121.
(In pads of 100.)
No. of Message..........

Prefix........Code........m	Words.	Charge.	This message is on a/c of:	Recd. at .... m.
Office of Origin and Service Instructions.	Sent		..............Service.	Date...............
	At..........m.		APP. XXXVI	From.............
	To..........			
	By..........		(Signature of "Franking Officer.")	By.............

TO	56 Div.		

Sender's Number.	Day of Month.	In reply to Number.	
G.310	28		A A A

The Army Commander desires me to convey to the 56th Divn his high appreciation of the gallantry and tenacity shewn by them during to-day's fight against greatly superior odds.

From: 13 Corps
Place:
Time: 10.25 p.m.

The above may be forwarded as now corrected. (Z)

....
Censor. Signature of Addressor or person authorised to telegraph in his name.

* This line should be erased if not required.
(3198.) Wt. W 12952/M 1294. 375,000 Pads. 1/17. H. W. & V., Ld. (E. 818.)

"A" Form.
MESSAGES AND SIGNALS.

Army Form C. 2121.
(In pads of 100.)

Prefix	Code	m	Words.	Charge.		No. of Message
Office of Origin and Service Instructions. PRIORITY to 167 Bde. (Sd.) F.B.Hurndall Major			Sent At .... m. By	This message is on a/c of: .... Service. APP. XXV. (Signature of "Franking Officer.")	Recd. at .... m. Date............. From .... By	

TO	167 Bde.	C.R.A.
	168 "	D.M.G.C.
	169 "	C.R.E.

Sender's Number. G.453	Day of Month. 28	In reply to Number.	AAA

Move your two battalions to a central position from which they can be able to reinforce POINT DU JOUR - THELUS Line and Ridge Posts AAA Kepp Bde. H.Q. as at present AAA Acknowledge and report completion AAA Addsd 167 reptd 168, 169, C.R.A. D.M.G.C. C.R.E.

From 56 Div.
Place
Time 8.5 a.m.

The above may be forwarded as now corrected.

(Sgd) F.B.Hurndall, Maj.G.S.

"A" Form.
MESSAGES AND SIGNALS.

Army Form C. 2121.
(In pads of 100.)

Prefix......Code........... m	Words.	Charge.	This message is on a/c of :	Recd. at .... m
Office of Origin and Service Instructions. PRIORITY to C.R.E. (Sgd) F.B.Hurndall Maj. G.S.	Sent At............m. By........		............................Service. (Signature of "Franking Officer.")	Date.......... From............ By..........

TO	C.R.E.		167 Bde.	
	168 Bde		C.R.A.	
	169 "			

Sender's Number.	Day of Month.	In reply to Number.	
G.455	28		A A A

Move your remaining two Field Companies
to an assembly position near JUNCTION
REDOUBT AAA They should send Officer to be
on telephone at 167 Bde H.Q. at G.6.d.8.6.
AAA Addsd. C.R.E. repeated Brigades and C.R.A.

From 56 Div.
Place
Time 8.15 a.m.

The above may be forwarded as now corrected.

(Z)
(Sgd.) F.B.Hurndall, Maj. G.S.
Censor. Signature of Addressor or person authorised to telegraph in his name.

* This line should be erased if not required.
(3796.) Wt. W492/M1647. 650,000 Pads. 5/17. H.W. & V., Ld.

"A" Form.
MESSAGES AND SIGNALS.

Army Form C. 2121.
(In pads of 100.)

Prefix	Code	m	Words.	Charge.	This message is on a/c of:	Recd. at .... m.
Office of Origin and Service Instructions.						Date ....
PRIORITY			Sent At .... m.		.... Service.	From ....
(Sd.) C.P.Robertson, Capt. for G.S.			By		(Signature of "Franking Officer.")	By ....

TO	167 Bde.	D.M.G.C.	3rd Can. Div.
	168 "	C.R.A.	
	169 "	4th Div.	

Sender's Number.	Day of Month.	In reply to Number.	
G.462	28		A A A

Enemy on ORANGE HILL AAA 4th Div. may have to switch back to meet flank attack AAA Right Bde. must hold RED LINE and switches back to MISSISSIPPI keeping touch with 4th Div. AAA 167 Bde. will send 1 bn. to come under orders of 169 Bde AAA Orders to go direct from 169 Bde through 167 Bde AAA 169 Bde may recall troops in front of RED LINE AAA RED LINE and switch to POINT DU JOUR to be held at all costs AAA D.M.G.C. will get in touch with Bn. of 167 going forward and will send 6 M.Gs to POINT DU JOUR AAA 167 Bde will hold its second Bn. in readiness to reinforce 169 Bde

From 56 Div.
Place
Time 10.30 a.m.

The above may be forwarded as now corrected.

(Z)
(Sgd.) F.B.Hurndall,
Major

Censor. Signature of Addressor or person authorized to telegraph in his name.

* This line should be erased if not required.
(3796.) Wt. W 492/M1647. 650,000 Pads. 5/17. H.W. & V., Ld.

"A" Form.
MESSAGES AND SIGNALS.

Army Form C. 2121.
(In pads of 100.)

Prefix Code m	Words.	Charge.	This message is on a/c of :	Recd. at m.
Office of Origin and Service Instructions. PRIORITY to 168 Bde. & 3rd Can.Div. (Sd.) C.W.Haydon, Capt.	Sent At m. To By		APP.XXVIII Service. (Signature of "Franking Officer.")	Date From By

TO	168 Bde.	3rd Can.Div.	C.R.A.
	167 "	13 Corps	D.M.G.C.
	169 "	83 H.A.	

Sender's Number.	Day of Month.	In reply to Number.	AAA
G.464.	28		

Withdraw your troops from front line system
to RED LINE which you will hold at all costs
AAA 169 Inf. Bde. also withdrawing to RED
LINE AAA Act in conjunction with Canadian
Brigade on your left making switch down
TIRED ALLEY if necessary AAA Addsd 168 Inf.
Bde. reptd. 167, 169 Inf. Bdes. 3rd Can. Div.
13 Corps 83 H.A. C.R.A. and D.M.G.C.

From: 56 Div.
Place:
Time: 11.40 a.m.

(Z)(Sgd.) C.W. Haydon, Capt.
G.S.

"A" Form.
MESSAGES AND SIGNALS.

Army Form C. 2121.
(In pads of 100.)

Prefix	Code	m	Words.	Charge.	This message is on a/c of :	Recd. at	m.
Office of Origin and Service Instructions.			Sent			Date	
URGENT OPERATIONS PRIORITY (Sd) C.P.Robertson, Capt.			At...........m. To........ By........		APP. XXIX. ....Service. (Signature of "Franking Officer.")	From By	

TO	167 Bde.	C.R.A.	3rd Can. Div.	
	168 "	C.R.E.	4 Div.	
	169 "	D.M.G.C.	13 Corps.	

Sender's Number.	Day of Month.	In reply to Number.	A A A
G.474	28		

C.R.E. will move one field coy to TONGUE POST and one field Coy to BLANCHE POST remainder to stop in JUNCTION REDOUBT AAA ADDSD. C.R.E. reptd. Inf.Bdes C.R.A. D.M.G.C. flank Divs. and 13 Corps.

From: 56 Div.
Place:
Time: 2 p.m.

The above may be forwarded as now corrected.

(Z)
(Sgd.) C.P.Robertson, Capt.

MESSAGES AND SIGNALS.

Army Form C. 2121.
(In pads of 100.)

Prefix	Code	m	Words	Charge	This message is on a/c of:	Recd. at ...... m.
Office of Origin and Service Instructions.			Sent			Date ......
D.R.L.S.			At ...... m.		APP.XXX ...... Service.	From ......
			To			
			By		(Signature of "Franking Officer.")	By ......

TO — Recipients 'A' & 'B' News Wires List

Sender's Number.	Day of Month.	In reply to Number.	
G.475	28		AAA

Corps Commander has informed First Army
56 Division are fighting splendidly. AAA
Stick to it.

From   G.O.C. 56th Div.
Place
Time   2.25 p.m.

General Staff.

"A" Form.
MESSAGES AND SIGNALS.

Army Form C. 2121.

PRIORITY

TO	167 Bde.	C.R.E.	4 Div.	C.R.A.
	168 "	"Q"	3 Can. Div.	13 Corps.
	169 "	D.M.G.C.	8 Can.Inf.Bde.	

Sender's Number.	Day of Month.	In reply to Number.	A A A
G.484	28		

167 Bde will relieve 169 Bde tonight in the right section AAA Details of relief to be arranged by B.Gs. concerned AAA 5th Can.Bn. has been ordered to move up and occupy during this relief the line POINT DU JOUR Redoubt inclusive as far as Railway Line at B.27.a.0.4 in addition to the existing garrison of that line AAA As soon as this Bn. arrives the responsibility for holding this portion of the POINT DU JOUR Line will rest entirely with its Bn. Commander who will be independent and NOT under the orders of B.G.C. 169 or 167 Bdes AAA The G.O.C. sanctions the relief being commenced before the arrival of this Cdn.Bn. provided that B.G.C. 169 Bde understands that he must be entirely responsible for the adequate protection of the POINT DU JOUR Redoubt and THELUS Line in his section until that Bn. arrives AAA Completion of relief to be reported AAA Addsd.Bdes C.R.A.C.R.E."Q" D.M.G.C. 13 Corps 4th Div. 3rd Cdn.Div. and 8th Cdn.Inf.Bde.

From: 56 Div.
Place:
Time: 10.10 p.m.

(Sgd.) F.B.Hurndall, Maj. G.S.

"A" Form.
MESSAGES AND SIGNALS.

Army Form C. 2121.
(In pads of 100.)

Prefix........Code.........m	Words.	Charge.	This message is on a/c of:	Recd. at.........m.
Office of Origin and Service Instructions. PRIORITY to 169 Bde. (Sd.) F.B.Hurndall, Major	Sent At.........m. To.........		.........Service. (Signature of "Franking Officer.")	Date......... From......... By.........

TO	167 Bde.	C.R.A.	
	168 "	C.R.E.	
	169 "		

Sender's Number.	Day of Month.	In reply to Number.	
* G.488	28		A A A

Warning Order AAA If situation permits
167 Bde will tonight relieve 169 Bde AAA
Orders follow if situation favourable AAA
Addsd. Bdes C.R.A. C.R.E.

From 56 Div.
Place
Time 7.5 p.m.

The above may be forwarded as now corrected.
.... (sgd.) F.B.Hurndall, Major
Censor.   Signature of Addressor or person authorised to telegraph in his name.

* This line should be erased if not required.

"A" Form.
MESSAGES AND SIGNALS.

Army Form C. 2121.
(In pads of 100.)

TO	169 Bde.
	167 "

Sender's Number.	Day of Month.	In reply to Number.	A A A
G.491	28		

Particular attention is to be paid to defence of GAVRELLE Road AAA Knife rests must be got in position and a trench dug across road AAA Addsd. 169 Bde reptd 167 Bde

From: 56 Div.
Place:
Time: 8.45 p.m.

(Z)(Sgd.) F.B.Hurndall, Major
G.S.

"A" Form.
MESSAGES AND SIGNALS.

Army Form C. 2121.
(In pads of 100.)

URGENT
OPERATIONS
PRIORITY
(Sd) F.B.Hurndall, Maj.

TO: 167 Bde.
168 "
169 "

Sender's Number: G.495
Day of Month: 28
AAA

In continuation of G.484 of this date 169 Bde will form Div. Reserve on relief and will eventually assume same dispositions as the bat'alion 167 Bde which was placed ready to counter attack on POINT DU JOUR AAA 169 Bde will arrange to relieve as soon as possible the two Coys of 167 Bde now attached to 168 Bde AAA These latter two Coys will rejoin 167 Bde AAA Until they rejoin 169 Bde will continue to keep two Coys. at the disposal of 167 Bde but B.G.C. 167 Bde must be prepared for their eventual withdrawal into Div. Res. when the relief is complete AAA Acknowledge AAA Addressed three Bdes

From: 56 Div.
Place:
Time: 11.10 p.m.

(Sgd.) F.B.Hurndall, Maj.H.S.

APPENDIX XXVII.

Orders & Instructions issued during the Operations, 29th March, 1918.

"A" Form.
MESSAGES AND SIGNALS.

Army Form C. 2121.
(In pads of 100.)
No. of Message...............

Prefix........Code...........m	Words.	Charge.	This message is on a/c of :	Recd. at ....m.
Office of Origin and Service Instructions.				
PRIORITY (Sd) B.Pakenham Lt.Col.	Sent At.........m. To........ By........		.................Service. APP.XXVII (Signature of "Franking Officer.")	Date............ From .... By........

TO	169 Bde.			
	167 "			

Sender's Number.	Day of Month.	In reply to Number.	
G.506	29		A A A

On conclusion of relief of GAGE by ICEBERG GAGE (less the two Cos of GAP who are being sent to relieve two Cos. of ICEBERG in area of HABIT) will be responsible for carrying out a counter attack on POINT DU JOUR Redoubt should it become necessary AAA He will place his troops accordingly and report briefly his dispositions to Div. H.Q. AAA As soon as the 2 relieved Coys of ICEBERG arrive from HABITS ar a ICEBERG will replace at disposal of GAGE the two Coys of GAP now temporarily attached to him AAA Completion of this to be reported by GAGE and ICEBERG so that the Canadian Bn. can be released AAA Addsd ICEBERG and GAGE.

From 56 Div.
Place
Time 6.17 a.m.

The above may be forwarded as now corrected.
.... (Z)
Censor. (Sd) B.Pakenham, Lt.Col. G.S.
Signature of Addressor or person authorised to telegraph in his name.

* This line should be erased if not required.
(3796.) Wt. W 492/M1647. 650,000 Pads. 5/17. H.W.&V., Ld. (E. 1101.)

"A" Form.
MESSAGES AND SIGNALS.

Army Form C. 2121.
(In pads of 100.)

Prefix........Code..........m	Words.	Charge.	This message is on a/c of:	Recd. at........m.
Office of Origin and Service Instructions. PRIORITY by Fullerphone (Sd.) F.B.Hurndall	Sent At........m. By		..................Service. APP.XXXIX (Signature of "Franking Officer.")	Date............... From............... By...............

TO	167 Bde.	C.R.E.	
	168 Bde.	D.M.G.C.	
	169 Bde.		

Sender's Number.	Day of Month.	In reply to Number.	
* G.511	29		A A A

Warning Order AAA If tactical situation permits the Division will be relieved tonight by 4th Can. Div. AAA 167th Bde. y 12th Bde and 168 Bde by 11th Bde AAA 169 Bde will not be directly relieved but will be withdrawn on conclusion of relief of other Bdes when ordered by Div. H.Q. AAA Orders follow AAA Addsd. 167 168, 169 Bdes C.R.E. & D.M.G.C.

From 56 Div.
Place
Time 11.26 a.m.

The above may be forwarded as now corrected. **(Z)** (Sgd.) B.Pakenham, Lt.Col.

"A" Form.
MESSAGES AND SIGNALS.

Army Form C. 2121.
(In pads of 100.)

Prefix......... Code........... Words. Charge.
Office of Origin and Service Instructions.

PRIORITY

(sd.) F.B.Hurndall

This message is on a/c of:

APP. XLI

(Signature of "Franking Officer.")

TO
- 167th Inf. Bde. C.R.A. & all recipients
- 168th Inf. Bde. C.R.E. of order No.158
- 169th Inf. Bde. "Q"

Sender's Number.	Day of Month.	In reply to Number.	
G.529	29		A A A

Moves ordered in Div. Order No. 158. will be carried out tonight AAA Addsd. recipients of Order.

From: 56 Div.
Place:
Time: 6.15 p.m.

(Z)(Sd.) F.B.Hurndall, Major

SECRET   56th DIVISION ORDER No. 157.   Copy No. 19

29th March, 1918

1. Until further orders the line will be held as follows by Brigades etc. within their respective boundaries.

   Right Section. by 167th Inf. Bde. with attached Tunnellers and Pioneers.
   The following lines will be held:-
   (a) BAILLEUL - WILLERVAL Line, where junction will be maintained with 4th Division.
   (b) New Switch Line from above line (K. Trench) via TOWY Alley and along line of posts between TOWY Alley about H.3.b.9.9. to H.4.c.2.7. where junction will be made and maintained with 4th Division in MISSOURI and MISSISSIPPI Trenches.
   FARBUS Line. Junction to be made with 168th Inf. Bde.
   POINT DU JOUR Line. The Tunnelling Coy. detachment will not be used in front of this line.

   Left Section. by 168th Inf. Bde. with attached two Companies of 169th Inf. Bde. and attached Pioneers.
   (a) BAILLEUL - WILLERVAL Line   )
   (b) BAILLEUL Defences   ) Touch to be kept on both flanks.
   (c) FARBUS Line   )
   (d) POINT DU JOUR Line   )
   The two attached Coys. of 169th Inf. Bde. will not be employed in front of the POINT DU JOUR - THELUS Line and BRIERLEY Hill.

   Divisional Reserves.
   (a) 169th Inf. Bde. with 3 machine guns detailed by D.M.G.O. will be placed in such a position as to be able to make an immediate counter-attack on POINT DU JOUR Redoubt, should the necessity arise, without reference to Div. H.Q.
   (b) B. Reserve Bde. (under C.R.E. but troops located in Bde. Sections to be under the tactical command of the B.G.C. that Section)
   Pioneer Battn. (less 1 Coy. with 167th Inf. Bde. and 2 Platoons with 168th Inf. Bde.)
       1 Coy. RIDGE POST.
       2 Platoons RAILWAY POST.
   R.E. Battn.
       1 Field Coy. TONGUE POST.
       1   "   "   BLANCHE POST.
       1   "   "   in Reserve.
   Tunnelling detachment - POINT DU JOUR Redoubt.
   Spare Personnel Battn.
       In vicinity of Div. H.Q.

2. The following lines are being held in rear by other troops.
   (a) LONE TREE POST - ASHFORD POST - JUNCTION POST - CHANTECLER POST - to about G.12.b.2.3. by 2 Battns. 8th Cdn. Inf. Bde., with 2 Battns. in Brigade Reserve near Div. H.Q. (1 Bn. is temporarily in the POINT DU JOUR Line but is to be withdrawn on conclusion of relief.)
   (b) JUNCTION POST - VICTORY Redoubt - FLANK POST (ST. CATHERINE Switch) by dismounted personnel of Tank Corps with 72 L.Gs.

3. It is essential that touch should be obtained and kept with Brigades on both flanks.
   Liaison patrols should be frequently sent, and Liaison officers sent between Brigade H.Qrs.

4. There is to be no withdrawal from the BAILLEUL - WILLERVAL Line.

5. ACKNOWLEDGE.

B Pakenham
Lieut-Colonel,
General Staff.

Issued at 10 a.m.

```
Copy No.  1 to 167th Infantry Brigade.
          2     168th Infantry Brigade.
          3     169th Infantry Brigade.
          4     1/5th Cheshire Regt.
          5     C.R.A.
          6     C.R.E.
          7     56th Div. M.G.Battn.
          8     56th Div. Signal Coy.
          9     A.D.M.S.
         10     "Q"
         11     A.P.M.
         12     56th Div. Train
         13     A.D.C.
         14     XIII Corps.
         15     3rd Cdn. Div.
         16     8th Cdn. Inf. Bde.
         17     4th Cdn. Div.
         18     4th Div.
         19 )
              War Diary
         20 )
         21     File.
```

SECRET   Copy No. 26

56th DIVISION ORDER No. 158

29th March, 1918.

1. If the tactical situation permits 56th Division (less Artillery) will be relieved tonight (29th/30th inst.) by 4th Canadian Division (less Artillery). The relief to be completed before daylight 30th inst.

2. 167th Inf. Bde. and attached Tunnellers will be relieved by 12th Canadian Inf. Bde. in the right section.
168th Inf. Bde. and attached troops will be relieved by 11th Canadian Inf. Bde. in the left section.
169th Inf. Bde. (Divisional Reserve) will be withdrawn by orders from Div. H.Q. when the relief has been completed.

3. All details of relief will be settled between Brigadiers concerned.

4. Arrangements for the relief of R.E. and Pioneers, Machine Guns and Medical units, will be made direct between C.R.E's, D.M.G.C's. and A.D's.M.S. concerned; except where it is arranged for Infantry to take over defences now held by R.E. and Pioneers, when the arrangements will be made by Infantry Brigadiers concerned in conjunction with the C.R.E. 56th Division.

5. All maps and plans will be handed over.

6. 4th Canadian Div. Artillery will be placed into line as soon as possible. 56th Div. Artillery will be withdrawn under orders of First Army.

7. The following personnel will remain in the line with relieving units for 24 hours after the relief.

   1 Officer from Bde. H.Q.
   1 Officer from Bn. H.Q. who knows the line taken over by the units to which they are attached.

8. On conclusion of the relief troops of 56th Div. will be located as shown in the Table which will be issued later.

9. Completion of reliefs and moves to be reported to Div. H.Q.

10. ACKNOWLEDGE BY WIRE.

F. B. Hurndall Major
for Lieut-Colonel,
General Staff.

Issued at 12 noon

Copy No. 1. 167th Inf. Bde.
2. 168th Inf. Bde.
3. 169th Inf. Bde.
5. C.R.A.
6. C.R.E.
7. 56th Div. M.G.Battn.
8. 56th Div. Signal Co.
9. 56th Div. Gas Offr.
10. A.D.M.S.
11. "Q"
12. A.P.M.
4. 1/5th Cheshire Regt.

Copy No. 13. D.A.D.O.S.
14. D.A.D.V.S.
15. 56th Div. Train.
16. 56th Div. M.T.Coy.
17. A.D.C.
18. Camp Commandant.
19. 56th Div. Employment Co.
20. French Mission.
21. XIII Corps "G"
22. XIII Corps "Q"
23. 4th Cdn. Div.
24. 3rd Cdn. Div.
25. 4th Division.
26-27 War Diary.
28 File.

SECRET   56th Divn. No. G.3/194.

LOCATION TABLE TO ACCOMPANY 56th DIV. ORDER No. 158.

167th Infantry Brigade.
```
    H.Q. and T.M.Battery    -   VILLERS AU BOIS
    2 Battalions            -   VILLERS AU BOIS
    1 Battalion             -   CAMBLAIN L'ABBE.
```

BUT if no trains are available

```
    Brigade H.Q. )
    2 Battns.    )  MAROEUIL
    L.T.M.Bty.   )
    1 Battalion  -  BRAY.
```

168th Infantry Brigade.
```
    H.Q.        -   MONT ST. ELOY
    1 Battn.    -   OTTAWA Camp.
    1 Battn.    -   LANCASTER Camp.
    1 Battn.    -   BOIS DES ARLEUX
    L.T.M.Bty.  -   DURHAM Camp.
```

169th Infantry Brigade
```
    H.Q.        )
    L.T.M.Bty.  )   NEUVILLE ST. VAAST
    3 Battns.   )   Liable to be changed.
```

```
    416th Field Coy. R.E. )
    512th    "    "   "   )   ANZIN
    513th    "    "   "   )
```

```
    1/5th (E. of C.) Bn. Cheshire Regt. Pioneers )  To be notified
    56th Bn. M.G.Corps                           )  by "Q"
```

A.D.M.S. will arrange for Field Ambulances to take over accommodation vacated by Field Ambulances 4th Canadian Division.

Acknowledge.

29th March, 1918.

for Lieut-Colonel,
General Staff, 56th Division.

Distribution:-

```
167th Inf. Bde.              D.A.D.V.S.
168th Inf. Bde.              56th Div. Train.
169th Inf. Bde.              56th Div. M.T.Coy.
C.R.A.                       A.D.C.
C.R.E.                       Camp Commandant.
56th Div. M.G.Battn.         56th Div. Employment Co.
56th Div. Signal Coy.        French Mission.
56th Div. Gas Officer        XIII Corps "G"
A.D.M.S.                     XIII Corps "Q"
"Q"                          4th Cdn. Div.
A.P.M.                       3rd Cdn. Div.
1/5th Cheshire Regt.         4th Division.
D.A.D.O.S.                   War Diary
                             File.
```

War Diary Appendix

SECRET   56th Div. No. G.3/195.

ADDENDUM No. 1 to 56th DIV. ORDER No. 158.
----

1.   G.O.C. 4th Canadian Division will assume command of the Sector on completion of relief.

2.   56th Div. H.Q. will remain at VICTORY Camp after completion of relief until 10 a.m., at which hour it will open at ACQ.

3.   56th Div. Artillery will be transferred to Canadian Corps on completion of relief, until relieved by 4th Canadian Div. Artillery.

4.   ACKNOWLEDGE.

                                     Y. B. Hurndall Major

                                                 Lieut-Colonel,
29th March, 1918.   General Staff, 56th Division.

To all Recipients of Order No. 158.

WAR DIARY

Instructions regarding War Diaries and Intelligence Summaries are contained in F.S. Regs., Part II. and the Staff Manual respectively. Title pages will be prepared in manuscript.

Army Form C. 2118.

WAR DIARY
or
INTELLIGENCE SUMMARY.
(Erase heading not required.)

56th Division.   **March, 1918.**

Place	Date	Hour	Summary of Events and Information	Remarks and references to Appendices
VICTORY CAMP.	March 1st.		Quiet day. Considerable hostile aerial activity.	
	2nd		Weather very cold, snow and hail with bright intervals.	
	3rd		Quiet day. Visibility very good between snow showers.	
	4th		Quiet during day. At 10 p.m. the enemy bombarded BAILLEUL heavily for 30 minutes with H.E. and gas shell. Our Artillery (counterbattery) replied. At 2.15 a.m. the enemy repeated his bombardment of BAILLEUL and scattered gas shell along the BAILLEUL - WILLERVAL Line. Quiet during the day time. Weather wet cold and misty. 167th Infantry Brigade carried out an inter-battalion relief.	
	5th		Quiet day beyond usual shelling of BAILLEUL and GAVRELLE. Our artillery carried out a retaliatory concentrated shoot on enemy H.Q. just N. of NEUVIREUIL. 168th and 169th Infantry Brigades carried out inter-battalion reliefs.	
	6th		Quiet day. Considerable hostile aerial activity. Weather sunny.	
	7th		Quiet day. Visibility poor. Sunny weather. Our artillery carried out a harassing programme at night. German relief suspected.	
	8th		Quiet day. Enemy shelled BAILLEUL and vicinity with gas shells from 9 p.m. to 11 p.m. 167th Infantry Brigade carried out an inter-battalion relief.	APP. I.
	9th		At 6.45 a.m. the 13th (Kensingtons) London Regiment carried out a very successful raid on enemy trenches just N. of OPPY. About 20 Germans were killed and 4 brought back as prisoners. Identification normal. Prisoners gave information which tended to show that an offensive was imminent. Our casualties were 1 killed and two wounded. A dummy smoke raid was carried out at the same time S. of OPPY which deceived the enemy.	
	10th		Quiet day. Visibility poor.	
	11th		Quiet day. Enemy fired gas shell on to the usual areas during the evening. Weather warm and hazy. Situation normal. Enemy fired about 200 rounds on to TOWY ALLEY and DITCH POST in 169th Infantry Brigade area. Also shelled Div. H.Q. intermittently during afternoon and evening with a H.V. gun. Our artillery retaliated. 169th Infantry Brigade and 168th Infantry Brigade carried out inter-battalion reliefs.	APP. I.
	12th		At 11.45 p.m. Div. H.Q. was again shelled direct hits being obtained on huts. Situation normal. Owing to amount of German movement seen and prisoners' statements a division relief opposite this front is suspected. Our artillery carried out harassing fire. Prisoners also stated German offensive imminent. The Battalion in Div. Reserve i.e. 2nd London Regiment was moved up from ST.AUBIN to CHANTECLER in close reserve. Orders	

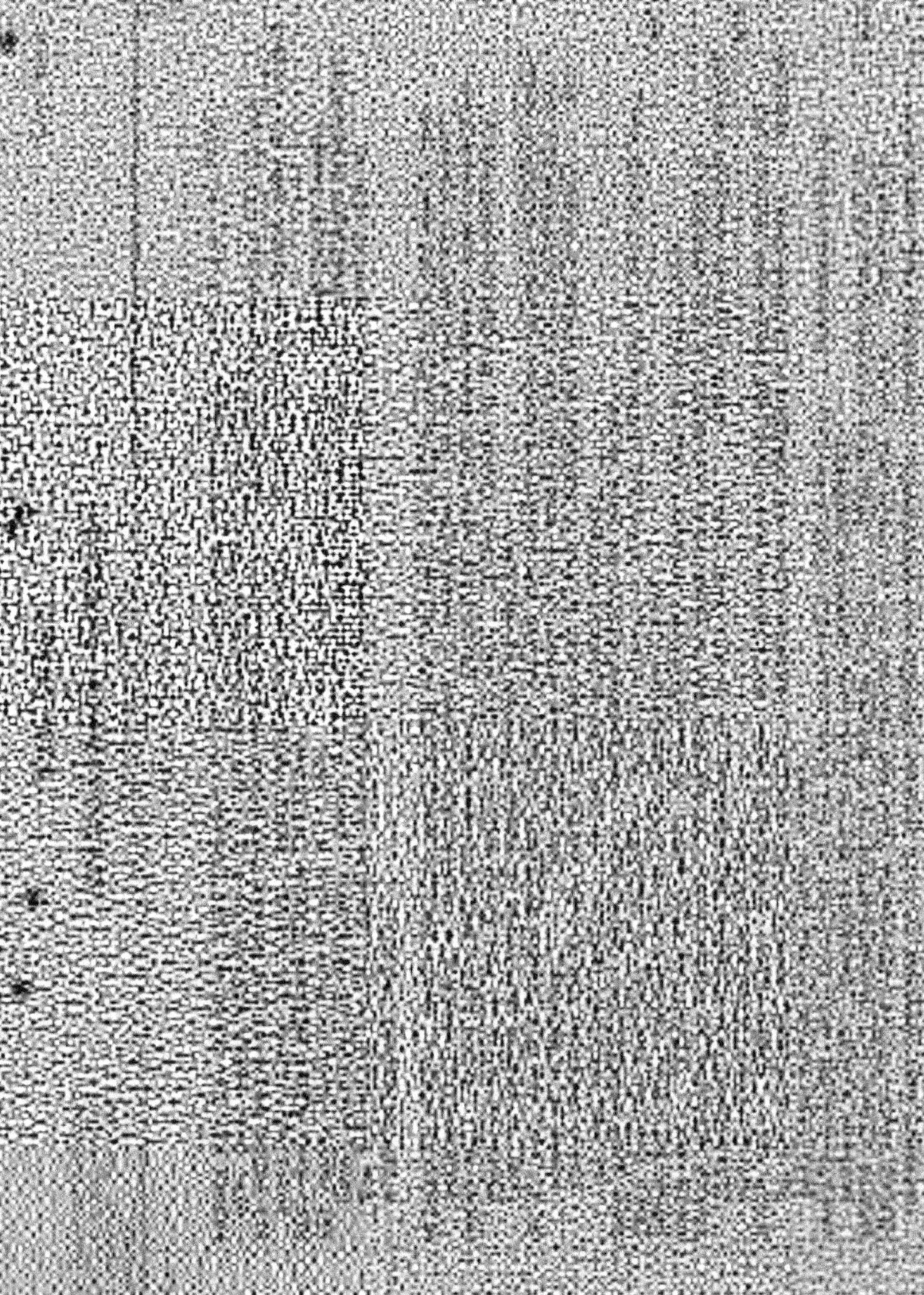

WAR DIARY
or
INTELLIGENCE SUMMARY.
(Erase heading not required.)

Army Form C. 2118.

Place	Date	Hour	Summary of Events and Information	Remarks and references to Appendices
VICTORY CAMP.	20th (ctd)		in morning. Order No. 151 issued re relief of 56th Div. by 62nd Division.	APP.III.
	21st		Front reorganised on 2 Brigade basis at night. 167th Brigade being in Divisional Reserve at ST.AUBIN.	APP. I
		a.m. 5.5. 6.45	Hostile artillery developed sudden activity at 5.5. a.m. with 4.2" and 5.9" and at 6.45 a.m. fire was opened on TOWY POST. GAVRELLE was heavily shelled and at 6.45 a.m. fire was opened on TOWY POST. Poison shell fell on BAILLEUL - WILLERVAL Line. At 5.45 a.m. an intense bombardment was opened by hostile M.T.Ms. on MILL POST C.19.c.8.8. and on wire between MILL and BRADFORD POSTS. Trenches and wire badly damaged. Repairs were made to wire at night and in anticipation of raid our Artillery carried out harassing fire during night. Enemy attached South of XIII Corps Front. Several Heavy H.V. guns were noticed firing opposite Divisional front in particular one at D.16.d.2.7. probably the one firing on ARRAS. Hostile aircraft were very active both by day and night. Bombs were dropped near THELUS. Several low flying aeroplanes were noticed. Addendum to Order No. 151 dated 20.3.18 issued. Order No. 151 was cancelled on receipt of Order from XIII Corps cancelling relief of 56th Division by 62nd Division.	APP.III b. APP.III c.
	22nd		Misty morning though fair visibility later. Hostile T.Ms. were active on Divisional front during day. Few low flying E.A. seen. Warning received from XIII Corps that Division was to be relieved by 2nd Canadian Division. Order No. 152. re relief issued. Representatives of 2nd Canadian Division arrived to take over. Divisional Artillery carried out programme of harassing fire on roads and tracks back areas at night. BAILLEUL was shelled with 4.2" and 5.9". 56th Division letter No. G.3/132 sent to Brigades re employment of switch from BEATTY POST - TOWY ALLEY GREEN LINE as line of resistance in event of enemy advance N. of SCARPE RIVER.	APP.IV. APP.V.
	23rd		Relief by 2nd Canadian Division cancelled. Order No. G.261 sent to Brigades. 167th Brigade H.Q. moved from ST.AUBIN to TRAFALGAR CAMP. 8th Middlesex Regt. moved to AUBREY CAMP. Order No. G.251. Letter G.3/135 sent to Brigades re eventualities in case of adoption of Switch Line referred to in G.3/132 of 22.3.18. Letter G.3/136 issued giving fuller instructions re employment of Switch Line as line of defence.	APP.IV. APP.I & VIII APP.VI APP.VII

Army Form C. 2118.

WAR DIARY
or
INTELLIGENCE SUMMARY.
(Erase heading not required.)

Instructions regarding War Diaries and Intelligence Summaries are contained in F. S. Regs., Part II. and the Staff Manual respectively. Title pages will be prepared in manuscript.

Place	Date	Hour	Summary of Events and Information	Remarks and references to Appendices
VICTORY CAMP.	March 23rd.		Divisional Artillery carried out programme of harassing fire on enemy's trenches at night particularly the FRESNES - ROUVROY Line where a good deal of movement had been seen. 100 rounds B.N.C. fired into C.15.c.9.1. and C.27.d. Hostile Artillery very active during day. Enemy exploded Land Mine under wire of TOWY POST about 5.12.p.m.	
		7.50.p.m.	Order No. G.276 sent by telegram to Brigades re method of holding TOWY POST and warning Right Brigade of action to be taken by Artillery in event of GAVRELLE being entered by enemy.	Appdx. IX.
		10.15. P.M.	Order sent out to Reserve Brigade re standing to at 5.a.m. in morning. Telegraphic Order No. G.283.	APP. X.
	24th		168th Infantry Brigade (Left Brigade) carried out an inter-battalion relief.	
		5 a.m.	At various times during night and early morning our artillery laid down heavy harassing fire on enemy's trenches. Situation quiet on front during day. Hostile aircraft very active many low flying E.A. passed over Divisional forward area. A good deal of movement seen in FRESNES - ROUVROY Line.	APP. I.
		1.15 pm.	Order G.283 re continuation of procedure laid down in G.283 of 23-3-18 was issued. Order No. 153 re relief of 169th Brigade by 167th Brigade on 28-3-18 was issued.	APP. XI APP. XII
		8 pm	Warning G.312 was issued re similar artillery programme for night 24/25th as for previous night vide G. 276 of 23-3-18. TOWY POST was shelled and trench mortared during afternoon. Left Brigade captured wounded prisoner of 471 Inf. Regt. 240th Division near MILL POST.	APP. XIII
	25th		A great deal of movement seen during day by observers. Forward observation balloon on ground at C.19.d.65.92 was destroyed by our artillery which also fired on many moving targets - both men and Light Railway trains. A battalion was seen to detrain at VITRY and march S.W. Indications of a relief.	
		4.15 pm.	Later report received from Army via XIII Corps on examination of Prisoner of 471 I.R. who stated attack was to be made on morning of 26th and that 219th and 23rd Res. Division had been brought up for purpose. These troops being accommodated in the DROCOURT - QUEANT Line (WOTAN STELLUNG). Many T.Ms. were to be used. All preparations were made to anticipate this attack by artillery fire on chosen targets and areas throughout the night and active patrolling by units holding the line. G.O.C. held a Conference at 6.30 p.m.	APP. XIV

Army Form C. 2118.

WAR DIARY
or
INTELLIGENCE SUMMARY.
(Erase heading not required.)

Instructions regarding War Diaries and Intelligence Summaries are contained in F. S. Regs., Part II. and the Staff Manual respectively. Title pages will be prepared in manuscript.

Place	Date	Hour	Summary of Events and Information	Remarks and references to Appendices
VICTORY CAMP.	March 25th	a.m. 1.15	Wire G.339 sent to 169th Inf. Bde. re capture if possible of another prisoner.	APP. XV
		7.45	Wire G.352 sent to 168th and 169th Inf. Bdes. and C.R.A. re Field Guns to sweep enemy's front line with H.E. between 4.30 a.m. and 5 a.m. 26th.	APP. XVI.
		8 p.m.	G.3/146 sent to all concerned re further action to be taken in view of possibility of hostile attack.	APP. XVII.
		8.30	Station Code Calls ordered to be taken into use from 6 a.m. 26th.	
		9.14	169th (Right) Inf. Bde. report garrison of GAVRELLE POST found to be missing by relief.	
	26th	a.m.	Quiet night. Our Artillery carried out harassing fire, retaliation to which was slight. Expected hostile attack did not develop.	
		10.45	169th Inf. Bde. (right) report relief for GAVRELLE POST found 2 dead men of garrison in dugout. Stick bombs lying about and signs of struggle having taken place. No signs of remainder of garrison.	
		p.m. 2.19	169th Inf. Bde. report 1 O.R. wounded and missing from MILL POST during night.	
		4.25	168th Inf. Bde. (Left) report low flying albatross (hostile) 'plane was forced to descend in N.15.a. at 4 p.m. Pilot and observer seen to surrender.	
			G.O.C. visited two Brigades in the line during morning to discuss details of raids ordered to be carried out tonight.	APP. XVIII. APP. XIX.
		7.30	G.395 (wire) to all Brigades warning against possibility of enemy agents being active	
		3.0	56th Div. Order No. 154 issued ordering Brigades in line to carry out raids tonight. 169th Inf. Bde. to do 3 raids. 168th Inf. Bde. to do 2 raids, object being to secure identifications. ZERO fixed 10.30 p.m.	
			Movement reported slightly above normal throughout the day. Weather sunny, Wind N. rather colder.	
			Lieut-Colonel G.de la P.B.Pakenham, D.S.O. (G.S.O.I 56th Divn.) rejoined, having been recalled from leave.	
			Lieut-Colonel W.R.Pinwill, D.S.O. acting G.S.O.I departed.	
	27th	a.m. 12.45	From 169th Bde. BM.485 Left Bn. reports at midnight. Our raiding party seen getting through our wire. Enemy opened M.G. and T.M.fire and rifle grenade. On fire dying down party went out again. 1 Officer & 15 O.R. crawled out in original direction. Party still out.	
		1. 6	From 169 Bde. BM.487 Reporting parties all returned casualties in wounded. Second attempt got within 100 yds. enemy's front line. Enemy very alert. Front line strongly held strongly. Casualties Killed one, wounded one.	
		1.34	" " BM.488 1/16th London Regt. (Q.W.R.) patrol reports at 1.5 a.m. Enemy holding trenches " 169 " " " 168 " " Situation quiet. 1/13th Londons (Kensingtons) patrol returned. No.prisoners. 1/14 London Scottish patrol still out.	

Army Form C. 2118.

WAR DIARY
or
INTELLIGENCE SUMMARY.
(Erase heading not required.)

Instructions regarding War Diaries and Intelligence Summaries are contained in F.S. Regs., Part II, and the Staff Manual respectively. Title pages will be prepared in manuscript.

Place	Date	Hour	Summary of Events and Information	Remarks and references to Appendices
VICTORY CAMP.	March 27th	a.m. 3.15	To XIII Corps. G.400. reporting all patrols sent out now returned. None succeeded in entering enemy's trenches. Enemy very alert. Further attempt being made by 1 patrol. Enemy reported attempting to repair gaps.	
		3.41	From 169 Bde. BM.489 Right Bn. report Bn. on their right sent up S.O.S. R.A. warned.	
		4.3.	" 169 " BM.490 Situation quiet. Bombardment on right now dies down.	
		4.35	To XIII Corps G.401 Reporting situation quiet. Further attempt to enter enemy's trenches was not made owing to enemy lying up in wait for party.	
		5.10	From 169 Bde. BM.491 Left Bn. reports MILL POST being heavily shelled also NAVAL Trench line.	
		5.30	To XIII Corps G.402 Reporting 169 Bde. report re MILL POST.	
		10.10	From XIII Corps G.219 Warning Order re XIII Corps assuming command up to SOUCHEZ River at 12 noon to-day. 56th Division to take over command from present S. boundary to TIRED ALLEY inclusive. BAILLEUL - WILLERVAL system to be taken as front line, present front line to be considered outpost line. Redistribution to be complete at 4 a.m.	
		11.30	To usual recipients of Operation Orders. W.O.No. 155. Re redistribution. Inter-brigade boundary to run BIRD POST - BAILLEUL EAST POST - RAILWAY POST all inclusive to Southern Brigade.	APP. XX.
		p.m. 12.30.	do. O.O.No.156. Ordering redistribution to be taken up.	APP. XXI.
		3.35	do. G.421. Cancelling portions of O.O.No.156.	APP. XXII.
		4. 0	To 168, 169th Bdes & C.R.A. G.422. Gaps cut last night in enemy's wire to be kept open.	
		5.30	To all recipients G.424. Ordering relief (cancelled by O.O. No. 156) to take place as Order No.153.	APP. XXIII.
		6.10	From 168 Bde. B.M.566 .... Brigade order re redistribution.	
		6.16	" 169 " I.O.510. .... Reporting considerable movement in FRESNES Line.	
		8.45	To 168th Bde. C.R.A., 3rd Canadian Division, as result of verbal information from XIII Corps. G.430. in order to conform to dispositions of Division on our left ARLEUX POST to be treated as an outpost and troops holding it will, if heavily attacked, withdraw fighting. Main defensive line in new position taken over to night from TOMMY POST inclusive along ARLEUX LOOP SOUTH to junction with left Division at TIRED ALLEY T.15.a.5.8.	APP. XXIV.

Army Form C. 2118.

WAR DIARY
or
INTELLIGENCE SUMMARY.
(Erase heading not required.)

Instructions regarding War Diaries and Intelligence Summaries are contained in F. S. Regs., Part II. and the Staff Manual respectively. Title pages will be prepared in manuscript.

Place	Date	Hour	Summary of Events and Information	Remarks and references to Appendices
VICTORY CAMP.	March 28th		At 3.35 p.m. 169th Infantry Brigade reported heavy hostile shelling, and at 5.35 a.m. S.O.S. was sent by Power Buzzer from TOWY POST (Right Brigade). The story of the battle which followed is attached.	APP. XXV APP. XXX
	"	6 am	Map issued shewing Boundaries and Headquarters.	APP. XXVI
			All important Orders and Instructions issued during the Operations are attached.	
	29th		See Report on Operations.	APP. XXV
			All important orders and instructions issued during the Operations are attached.	APP. XXVII
	30th	a.m.	Quiet night. From 168th Brigade Relief complete.	
		3.25	From 167th Brigade Relief complete.	
		5.50	" Brigades Situation normal.	
		5.50	To 13th Corps. Relief of 56th Division by 4th Canadian Division complete (less Div. Arty. and M.G.Bn.) Command of the Sector passed to G.O.C. 4th Can. Div. 56th	
		6.50	Div. Artillery remains in line.	
ACQ.		10.0	Divisional H.Qrs. established.	
			Infantry Brigades disposed 167th Infantry Brigade VILLERS AU BOIS Area.	
			168th do. MONT ST. ELOI Area.	
			169th do. ECOIVRES Area.	
			M.G.Bn. ROCLINCOURT.	
			G.O.C. visited First Army Headquarters with XIII Corps Commander, where he was personally congratulated by the Army Commander on the result of the battle on the 28th inst. The G.O.C. further had the honour of being received by His Majesty The King.	
		p.m. 7.45	Further congratulatory message received from XIII Corps Commander. First Army Commander visited H.Qrs. 167th & 168th Infantry Brigades during afternoon. 13th Corps Order 56th Division to be prepared to move from Corps area by train during afternoon of 2nd April.	APP. XXVIII
			All units notified. 13th Corps wire in all probability 56th Division/would rejoin the Division from the line to-morrow, 31st.	APP. XXIX

Army Form C. 2118.

WAR DIARY
or
INTELLIGENCE SUMMARY.
(Erase heading not required.)

Instructions regarding War Diaries and Intelligence Summaries are contained in F. S. Regs., Part II. and the Staff Manual respectively. Title pages will be prepared in manuscript.

Place	Date	Hour	Summary of Events and Information	Remarks and references to Appendices
ACQ.	March. 31st	2.5 a.m.	Relief of 56th Div. M.G.Bn. by 4th Canadian M.G.Bn. reported complete. H.Q. 56th Div. M.G.Bn. established at VICTORY CAMP G.3.b.8.3.	
			Corps Commander visited G.O.C. during afternoon and told him that in all probability 56th Division would not leave XIII Corps Area.	
			All Brigades employed in bathing and generally re-equipping.	

4th April, 1918.

[signature]
Major-General,
Commanding 56th Division.

APPENDICES

I to XXX.

56th Div. LOCATION TABLE at 6 p.m. March 1918. Appendix 1

	1	2	3	4	5	6	7	8	9	10	11	12	13	14	15
Div. H.Q.	VICTORY CAMP G3b 73														
167th Inf. Bde. H.Q.	B27a 78														
1st Lon. Rgt.	Reserve				Support				Line						Reserve
~~2nd~~ "	Line				Reserve				Support						Line
7th Midx. "	Support				Line				Reserve						Support
8th "															
168th Inf. Bde. H.Q.	B20b 15														
4th Lond. Rgt.	Reserve					Support						Line			
~~12th~~ 13th "	Support					Line						Reserve			
14th "	Line					Reserve						Support			
169th Inf. Bde. H.Q.	Maison Blanche H1d 38														
2nd Lond. Rgt.	Line					Support						Reserve			
5th "	Reserve					Line						Support			
~~9th~~ 16th "	Support					Reserve						Line			
Div. Arty. H.Q.	VICTORY CAMP														
280 Bde.	H1c 80														
281 "	B21a 95.25.														
Pioneers.	St. Catherine														
M.G. Batln.	Trafalgar Camp														

56th DIVISION   LOCATION TABLE at 6 p.m.   MARCH. 1918

	16	17	18	19	20	21	22	23	24	25	26	27	28	29	30	31
Div. H.Q.	VICTORY CAMP	—	—	—	—	—	—	—	—	—	—	—	—	—	ACQ.	—
167th Inf. Bde. H.Q.	B27a.7.8. (Centre)	—	—	—	—	—	—	ST AUBIN TRAFALGAR CAMP (G3.1.78)	—	—	—	—	CHANTECLER H.1.d.58	—	CAMBLAIN L'ABBE	—
1st Lond. Rgt.	RESERVE	—	—	—	—	—	—	B27a.A.80.	—	—	—	—	BRIERLY HILL (B16.a.20)	LINE	VILLERS AU BOIS	—
3rd "	LINE	—	—	—	—	—	—	WAKEFIELD CAMP	—	—	—	—	B 25 b.			
7th Middx. "	SUPPORT	—	—	—	—	—	—	AUBREY CAMP (G4.a.28)	—	—	—	—	POINT DU JOUR REDOUBT			
8th "								ST AUBIN								
168th Inf. Bde. H.Q.	B27b.15. (Left)	—	—	—	—	—	—	—	—	—	—	—	—	—	MONT ST ELOI	—
4th Lond. Rgt.	LINE	RES.	—	—	—	SUP.	—	—	LINE (L)	—	—	—	SUP.	—	ECOIVRES	—
12th "	RES.	SUP.	—	—	—	LINE (R)	—	—	—	—	—	—	—	—	ECOIVRES	—
13th "	SUP.	LINE	—	—	—	LINE (L)	—	—	SUP.	—	—	—	LINE (L)	—	MONT ST ELOI	—
14th "																
169th Inf. Bde. H.Q.	MAISON BLANCHE (H.1.d.38.(Right))	—	—	—	—	—	—	—	—	—	—	—	—	CHANTECLER ECOIVRES	—
2nd Lond. Rgt.	RES.	—	LINE	—	—	LINE (R)	—	—	—	SUP.	—	—	—	POINT DU JOUR	BOIS DES ALLEUX	—
5th "	SUP.	—	RES.	—	—	LINE (L)	—	—	—	—	—	—	—	ST ELOIS LINE	"	"
9th "	LINE	—	SUP.	—	—	—	—	—	LINE (R)	—	—	—	—	ROUNDHAY CAMP	"	"
16th "																
Div. Arty. H.Q.	VICTORY CAMP H.I.C.80	—	—	—	—	—	—	—	—	—	—	—	—	—	ACQ.	—
280 Bde.	B21a.05.15	—	—	—	—	—	—	—	—	—	—	—	—	—	—	—
281																
Pioneers.	ST CATHERINE	—	—	—	—	—	—	—	—	—	—	—	—	—	ST. ESTREES CATHERINE CAUCHIE	—
D.M.G. Btn.	TRAFALGAR CAMP	—	—	—	—	—	—	—	—	—	—	—	—	VICTORY CAMP	ST AUBIN	—

SECRET.

Appendix II

		56th Division G.3/96.
167th Infantry Brigade.		
168th Infantry Brigade.		
169th Infantry Brigade.	XIII Corps.	
C.R.A.	62nd Division.	
C.R.E.	31st Division.	for information.
D.M.G.C.	4th Division.	
1/5th Cheshire Regt.	Guards Division.	
A.D.M.S.	"Q".	

XIII Corps - Right Division
Re-organisation on a 2 Brigade Front.

1. The Area allotted to the Right Division will be held on a 2 Infantry Brigade Front, each Brigade having 2 Battalions in Front Line and 1 Battalion in Reserve. 1 Infantry Brigade will be in Divisional Reserve.
    The necessary moves will take place as soon as possible and will be complete by 5 a.m. 22nd March.

2. The inter-Brigade boundary will run as follows :-
    Junction of CADORNA and CHARLES Trenches - along N. side of BROUGH ALLEY to its junction with MARINE Tr. - N.E. corner of BAILLEUL POST (B.28.b.9.5.) - B.28.b.2.8. - B.27.b.5.5. - thence due W to the Railway.

3. The area now held by the 167th Infantry Brigade will be taken over by the 168th & 169th Infantry Brigades respectively under arrangements to be made by Brigadiers concerned. On relief 167th Infantry Brigade will come into Divisional Reserve with Headquarters at ST.AUBIN. One Battalion will remain East of the Ridge, and will find working parties - 2 Companies to each front line Brigade. 168th Infantry Brigade will accommodate the H.Q. of this Battalion.

4. The Divisional Artillery will be organised in 2 Groups, one Group covering each Infantry Brigade.

5. The Divisional Machine Gun Battalion will be disposed :-

    (a) One Company to each Infantry Brigade.
    (b) One Company manning certain guns West of the RED LINE.
    (c) One Company in Divisional Reserve.
    The necessary re-adjustment will be carried out by the D.M.G.C. in consultation with Brigadiers concerned.

6. (a) The present system of defence will be adhered to. All details regarding defence will be handed over on relief by 167th Infantry Brigade to 168th & 169th Infantry Brigades respectively.

    (b) The two Infantry Companies 167th Infantry Brigade left with each front line Brigade for work, will be at the disposal of these Brigades for defence purposes.

7. The completion of the moves ordered in paras. 3 & 5 will be notified to Div. H.Q. by Code word "CHALK".

8. ACKNOWLEDGE.

H.Q. 56th Divn.
19.3.18.

Lieut-Colonel,
General Staff.

War Diary   *Appendix III*

SECRET   Copy No. 28

56th (LONDON) DIVISION ORDER No. 151
20th March, 1918.

Ref. Map 51 b 1/40,000
     Lens 11 1/100,000

1. (a) The 56th Division will be relieved in the Right Sector of the XIII Corps Front by the 62nd Division as follows:-

    23rd - 25th March - R.E., Infantry, M.G. Battn. Pioneers and Medical Units.
    26th - 28th March - Divisional Artillery.

  (b) On relief, the 56th Division will move to the VILLERS CHATEL Area, where it will be in G.H.Q. Reserve at 12 hours notice to move by rail or bus (48 hours notice while relief is in progress).

2. (a) Relief will be effected in accordance with the Attached Table. No Formation or Unit will move back from the Divnl. Reserve Area until it is actually relieved in that Area. Two Machine Gun Companies will be in Divnl. Reserve during relief.
  (b) Advanced Parties of 1 Officer per Coy. and 1 N.C.O. per Platoon of Battalions, 62nd Division, going into the Line are being sent forward 24 hours in advance. These will be attached to corresponding Units of the 56th Division.
  (c) The D.M.G.O. will arrange to leave 1 N.C.O. or man for each M.G. in position; also guides to reinforcing positions for the M.G. Companies in Divnl. Reserve; the above to remain behind for 24 hours after relief.
    M.G. Companies attached to Infantry Brigades will be relieved the day before the Infantry relief takes place.
  (d) All Maps, Air photos, Log books, Schemes of Defence and Programmes of Work will be handed over on relief.
  (e) All further details of relief will be arranged between Brigadiers and Commanders concerned.
  (f) Transport arrangements to the VILLERS CHATEL Area will be notified by 56th Div. "Q"

3. The relief of Divnl. Artillery, Field Coys. R.E., and Medical Units will be carried out under arrangements made by the C.R.A., C.R.E. and A.D.M.S. respectively.
    Moves of Units not referred to above and of Transport Lines will be arranged by 56th Div. "Q".

4. Employed men will be relieved on the 23rd March.

5. All Troops, 62nd Division, in the Right Sector, come under the orders of the G.O.C., 56th Division, till the command of the Sector passes to the G.O.C. 62nd Division.

6. The Command of the Right Sector, XIII Corps Front, will pass to the G.O.C. 62nd Division at 3 p.m. 25th March, at which hour Headquarters, 56th Division, will close at VICTORY CAMP and re-open at VILLERS CHATEL.

7. ACKNOWLEDGE.

                                                    Lieut-Colonel,
                                         General Staff, 56th Division.

20th March, 1918.

P.T.O.

Issued at

Distribution:-

Copy No.1.	167th Infantry Brigade.	Copy No.16.	56th Div.Supply Col.
2.	168th Infantry Brigade.	17.	No. 56 Am.Sub Park.
3.	169th Infantry Brigade.	18.	A.D.C.
4.	1/5th Cheshire Regt.	19.	Camp Commandant.
5.	C.R.A.	20.	56th Div.Employ.Co.
6.	C.R.E.	21.	French Mission.
7.	56th Div. M.G.Battn.	22.	XIII Corps "G"
8.	56th Div. Signal Coy.	23.	XIII Corps "Q"
9.	56th Div. Gas Officer.	24.	62nd Division.
10.	A.D.M.S.	25.	31st Division.
11.	"Q"	26.	Guards Division.
12.	A.P.M.	27.	4th Division.
13.	D.A.D.O.S.	28.)	War Diary.
14.	D.A.D.V.S.	29.)	
15.	56th Div. Train.	30.	File.

SECRET

TABLE OF RELIEFS TO ACCOMPANY 56th DIVISION ORDER No. 151

SERIAL NO.	DATE	FORMATION OR UNIT	FROM	TO	ON RELIEF BY	REMARKS
1.	March 22nd	1 M.G.Coy.56th Div.	Right Subsection	Div. Reserve	1 M.G.Coy.62nd Div.	
2.	23rd	169th Inf. Bde.	Right Subsection	ST. AUBIN	187th Inf. Bde.	
3.		167th Inf. Bde.	ST. AUBIN	Res. Area	169th Inf. Bde.	
4.		1 M.G.Coy.56th Div.	Left Subsection	Div. Reserve	1 M.G.Coy.62nd Div.	
5.		1 M.G.Coy.56th Div.	Div. Reserve	Res. Area	1 M.G.Coy.56th Div.	
6.	24th	168th Inf. Bde.	Left Subsection	ST. AUBIN	185th Inf. Bde.	
7.		139th Inf. Bde.	ST. AUBIN	Reserve Area	138th Inf. Bde.	
8.		1 M.G.Coy.56th Div.	E. of GREEN Line	Div. Reserve	1 M.G.Coy.62nd Div.	
9.		1 M.G.Coy.56th Div.	Div. Reserve	Res. Area	1 M.G.Coy.56th Div.	
10.	25th	168th Inf. Bde.	ST. AUBIN	Res. Area	185th Inf. Bde.	
11.		H.Q. & 2 Coys. 56th Div.M.G.Bn.	Div. Reserve	Res. Area	1 M.G.Coy.62nd Div.	
12.		1/5th Cheshire Rgt. Pioneers.	Line	Orders Later.	9th D.L.I. (Pioneers)	
13.		Div.H.Q. 56th Div.	VICTORY CAMP	VILLERS CHATEL	Div.H.Q. 62nd Div.	Command passed at 3 pm.

The completion of each serial number will be wired to Divisional Headquarters.

War Diary   *Appendix III b*

SECRET.   56th Division G.3/110.

ADDENDUM No. 1 to 56th (LONDON) DIVISION ORDER No. 151 dated 20th March, 1918.

1. On relief by Field Companies R.E. of 62nd Division, two Field Companies, R.E. 56th Division will be placed at the disposal of the C.E., XIII Corps for work on Corps Defences.

2. The last sentence of para. 2 (a) is cancelled.
Two Companies 56th Div. M.G.Battalion on relief by Two Companies 62nd Div. M.G.Battalion, will be accommodated in CUBITT CAMP until 26th March, when they will rejoin their Battalion in the Reserve Division Area under orders to be issued later. This Camp is being connected by wire direct to Corps H.Q.

The following amendments will be made to Table annexed to 56th Div. Order No. 151. -

Serial No. 1 Col. 5 for Divisional Reserve read CUBITT CAMP.
" No. 4 " 5 " " " " CUBITT CAMP.
" No. 5 is cancelled.
" No. 9 " "

3. Para. 2 (a). The number of Battalions in the Divisional Reserve Area will not be reduced during relief, i.e. no Battalion will be moved to the Reserve Area till its relieving Battalion has arrived in the Divisional Reserve Area. Each Brigade coming into Divisional Reserve will leave one Battalion forward of the GREEN LINE for work and for defence as directed in 56th Div. G.3/96 dated 19.3.18, paras. 3 & 6 (b).

4. ACKNOWLEDGE.

H.Q. 56th Divn.   Lieut-Colonel,
21.3.18.   General Staff.

Issued to all recipients of 56th Div. Order No. 151.

"A" Form
MESSAGES AND SIGNALS.

Army Form C. 2121
(In pads of 100.)

Sender's Number.	Day of Month.	In reply to Number.	
* G. 193	21		AAA

56 Div. Order No. 151 is postponed till further orders AAA Addsd all recipients of Order AAA Acknowledge.

From 56th Div.

(sd) G.P.CROWDEN,
General Staff.

SECRET.   Copy No. 27

56th DIVISION WARNING ORDER No. 152.

                                                          22nd March, 1918.

1.   The 56th Division will probably be relieved by the 2nd Canadian Division commencing on or about the 24th March.
        On relief the 56th Division will come into G.H.Q. Reserve at 12 hours notice to move by rail or bus.

2. (a) The 6th Canadian Infantry Brigade will relieve the 169th Infantry Brigade in the Right Sub-sector.
        The 5th Canadian Infantry Brigade will relieve the 168th Infantry Brigade in the Left Sub-sector.
        The 4th Canadian Infantry Brigade will relieve the 167th Infantry Brigade in Divisional Reserve.

   (b) The Machine Gun Companies in the line will as far as possible not be relieved on the same day as the Infantry Brigades they cover.

   (c) Companies of the Battalion 167th Infantry Brigade quartered East of the Ridge will be withdrawn with the Infantry Brigades to whom they are attached.

3.   The Brigade in the Right Sub-sector will be the first to be relieved.

4.   Brigadiers, C.R.A., C.R.E., A.D.M.S. and O.C. Pioneers will make all possible preliminary arrangements with a view to relief at short notice.
        All maps, air photos, log-books and programmes of work will be handed over.

5.   ACKNOWLEDGE.

                                                Lieut-Colonel,
                                                General Staff, 56th Division.

Issued at

Distribution :-
Copy No. 1. 167th Infantry Brigade.   No. 18. Camp Commandant.
        2.   168th Infantry Brigade.   19. 56th Div. Employment
        3.   169th Infantry Brigade.   Coy.
        4.   1/5th Cheshire Regt.   20. French Mission.
        5.   C.R.A.   21. XIII Corps "G".
        6.   C.R.E.   22. XIII Corps "Q".
        7.   56th Div. M.G.Bn.   23. 2nd Canadian Divn.
        8.   56th Div. Signal Coy.   24. 4th Division.
        9.   56th Div. Gas Officer.   25. 62nd Division.
       10.   A.D.M.S.   26. 3rd Canadian Divn.
       11.   "Q".   27.) War Diary.
       12.   A.P.M.   28.)
       13.   D.A.D.O.S.   29. File.
       14.   D.A.D.V.S.
       15.   56th Div. Train.
       16.   56th Div. M.T.Coy.
       17.   A.D.C.

"A" Form
MESSAGES AND SIGNALS.

Army Form C. 2121
(In pads of 100.)

Prefix	Code	Words	Charge		No. of Message
Office of Origin and Service Instructions				This message is on a/c of:	Recd. at .... m.
		Sent At .... m.		*Appendix 16*	Date
		To		Service.	From
		By		(Signature of "Franking Officer.")	By

TO

Sender's Number.	Day of Month.	In reply to Number.	
G 261	23		AAA

Warning cancelled	Order	152	is

From **56 Div.**
Place
Time **1.15 bn** ⚹ 13 Midnight

The above may be forwarded as now corrected. (Z)

Censor. Signature of Addressor or person authorised to telegraph in his name.
General Staff

Appendix V

SECRET & URGENT.   56th Division G.3/132.

167th Infantry Brigade.   XIII Corps for information.
168th Infantry Brigade.
169th Infantry Brigade.
C.R.A.
C.R.E.
O.C. 56th Div. Signals.
"Q"
D.M.G.C.

The following is for the personal information of Brigadiers, C.R.A., C.R.E., Signals, D.M.G.C. It is not to be communicated to the troops till the necessity arises and is sent out to enable Commanders to think out their plans.

1. The XVII Corps has been ordered to withdraw to its 3rd system which corresponds to our GREEN LINE: but continuing to hold MONCHY lightly. The Division on our right will not withdraw its troops north of the SCARPE till compelled to do so by the capture of MONCHY.
Should the 4th Division withdraw his troops N. of the SCARPE to the GREEN LINE a readjustment of our line will become necessary.

2. This readjustment will be the occupation of the Switch BEATTY POST - N. TYNE ALLEY - RED LINE - TOWY ALLEY - GREEN LINE.
The junction between Brigades will be as at present, i.e. the N.E. corner of BAILLEUL POST (which is inclusive to the Right Brigade.)

3. Brigadiers will consider the question of withdrawing to in the line this line, holding such posts in advance of it as will give it depth and assist in breaking up any hostile attack.

4. The D.M.G.C. will consider the question of withdrawing the Machine Guns forward of this line and placing them in position to cover the new line.

5. O.C. Signals will arrange for the destruction of the buried cable E. of the RED LINE should necessity arise.

6. The O.C. Right Brigade will at once get in touch with the Left Brigade, 4th Division, and arrange details as to the exact point of junction on the GREEN LINE.

7. As much ammunition will be brought back as possible.

8. ACKNOWLEDGE BY WIRE.

H.Q. 56th Divn.
22.3.18.
                                                    Lieut-Colonel,
                                                    General Staff.

SECRET & URGENT.   56th Division G.3/135.

Appendix VI

167th Infantry Brigade.
168th Infantry Brigade.
169th Infantry Brigade.   O.C. 56th Div. Signals.
C.R.A.   "Q"
C.R.E.   XIII Corps (for information).
D.M.G.Commander.

Reference 56th Division G.3/132 dated 22nd March 1918.

1. The scheme indicated in the above quoted memo is to be looked on purely as a possibility which may arise, and such work will be proceeded with as is necessary to effectively carry it out at short notice.

2. The G.O.C. also wishes the Brigadier, Right Brigade and the D.M.G.C. to consider the question of switching from MILL POST (inclusive) along BELVOIR ALLEY - thence along MARINE & NAVAL Trench to connect with the Division on our right, and also from NAVAL and MARINE Trench along TOWY ALLEY.

It is probable that this switch would be taken into use as a preliminary step to adopting the scheme referred to in para. 1 should this latter become necessary.

3. Work on dugouts is to be stopped until further orders and the C.R.E. will, in consultation with Brigadiers concerned, utilize all available engineers and pioneers in connection with the two switches referred to above.

Brigadiers concerned will give all possible assistance in the matter of labour.

H.Q. 56th Divn.   (Sgd.) W.R.Pinwill,
23.3.18.   Lieut-Colonel,
                                                  General Staff.

Appendix VII.

SECRET

56th Division No. G.3/136.

167th Infantry Brigade.	56th Div. M.G. Battn.
168th Infantry Brigade.	56th Div. Signal Coy.
169th Infantry Brigade.	"Q"
C.R.A.	XIII Corps.
C.R.E.	4th Division.

The following is in amplification of 56th Div. No. G.3/132 and G.3/135 dated 22nd and 23rd March respectively.

1. The 4th Division on our Right do not intend to withdraw from their positions N. of the SCARPE, unless definitely ordered to do so. They will fight the following successive lines:-
   (a) 1st Line of Resistance, CHICKEN RESERVE - CHALK RESERVE.
   (b) 2nd Line of Resistance, the BAILLEUL-WILLERVAL Line and thence along CLYDE Avenue from H.5.d.0.5. to H.12.c.5.9.
   (c) The 3rd System of which the Front Line starts at H.4.c.1.6 on the POINT DU JOUR - GAVRELLE Road, and runs in a S.E. direction. The Support Line is approx. 300 yds. in rear of the Front Line. This system connects with our GREEN Line.

2. With reference to (a) :- This will be fought in conjunction with MILL POST (incl.) BELVOIR ALLEY and NAVAL MARINE Trench: with possibly outposts at TOWY, WATER and GAVRELLE POSTS.
   Should the Line CHALK RESERVE, CHICKEN RESERVE, be forced TOWY ALLEY will be manned as a switch to connect NAVAL and MARINE Trench with the RED LINE.
   Should MILL POST be lost, the NAVAL, MARINE, EARL, MARQUIS Line, will be held in conjunction with such Front Line Posts as are holding out.
   A break in the NAVAL MARINE Line will be met by the occupation of the North TYNE ALLEY Switch.

3. With reference to 1 (b):- Line
   A break in the BAILLEUL-WILLERVAL / on or South of the Divl. boundary will be met by the occupation of the TOWY ALLEY - POINT DU JOUR Switch.

4. In connection with the above work on the following is considered important:-

   a. (BELVOIR ALLEY, North TYNE ALLEY and Supporting
   (Points, NAVAL and MARINE Line.
   (TOWY ALLEY - POINT DU JOUR Switch and Supporting
   (Points
   (Doubling the RED LINE.

   b. (OUSE ALLEY Switch W. of RED LINE - of secondary
   (importance.

5. The main Lines of Defence for the/Divisions are:-

   The NAVAL and MARINE, EARL, MARQUIS Line.
   The RED LINE.
   The BROWN and GREEN LINES.
   with their connecting switches.

   These Lines and their Supporting Posts are to be fought for, and no withdrawal is to be made except on definite orders.

23rd March, 1918.

Lieut-Colonel,
General Staff, 56th Division.

"A" Form
MESSAGES AND SIGNALS.

Army Form C. 2121
(In pads of 100.)

No. of Message..........

TO	167th Inf Bde	"Q"	
	168th Inf Bde	Sigs	
	169th Inf Bde		

Sender's Number.	Day of Month.	In reply to Number.	
G. 251	23		AAA

H.Q. and one Battalion 167th Inf Bde now at ST. AUBIN will move as follows aaa Bde H.Q. to TRAFALGAR CAMP 1 Battn to AUBREY aaa L.T.M.B. remains ANZIN aaa Move when ready by march route aaa "Q" will arrange tspt aaa ackdge aaa Addressed 167 Bde reptd 168 169 "Q" and Sigs

From: 56th Div
Time: 10 am

(sd) T.W. PINWILL.
Lt. Col. for G.S.

"A" Form
MESSAGES AND SIGNALS.

Army Form C. 2121
(In pads of 100.)

No. of Message. IX

Prefix........Code........m, Words. Charge. This message is on a/c of: Recd. at............m.
Office of Origin and Service Instructions

Sent
At................m.
To................
By................ (Signature of "Franking Officer.")

Date................
From................
By................

TO	167th Inf Bde	C.R.A.	62nd Division
	168th Inf Bde	C.R.E.	4th Division
	169th Inf Bde	D.M.G.O.	

Sender's Number.	Day of Month.	In reply to Number.	
G. 276	23rd		AAA

The enemy appears to be manning the FRESNES - ROUVROY Line opposite the Divnl front more thickly than usual aaa He has also displayed considerable activity in No Mans Land and has cut some of our wire by means of a land mine aaa The Brigadier 169th Inf Bde may at his discretion thin out TOWY POST and hold it with outposts only aaa In the event of GAVRELLE being entered by the enemy he will inform the artillery and Div. H.Q. aaa On this information the Artillery will shell GAVRELLE aaa During the night the heavy artillery will shell at intervals the area in rear of the enemy's front line system aaa At 5 am the heavy artillery will put down a S.O.S. barrage along the whole front of the

From
Place
Time

The above may be forwarded as now corrected. (Z)
.... Censor. Signature of Addressor or person authorised to telegraph in his name.
* This line should be erased if not required.
(7981) Wt. W493/M1647 130,000 Pads 5/17 D. D. & L. E1187

"A" Form
MESSAGES AND SIGNALS.

Army Form C. 2121
(In pads of 100.)

TO (2)

* AAA

~~SxOxSxxbx~~
Div. using 106 fuzes aaa Men in the front trenches are to be warned that some splinters may reach them and that they should not expose themselves more than is necessary to keep a good look out aaa The Field Artillery will not open a S.O.S. barrage unless it is called for aaa Addsd Inf Bdes C.R.A. C.R.E. D.M.G.C. reptd Flank Divns

From 56th Div
Time 7.50 p.m.   (sd) F.B.HURNDALL,
(Z) Major, G.S.

"A" Form
MESSAGES AND SIGNALS.

Army Form C. 2121
(In pads of 100.)

TO: 167 Inf Bde C.R.E. D.M.G.C.

Sender's Number: G. 283
Day of Month: 23

AAA

Troops in Div. Reserve will stand to at 5 am tomorrow except Field Companies and the Inf Battn working tonight aaa These latter will be at one hours notice aaa ackdge Addsd 167 Bde D.M.G.C. and C.R.E.

From: 56th Div
Time: 10.15 pm

(sd) W.R. PINWILL,
Lt. Col.

"A" Form
MESSAGES AND SIGNALS.

Army Form C. 2121
(in pads of 100).
No. of Message..............

Prefix......Code........m.	Words.	Charge.	This message is on a/c of:	Recd. at..........m.
Office of Origin and Service Instructions.	Sent		**APPENDIX XI**	Date..............
....	At..........m.		...............Service.	From..............
....	To..........			
....	By..........		(Signature of "Franking Officer.")	By..............

TO	167 Bde.			
	C.R.E.			
	D.M.G.C.			

Sender's Number.	Day of Month.	In reply to Number.	AAA
G.302	24		

G.283 of 23rd will hold good until
further orders.

From 56 Div.
Place
Time 1.15 p.m.

(Sgd.) F.B.Hurndall

SECRET.

War Diary — *Appendix XII* — Copy No. 23

56th DIVISION ORDER No. 153.

24th March, 1918.

1. 167th Infantry Brigade will relieve 169th Infantry Brigade on the present front on 28th March.

2. Details of relief will be arranged between Brigadiers concerned.

3. Maps, air photos, Log-books, Defence Schemes, Trench Stores and Dumps will be handed over on relief.

4. On relief 169th Infantry Brigade will become Divisional Reserve and will take over accommodation vacated by 167th Infantry Brigade. All working parties found by 167th Infantry Brigade will be taken over by 169th Infantry Brigade.

5. The completion of relief will be wired to Div. H.Q.

6. The Command of the front will pass from 169th Infantry Brigade to 167th Infantry Brigade on completion of relief.

7. ACKNOWLEDGE.

F. B. Hurndall Major
for Lieut-Colonel,
General Staff.

Issued at 11.30 p.m.

Copy No. 1 to 167th Infantry Brigade.
2 " 168th Infantry Brigade.
3. " 169th Infantry Brigade.
4. " 1/5th Cheshire Regt.
5. " C.R.A.
6. " C.R.E.
7. " 56th Div. M.G.Bn.
8. " 56th Div. Signal Coy.
9. " 56th Div. Gas Officer.
10. " A.D.M.S.
11. " "Q"
12. " A.P.M.
13. " D.A.D.O.S.
14. " D.A.D.V.S.
15. " 56th Div. Train.
16. " 56th Div. M.T.Coy.
17. " A.D.C.
18. " Camp Commandant.
19. " 56th Div. Employment Coy.
20. " French Mission.
21. " 4th Division.
22. " XIII Corps.
23.) " War Diary.
24.)
25. " File.

"A" Form
MESSAGES AND SIGNALS.

Army Form C. 2121 (in pads of 100).

This message is on a/c of:
APPENDIX XIII

TO	167 Inf. Bde.	C.R.A.	4th Divn.
	168 Inf. Bde.	C.R.E.	* 3rd Cdn. Divn.
	169 Inf. Bde.	D.M.G.C.	

Sender's Number.	Day of Month.	In reply to Number.	
* G.312	24		AAA

Reference G.276 dated 23rd similar action by artillery tonight with exception that barrage by heavy artillery will be put down at 4.30 a.m. instead of 5 a.m. AAA
Acknowledge

*G.276 sent to 62nd Div. on 23rd.

From 56 Div.
Place
Time 8 p.m.

(Sd.) F.B. Hurndall,
Maj.

* This line should be erased if not required.

Appendix XIV

XIII Corps Intelligence Report taken 4.15 p.m.

Examination at Army of prisoner of 471st I.R. as follows :-

Prisoner states WOTAN STELLUNG occupied last night by 101st Res. and 102nd Res. Regiment from RIGA belonging to 219th Division and 23rd Res. Divn. 240th Divn. is to be relieved tonight by these troops. They will occupy mine shafts and dugouts to avoid barrage. Men of 240th Division will occupy shell craters. Attack to take place tomorrow morning by these Russian Divisions plus the 240th and 5th Bav. Res. Divn. This was told him by a man of the 12th Bav. Res. Regt. and also by men from Russia in WOTAN STELLUNG. Objective to a depth of 4 kilos. Right Flank OPPY, then swing round towards VIMY. Battalion Section of 471st Regt. have already 60 T.M's and eight more T.M. Coys. arriving tonight; ammunition already there.

Note. - This prisoner is definite about an attack and his statements agree with the evidence from other prisoners re an attack at LA BASSEE tomorrow.

(WOTAN STELLUNG = QUEANT - DROCOURT LINE.)

H.Q., 56th Divn.
25. 3. 1918.

"A" Form
MESSAGES AND SIGNALS.

Army Form C. 2121 (in pads of 100).

This message is on a/c of:
APPENDIX XV

TO: 168th Inf. Bde.

Sender's Number: G.339
Day of Month: 25
AAA

G.O.C. very anxious obtain another identification tonight AAA Do what you can with an enterprising small party lying up on enemy parapet or other suitable spot AAA Acknowledge.

From: 56 Div.
Time: 1.15 p.m.

(Z) (Sgd.) W.R. Pinwill,
General Staff.

"A" Form
MESSAGES AND SIGNALS.

Army Form C. 2121 (in pads of 100).

SECRET

TO: 168 Inf. Bde.
169 "
C.R.A.

Sender's Number: G.352
Day of Month: 25

AAA

Our Field Guns will sweep the enemy's front line trenches with H.E. to-morrow between 4.30 a.m. and 5 a.m. AAA Patrols should be warned accordingly AAA Acknowledge by wire AAA Addsd 168, 169 Bdes repeated C.R.A.

From: 56 Div.
Time: 7.45 p.m.

(Sd.) W.N.Pinwill, Lt.Col

War Diary Append. XVII

SECRET. 56th Division 1.3/149.

167th Infantry Brigade.
168th Infantry Brigade.
169th Infantry Brigade.
C.R.A.
C.R.E.
D.M.G.C.
1/5th Cheshire Regt.
"Q"
A.D.M.S.
4th Division.
3rd Canadian Division

In view of the information given by the German prisoner of the 471 I.R. captured last night (our G.2/151) the following action will be taken :

(a) Field and Heavy Artillery and Machine Guns will harass roads, tracks and possible assembly positions at intervals. Machine guns will draw additional ammunition for this purpose.

(b) Heavy Artillery and 4.5" How. Batteries will be ready to heavily barrage known and suspected T.M.Emplacements should the enemy open a T.M.Barrage on our line. The call for this will be "Anti T.M.Barrage" sent to Artillery and Div. H.Q.

(c) Brigadiers will ensure that the Companies 167th Infantry Brigade attached to them are available to occupy their positions at short notice.

(d) Special vigilance will be maintained by patrols and listening posts with a view to ascertaining if the enemy is cutting his own wire to make gaps for attack. All information gained will be transmitted immediately. Negative information will be sent in should nothing suspicious be noticed.

(e) Troops (including Divnl. Reserves) will stand to arms at 5 a.m. as usual. All troops in Divisional Reserve will be prepared to move at 30 minutes notice from 4 a.m. - 167th Infantry Brigade H.Q. to the vicinity of CHANTECLER: troops to the vicinity of JUNCTION REDOUBT just West of the Crest of the Ridge.

H.Q. 56th Divn.
25.3.18.

Lieut-Colonel,
General Staff.

"A" Form.
MESSAGES AND SIGNALS.

Army Form C. 2121.
(In pads of 100.)

This message is on a/c of:
APPENDIX XVIII

TO	167th Inf. Bde.
	168th Inf. Bde.
	169th Inf. Bde.

Sender's Number.	Day of Month.	In reply to Number.	
G.395	26		AAA

In view possible appearance enemy agents warn all ranks against use of word RETIRE AAA Any person using this word before or during an attack to be shot.

From 56 Div.
Place
Time 7.30 p.m.

(Sgd.) W.R.Pinwill,

SECRET   Copy No. 25

56th DIVISION ORDER NO. 154.

26th March, 1918.

1. In order to ascertain the German dispositions opposite the 56th Division and to secure identifications, simultaneous raids will be made into the enemy's front system on the night 26th/27th March, by 168th Inf. Bde. at 2 points, by 169th Inf. Bde. at 3 points.

2. Details regarding the numbers to be employed, the exact points of entry and artillery co-operation, will be arranged by the Brigadiers concerned.

3. Zero hour will be fixed by the Brigadier, 169th Inf. Bde. and notified to all concerned. An officer from Divisional H.Q. will attend at each Infantry Brigade H.Q. to synchronize watches.

4. During the night 26th/27th March, a programme of harassing fire will be carried out. This will be so arranged as not to interfere with the Raids.

5. ACKNOWLEDGE.

                                                        Lieut-Colonel,
                                        General Staff, 56th Division.

Issued at 3/-.

Copy No. 1 to 167th Infantry Brigade.
           2 " 168th Infantry Brigade.
           3 " 169th Infantry Brigade.
           4 " 1/5th Cheshire Regt.
           5 " C.R.A.
           6 " C.R.E.
           7 " 56th Div. M.G.Bn.
           8 " 56th Div. Signal Coy.
           9 " 56th Div. Gas Officer.
          10 " A.D.M.S.
          11 " "Q"
          12 " A.P.M.
          13 " D.A.D.O.S.
          14 " D.A.D.V.S.
          15 " 56th Div. Train
          16 " 56th Div. M.T.Coy.
          17 " A.D.C.
          18 " Camp Commandant
          19 " 56th Div. Employment Coy.
          20 " French Mission.
          21 " 4th Division.
          22 " 3rd Can. Div.
          23 " 2nd Can. Div.
          24 " XIII Corps.
          25) " War Diary.
          26)
          27 " File.

SECRET.   *War Diary Appendix XX*   Copy No. 25

56th DIVISION WARNING ORDER No. 155

27th March 1918.

1. XIII Corps Boundary is being extended North to the SOUCHEZ River.

2. 3rd Canadian Division comes under orders of XIII Corps at noon to-day.

3. Redistribution of the Front will take place as follows: 56th Division will extend North and Northern Divisional Boundary will be along TIRED ALLEY inclusive to 56th Division.

    Southern Boundary will remain as before.

    The Inter-Brigade Boundary will run from BIRD POST - BAILLEUL EAST - RAILWAY POST, all inclusive to Southern Brigade.

4. BAILLEUL - WILLERVAL Line will be considered the front system. The present front system will be held as an outpost Line. Redistribution to be completed by 4 a.m. 28th.

5. 56th Div. Order No. 153 is postponed.

6. ACKNOWLEDGE.

                                    F. B. Hurndall
                                         Major
                                    Lieut-Colonel,
                                    General Staff.

Issued at 11.30 a.m.

Copy No. 1 to 167th Infantry Brigade.
       2.   168th Infantry Brigade.
       3.   169th Infantry Brigade.
       4.   1/5th Cheshire Regt.
       5.   C.R.A.
       6.   C.R.E.
       7.   56th Div. M.G.Bn.
       8.   56th Div. Signal Coy.
       9.   56th Div. Gas Officer.
      10.   A.D.M.S.
      11.   "Q"
      12.   A.P.M.
      13.   D.A.D.O.S.
      14.   D.A.D.V.S.
      15.   56th Div. Train.
      16.   56th Div. M.T.Coy.
      17.   A.D.C.
      18.   Camp Commandant.
      19.   56th Div. Employment Coy.
      20.   French Mission.
      21.   4th Division.
      22.   3rd Can. Div.
      23.   XIII Corps "G".
      24.   XIII Corps "Q"
      25.)
      26.)   War Diary.
      27.   File.

SECRET.   Copy No. 25

56th DIVISION ORDER No. 156.

Ref. 1/20,000 Map MAROEUIL.

War Diary Appendix XXI
27th March 1918

1. In accordance with orders received 56th Division will tonight relieve 3rd Canadian Division up to ARLEUX POST (inclusive) in the front line, the Northern Boundary thence being TIRED ALLEY (inclusive)
   At the same time 56th Division will withdraw to the BAILLEUL-WILLERVAL System which will become the front system, but will keep outposts in our original front line posts, whose mission will be to deceive the enemy and conceal the fact of our withdrawal. These outposts will only withdraw when ordered or in case of a general hostile attack, when they will withdraw fighting.

2. 169th Infantry Brigade will take over tonight from 168th Infantry Brigade as follows :-
   Front line - up to BIRD POST (inclusive)
   BAILLEUL - WILLERVAL Line - up to BAILLEUL EAST POST (inclusive).
   FARBUS Line - up to BAILLEUL Road B.21.d.20.98 (inclusive)
   POINT DU JOUR - THELUS Line - up to RAILWAY POST (inclusive).

   168th Infantry Brigade will relieve 3rd Canadian Division tonight up to the new boundary.

3. Both Brigades in the line will arrange to relieve such R.E. and Pioneers as are holding Posts in front of the POINT DU JOUR Line.
   R.E. and Pioneers will occupy the POINT DU JOUR Line under orders from the C.R.E. and continue work thereon.
   One Company Pioneers will be quartered in each of the following posts : RIDGE POST - RAILWAY POST - POINT DU JOUR Redoubt.
   All R.E. and Pioneers in the POINT DU JOUR Line will come under the tactical command of the Brigadier Commanding the Infantry Brigade in whose section they are located, and will send officers to report their locations and dispositions.
   In the event of hostile attack arrangements will be made for the relief of R.E. & Pioneers and their formation as Divisional Reserve.

4. It is of the utmost importance that the withdrawal of troops to the BAILLEUL - WILLERVAL Line should be concealed from the enemy.
   The withdrawal will, therefore, not commence till dusk and will be complete by 4 a.m. tomorrow.
   All S.A.A., Trench Mortars and ammunition and Trench Stores will be withdrawn.

5. B.Gs.C. 169th & 168th Infantry Brigades will arrange to leave weak outposts in the old front posts, who will carry on the usual routine firing of lights. Arrangements should be made to send out usual patrols from troops in rear, and to send up machine guns and Stokes Mortars occasionally to fire from the usual places and then again withdraw.

6. Brigadiers in the line will consider and report on the question of holding such posts close to and in advance of the BAILLEUL - WILLERVAL Line as will give it depth and assist in breaking up any hostile attack. HOW TRENCH will be held as part of the BAILLEUL - WILLERVAL Line System.

7. The C.R.A. will withdraw tonight all guns and trench mortars in front of the BAILLEUL - WILLERVAL Line and will arrange for barrages in case of attack in conformity with this withdrawal.

8. Infantry Brigadiers in the line will arrange for the retirement of the outposts in case of attack down fixed communication trenches, and will inform their Group Commanders so that the barrage can be arranged accordingly.

/9.

9.   The D.M.G.C. will arrange for the withdrawal of machine guns forward of the BAILLEUL - WILLERVAL Line, and for placing them in positions tonight to cover it, also for relieving guns of 3rd Can.Divn.

10.   O.C. Signals will arrange for the destruction of the buried cable East of the BAILLEUL - WILLERVAL Line.

11.   G.O.C. Right Brigade will at once get in touch with G.O.C. Left Brigade, 4th Division and arrange point of junction in the new front line.
      G.O.C. Left Brigade will at once get in touch with G.O.C. 3rd Canadian Division and arrange details of relief.

12.   Order No. 153 is postponed.

13.   ACKNOWLEDGE.

B.Pakenham
Lieut-Colonel,
General Staff.

Issued at 12.30 p.m.

Copy No. 1 to 167th Infantry Brigade.
     2.   168th Infantry Brigade.
     3.   169th Infantry Brigade.
     4.   1/5th Cheshire Regt.
     5.   C.R.A.
     6.   C.R.E.
     7.   56th Div. M.G.Bn.
     8.   56th Div. Signal Coy.
     9.   56th Div. Gas Officer.
    10.   A.D.M.S.
    11.   "Q"
    12.   A.P.M.
    13.   D.A.D.O.S.
    14.   D.A.D.V.S.
    15.   56th Div. Train.
    16.   56th Div. M.T.Coy.
    17.   A.D.C.
    18.   Camp Commandant.
    19.   56th Div. Employment Coy.
    20.   French Mission.
    21.   4th Division.
    22.   3rd Can. Divn.
    23.   XIII Corps "G".
    24.   XIII Corps "Q".
    25.)
          War Diary.
    26.)
    27.   File.

"A" Form.
MESSAGES AND SIGNALS. Army Form C. 2121.

Prefix	Code	Words	Charge	This message is on a/c of:	Recd. at	m.
Office of Origin and Service Instructions.		Sent			Date	
		At		Service.	From	
		To				
		By		(Signature of "Franking Officer.")	By	

TO: *All recipients of Order 156*

| Sender's Number. | Day of Month. | In reply to Number. | AAA |

C. 421   27th

Following portions of O.O. 156 are
cancelled aaa Last six lines of para 1
aaa Whole of paras 3,4,5,6,7,8,9,10 aaa
First three lines of para "11" aaa Staff
officer visiting 188th and 189th Inf. Bdes.
to explain aaa ~~C.3/1-- of today b also
cancelled aaa~~ Acknowledge

X To 2 Bdes only

From 58th Div.
Place
Time 3.35 pm

Robert Carr

"A" Form.
MESSAGES AND SIGNALS.

Army Form C. 2121.
(In pads of 100.)

APP. XXIII

TO - All recipients of Order 153

Sender's Number.	Day of Month.	In reply to Number.	A A A
G.424	27		

Continuation our G.421 of today AAA Para. 12 O.O.156 cancelled AAA Moves will take place as ordered in O.O.153 AAA Acknowledge.

From 56 Div.
Place
Time 5.30 p.m.

(Z)
(Sgd) C.W. Haydon, Capt.
G.S.

"A" Form.
MESSAGES AND SIGNALS.

Army Form C. 2121.
(In pads of 100.)
No. of Message..............

Prefix........Code........m	Words.	Charge.		
Office of Origin and Service Instructions.			This message is on a/c of:	Recd. at........m.
PRIORITY	Sent		APP. XXIV	Date...........
by Fullerphone	At........m.		..........Service.	From...........
	To........			
	By........		(Signature of "Franking Officer.")	By........

TO: 168th Inf. Bde.   3rd Can. Div.
    C.R.A.

Sender's Number.	Day of Month.	In reply to Number.	
G.430	27		A A A

In order to conform to dispositions of
Div on our left ARLEUX POST will be treated
as an outpost and troops holding it will if
heavily attacked withdraw fighting AAA Our
main defensive line in new portion taken over
tonight will run from TOMMY POST inclusive
along ARLEUX LOOP SOUTH to junction with
left Division at TIRED ALLEY T.5.c.6.8. AAA
Acknowledge AAA Addsd. QJA reptd. C.R.A. and
CYC.

From 56 Div.
Place
Time 8.45 p.m.

(Z)
(Sgd.) B. Pakenham, Lt. Col.

APPENDIX XXV.

Report on the Operations of 56th Division in the vicinity of OPPY & GAVRELLE, 28th & 29th March, 1918.

(Note:- This Appendix precedes the War Diary.)

APPENDIX XXVI.

Orders & Instructions issued during the Operations, 28th March, 1918.

(Note:- This Appendix precedes the War Diary).

A P P E N D I X   X X V I I.

Orders & Instructions issued during the Operations 29th March, 1918.

(<u>Note</u>:- This Appendix precedes the War Diary).

"A" Form.
MESSAGES AND SIGNALS.

Army Form C. 2121.
(In pads of 100.)

This message is on a/c of:

APP. XXVIII

TO	56 Div.

Sender's Number.	Day of Month.	In reply to Number.	A A A
G.363	30		

The Corps Commander wishes you to convey to the troops of BRAMBLE his appreciation of their gallant conduct and resulute action in the defence of the VIMY RIDGE on 28th March AAA Though greatly outnumbered and opposed to overwhelming ordnance they maintained the line intact until ordered to withdraw to the main line of resistance where two attacks of the enemy were completely repulsed with heavy losses AAA This fine work has greatly added to the high reputation already gained by your division

From 13 Corps
Place
Time 5.30 p.m.

Appendix XXIX

SECRET

56th Div. No: G.3/206

167th Infantry Brigade.
168th Infantry Brigade.
169th Infantry Brigade.
C.R.A.
C.R.E.
56th Div. M.G.Battn.
56th Div. Signal Coy.
56th Div. Gas Officer.
A.D.M.S.
"Q".
A.P.M.
1/5th Cheshire Regt.
D.A.D.O.&S.

D.A.D.V.S.
56th Div. Train.
56th Div. M.T.Coy.
A.D.C.
Camp Commandant.
56th Div. Employment Coy.
French Mission.
XIII Corps "G"
XIII Corps "Q"
War Diary.
File.

The Division will be prepared to entrain from XIII Corps area any time after 12 noon, 2nd April.

Details of move will be notified as soon as received.

F. B. Hurnall [?]
for Lieut-Colonel,
General Staff.

H.Q. 56th Divn.
30.3.18.

A P P E N D I X   X X X.

Map shewing Boundaries & H.Qs. 56th Division. 6 a.m. 28.3.18.

(Note:- This Appendix precedes the
War Diary.)

Headquarters,　　　　　　　　　　　162th. Inf. Bde. G.93
58th. Division.　3/53
　　　　　　　　　　15.11.18.

　　　　　　　Herewith Report on Operations from
31st. October to 7th. November, as requested.

　　　　　　　　　　　　R.C.Boyle

　　　　　　　　　　　　　　　　Captain,
　　　　　　　　　　　　for Brigadier General,
　　　　　　Commanding 163th. Infantry Brigade.

14.11.18.　　　　　　　　　　B.F. 169 Bdes Relat
　　　　　　　　　　　　　　　into this town

SECRET.   56th Division G.S/232.

REPORT ON THE OPERATIONS of 56th DIVISION in the vicinity of OPPY & GAVRELLE, 28th & 29th March, 1918.

Reference Map MAROEUIL 1/20,000.

On 18th March information was received that an offensive by the enemy on a large front, which might include the VIMY Ridge, was imminent.

From this date Brigades in the line were ordered to be extremely alert and the whole Division stood to arms at 5 a.m. each morning.

Counter offensive shoots by the Artillery were carried out almost daily, especially at night and just prior to dawn, so as to disorganise any possible assembly of troops for attack.

On 21st March the enemy offensive South of the R.SCARPE commenced and by 27th he was in occupation of the VILLAGE of MONCHY, which commanded the ground on the North of that river.

During this time it became apparent that the enemy would endeavour to envelop ARRAS, and to capture the VIMY RIDGE from the South, and much work was done in improving the defensive switches facing South.

Night 27th/28th March.

On the night 27th/28th March the Division was ordered to extend its left flank and relieve the troops of the 3rd Canadian Division for a distance of approximately 1500 yards. This entailed an extension of the front of the Right (169th) Infantry Brigade to include BRADFORD & BIRD POSTS, and the taking over by the Left (168th) Infantry Brigade of TOMMY & ARLEUX POSTS.

The dispositions of the two Brigades in the line were then -

169th Infantry Brigade.

Right Battn. 1/16th London Regt. (Queens Westminsters) holding TOWY POST.

Left Battn.   8th London Regt. (London Rifle Brigade) holding HILL, BRADFORD & BIRD POSTS.

In BAILLEUL - WILLERVAL Line - 2nd Bn. London Regiment.
In FARBUS Line.   - 1 Coy. 1/5th Cheshire Regt.
                                   (Pioneers).
In Brigade Reserve   - 2 Cos. 1st London Regt. (attached)
                                   from 167th Infantry Brigade).
                                Detachment of 176th Tunnelling Coy.
                                R.E. (in POINT DU JOUR Redoubt).

168th Infantry Brigade.

Right Battn. - 4th London Regt. - holding BEATTY, WOOD & OPPY Posts.
Left Battn. 1/13th London Regt. (Kensingtons) - holding TOMMY & ARLEUX Posts.

In BAILLEUL - WILLERVAL Line - 1/14th London Regt. (London Scottish)
In CHESTER Post (B.15.d.)   - 2 Platoons 1/5th Cheshire Regt.
                                   (Pioneers).
In POINT DU JOUR Line & BRIMLEY HILL - 2 Cos. 1st London Regt.
                                   (attached from 167th Infantry Bde.)
                                   and 1½ Cos. 1/5th Cheshire Regiment.

In Divisional Reserve   - 167th Inf. Bde. (less 1 Bn.) and
                                   3 Field Coys. R.E.

The above extension was ordered under XIII Corps Order No. 122, which laid down that the BAILLEUL - WILLERVAL Line was to be held as our front line, and our old front line system to be considered as an outpost line.

This was subsequently cancelled by XIII Corps Order No. 123, which ordered our front line system to be held as such in order to conform to the 4th Division on our right (XVII Corps).

/At

At 8.45 p.m. however, as a result of verbal orders from XIII Corps, this was modified as regards ARLEUX Post, in order to conform to the defensive line of the 3rd Canadian Division on our Left, and the troops holding this were ordered, if heavily attacked, to withdraw fighting to the ARLEUX LOOP SOUTH, switching back from TOWY POST.

The reliefs resultant on this redistribution had not been completed at 5 a.m. when a heavy hostile bombardment opened.

At that hour the L.R.B. (169th Bde.) had not taken over BAILLEUL EAST Post, and one Company of the 1st Canadian Mounted Rifles had not been relieved from SUGAR POST. This latter Company remained in SUGAR POST throughout the battle, being placed by the courtesy of the G.O.C. 8th Canadian Infantry Brigade under the orders of 168th Infantry Brigade.

Commencement of the Battle.

At 5 a.m. the enemy opened a heavy bombardment consisting of heavy gas shelling of our rear lines of defence and Headquarters, followed later by H.E. on the BAILLEUL - WILLERVAL Line and FAMPUX Line.

At about 6 a.m. a very heavy artillery and Trench Mortar bombardment was opened on our front line system and forward posts, which continued until about 7 a.m.

At 6.35 a.m. the S.O.S. was sent by Power Buzzer from TOWY Post but no infantry attack developed then.

Owing to the continuous enemy shelling there seemed to be no doubt that an attack was imminent, and, therefore, at about 6.15 a.m. H.Q. & 1 Bn. of 187th Infantry Brigade were sent forward to the neighbourhood of CHANTECLER together with all the Reserve Machine Guns of the Division.

At 6.40 a.m. counter preparation was ordered to be carried out by Heavy and Field Artillery.

At about 7.5 a.m. the S.O.S. Signal was again sent up from TOWY POST, and was almost immediately followed by the S.O.S. along the whole line up to and including OPPY Post. The remaining battalion of the 187th Infantry Brigade was ordered forward to the vicinity of CHANTECLER.

The enemy attack.

Under cover of a creeping barrage the enemy's infantry moved forward apparently about 7.5 a.m.

The Heavy T.M. & Artillery bombardment had obliterated the bulk of the forward posts from our Southern boundary to OPPY POST (inclusive). With the exception of TOWY POST and of WOOD POST, in which the dispositions had been changed a day or two previously, the garrisons were apparently wiped out. There was only one survivor of the garrison of MILL POST, who reported that when he left the trenches were almost blotted out, and that the entrances to the large dug-out had already been smothered.

The garrisons of TOWY and WOOD Posts put up a gallant fight.

In the neighbourhood of GAVRELLE the enemy appears to have got into a pocket formed by TOWY and WATER Posts and by NAVAL Trench, and in this pocket he was exposed to the indirect fire of 14 machine guns, which were designed to bring S.O.S. fire on this area.

WOOD POST held out for about an hour, inflicting heavy casualties.

The garrison of TOWY POST made a stand in the Support Trench.

By 7.30 a.m. the enemy was attacking heavily in front, had passed over the Support Trench on either flank and was bombing up towards the Post from TOWY ALLEY in rear.

As it was manifest that there would soon be a shortage of bombs, the garrison after a stiff and splendid resistance, in which they were reduced to 3 Officers and 20 O.R., succeeded in fighting their way back down TOWY Trench and through the enemy back into the NAVAL Line. Meanwhile on the left of the 169th Brigade Section the enemy

/swarmed

swarmed over our forward posts and was soon pressing through gaps in the wire and down old C.Ts. into the NAVAL - MARINE Line.

Very soon after the attack had begun the L.R.B. Headquarters personnel under Lieut-Colonel HUSEY, D.S.O., M.C. found themselves repelling a massive onset delivered in 3 successive moves on MARINE Trench.

The wire in front of this line, which had recently been thickened, caused the enemy considerable discomfiture and great losses were caused to him by rifle, Lewis Gun and Machine Gun fire, but such were his numbers that this party was soon outflanked from the North.

The B.G.C. 169th Inf. Bde. therefore ordered Lieut-Colonel, HUSEY to fight his way to the junction of THAMES ALLEY and MARINE Trench and to withdraw slowly down THAMES ALLEY to the BAILLEUL - WILLERVAL Line, and by 10.30 a.m. the remains of his Battalion, numbering 4 Officers and 84 O.R. had taken up a position in the BAILLEUL - WILLERVAL Line.

Up to now the Q.W.R. under Lieut-Colonel GLASIER, D.S.O. on the right of 169th Inf. Bde. had been able to hold on to NAVAL Trench from their Southern boundary up to the GAVRELLE Road, and as long as the enemy were being held on the flanks by the L.R.B. and the Lancashire Fusiliers of the 4th Division, they were able successfully to ward off the enemy, inflicting great casualties on him.

Increasing pressure on both flanks soon rendered this position untenable and the enemy, who had been kept well in check, gradually surrounded the remainder of the garrison, and worked round to the right rear. Meanwhile information had been received that ORANGE HILL (S. of the SCARPE) had fallen.

The Corps Commander visited Divisional H.Q. and as a result of his verbal orders a wire was sent out at 10.30 a.m. ordering the withdrawal of 169th Inf. Bde. to the BAILLEUL - WILLERVAL Line, which was to be held at all costs.

1 Battalion of 167th Inf. Bde. was placed under the orders of 169th Inf. Bde. and 6 M.Gs. were sent forward to POINT DU JOUR to strengthen the right flank and our junction with 4th Division. 2 Field Coys. R.E. were also ordered up to strengthen the right flank by holding TONGUE and BLANCHE Posts. These orders were also telephoned to 169th Inf.Bde. and the withdrawal was carried out by the Q.W.R., who fought their way slowly back.

As regards the 168th Inf. Bde. the 4th London Regt. had been putting up a gallant defence on the MARQUIS Line. The Reserve Coy. had been moved forward from BOW Trench at 8.5 a.m. to counter-attack the enemy who had penetrated MARQUIS Trench. Heavy fighting occurred in DUKE Street and the Bn. H.Q. there was lost and regained.

At 10.30 a.m. the Brigade was ordered to be prepared to withdraw from our front line system in conjunction with the 3rd CANADIAN DIVISION.

By 11.30 a.m. the position was critical, both flanks of the Battalion being turned, while some of the enemy were even in OUSE ALLEY, the only trench open for a withdrawal.

The remnants of the garrison therefore commenced their withdrawal over the open under the cover of the Reserve Company, which manned the OUSE ALLEY Switch.

At 11.40 a.m. in consequence of orders received from the Corps, an order was sent to 188th Inf. Bde. to withdraw the remainder of its troops (Kensington Regt.) from TOMMY and ANZHEK Posts, in conjunction with 3rd Canadian Division, who similarly received orders to withdraw in co-operation with the Brigade to the BAILLEUL - WILLERVAL Line.

After the withdrawal of 4th London Regt. the enemy made a strong bombing attack on the block in OUSE ALLEY near BOW TRENCH which was, however, effectively stopped by a Lewis Gun covering the block.

Meanwhile, as early as 7.30 a.m. while the 4th London Regt. were still fighting in the front system, enemy bombing parties had broken through on their right by TYNE and N.TYNE ALLEYS, captured the two machine guns in position about 100 yds. East of BAILLEUL EAST Post and attacked the post which was held by the London Scottish.

A counter-attack was promptly organized, the enemy was driven back 150 yds. the machine gun crews released from their dugout, and a new block formed in advance of their position.

Repeated attacks were made on this block, but assisted by the fire of Stokes and 6" Newton Mortars these were all repulsed, as also several attacks made over the open astride of the BAILLEUL-GAVRELLE Road.

During the whole morning the situation of the 4th Division on our right was very obscure, the Division being reported to have lost touch with its own Brigades, while the lateral line between 189th Inf. Bde. and 12th Inf. Bde. was also cut. At about noon, however, we were in touch in the BAILLEUL - WILLERVAL Line and later definite touch was also obtained in the POINT DU JOUR - THELUS Line and in the Switch from TOWY ALLEY to MISSOURI Trench.

Up to about 2 p.m. tentative attacks were made by various groups of the enemy on the BAILLEUL - WILLERVAL Line; the enemy method of advance appears to have been to throw their rifles forward into the nearest shell-hole, to hold up their hands in surrender, and then drop down alongside their rifles.

At 2 p.m. another severe bombardment broke out all along the BAILLEUL - WILLERVAL Line, and it was evident that the wire was being cut. During this period low flying enemy planes caused much trouble to the garrison.

At 5 p.m. a heavy attack developed on BAILLEUL EAST POST, which was however repulsed by concentrated artillery and small-arm fire.

By 8 p.m. the situation had become more or less quiet and arrangements were made for the relief of 189th Inf.Bde. by 187th Inf.Bde. when the situation permitted. This relief was eventually carried out, one Battalion of 8th Canadian Inf. Bde. (5th C.M.R.) being sent by the Corps to man and be responsible for the line POINT DU JOUR - Railway in B.27.a.

29th March.
During the night 28th/29th the R.E. were employed on blocking and filling in C.T's in front of the new front line and patrolling was actively carried out, the 13th London Regt. (Kensington Regt.) penetrating into ARLEUX LOOP SOUTH - KENT Road and the junction of TOMMY and BARON.

During the morning our patrols on the left were as active, and dominated those of the enemy, driving him right back to RAILWAY Trench, and even salved ammunition and equipment from the dugouts there.

In fact, on our left the enemy was slow to realize that a withdrawal had been made, and it was not until about 3 p.m. that he established a post in the Gun Pits about B.8.d.2.5.

On the remainder of the front there was much hostile movement, during the whole day and many reports were received of his massing, while a prisoner we captured stated that the attack was to be renewed.

Later it became evident that the enemy was relieving the troops who had attacked.

Night 29th/30th.
On the night 29th/30th the Division (less Artillery) was relieved by 4th Canadian Division, the relief being completed by about 5 a.m.

Casualties.

The total casualties in the action were :-

Observation.

For the first couple of hours the battle field was covered by smoke.

When this cleared excellent observation was obtained from the Ridge, and it was largely due to this that every effort to advance was frustrated. At one time hostile batteries came into action in the open near BRADFORD POST and just West of the NAVAL - MARINE Line, but were promptly destroyed.

Communications.

The Corps buried cable system was invaluable and communication was maintained to forward battalions until they had to leave their H.Q. As the withdrawal proceeded, wires were cut.

Supply of Ammunition, etc.

The system of keeping all Reserve Ammunition in deep dugouts proved thoroughly sound, as otherwise large quantities would have been destroyed or buried.

There was no shortage of S.A.A. or bombs during the action.

Bearing of the enemy.

It was widely remarked that the enemy approached in a slow dazed manner. This may have been due to the great weight carried and that he was searching for gaps in our wire.

With one exception, where he was reported to have fired rifle grenades from the hip, the enemy infantry did not use their rifles.

They were reported, however, to have sent out light M.Gs. in front.

The clearest description of the enemy's formation is given by the 18th London Regiment (Q.W.R.) who report that he was in about 8 lines, almost shoulder to shoulder.

Enemy losses.

All reports agree that the enemy losses were extremely heavy, and that they might have been even heavier were it possible to get more time for individual training of men to get full value out of their weapons.

Machine Guns.

A captured German Officer of 152 Inf.Regt. stated that one of the main causes of the failure of the attack was the intensity of the M.G. barrage, which caused heavy casualties. Numerous targets were obtained for direct fire. Machine Guns were attacked in several instances by low flying aeroplanes, one being knocked out by a bomb, while others were destroyed by Artillery with aeroplane observation.

The total casualties in machine guns were 19, of which only 2 were lost to the enemy, the remainder being destroyed.

(Sgd.) F.A.HUDSON,
Major-General,
Commanding 58th Division.

4th April, 1918.

		Officers.	Other Ranks.
Killed	*****	11	159
Wounded	*****	19	406
Missing	*****	25	293
	Total	55	1258

General.
The Division received the congratulations of the Corps and Army Commanders on its defence, and the G.O.C. on 30th March had the honour of being received by H.M. the King, who was pleased to express his appreciation of its behaviour.

NOTES.

Artillery (1)   The frontage of the Division (about 5,000 yds.) was covered by 48 18-pdr. and 12 4.5" Hows. (including 9 18-pdr. of 3rd Canadian Division covering the front taken over on the night 27th/28th March).

From 5 a.m. to 7.15 a.m. our artillery fired heavily on the enemy's front system, special concentrations being put down, in co-operation with the Heavy Artillery, on lines of organized shell-holes, considered at the time to be T.M. emplacements.

From 6.45 a.m. 'counter-preparation' was put into effect and at 7.15 a.m. the S.O.S. barrage was put down.

From then until the withdrawal to the BAILLEUL - WILLENVAL Line was complete, barrage lines were adjusted with Brigade Commanders in accordance with the situation.

During the afternoon many excellent targets were presented, but owing to the limited number of guns, only a few could be taken off the barrage at one time to deal with them.

This was particularly unfortunate, as masses of Infantry, transport and batteries in the open were visible in all directions.

All battery positions were heavily shelled throughout the day and 12 18-pdrs. were destroyed or put out of action by shell fire.

Two 18-pdrs., forming an enfilade section near ABLEUX, obtained many targets with direct observation, until our infantry were ordered to withdraw.

The detachments then damaged the guns, removed dial sights and breechblocks, set the dugouts on fire and retired in accordance with orders.

During the night 29th/30th the artillery were withdrawn, gun by gun, to a range of 3600 yds. from our new front line. Allowing for the 14 guns put out of action, the average expenditure of ammunition was 750 rds. per gun and 680 rounds per Howitzer.

The Heavy Artillery did invaluable work in breaking up enemy masses and in counter battery work, and were assisted by 40 infantry

Our Defensive Wire.
Much extra wire had been put out in the 6 weeks the Division had been in the line.

There were 3 belts of double apron wire on the NAVAL - MARINE Line. This stood the bombardment well and the enemy was seen to be greatly impeded by it.

/Observation.

- 2 -

At 8.45 p.m. however, as a result of verbal orders from XIII Corps, this was modified as regards ARLEUX Post, in order to conform to the defensive line of the 3rd Canadian Division on our Left, and the troops holding this were ordered, if heavily attacked, to withdraw fighting to the ARLEUX LOOP SOUTH, switching back from TOMMY POST.

The reliefs resultant on this redistribution had not been completed at 3 a.m. when a heavy hostile bombardment opened.

At that hour the L.R.B. (169th Bde.) had not taken over BAILLEUL EAST Post, and one Company of the 1st Canadian Mounted Rifles had not been relieved from SUGAR POST. This latter Company remained in SUGAR POST throughout the battle, being placed by the courtesy of the B.G.C. 8th Canadian Infantry Brigade under the orders of 169th Infantry Brigade.

Commencement of the Battle.

At 3 a.m. the enemy opened a heavy bombardment consisting of heavy gas shelling of our rear lines of defence and Headquarters, followed later by H.E. on the BAILLEUL - WILLERVAL Line and FARBUS Line.

At about 5 a.m. a very heavy artillery and Trench Mortar bombardment was opened on our front line system and forward posts, which continued until about 7 a.m.

At 6.35 a.m. the S.O.S. was sent by Power Buzzer from TOWY Post but no infantry attack developed then.

Owing to the continuous enemy shelling there seemed to be no doubt that an attack was imminent, and, therefore, at about 6.15 a.m. H.Q. & 1 Bn. of 187th Infantry Brigade were sent forward to the neighbourhood of CHANTECLER together with all the Reserve Machine Guns of the Division.

At 6.40 a.m. counter preparation was ordered to be carried out by Heavy and Field Artillery.

At about 7.5 a.m. the S.O.S. Signal was again sent up from TOWY POST, and was almost immediately followed by the S.O.S. along the whole line up to and including OPPY Post. The remaining battalion of the 187th Infantry Brigade was ordered forward to the vicinity of CHANTECLER.

The enemy attack.

Under cover of a creeping barrage the enemy's infantry moved forward apparently about 7.5 a.m.

The Heavy T.M. & Artillery bombardment had obliterated the bulk of the forward posts from our Southern Boundary to OPPY POST (inclusive). With the exception of TOWY POST and of WOOD POST, in which the dispositions had been changed a day or two previously, the garrisons were apparently wiped out. There was only one survivor of the garrison of MILL POST, who reported that when he left the trenches were almost blotted out, and that the entrances to the large dug-out had already been smothered.

The garrisons of TOWY and WOOD Posts put up a gallant fight.

In the neighbourhood of GAVRELLE the enemy appears to have got into a pocket formed by TOWY and WATER Posts and by NAVAL Trench, and in this pocket he was exposed to the indirect fire of 14 machine guns, which were designed to bring S.O.S. fire on this area.

WOOD POST held out for about an hour, inflicting heavy casualties.

The garrison of TOWY POST made a stand in the Support Trench.

By 7.30 a.m. the enemy was attacking heavily in front, had passed over the Support Trench on either flank and was bombing up towards the Post from TOWY ALLEY in rear.

As it was manifest that there would soon be a shortage of bombs, the garrison after a stiff and splendid resistance, in which they were reduced to 2 Officers and 25 O.R., succeeded in fighting their way back down TOWY Trench and through the enemy back into the NAVAL Line. Meanwhile on the left of the 169th Brigade Section the enemy

/swarmed

SECRET.   56th Division G.S/223.

REPORT ON THE OPERATIONS of 56th DIVISION in the vicinity of OPPY & GAVRELLE, 28th & 29th March, 1918.

Reference Map MAROEUIL 1/20,000.

On 12th March information was received that an offensive by the enemy on a large front, which might include the VIMY Ridge, was imminent.

From this date Brigades in the line were ordered to be extremely alert and the whole Division stood to arms at 5 a.m. each morning.

Counter offensive shoots by the Artillery were carried out almost daily, especially at night and just prior to dawn, so as to disorganise any possible assembly of troops for attack.

On 21st March the enemy offensive South of the R.SCARPE commenced and by 27th he was in occupation of the VILLAGE of BOISEUX, which commanded the ground on the North of that river.

During this time it became apparent that the enemy would endeavour to envelop ARRAS, and to capture the VIMY RIDGE from the South, and much work was done in improving the defensive switches facing South.

Night 27th/28th March.

On the night 27th/28th March the Division was ordered to extend its left flank and relieve the troops of the 3rd Canadian Division for a distance of approximately 1500 yards. This entailed an extension of the front of the Right (169th) Infantry Brigade to include BRADFORD & BIRD POSTS, and the taking over by the Left (168th) Infantry Brigade of TOMMY & ARLEUX POSTS.

The dispositions of the two Brigades in the line were then -

169th Infantry Brigade.

Right Battn. 1/16th London Regt. (Queens Westminsters) holding TOWY POST.

Left Battn.   5th London Regt. (London Rifle Brigade) holding HILL, BRADFORD & BIRD POSTS.

In BAILLEUL - WILLERVAL Line - 2nd Bn. London Regiment.
In FARBUS Line.   - 1 Coy. 1/5th Cheshire Regt.
                                                     (Pioneers).
In Brigade Reserve   - 2 Cos. 1st London Regt. (attached
                                from 167th Infantry Brigade).
                                Detachment of 176th Tunnelling Coy.
                                R.E. (in POINT DU JOUR Redoubt).

168th Infantry Brigade.

Right Battn. - 4th London Regt. - holding BEATTY, WOOD & OPPY Posts.
Left Battn. 1/13th London Regt. (Kensingtons) - holding TOMMY &
                                                 ARLEUX Posts.

In BAILLEUL - WILLERVAL Line - 1/14th London Regt. (London Scottish)
In CHESTER Post (B.15.d.)   - 2 Platoons 1/5th Cheshire Regt.
                                                   (Pioneers).
In POINT DU JOUR Line & BRIERLEY HILL - 2 Cos. 1st London Regt.
                                (attached from 167th Infantry Bde.)
                                and 1½ Cos. 1/5th Cheshire Regiment.

In Divisional Reserve   - 167th Inf. Bde. (less 1 Bn.) and
                                3 Field Coys. R.E.

The above extension was ordered under XIII Corps Order No. 122, which laid down that the BAILLEUL - WILLERVAL Line was to be held as our front line, and our old front line system to be considered as an outpost line.

This was subsequently cancelled by XIII Corps Order No. 125, which ordered our front line system to be held as such in order to conform to the 4th Division on our right (XVII Corps).

/At

captured the two machine guns in position about 100 yds. East of BAILLEUL EAST Post and attacked the post which was held by the London Scottish.

A counter-attack was promptly organized, the enemy was driven back 150 yds. the machine gun crews released from their dugout, and a new block formed in advance of their position.

Repeated attacks were made on this block, but assisted by the fire of Stokes and 6" Newton Mortars these were all repulsed, as also several attacks made over the open astride of the BAILLEUL-GAVRELLE Road.

During the whole morning the situation of the 4th Division on our right was very obscure, the Division being reported to have lost touch with its own Brigades, while the lateral line between 150th Inf. Bde. and 12th Inf. Bde. was also cut. At about noon, however, we were in touch in the BAILLEUL - WILLERVAL Line and later definite touch was also obtained in the POINT DU JOUR - THELUS Line and in the Switch from TOMMY ALLEY to MISSOURI Trench.

Up to about 2 p.m. tentative attacks were made by various groups of the enemy on the BAILLEUL - WILLERVAL Line; the enemy method of advance appears to have been to throw their rifles forward into the nearest shell-hole, to hold up their hands in surrender, and then drop down alongside their rifles.

At 2 p.m. another severe bombardment broke out all along the BAILLEUL - WILLERVAL Line, and it was evident that the wire was being cut. During this period low flying enemy planes caused much trouble to the garrison.

At 5 p.m. a heavy attack developed on BAILLEUL EAST POST, which was however repulsed by concentrated artillery and small-arm fire.

By 9 p.m. the situation had become more or less quiet and arrangements were made for the relief of 109th Inf.Bde. by 107th Inf.Bde. when the situation permitted. This relief was eventually carried out, one Battalion of 8th Canadian Inf. Bde. (5th C.M.R.) being sent by the Corps to man and be responsible for the line POINT DU JOUR - Railway in B.27.a.

29th March.

During the night 28th/29th the R.E. were employed on blocking and filling in C.T's in front of the new front line and patrolling was actively carried out, the 13th London Regt. (Kensington Regt.) penetrating into ARLEUX LOOP SOUTH - KENT Road and the junction of TOMMY and BARON.

During the morning our patrols on the left were as active, and dominated those of the enemy, driving him right back to RAILWAY Trench, and even salved ammunition and equipment from the dugouts there.

In fact, on our left the enemy was slow to realise that a withdrawal had been made, and it was not until about 5 p.m. that he established a post in the Gun Pits about S.5.d.3.5.

On the remainder of the front there was much hostile movement, during the whole day and many reports were received of his massing, while a prisoner we captured stated that the attack was to be renewed.

Later it became evident that the enemy was relieving the troops who had attacked.

Night 29th/30th.

On the Night 29th/30th the Division (less Artillery) was relieved by 4th Canadian Division, the relief being completed by about 5 a.m.

Casualties.

The total casualties in the action were :-

swarmed over our forward posts and was soon pressing through gaps in the wire and down old C.Ts. into the NAVAL - MARINE Line.

Very soon after the attack had begun the L.R.B. Headquarters personnel under Lieut-Colonel HUSEY, D.S.O., M.C. found themselves repelling a massive onset delivered in 5 successive moves on MARINE Trench.

The wire in front of this line, which had recently been thickened, caused the enemy considerable discomfiture and great losses were caused to him by rifle, Lewis Gun and Machine Gun fire, but such were his numbers that this party was soon outflanked from the North.

The B.G.C. 169th Inf. Bde. therefore ordered Lieut-Colonel HUSEY to fight his way to the junction of JAMES ALLEY and MARINE Trench and to withdraw slowly down JAMES ALLEY to the BAILLEUL - WILLERVAL Line, and by 10.30 a.m. the remains of his Battalion, numbering 4 Officers and 64 O.R. had taken up a position in the BAILLEUL - WILLERVAL Line.

Up to now the Q.W.R. under Lieut-Colonel GLASIER, D.S.O. on the right of 169th Inf. Bde. had been able to hold on to NAVAL Trench from their Southern boundary up to the GAVRELLE Road, and as long as the enemy were being held on the flanks by the L.R.B. and the Lancashire Fusiliers of the 4th Division, they were able successfully to ward off the enemy, inflicting great casualties on him.

Increasing pressure on both flanks soon rendered this position untenable and the enemy, who had been kept well in check, gradually surrounded the remainder of the garrison, and worked round to the right rear. Meanwhile information had been received that ORANGE HILL (S. of the SCARPE) had fallen.

The Corps Commander visited Divisional H.Q. and as a result of his verbal orders a wire was sent out at 10.30 a.m. ordering the withdrawal of 169th Inf. Bde. to the BAILLEUL - WILLERVAL Line, which was to be held at all costs.

1 Battalion of 167th Inf. Bde. was placed under the orders of 169th Inf. Bde. and 6 M.Gs. were sent forward to POINT DU JOUR to strengthen the right flank and our junction with 4th Division. 2 Field Coys. R.E. were also ordered up to strengthen the right flank by holding TONGUE and MANCHE Posts. These orders were also telephoned to 169th Inf.Bde. and the withdrawal was carried out by the Q.W.R., who fought their way slowly back.

As regards the 168th Inf. Bde. the 4th London Regt. had been putting up a gallant defence on the MARQUIS Line. The Reserve Coy. had been moved forward from BOW Trench at 6.3 a.m. to counter-attack the enemy who had penetrated MARQUIS Trench. Heavy fighting occurred in DUKE Street and the Bn. H.Q. there was lost and regained.

At 10.30 a.m. the Brigade was ordered to be prepared to withdraw from our front line system in conjunction with the 3rd CANADIAN DIVISION.

By 11.30 a.m. the position was critical, both flanks of the battalion being turned, while some of the enemy were even in OUSE ALLEY, the only trench open for a withdrawal.

The remnants of the garrison therefore commenced their withdrawal over the open under the cover of the Reserve Company, which manned the OUSE ALLEY Switch.

At 11.40 a.m. in consequence of orders received from the Corps, an order was sent to 168th Inf. Bde. to withdraw the remainder of its troops (Kensington Regt.) from TOMMY and ARLEUX Posts, in conjunction with 3rd Canadian Division, who similarly received orders to withdraw in co-operation with the Brigade to the BAILLEUL - WILLERVAL Line.

After the withdrawal of 4th London Regt. the enemy made a strong bombing attack on the block in OUSE ALLEY near BOW TRENCH which was, however, effectively stopped by a Lewis Gun covering the block.

Meanwhile, as early as 7.30 a.m. while the 4th London Regt. were still fighting in the front system, enemy bombing parties had broken through on their right by TYNE and N.TYNE ALLEYS.

Observation.

For the first couple of hours the battle field was covered by smoke.

When this cleared excellent observation was obtained from the Ridge, and it was largely due to this that every effort to advance was frustrated. At one time hostile batteries came into action in the open near BRADFORD POST and just West of the NAVAL - MARINE Line, but were promptly destroyed.

Communications.

The Corps buried cable system was invaluable and communication was maintained to forward battalions until they had to leave their H.Q. As the withdrawal proceeded, wires were cut.

Supply of Ammunition, etc.

The system of keeping all Reserve Ammunition in deep dugouts proved thoroughly sound, as otherwise large quantities would have been destroyed or buried.

There was no shortage of S.A.A. or bombs during the action.

Bearing of the enemy.

It was widely remarked that the enemy approached in a slow dazed manner. This may have been due to the great weight carried and that he was searching for gaps in our wire.

With one exception, where he was reported to have fired rifle grenades from the hip, the enemy infantry did not use their rifles.

They were reported, however, to have sent out light M.Gs. in front.

The clearest description of the enemy's formation is given by the 16th London Regiment (Q.W.R.) who report that he was in about 6 lines, almost shoulder to shoulder.

Enemy losses.

All reports agree that the enemy losses were extremely heavy, and that they might have been even heavier were it possible to get more time for individual training of men to get full value out of their weapons.

Machine Guns.

A captured German Officer of 152 Inf.Regt. stated that one of the main causes of the failure of the attack was the intensity of the M.G. barrage, which caused heavy casualties. Numerous targets were obtained for direct fire. Machine Guns were attacked in several instances by low flying aeroplanes, one being knocked out by a bomb, while others were destroyed by Artillery with aeroplane observation.

The total casualties in machine guns were 12, of which only 2 were lost to the enemy, the remainder being destroyed.

4th April, 1918.

(Sgd.) F.A. DUDGEON,
Major-General,
Commanding 38th Division.

	Officers.	Other Ranks.
Killed	11	155
Wounded	19	405
Missing	25	893
Total	55	1453

General.

The Division received the congratulations of the Corps and Army Commanders on its defence, and the G.O.C. on 30th March had the honour of being received by H.M. the King, who was pleased to express his appreciation of its behaviour.

NOTES.

Artillery (i) The frontage of the Division (about 5,000 yds.) was covered by 45 18-pdr. and 12 4.5" Hows. (including 9 18-pdr. of 3rd Canadian Division covering the front taken over on the night 27th/28th March).

From 5 a.m. to 7.15 a.m. our artillery fired heavily on the enemy's front system, special concentrations being put down, in co-operation with the Heavy Artillery, on lines of organized shell-holes, considered at the time to be T.M. emplacements.

From 6.45 a.m. 'counter-preparation' was put into effect and at 7.15 a.m. the S.O.S. barrage was put down.

From then until the withdrawal to the BAILLEUL - WILLERVAL Line was complete, barrage lines were adjusted with Brigade Commanders in accordance with the situation.

During the afternoon many excellent targets were presented, but owing to the limited number of guns, only a few could be taken off the barrage at one time to deal with them.

This was particularly unfortunate, as masses of Infantry, transport and batteries in the open were visible in all directions.

All battery positions were heavily shelled throughout the day and 12 18-pdrs. were destroyed or put out of action by shell fire.

Two 18-pdrs., forming an enfilade section near ACHEUX, obtained many targets with direct observation, until our infantry were ordered to withdraw.

The detachments then damaged the guns, removed dial sights and breechblocks, set the dugouts on fire and retired in accordance with orders.

During the night 28th/29th the artillery were withdrawn, gun by gun, to a range of 3800 yds. from our new front line. Allowing for the 14 guns put out of action, the average expenditure of ammunition was 750 rds. per gun and 250 rounds per Howitzer.

The Heavy Artillery did invaluable work in breaking up enemy masses and in counter battery work, and were assisted by 40 infantry

Our Defensive Wire.

Much extra wire had been put out in the 6 weeks the Division had been in the line.

There were 3 belts of double apron wire on the NAVAL - MARINE Line. This stood the bombardment well and the enemy was seen to be greatly impeded by it.

/Observation.

XVII CORPS

WAR DIARY

GENERAL STAFF

56th DIVISION

APRIL 1918.

Appendices attached :-
    Relief & Move orders.
    Disposition Table.
    Map showing boundaries etc.

SECRET.   "G" 56th DIVISION.

Army Form C. 2118.

WAR DIARY
or
INTELLIGENCE SUMMARY.
(Erase heading not required.)

April 1918

Instructions regarding War Diaries and Intelligence Summaries are contained in F. S. Regs., Part II. and the Staff Manual respectively. Title pages will be prepared in manuscript.

Place	Date	Hour	Summary of Events and Information	Remarks and references to Appendices
ACQ	1st		All units notified of the possibility of the 56th Div. not leaving the XIII Corps area. Later as a result of visit to 56th Div. H.Qrs. of G.S.O.II, First Army, all units informed that from information received there is a possibility of the Division moving shortly, all to be warned accordingly.	APP. II
			Letter sent to all concerned giving further congratulations from XIII Corps Commander, also informing all concerned of the G.O.C. having been received by His Majesty the King on the 30th ult. Army Commander also personally expressed his appreciation of the work done by the Division and of its tenacious defence on the 28th March.	APP.III APP.III APP.IV.
			Further information received that 56th Division not likely to move early— previous warning letter (Appendix II) accordingly cancelled.	APP. V.
			168th Infantry Brigade supplied working party of 1200 men for work on HAUTE AVESNES Switch. G.O.C. visited work.	
	2nd		Corps Commander visited Divisional H.Qrs. during morning. 167th Infantry Brigade supplied working party of 1400 men and 168th Infantry Brigade 1200 for work in HAUTE AVESNES and HABARCQ Switches, also at VILLERS AU BOIS. G.O.C. and G.S.O.I visted 1st Corps H.Qrs. G.S.O. II visited XI Corps H.Qrs. and H.Qrs. 55th Division.	
	3rd		169th Infantry Brigade supplied working party of 1200 men for work on HAUTE AVESNES Switch also HARBARCQ Switch. 167th and 168th Infantry Brigades training.	
	4th		169th Infantry Brigade supplied working party of 1500 men for work on Switches 167th " " " " " " 1400 " " " " " 168th Infantry Brigade Training.	
	5th		3 Field Coys. R.E. moved from ANZIN to ESTREE CAUCHIE and 56th M.G.Bn. moved from ST.AUBIN to CHATEAU DE LA HAIE. 168th Infantry Brigade supplied 1200 men for work on Switches	
		11.30 p.m.	Information received from XIII Corps that 56th Division will be required to relieve 1st Canadian Division XVII Corps in the line on night 7th/8th April. Warning Order G.597 issued.	APP.VI.

SECRET.   Army Form C. 2118.

Instructions regarding War Diaries and Intelligence Summaries are contained in F.S. Regs., Part II. and the Staff Manual respectively. Title pages will be prepared in manuscript.

WAR DIARY
or
INTELLIGENCE SUMMARY.
(Erase heading not required.)

"G" 56th DIVISION.   **April 1918.**

Place	Date	Hour	Summary of Events and Information	Remarks and references to Appendices
ACQ.	6th	a.m. 2.15	Operation Order No. 159 issued. G.O.C. & G.S.O.I visited H.Qrs. XVII Corps & 1st Canadian Division. 167th Infantry Brigade moved to DAINVILLE Area, and 168th Infantry Brigade moved to AGNEZ LES DUISANS Area.	APP. VII
		2.30	Operation Order No. 160 issued.	APP. VIII
	7th		Further moves in connection with relief of 1st Canadian Division were carried out. G.O.C. & G.S.O.I visited some portions of front held by 1st Canadian Division.	APP. I.
WARLUS.	8th		Relief of 1st Canadian Division (less Artillery) complete and command of sector passed to G.O.C., 56th Division at 12 noon, Divisional front being from N.7.d.0.0. to H.31.d.8.0. (BOIS des BOEUFS). Information received that XVII Corps passed under command of First Army from Third Army.	
	8th		Locations of Units as shown in APPENDIX I. Rain fell most of the day.	APP. I.
	9th		Fairly quiet night. Hostile artillery increased in back areas from dawn onwards, much poison being used. Enemy put down Light T.M. and shell barrage on front system in the neighbourhood of TILLOY at 9 a.m., this quietened down gradually until becoming quiet at 9.30 a.m. Quiet during remainder of day.	
	10th		Quiet night. Hostile shelling on to DAINVILLE necessitated the moving of the Reserve Bde. H.Qrs. from that place to BERNEVILLE. Conference of senior representatives of departments of Divnl. H.Qrs. held at 6.30 p.m. attended by G.O.C. was present and following attended : G.S.O.I, G.S.O.II, A.A.& Q.M.G., C.R.E., D.M.G.C., A.D.M.S. Conference to be held nightly.	
	11th	a.m. 6.15	Enemy shelled heavily front and rear areas of Bn. on right of Divnl. Sector, shelling extended Northwards, TELEGRAPH HILL and Area G.35.c. & d. being chief places shelled in this area. Situation quiet by 9.30 a.m. All units ordered to "STAND TO" at 9.10 a.m. and "STAND DOWN" at 10.25 a.m. Between 6 a.m. and 9 a.m. our outpost at N.2.c.5.9. (8th Middlesex Regt.) was attacked by two strong parties of enemy who approached under cover of T.M. fire, the garrison was forced to retire to our front line. This outpost was re-established during early evening.	

SECRET. "G" 56th DIVISION. April 1918.

Army Form C. 2118.

WAR DIARY
or
INTELLIGENCE SUMMARY.
(Erase heading not required.)

Instructions regarding War Diaries and Intelligence Summaries are contained in F.S. Regs., Part II. and the Staff Manual respectively. Title pages will be prepared in manuscript.

Place	Date	Hour	Summary of Events and Information	Remarks and references to Appendices
WARLUS.	11th	8.45 a.m.	56th Div. Order No. 161 issued for relief of 167th Infantry Brigade in front line by 168th Infantry Brigade on night 13th/14th. 169th Infantry Brigade to move into Support and 167th Infantry Brigade into Divnl. Reserve on 14th inst.	APP.IX.
	12th		167th Infantry Brigade report officer of 8th Middlesex Regiment missing from patrol during night 11th/12th. Quiet night. Harassing fire as usual was carried out on enemy back areas. Orders received from XVII Corps for reconnaissance to be carried out of 15th Divnl. front (on left) in case of 15th Division being withdrawn and 56th Division taking over whole Corps front. Similarly 15th Division to reconnoitre 56th Divnl. front, in case 56th Division should be withdrawn.	
	13th		Quiet night. Weather dull early morning, sunny later.	
	14th		Quiet night. 168th Infantry Brigade relieved 167th Infantry Brigade in the line during night. 4th Bn. London Regt. to Left, 14th Bn. London Regt. (London Scottish) to Right, 13th Bn. London Regt. (Kensingtons) to Support, 7th Bn. Middlesex Regt. (167th Inf.Bde) came under command of B.G.C. 168th Infantry Brigade as Reserve Battalion. 167th Infantry Brigade moved into Divnl. Support.	APP.I.
	15th		Quiet night. Our artillery carried out harassing fire as on previous nights. 169th Infantry Brigade relieved 167th Infantry Brigade in Support, which Brigade moved back to BERNEVILLE Area and came into Divnl. Reserve. 5th Bn. London Regt. (L.R.B.) relieved 7th Bn. Middlesex Regt. as Reserve Bn. to 168th Infantry Brigade (in Line). G.O.C. & G.S.O.I attended Conference at XVII Corps H.Qrs. Dispositions of troops in Defence discussed. Escaped British prisoner stopped at ACHICOURT Bridge. Corporal of 15th Bn. Royal Scots captured in front CROSILLES on 22nd March; he had escaped from ECOUST - ST.MEIN on night 14th/15th inst.	APP.I.
	16th		Quiet night. Our artillery harassed selected points in rear of enemy lines. Our patrols active but no enemy patrols encountered.	

SECRET.   "G" 56th DIVISION.   WAR DIARY or INTELLIGENCE SUMMARY.   April 1918.   Army Form C. 2118.

Instructions regarding War Diaries and Intelligence Summaries are contained in F. S. Regs., Part II. and the Staff Manual respectively. Title pages will be prepared in manuscript.

(Erase heading not required.)

Place	Date	Hour	Summary of Events and Information	Remarks and references to Appendices
WARLUS.	17th		Quiet night. Our artillery active with harassing fire. No enemy patrols encountered by our patrols who were out during the whole of the night. 56th Divnl. Order No. 162 issued, ordering relief of 168th Infantry Brigade in the line by the 169th Infantry Brigade on night 19th/20th April, and 167th Infantry Brigade to relieve 168th Infantry Brigade in Support on the 20th April. 168th Infantry Brigade to move back to Divnl. Reserve.	APP.X.
	18th		Quiet night. Wet day and milder. Usual harassing fire carried out by our Artillery.	
	19th	4.30 a.m.	A very successful enterprise was carried out on the enemy trenches in N.2.c and N.8.a. These trenches were stormed by troops of the 14th Bn. London Regiment (London Scottish) and 4th Bn. London Regt. (Royal Fusiliers) 168th Infantry Brigade, the enemy being completely surprised. One W.O. 3 O.R. (1 since died) of the 65 I.R., 185th Division were captured together with 9 M.Gs. and 1 Granatenwerfer. The line N.8.a.2.0., N.8.a.5.6., N.8.a.9.3., N.2.c.7.2., N.2.a.8.1. being consolidated.	
		8 p.m.	The enemy counter-attacked our raiding party in N.2.c. before it could be withdrawn as arranged. He got in between 2 platoons which were occupying the trench junction N.2.c.7.2. and the Supporting Platoon which was forced back to its old post at N.8.a.0.5. The 2 platoons at N.2.c.7.2. were engaged in heavy bomb fighting, but maintained their position at N.2.c.7.2. A counter-attack was being organised when ordered to withdraw. During the counter-attack the Germans sent up Green Lights from the PILL BOX at N.8.a.9.5. and vicinity which brought down our S.O.S. barrage. No S.O.S. Signal was sent up by us.	
			Warning Order received from XVII Corps for 56th Div. to be prepared to take over front held by 15th Division at short notice. 56th Div. Warning Order No. 163 issued.	APP.XI.
	20th		169th Infantry Brigade relieved 168th Infantry Brigade in the Line during night. 168th Infantry Brigade moved into Divnl.Support.	APP.I.
	21st		Quiet night. 167th Infantry Brigade relieved 168th Infantry Brigade in Divnl. Support during night. 168th Infantry Brigade moved back into Divnl. Reserve.	APP.I.

SECRET.

Army Form C. 2118.

WAR DIARY
or
INTELLIGENCE SUMMARY.
(Erase heading not required.)

"G" 56th DIVISION.   April 1918.

Instructions regarding War Diaries and Intelligence Summaries are contained in F. S. Regs., Part II. and the Staff Manual respectively. Title pages will be prepared in manuscript.

Place	Date	Hour	Summary of Events and Information	Remarks and references to Appendices
WARLUS.	22nd		Quiet night. Fine and sunny all day. XVII Corps Order No. 130 received ordering 56th Divn. to extend to the left and take over the left sector of Corps front from 15th Division who are to be withdrawn. Relief to be complete by 5 a.m. 24th April, at which hour G.O.C. 56th Division is to assume command of whole of XVII Corps front. 56th Division O.No.164 issued. Enemy deserter taken at 7 a.m. near one of our outposts. Identification 161st I.R. 185th Division (normal).	APP.XII
	23rd		Quiet night. Relief of 15th Division by 56th Division extending to the left commenced.	
	24th		Quiet night. Relief of 15th Division completed by 5 a.m. at which hour G.O.C. 56th Division assumed command of whole of XVII Corps front. At an early hour this morning 3 escaped British prisoners of 1st Bn. Shropshire Light Infantry approached our L.G. Post South of CAMBRAI road from enemy line.	APP.I.
		p.m. 6.40	Enemy started shelling WARLUS with light high velocity gun. About 15 to 20 in all, lasting until approx. 9.30 p.m.	
		9.15	2nd Bn. London Regt. (169th Infantry Brigade) holding left sub-sector of Right Brigade front attempted a raid on enemy trenches from N.2.a.7.1. to N.2.c.5.9. Hostile M.Gs. greatly hampered the raiding party. No identifications were obtained.	
		9.50	Enemy raided our outpost in gunpit in H.27.c.85.35. under cover of a heavy artillery and medium T.M.Barrage. He occupied the gunpit after a severe struggle, we reoccupied the position later. Enemy did not secure any identification.	
	25th		Identifications secured from enemy dead after the hostile raid 28th R.I.R., 185th Division (normal). Two prisoners captured in vicinity of BROKEN HILL belonging to 14th Bav.I.R. 16th Bavarian Division, thus indicating a relief of 185th Division by 16th Bav.Division during night 24th/25th. Instructions received from XVII Corps for urgency in the economising of man power in Artillery. Army Commander therefore orders harassing fire and counter-battery work to cease unless urgently required, on this front. Major-General F.A.DUDGEON, C.B., Commanding 56th Division evacuated to hospital sick. Brigadier-General G. FREETH, C.M.G., D.S.O., Commanding 167th Infantry Brigade assumed temporary command of 56th Division.	

SECRET. "G" 56th DIVISION. April 1918. Army Form C. 2118.

WAR DIARY
or
INTELLIGENCE SUMMARY.
(Erase heading not required.)

Instructions regarding War Diaries and Intelligence Summaries are contained in F. S. Regs., Part II. and the Staff Manual respectively. Title pages will be prepared in manuscript.

Place	Date	Hour	Summary of Events and Information	Remarks and references to Appendices
WARLUS.	26th		Quiet night. 56th Division Order No. 165 issued ordering relief of 169th Infantry Brigade in the right sector of 168th Infantry Brigade on night 28th/29th April.	APP. XIII
	27th	p	Quiet night. Enemy again shelled WARLUS during evening.	
	28th		Our artillery carried out harassing fire during the night as an enemy relief was suspected, also fired in support of a raid carried out by 1st Canadian Division on left of 56th Divn.	APP. I
	29th		Quiet night. 168th Infantry Brigade relieved 169th Infantry Brigade in right sector during night 28th/29th. 169th Infantry Brigade on relief moved back to BERNEVILLE area into Divl. Reserve. Orders received from XVII Corps for withdrawal of 15th Divisional Artillery during night 29th/30th. 56th Division Order No. 166 issued.	APP. XIV
	30th		Quiet night. 15th Divnl. Artillery withdrawn from 56th Divnl. front. 311th A.F.A. Bde. moved into Divnl. front and came under orders of G.O.C., 56th Division.	

4th May, 1918.

A Hull
Major-General,
Commanding 56th Division.

56th DIVISION. LOCATION TABLE at 6 p.m. APRIL 1918. APPENDIX I

	1	2	3	4	5	6	7	8	9	10	11	12	13	14	15	16
Div. H.Q.	ACQ															
167th Inf.Bde.H.Q.		VILLERS-AU-BOIS				DAINVILLE		WARLUS	G27b8.3 G28d1.3					G28d1.3	BERNEVILLE	
1st London Regt.		CAMBLAIN L'ABBÉ				WARLUS			N7a28 LINE (R)						Ronville Caves	
7th Middx. Regt.		VILLERS-AU-BOIS				DAINVILLE			M10a57 LINE (S)						M10a3,2 (Res)	DAINVILLE
8th		VILLERS-AU-BOIS		CHATEAU DE LA HAIE		DAINVILLE			N1a63 LINE (L)						Ronville Caves	BERNEVILLE
168th Inf.Bde.H.Q.		MONT ST. ELOI				AGNEZ-lès-Duisans		G27b6.2						G34b5.95		
4th London Regt.		ECOIVRES			VILLERS AU BOIS	AGNEZ-LES DUISANS		Ronville Caves							LINE (L)	
13th		ECOIVRES				DUISANS		M10a32 (Res)							LINE (S)	
14th		MONT ST. ELOI				Camp L2 central		Ronville Caves							LINE (R)	
169th Inf.Bde.H.Q.		ECOIVRES						DAINVILLE		BERNEVILLE				G28d1.3		
2nd London Regt.		BOIS DES ALLEUX						DAINVILLE							Ronville Caves	
5th		BOIS DES ALLEUX						BERNEVILLE							M10a32(Res)	
13th		BOIS DES ALLEUX						DAINVILLE							Ronville Caves	
Div. Arty. H.Q.	ACQ	BERLES						WARLUS								
290th Bde.		H1c80						M8b75.12				G28d1.3				
281st		B21a05.45						G35b00.75								
Pioneers.		ESTREE-CAUCHIE			ANZIN-ST.AUBIN				Ronville Caves							
M.G.Battn.H.Q.		ST. AUBIN			CHATEAU DE LA HAIE		WARLUS	WARLUS								

LINE (R) = Right Bn. of Bde. in Line
LINE (L) = Left " " " "
LINE (S) = Support " " " "
LINE (Res) = Reserve Bn. to Bde in Line (detached from it's own Bde.)

BLUE — Whole Division out of Line
RED — Units in Line.
GREEN — Support
PURPLE — Reserve.

56th DIVISION. LOCATION TABLE at 6 p.m. APRIL 1918.

APPENDIX I

	17	18	19	20	21	22	23	24	25	26	27	28	29	30
Div. H.Q.	WARLUS													
167th Inf. Bde. H.Q.	RESERVE				SUPPORT			LINE (L)						
1st London Regt.	DAINVILLE				Ronville Caves			LINE (R)			LINE (S)			
7th Middx. Regt.	DAINVILLE				Ronville Caves			LINE (L)			LINE (L)			
8th " "	BERNEVILLE				LINE (Res)			LINE (S)			LINE (R)			
168th Inf. Bde. H.Q.	LINE			SUPPORT	RESERVE			RESERVE				LINE (R)		
4th London Regt.	LINE (L)			Ronville Caves	DAINVILLE			Ronville Caves				LINE (L)		
13th " "	LINE (S)			LINE (Res)	DAINVILLE			St. Sauveur Caves				LINE (R)		
14th " "	LINE (R)			Ronville Caves	BERNEVILLE			Ronville Caves				LINE (S)		
169th Inf. Bde. H.Q.	SUPPORT			LINE				LINE (R)				BERNEVILLE		
2nd London Regt.	Ronville Caves			LINE (L)				LINE (L)				DAINVILLE		
5th " "	LINE (Res)			LINE (S)				LINE (S)				DAINVILLE		
16th " "	Ronville Caves			LINE (R)				LINE (R)				BERNEVILLE		
Div. Arty. H.Q.	WARLUS													
280th Bde.	M8b75.42			G34b2.9										
281st	G28d1.3													
Pioneers.	Ronville Caves							Ronville Caves						
M.G.Battn. H.Q.	WARLUS													

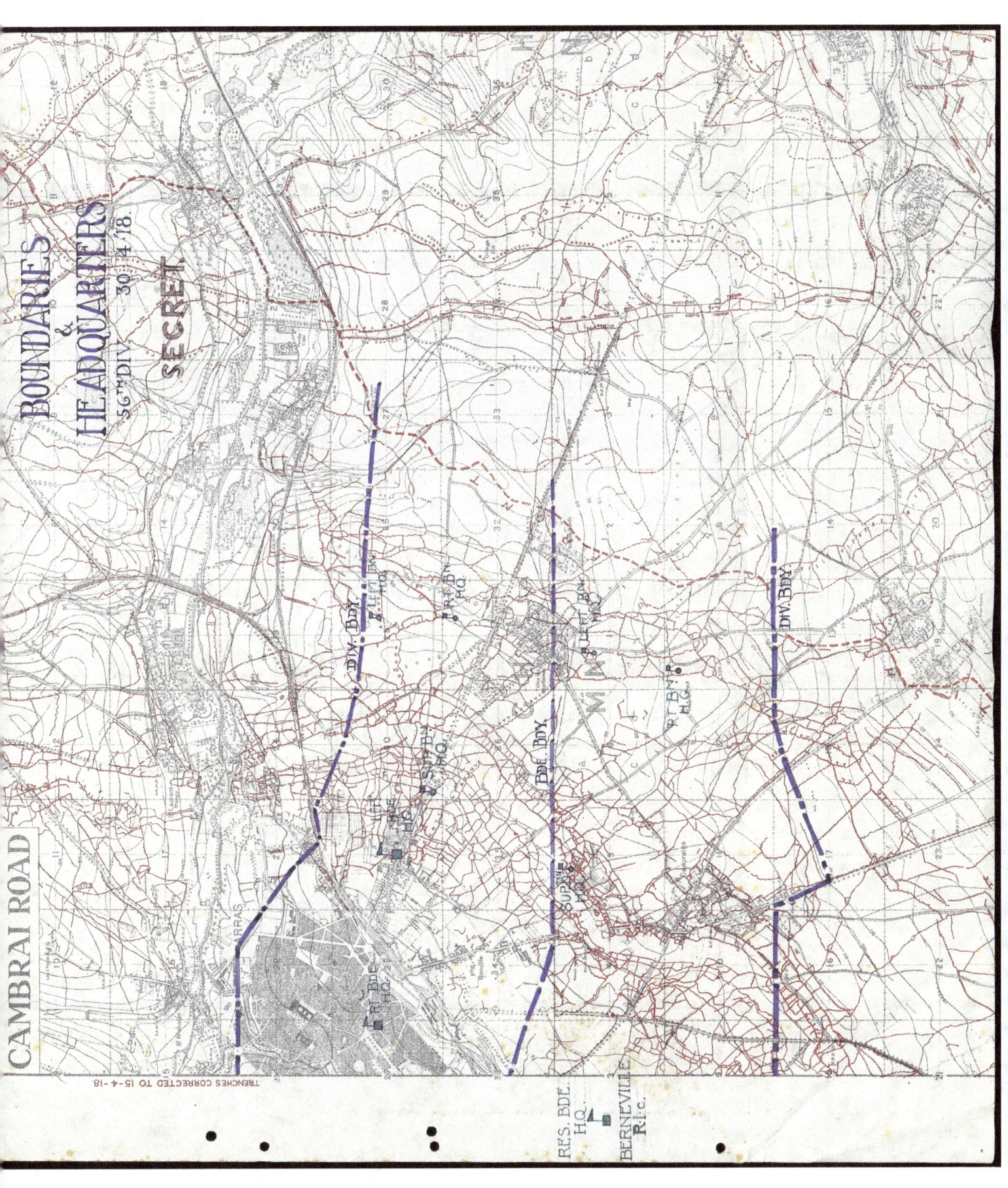

SECRET. 56th Divn. G.3/210.

167th Infantry Brigade.
168th Infantry Brigade.
169th Infantry Brigade.
C.R.A.
C.R.E.
D.M.G.C.

      The attached copy of 56th Div. letter No. G.3/210 of 2nd April is forwarded for your information.

H.Q. 56th Divn.
2nd April, 1918.

                                Lieut-Colonel,
                                General Staff.

Encl.

SECRET   56th Division No. G.3/210

XIII Corps.

In reply to XIII Corps No. 1377/6 (G.A.) of 31st March, the notes contained in First Army 1888 (G) of 30th March are fully borne out by the experience of this Division in the fighting of the 28th March, especially as regards:-

(a) Use of the rifle. The attack of the German Infantry gave the impression that they had been 'doped'. They paid almost no attention to their losses and came steadily along, filing along the wire to find gaps and scarcely firing a shot.
Even more training is required in individual rapid shooting than is now given. It is felt that the German losses might have been even heavier had the shooting been better.

(b) The post system of holding the line is a failure. Attacking as the Germans did, in masses, they invariably succeeded in filtering round the posts in the front line and the small supporting posts in rear. The enemy, after a long period of trench warfare, gets to know their location intimately, in spite of all efforts to deceive him as to their position, and the system, therefore, merely enables him to concentrate his artillery on a series of small targets instead of a wide one. All our posts were blotted out by T.M. fire except TOWY POST and one other (WOOD) which changed its dispositions at the last moment.

(c) A wide No Mans Land is essential - it is of vital importance to ensure that one's line of defence is not within trench mortar range.

2.   The following further lessons appear to stand out:-

(a) In the case of the OPPY and GAVRELLE Sections, the site of the front line trenches was not suited for effective artillery support when the artillery had been drawn back for defensive as opposed to offensive reasons.

(b) Machine gun posts should invariably have Infantry attached to them, especially if sited off communication trenches. Cases occurred of M.Gs. being put out of action by hostile bombing parties.

(c) The Division had only a few 'anti-raid' machine guns in the front line system, the rest being distributed in depth in pairs and batteries behind. The fact that only 2 guns were lost shows the value of this system.

(d) The system of siting Infantry and M.G. defences in depth not only delayed and broke up the German attack, but materially assisted the survivors in the front line system to withdraw to the BAILLEUL - WILLERVAL Line.

(e) A sudden extension of front when a battle is expected is dangerous, as it upsets the M.G. defence. In the case of this Division the M.G. defence in depth behind the BAILLEUL - WILLERVAL Line had to be abandoned, owing to the necessity for finding guns to cover the increased front taken over, and this left the defence of the BAILLEUL - WILLERVAL Line weaker than it was planned.

(f) The lines of defence at the junction of Armies require careful co-ordination beforehand. The Division was committed to fight in an unfavourable position, in order to conform to the Third Army line of resistance.

(g) Tracer bullets for anti-aircraft M.G. and Lewis Guns are essential to save undue waste of ammunition and give good results.

(h) Some form of mustard gas for 18-pdr. guns is desirable. A bombardment of the enemy's assembly area with this gas would inflict heavy casualties.

SECRET.

S/CRA/15/371.
1-4-18.

56th Division "G".

With reference to your G.3/210, the points in connection with Artillery work in recent operations which appear to me to be outstanding are as follows :-

1.   The value of having batteries superimposed on the barrage and available to deal with favourable targets at short notice.
   During the German attack on the 28th March the guns available to cover the front of the Division were so few that it was rarely possible to take any off the barrages, though wonderful targets were repeatedly offered.

2.   The absolute necessity of having buried lines to O.Ps - at least to one O.P. per Group.
   It was found impossible to keep communication on 23rd March to O.Ps by air lines.

3.   The value of having reinforcing and "2nd line" battery positions arranged for, and if possible partially prepared with a proportion of ammunition dumped and map boards ready.
   During the night of the 28th March the greater part of the Divisional Artillery moved back to reinforcing positions where platforms had been made, shelters for personnel erected and 200 rounds per gun already dumped.
   Map boards had been held in hand at Div. Arty. H.Q.

Brigadier-General, R.A.,
Commanding Royal Artillery,
56th Division.

1st April, 1918.

First Army No: 1889 (G).

XIII Corps.
───────────

　　　　Will you please obtain from any Divisions in your Corps, recently engaged, any information as to Artillery or other tactical lessons to be learnt from these operations.
　　　　This information should be forwarded to Army Headquarters in as brief a form as possible, so that it may be circulated to other formations.

First Army.　　　　　　(Sd.) W.M.M. CRICHTON, Lt-Col; GS
30th March, 1918.　　　　　　for Major-General,
　　　　　　　　　　　　　　General Staff, First Army.

58th Division.
───

No: 1577/G (G.A.).　　　31st March, 1918.
───

　　　　Please forward a short report in accordance with the above, so as to reach Corps Headquarters by April 3rd.

XIII Corps.
　　　　　　　　　　　for Brig-Genl; General Staff.

Appendix II

SECRET
56th Division G.3/215.

167th Infantry Brigade.
168th Infantry Brigade.
169th Infantry Brigade.
C.R.A.
C.R.E.
56th Div. M.G.Bn.
56th Div. Signal Coy.
56th Div. Gas Officer.
A.D.M.S.
"Q"
A.P.M.
1/5th Cheshire Regt.
D.A.D.O.S.

D.A.D.V.S.
56th Div. Train.
56th Div. M.T.Coy.
A.D.C.
Camp Commandant.
56th Div. Employment Coy.
French Mission.
XIII Corps "G"
XIII Corps "Q"
War Diary.
File.

56th Division No. G.3/206 dated 30.3.18 is cancelled and the following substituted :-

As far as can be forecasted at present the 56th Division will remain in the XIII Corps area.

F. B. Hurndall Hayn
for Lieut-Colonel,
General Staff.

H.Q. 56th Divn.
1st April, 1918.

War Diary   *Appendix III*

SECRET   56th Division No. G.3/217

167th Infantry Brigade.	D.A.D.V.S.
168th Infantry Brigade.	56th Div. Train.
169th Infantry Brigade.	56th Div. M.T. Coy.
C.R.A.	A.D.C.
C.R.E.	Camp Commandant.
56th Div. M.G.Bn.	56th Div. Employment Coy.
56th Div. Signal Coy.	French Mission.
56th Div. Gas Officer.	XIII Corps "G"
A.D.M.S.	XIII Corps "Q"
"Q"	War Diary.
A.P.M.	File.
1/5th Cheshire Regt.	
D.A.D.O.S.	

       Information has been received that, although nothing definite has been settled, there is a possibility of the Division being moved shortly.

       Consequently, units will be warned to be ready to move at short notice.

                                                        B Pakenham

                                                           Lieut-Colonel,

1st April, 1918.   General Staff, 56th Division.

War Diary. Appendix IV

CONFIDENTIAL. 56th Division No. G.3/207.

56th Division.

XIII Corps No. 1377/7 G.A. 30-3-18.

      The Corps Commander wishes you to convey to the troops of the 56th Division his appreciation of their gallant conduct and resolute action in the defence of the VIMY RIDGE on the 28th March 1918.

      Though greatly outnumbered and opposed to overwhelming ordnance, they maintained the line intact until ordered to withdraw to the main line of resistance, where the attacks of the enemy were completely repulsed with heavy losses.

      This fine work has greatly added to the high reputation already gained by your Division.

              (Sgd.) IAN STEWART.
                         Brigadier-General,
XIII Corps.   General Staff.

(-2-)

167th Infantry Brigade.	"Q".
168th Infantry Brigade.	A.P.M.
169th Infantry Brigade.	D.A.D.V.S.
C.R.A.	56th Div. Train.
C.R.E.	56th Div. M.T. Coy.
1/5th Cheshire Regt.	Camp Commandant.
56th Div. M.G. Battn.	56th Div. Employment Coy.
56th Div. Signal Coy.	French Mission.
56th Div. Gas Officer.	
A.D.M.S.	
D.A.D.O.S.	

      Forwarded for information.

      The Army Commander personally expressed to the G.O.C. Division his appreciation of the good work done by the Division and of its tenacious defence.

      The G.O.C. Division also had the honour of being received by His Majesty the King, who was pleased to graciously express his approval of the gallantry displayed by all ranks of the 56th Division.

H.Q., 56th Divn.,   Lieut-Colonel.
1st April 1918.   General Staff.

"A" Form.
MESSAGES AND SIGNALS.

Army Form C. 2121.
(In pads of 100.)
No. of Message..........

Prefix.....Code.....m	Words.	Charge.	This message is on a/c of:	Recd. at........m.
Office of Origin and Service Instructions.	Sent		..........Service.	Date..........
....	At.........m.			From..........
	To..........			
	By..........		(Signature of "Franking Officer.")	By..........

TO — All recipients of G.3/217

Sender's Number.	Day of Month.	In reply to Number.	A A A
* G. 563	1st		

Cancel G.3/217 of today

From: 56th Div

Place:

Time:

(sd) F.B. HURNDALL,
Major, General Staff
for

* This line should be erased if not required.

"A" Form.
MESSAGES AND SIGNALS.

Army Form C.2121 (in pads of 100).

Sender's Number.	Day of Month.	In reply to Number.	
G.597	6		A A A

Warning Order AAA 167 & 168 Bde Group will be moving 6 inst AAA 167 Bde to DAINVILLE with 1 Bn. at WARLUS AAA 168 Bde to DUISANS & AGNEZ LES DUISANS AAA On night 7/8 April 167 Bde will relieve 1st Can. Div. with possibly 1 bn. of 168 in close support AAA Remainder of 168 to RONVILLE CAVES AAA 169 Bde to DUISANS & AGNEZ LES DUISANS AAA Lorries will be provided tomorrow for reconnaissance officers as follows AAA One for 167 Bde at 9 a.m. at cross roads VILLERS AU BOIS K.19.b.0.3. AAA One for 168 Bde at WHITE HOUSE MONT ST ELOI at 9 a.m. AAA One for M.G.Bn. at road junction W.19.c.1.3. at 9 a.m. AAA Reconnaissance parties report to H.Q. 1st Can. Div. at WARLUS AAA One M.G. Coy and One Field Coy. will also be required to move 6th inst. with each Bde AAA Units will be timed to arrive in new area about 3 p.m. AAA Addsd. all concerned

From: 56 Div.

General Staff.

SECRET.

Appendix VII

Copy No 27

56th DIVISION ORDER No. 159.

6th April, 1918.

Reference Maps 1/40,000 51B & 51C.

1. 56th Division is to relieve 1st Canadian Division (XVII Corps) on night 7/8th inst.

2. Moves in relief will take place as in attached Table.

3. The Divisional frontage will be taken over by 167th Inf. Bde & will be approximately from N.7.d.00. on the right flank to H.31.d.80 (BOIS DES BOEUFS) on the left flank.
   1 Bn. 168th Inf. Bde will probably be in close support and attached to 167th Brigade - remainder of 168th Inf. Bde. in Support in RONVILLE CAVES.
   169th Inf. Bde will be in Div. Reserve about AGNEZ LES DUISANS & DUISANS.

4. The relief will be completed before daylight on 8th inst., all details being arranged direct between Brigadiers concerned.

5. Command of Brigade Sections will be taken over on completion of relief.
   Command of the Divisional Sector will be taken over at 12 noon, 8th inst.

6. Reliefs of R.E. & Pioneers of Machine Guns and Medical units will be arranged direct between C.R.E's., D.M.G.C's & A.Ds.M.S. concerned.
   Moves of other units not specified in these orders will be arranged by A.A.& Q.M.G.

7. All trench maps will be taken over on relief.

8. H.Q. 56th Division will close at ACQ at 12 noon, 8th inst. and open at WARLUS at the same hour.

9. ACKNOWLEDGE.

Issued at 2.15 a.m.

C.Robertson Capt
for Lieut-Colonel,
General Staff.

Copy No. 1. 167th Inf. Bde.
2. 168th Inf. Bde.
3. 169th Inf. Bde.
4. 1/5th Cheshire Regt.
5. C.R.A.
6. C.R.E.
7. 56th Div. M.G.Bn.
8. 56th Div. Signal Coy.
9. 56th Div. Gas Officer.
10. A.D.M.S.
11. "Q"
12. A.P.M.
13. D.A.D.O.S.
14. D.A.D.V.S.
15. 56th Div. Train.
16. 56th Div. M.T.Coy.
17. A.D.C.
18. Camp Commandant.
19. 56th Div. Employ. Coy.
20. French Mission.
21. XIII Corps
22. XVII Corps "G"
23. XVII Corps "Q"
24. 1st Canadian Div.
25. Canadian Corps.
26.) War Diary.
27.)
28. File.

P.T.O.

MARCH TABLE TO ACCOMPANY 56th DIVISION ORDER No. 159.

Serial No.		Unit.	From.	To.	Route.	Remarks.
1	April 6th.	167th Inf.Bde. (less One Bn.) 1 M.G.Coy.	VILLERS AU BOIS Area.	DAINVILLE.	MAROEUIL.	To be clear of cross roads at F.8.d.4.1. by 1.30 p.m.
2	do.	1 Bn. 167th Inf. Bde.	VILLERS AU BOIS Area.	WARLUS.	HAUTE – AVESNES.	To be clear of ARRAS ST.POL road by 2.15 p.m.
3	do.	416th Field Coy. R.E.	ESTREE-CAUCHIE.	DAINVILLE	CAMBLAIN L'ABBE – FREVIN-CAPELLE – main ARRAS ST.POL Road.	Not to reach main ARRAS ST.POL Road before 2 p.m.
4	do.	168th Inf.Bde.	MONT ST ELOI	DUISANS AGNEZ LES DUISANS.	ECOIVRES Main ARRAS ST.POL Road.	Not to move before 1.45 p.m.
5	do.	1 M.G.Coy.	CHATEAU DE LA HAIE	DUISANS Area.	ACQ.	No restrictions as to time.
6	do.	512th Field Coy R.E.	ESTREE CAUCHIE.	DUISANS Area.	CAMBLAIN L'ABBE – FREVIN CAPELLE – Main ARRAS ST.POL Road.	Not to reach main ARRAS ST.POL Road before 3 p.m.

No units will arrive at their destinations before 3 p.m. Usual distances will be maintained.
A March Table for subsequent days will be issued later.

SECRET. Copy No. 27

56th DIVISION ORDER No. 160.

6th April, 1918.

1. In continuation of 56th Div. Order No. 159, the Divisional frontage will be taken over by 167th Infantry Brigade. B.G.C. 168th Infantry Brigade will place 1 Bn. at the disposal of B.G.C. 167th Infantry Brigade for the relief on the night 7/8th inst.

2. Moves in relief will take place in accordance with the attached March Table.

3. Locations of Brigade H.Q. -

    Bde. in Line (167th Inf. Bde.) St. SAUVEUR CAVE G.29.c.6.8.
    Support Brigade (168th Inf. Bde.) RONVILLE CAVES G.28.d.0.3.
    Reserve Brigade (169th Inf. Bde.) DAINVILLE.

4. The following troops will be accommodated in the RONVILLE CAVES :-

    168th Infantry Brigade (less 1 bn. detached to 167th Inf.Bde)
    1/5th Cheshire Regt. (Pioneers)
    512th Field Coy. R.E.

    These will come tactically under the Command of 168th Infantry Brigade.

    O.C., 1/5th Cheshire Regiment will place himself in communication with B.G.C. 168th Infantry Brigade at AGNEZ LES DUISANS to-day, and will ascertain the hour at which he will be required to arrive on the night 7/8th inst.

5. The D.M.G.C. will arrange to relieve the Support and Reserve Machine Gun Companies of 1st Canadian Division to-morrow.
    The 2 forward M.G.Companies will be relieved on the night 8/9th inst.

6. The Division will be covered by 1st Canadian Div. Artillery until further orders, under the Command of C.R.A. 56th Division.

7. B.G.C. 168th Infantry Brigade will arrange to have a careful reconnaissance made of the RONVILLE CAVES, and guides etc. detailed, so as to allow of troops being led out rapidly to their battle positions.

8. Defence Schemes will be taken over on relief.

9. The Brigades in Line and Support will not take nucleus personnel forward.
    The Reserve Brigade will arrange, if required to go into action, to leave its nucleus personnel behind.

10. Units of 56th Division arriving in 1st Canadian Divisional Area will come under orders of 1st Canadian Division, and will report arrival to that Division.

11. ACKNOWLEDGE.

F. B. Hurndall, Major
for Lieut-Colonel,
General Staff.

Issued at 2.30 p.m.

Copy No. 1. 167th Inf.Bde.
2. 168th Inf.Bde.
3. 169th Inf.Bde.
4. 1/5th Cheshire Regt.
5. C.R.A.
6. C.R.E.
7. 56th Div. M.G.Bn.
8. 56th Div. Signal Coy.
9. 56th Div. Gas Officer.

No.10. A.D.M.S.
11. "Q"
12. A.P.M.
13. D.A.D.O.S.
14. D.A.D.V.S.
15. 56th Div. Train.
16. 56th Div. M.T.Coy.
17. A.D.C.
18. Camp Commandant.

No.19. 56th D.Emp Coy.
20. French Mission.
21. XIII Corp
22. XVII Corp "G"
23. XVII Corp "Q"

24. 1st Canadian Div. 26) War Diary. 28 File.
25. Canadian Corps   27)

MARCH TABLE.

TO ACCOMPANY 56th DIVISION ORDER No. 180.

Serial No.	Date	Unit.	From.	To.	Route and Remarks.
5	Night 7/8th	167th Inf. Bde. (with 1 Bn.168th Inf. Bde.)	DAINVILLE, WARLUS, etc.	Line	In relief of 3rd Can. Inf. Bde.
3	"	415th Field Coy. R.E.	DAINVILLE, WARLUS Area.	AGNY.	To relieve forward Field Coy. of 1st Canadian Divn.
7	"	168th Inf.Bde. (less 1 Bn.) 512th Field Coy. R.E.	DUISANS Area.	RONVILLE Caves (Support Bde. position.) NO WARLUS	To relieve 2nd Can. Inf. Bde. To arrange with 137th Inf. Bde. NOT to clash during relief.
1	7th	H.Q. & 1 Coy. 56th M.G. Battn.	CHATEAU DE LA HAIE.	GOUVES.	To relieve 1st Can. Div. Reserve M.G.Coy. via HAUTE AVESNES.
2	7th	1 Coy. 56th M.G.Bn.	do.	Support M.G.Coy. position.	To relieve 1st Can Div. support M.G. Coy. No restrictions as to route.
5	7th	1/5th Cheshire Regt. Pioneers.	~~VILLAGE CAMP,~~ ~~ECOIVRES~~ ST AUBIN ESTREE CAUCHIE do.	RONVILLE CAVES.	To move in accordance with orders of B.G.C. 168th Inf. Bde. via ST. CATHERINE.
4	7th	513rd Field Coy. R.E.	do.	AGNEZ LES DUISANS.	For work under XVII Corps via HAUTE AVESNES.
8	8th	169th Inf. Bde.	BOIS DES ALLEUX and LE PENDU.	DAINVILLE (H.Q. & 2 Bns.) & BERNEVILLE (1 Bn).	To arrive at 2 p.m. Ens. for DAINVILLE via MAROEUIL. Bn. for BERNEVILLE via DUISANS.
6	Night 8/9th	2 Cos. 56th M.G.Bn.	DAINVILLE, DUISANS Areas.	Line	To relieve 2 forward M.G.Cos. of 1st Can. Div.
10	9th	H.Q. & 1 Coy. 56th M.G.Bn.	GOUVES	WARLUS	When WARLUS is vacated by 1st Can Div. M.G.Cos.

SECRET.   Copy No. 26

56th DIVISION ORDER No. 161.

11th April, 1918.

1. 168th Infantry Brigade will relieve 167th Infantry Brigade on its present front on the night 13th/14th April.

2. On relief 167th Infantry Brigade will be Brigade in Support, will take over dispositions of 168th Infantry Brigade and will place 1 Battalion at disposal of B.G.C. 168th Infantry Brigade.

3. On the 14th inst. 169th Infantry Brigade will relieve 167th Infantry Brigade, placing 1 Battalion at the disposal of B.G.C. 168th Infantry Brigade.

4. On relief, 167th Infantry Brigade will proceed to the DAINVILLE - BERNEVILLE Area, and become Divisional Reserve.

5. Details of relief, which must be arranged to interfere as little as possible with work in progress will be arranged between Brigadiers concerned. The hour of relief between 169th and 167th Infantry Brigades is left to the discretion of Brigadiers according to the visibility.

6. Maps, air-photos, defence schemes, trench stores and dumps will be handed over on relief.

7. Completion of reliefs will be sent to Div. H.Q. by wiring name of relieving B.G.C.

8. Command will pass in each case on completion of relief.

9. ACKNOWLEDGE.

F. B. Hurndall
Major
Lieut-Colonel,
General Staff.

Issued at 8.45 a.m.

Copy No. 1. 167th Infantry Brigade.
2. 168th Infantry Brigade.
3. 169th Infantry Brigade.
4. 1/5th Cheshire Regt.
5. C.R.A.
6. C.R.E.
7. 56th Div. M.G.Bn.
8. 56th Div. Signal Coy.
9. 56th Div. Gas Officer.
10. A.D.M.S.
11. "Q"
12. A.P.M.
13. D.A.D.O.S.
14. D.A.D.V.S.
15. 56th Div. Train.
16. 56th Div. M.T.Coy.
17. A.D.C.
18. Camp Commandant.
19. 56th Div. Employment Coy.

No. 20. French Mission.
21. XVII Corps.
22. 2nd Canadian Divn.
23. 15th Division.
24. 4th Division.
25.) War Diary.
26.)
27. File.

S.E.C.R.E.T.

War Diary Copies — Appendix X

Copy No. 25

56th DIVISION ORDER No. 162.

17th April, 1918.

1. 169th Infantry Brigade will relieve 168th Infantry Brigade on its present front on the night 19th/20th April.

2. On relief 168th Infantry Brigade will be Brigade in Support, will take over dispositions of 169th Infantry Brigade and will place 1 Battalion at disposal of B.G.C. 169th Infantry Brigade.

3. On the 20th inst. 167th Infantry Brigade will relieve 168th Infantry Brigade, placing 1 Battalion at the disposal of B.G.C. 169th Infantry Brigade.

4. On relief, 168th Infantry Brigade will proceed to the DAINVILLE - BERNEVILLE Area, and become Divisional Reserve.

5. Details of relief, which must be arranged to interfere as little as possible with work in progress will be arranged between Brigadiers concerned. The hour of relief between 168th and 167th Infantry Brigades is left to the discretion of Brigadiers according to the visibility.

6. Maps, air-photos, defence schemes, trench stores and dumps will be handed over on relief.

7. Completion of reliefs will be sent to Div. H.Q. by wiring name of relieving B.G.C.

8. Command will pass in each case on completion of relief.

9. ACKNOWLEDGE.

F. B. Hurndall
Major
for
Lieut.-Colonel,
General Staff.

Issued at 8.45 a.m.

Copy No. 1. 167th Infantry Brigade.
2. 168th Infantry Brigade.
3. 169th Infantry Brigade.
4. 1/5th Cheshire Regt.
5. C.R.A.
6. C.R.E.
7. 56th Div. M.G.Battn.
8. 56th Div. Signal Coy.
9. 56th Div. Gas Officer.
10. A.D.M.S.
11. "Q"
12. A.P.M.
13. D.A.D.O.S.
14. D.A.D.V.S.
No. 15. 56th Div. Train.
16. 56th Div. M.T.Coy.
17. A.D.C.
18. Camp Commandant.
19. 56th Div. Employment Coy.
20. French Mission.
21. XVII Corps.
22. "   "
23. 2nd Canadian Div.
24. 15th Division.
25.) War Diary.
26.)
20. File.

SECRET.   Copy No. 26.

56th DIVISION WARNING ORDER No. 163.

Ref. Maps 51C. N.E.
      51B. N.W.   19th April 1918.
      51B. S.W.

1.   56th Division is to be prepared to extend its left at short notice, so as to relieve the 15th Division (less Artillery).

2.   The Northern boundary after relief will be BROKEN MILL at H.27.b.22 (exclusive) - H.26.a.85 - (whole of TRIANGLE SWITCH inclusive to Canadian Corps) - G.23.d.85.33 - thence along Railway (exclusive) to G.23.d.25.20 - G.22.b.99.32 - thence along Railway G.22.b.25.65 (Railway inclusive) - ROND POINT G.21.b.45.70 (exclusive) - BOULEVARD DE LA LIBERTE (exclusive) - G.21.a.87 - BAUDIMONT GATE - road junction G.21.a.35.70 - G.21.a.00.83 (all inclusive) thence as shown on Corps Map No. 154.

3.   The relief will be carried out as follows :-

(a) The Support Brigade 56th Division will relieve the Brigade in the Line of 15th Division, and the Reserve Brigade 56th Division will move up Brigade H.Q. and 2 Bns. to RONVILLE CAVES and 1 Bn. to ST. SAUVEUR CAVES.

(b) In the event of the order being received whilst a relief on 56th Divn. front is in progress, or the Support Brigade has just come out of the line, the Reserve Brigade 56th Division will relieve the Line Brigade 15th Division, and will move up by day as a preliminary to the relief, having 1 Bn. in ST. SAUVEUR CAVES, 1 Bn. in ARRAS and 1 Bn. in DAINVILLE, with Brigade H.Q. in ARRAS, thus relieving the Support Brigade of 15th Division.
   In this eventuality, the Support Brigade of 56th Division will become the Reserve Brigade, and will arrange to place 1 Bn. in ST. SAUVEUR CAVES to replace the Battalion of the relieving Brigade when it goes forward.

(c) From the commencement of the relief, the battalion of Support Brigade 56th Division attached to the Brigade in Line 56th Division will come under the command of its own Brigade, and will not be replaced.

(d) All details of relief will be arranged direct between Brigadiers concerned and the necessary reconnaissances carried out forthwith.

(e) The reliefs will be so arranged that the number of battalions in Support is not allowed to fall at any time below its present number.

4.   The C.R.A. will be prepared for a redistribution of the artillery should either the 4th Div. Artillery or 15th Div. Artillery be withdrawn.

5.   The D.M.G.O. will arrange to take over the whole Divnl. front with 3 M.G. Coys. and move the Reserve M.G. Coy. to DAINVILLE.
   Relief of machine guns of 15th Division will be carried out on the day after the Infantry relief, except that guns which cannot be relieved by day will be relieved on the same night as the Infantry.

6.   The C.R.E. will take over all details of work and demolitions from C.R.E. 15th Divn. and move the R.E. Coy. from AGNY to ST. SAUVEUR CAVES.
   He will place 2 Platoons, 1/5th Cheshire Regt. (Pioneers) at the disposal of B.G.C. Left Sector, and afford such technical R.E. assistance as is desired by him and available.

                                                            P.T.O.   /7.

(-2-)

7. The A.D.M.S. will make the necessary medical arrangements with A.D.M.S. 15th Division.

8. Maps, air photos., defence schemes, trench stores and dumps will be taken over on relief.

9. Completion of reliefs will be reported to Div. H.Q. by wiring the name of the relieving Brigadier.

10. Command of the Left Sector will pass on completion of the Infantry reliefs, at which hour G.O.C. 56th Division will assume command of the new front.

11. ACKNOWLEDGE.

B Pakenham
Lieut-Colonel.
General Staff.

Issued at 2 pm

Copy No.	
1.	167th Infantry Brigade.
2.	168th Infantry Brigade.
3.	169th Infantry Brigade.
4.	1/5th Cheshire Regt.
5.	C.R.A.
6.	C.R.E.
7.	56th Bn. M.G.C.
8.	56th Div. Signal Coy.
9.	56th Div. Gas Officer.
10.	A.D.M.S.
11.	"Q".
12.	A.P.M.
13.	D.A.D.O.S.
14.	D.A.D.V.S.
15.	56th Div. Train.
16.	56th Div. M.T. Coy.
17.	A.D.C.
18.	Camp Commandant.
19.	56th Div. Employment Coy.
20.	French Mission.
21.	XVII Corps.
22.	" "
23.	2nd Canadian Divn.
24.	15th Division.
25. }	War Diary.
26. }	
27.	File.

SECRET.

Copy No. 26

War Diary Appendix XII

56th DIVISION ORDER No. 164.

22nd April 1918.

Ref. Map 1/20,000 51C N.E. 51E N.W., 51E S.W.

1. 56th Division will extend its left so as to take over the frontage held now by 15th Division, the relief to be completed by 5 a.m. 24th.

2. The Northern boundary of the Division will be BROKEN MILL at H.27.b.2.2. (Exclusive) - H.26.a.8.5. - (whole of TRIANGLE SWITCH inclusive to Division on our left flank) - G.23.d.85.33. - thence along Railway (exclusive) to G.23.d.25.20 - G.22.b.99.32 - thence along Railway G.22.b.25.65 (Railway inclusive) - ROND POINT G.21.b.45.70 (exclusive) - BOULEVARD DE LA LIBERTIE (exclusive) - G.21.a.8.7. - BAUDIMONT GATE - Road junction G.21.a.35.70. - G.21.a.00.85 (all inclusive), thence as shown on Corps Map 154.

3. 167th Infantry Brigade will relieve 44th Infantry Brigade in the line on the night 23rd/24th.
   All details of relief will be arranged direct between Brigades concerned.
   167th Infantry Brigade H.Qrs. will be at G.29.d.05.70. (ST. SAUVEUR CAVES).

4. 168th Infantry Brigade will be in Divisional Reserve and will establish its Headquarters at present Support Brigade H.Qrs. in RONVILLE CAVES.
   2 Battalions will be located in RONVILLE CAVES and 1 Bn. in ST.SAUVEUR CAVES.

5. B.G.C. 168th Infantry Brigade will arrange with B.G.C. 167th Infantry Brigade to move his 2 Battalions into RONVILLE CAVES as the battalions of 167th Infantry Brigade move out on relief.
   He will also arrange with the B.G.C. 46th Infantry Brigade for the relief of the battalion in ST.SAUVEUR CAVES at G.29.d.

6. From the commencement of the relief ordered in para. 3, the attached battalion of 167th Infantry Brigade will cease to be at the disposal of 169th Infantry Brigade nor will it be replaced.

7. The D.M.G.C. will arrange with D.M.G.C. 15th Division to relieve the most important guns in the sector to be taken over.
   3 M.G. Companies will be in the Line.
   1 M.G.Company will be in Reserve, and will move to DAINVILLE on the night 23rd/24th inst.

/8.

8. The C.R.E. will arrange to take over all details of work in the new Sector, and to move the R.E. Field Coys. at AGNY to ST.SAUVEUR CAVES.

He will place 2 Platoons of 1/5th Cheshire Regt. (Pioneers) at the disposal of B.G.C. 169th Infantry Brigade and afford him such R.E. technical assistance as he desires, and as is available.

9. The A.D.M.S. will make the necessary medical arrangements with A.D.M.S. 15th Division.

10. Maps, air-photos, Defence Schemes, Trench Stores and Dumps will be taken over on relief.

11. Command will pass on completion of relief, at which hour G.O.C. 56th Division will assume command of the whole XVII Corps front.

12. Completion of relief will be sent to Div. H.Qrs. by wiring name of relieving B.G.C.

13. ACKNOWLEDGE.

B Pakenham

Lieut-Colonel,
General Staff.

Issued at 9.15 p.m.

Copy No.		No.	
1.	167th Infantry Brigade.	18.	A.D.C.
2.	168th Infantry Brigade.	19.	Camp Commandant.
3.	169th Infantry Brigade.	20.	56th Div. Employ. Coy.
4.	1/5th Cheshire Regt.	21.	French Mission.
5.	C.R.A.	22.) & 23.)	XVII Corps.
6.	O.C. Right H.A. Group.		
7.	C.R.E.	24.	2nd Cand. Division.
8.	56th Div. M.G.Bn.	25.	15th Division.
9.	56th Div. Signal Coy.	26.) 27.)	War Diary.
10.	56th Div. Gas Officer.		
11.	A.D.M.S.	28.	File.
12.	"Q"		
13.	A.P.M.		
14.	D.A.D.O.S.		
15.	D.A.D.V.S.		
16.	56th Div. Train.		
17.	56th Div. M.T. Coy.		

SECRET   Appendix XIV   Copy No. 22

56th DIVISION ORDER No. 166.

29th April 1918.

1.   15th Divisional Artillery will be relieved to night April 29th/30th and will march to-morrow 30th instant, under orders to be issued later.

2.   311th Army Brigade R.F.A. will relieve 71st Brigade R.F.A., 15th Divisional Artillery to-night. Personnel may relieve in daylight. Guns will be taken over in situ stripped of stores and sights, except that A/71st Battery will retain their guns (fitted with air recuperators) and A/311th Battery will take their own guns into action. On completion of relief 311th Army Brigade R.F.A. will come under orders of C.R.A., 56th Division and 71st Brigade R.F.A. will withdraw to wagon lines (arrangements have already been made verbally with C.R.A.).

3.   311th and 277th Army Brigades R.F.A. will form a sub-group under command of Lieut-Colonel J.E.C.J.COCHRANE, D.S.O. R.F.A., to cover the left Infantry Brigade front of 56th Divn.

4.   Copies of XVII Corps R.A. defence orders in possession of 15th D.A. Hd.Qrs. and 70th and 71st Brigades, will be returned to R.A. XVII Corps.

5. CRA   will arrange to take over all ammunition in rear positions from 15th Divisional Artillery.

6.   15th Divisional Artillery will hand over medium trench mortars now in line to 56th Division and will take over corresponding number not in action from 56th Division under arrangements to be made between C.R.As concerned.

7.   ACKNOWLEDGE.

F. B. Hunnvall Major
for Lieut-Colonel,
General Staff.

Issued at
Copy No. 1. 167th Infantry Bde.   No. 11. "Q"
         2. 168th Infantry Bde.   12. A.P.M.
         3. 169th Infantry Bde.   13. 56th Div. Train.
         4. C.R.A.   14. 56th Div. M.T.Coy.
         5. Right H.A.Group.   15. A.D.C.
         6. C.R.E.   16. Camp Commandant.
         7. 56th Div.M.G.Bn.   17-18 XVII Corps.
         8. 56th Div.Signal Co.   19. 2nd Canadian Divn.
         9. 56th Div.Gas Offr.   20. 1st Canadian Divn.
        10. A.D.M.S.   21-22 War Diary.
                                           23. File.

SECRET.

Appendix XIII

Copy No 27

56th DIVISION ORDER No. 165.

26th April, 1918.

1. 168th Infantry Brigade will relieve 169th Infantry Brigade on its present front on the night 28th/29th April. All details of relief will be arranged between B.Gs.C. concerned.

2. On relief 169th Infantry Brigade will become Divisional Reserve, and will proceed to BERNEVILLE - DAINVILLE Area.

3. Maps, air photos, defence schemes, trench stores and dumps will be handed over on relief.

4. Command will pass on completion of relief.

5. Completion of relief will be wired to Div. H.Q. by the Code Word "BANANA".

6. ACKNOWLEDGE.

F. B. Hurnvall, Major

for Lieut-Colonel,
General Staff.

Issued at 2 p.m.

Copy No.		No.	
1.	167th Infantry Brigade.	16.	56th Div. Train.
2.	168th Infantry Brigade.	17.	56th Div.M.T.Coy.
3.	169th Infantry Brigade.	18.	A.D.C.
4.	1/5th Cheshire Regt.	19.	Camp Commandant.
5.	C.R.A.	20.	56th Div.Employ.Coy.
6.	Right H.A.Group.	21.	French Mission.
7.	C.R.E.	22.	XVII Corps.
8.	56th Div. M.G.Bn.	23.	" "
9.	56th Div. Signal Coy.	24.	2nd Canadian Divn.
10.	56th Div. Gas Officer.	25.	1st Canadian Divn.
11.	A.D.M.S.	26.)	War Diary.
12.	"Q"	27.)	
13.	A.P.M.	28.	File.
14.	D.A.D.O.S.		
15.	D.A.D.V.S.		

CONFIDENTIAL.

WAR DIARY

OF

GENERAL STAFF,

56th DIVISION.

From   1st MAY, 1918
To   31st MAY, 1918

* * * * * * *

WAR DIARY or INTELLIGENCE SUMMARY

56th Division.
'G' Branch.

May 1918.

Army Form C. 2118.

Place	Date	Hour	Summary of Events and Information	Remarks and references to Appendices
WARLUS.	1st		Quiet night. 56th Divnl. Order No. 167 issued ordering relief of 167th Infantry Brigade by 169th Infantry Brigade in the Left Sector of Divnl. front on night 4th/5th May.	App. II.
	2nd		Quiet night. XVII Corps order received notifying extension of Corps front. 56th Divnl. front to be extended North to ARRAS — DOUAI Railway (exclusive). This front to be taken over from 1st Canadian Division on night 3rd/4th May. 56th Divnl. Order No.168 issued.	App. II.
	3rd 4th		Our artillery carried out normal harassing fire during night 2nd/3rd. Quiet night. 56th Divnl. front extended North to ARRAS — DOUAI Railway (exclusive) during night 3rd/4th. Our artillery carried out normal harassing fire. Maj-Genl. Sir C.P.A.HULL, K.C.B. assumed Command of 56th vice Major-General F.A.DUDGEON, C.B., evacuated sick. Brigadier-General G.H.B.FREETH, C.M.G., D.S.O. resumed command of 167th Infantry Brigade.	Divn.
	5th		Harassing fire by our artillery was carried out. Our patrols were very active during the night but encountered none of the enemy. 169th Infantry Brigade relieved 167th Infantry Brigade in the Left Brigade front. 167th Infantry Brigade moved back to Divnl. Reserve at BERNEVILLE. 8th Middlesex Regt. (167th Infantry Brigade) retained in forward area for work in FEUCHY SWITCH.	App. I.
	6th		Quiet night. Normal harassing fire carried out at night. 1st Bn. London Regt. (167th Infantry Brigade) moved up to forward area for work.	
	7th		Quiet night. Normal harassing fire at night. Captain HAYDON, G.S.O.III, assumed duty as Brigade Major of 167th Infantry Brigade.	
	8th		Quiet night. During the night 3 escaped British prisoners of the 15th Division, taken on the 28th March entered our lines. They reported no signs of enemy preparations for attack. Our patrols were active during the night, but no enemy were encountered. 56th Div. Order No. 169 issued for relief of 168th Infantry Brigade on night 12th/13th May by 167th Infantry Brigade	App. II.
	9th		Quiet night. Usual harassing fire carried out at night. Our patrols were again active but no enemy movement detected.	

Army Form C. 2118.

WAR DIARY
or
INTELLIGENCE SUMMARY

(Erase heading not required.)

56th Division 'G' Branch.

May 1918.

Instructions regarding War Diaries and Intelligence Summaries are contained in F.S. Regs., Part II, and the Staff Manual respectively. Title pages will be prepared in manuscript.

Place	Date	Hour	Summary of Events and Information	Remarks and references to Appendices
WARLUS.	10th		Hostile artillery quiet. Our harassing fire carried out as usual.	
	11th		Hostile artillery rather more active.	
	12th		Quiet night. Hostile artillery normal. Usual harassing fire carried out by us. 167th Infantry Brigade relieved 168th Infantry Brigade in the Right Section.	App. I.
	13th		Hostile artillery less active. Weather very wet visibility poor.	
	14th		Enemy shelled ARRAS in region of Station and Levis Barracks heavily during evening. Situation normal.	
	15th		Visibility good. Situation quiet. Enemy shelled extreme left front with gas shell during evening considerably interfering with a working party digging an advanced trench near FEUCHY. Capt. T.L.G. HEALD assumed duties of G.S.O.III.	
	16th		Weather warm, visibility poor. Quiet day. Enemy shelled TILLOY WOOD with 4.2's during morning. Enemy aeroplane brought down in air fight over our lines and crashed just E. of BOIS DES BOEUFS.	
	17th		Weather hot and visibility poor. Patrols report enemy wiring his outpost line. Hostile Artillery shelled ARRAS during the afternoon. Enemy movement normal.	
	18th		Weather hot. Hostile artillery very active on our battery positions. Operation Order No. 170 issued for relief of 169th Infantry Brigade by 168th Infantry Brigade in Left Section on 21st/22nd May. 167th Infantry Brigade carried out an inter-battalion relief. G.O.C. and G.S.O.I attended Conference at Corps H.Q. During the night hostile aeroplane dropped two bombs on Div. H.Q. No damage done.	APP. II.
	19th		Weather warm. Visibility poor. Situation quiet. A message intercepted by the listening sets apparently giving indications of a German attack received at 10 p.m. Precautionary orders were issued.	

56th Division
'G' Branch.

WAR DIARY or INTELLIGENCE SUMMARY

Army Form C. 2118.

May 1918.

Place	Date	Hour	Summary of Events and Information	Remarks and references to Appendices
	19th (cont'd)		During the night three British prisoners made their way into our lines. They saw no signs of impending attack.	
	20th		Weather hot. Quiet day. Our guns active in counter battery and harassing fire. Enemy artillery fired gas shell in region of TILLOY during evening.	
	21st		At 2 a.m. 8th Middlesex carried out a successful raid on the enemy outpost line capturing 4 prisoners and 1 L.M.G. establishing the relief of the 16th Bav. Division by the 214th Divn. Weather fine and hot. The 168th Infantry Brigade relieved the 169th Infantry Brigade in the Left Section, the 169th Infantry Brigade moving into Divisional Reserve.	App. I.
	22nd		Weather hot. Situation quiet. Hostile aeroplane dropped bombs on DAINVILLE and BERNEVILLE during the night causing a few casualties. Our artillery carried out usual harassing fire.	
	23rd		Situation normal. Our artillery very active searching for hostile T.M. Dumps. Enemy artillery active with counter battery fire on batteries near BLANGY. G.O.C. visited new forward trench on extreme left with B.G.C. 168th Infantry Brigade.	
	24th		Situation quiet, weather wet. 167th Infantry Brigade carried out an inter-battalion relief.	App. I.
	25th		Visibility poor. Hostile artillery very active and shelled the region near TILLOY heavily all afternoon. The extreme left of our front line, ARRAS STATION and the BLANGY System were also shelled. Our heavies opened counter battery fire. All quiet about 6.30 p.m. G.O.C. and G.S.O. I attended a Corps Conference during the morning	
	26th		Hostile artillery very active all day. Commencing at 3 a.m. when he put a barrage on the front line, which ceased about 4 a.m. he has shelled persistently throughout the day, the region round TILLOY being most heavily shelled. The remainder of the shelling has been scattered. Our heavy artillery have been engaged in counter battery fire. At 7 p.m. the shelling is reported to have almost ceased.	

56th Division
'G' Branch.

WAR DIARY or INTELLIGENCE SUMMARY.

(Erase heading not required.)

Army Form C. 2118.

May 1918

Place	Date	Hour	Summary of Events and Information	Remarks and references to Appendices
WARLUS	27th		Hostile artillery quieter. About 2.45 a.m. a barrage lasting 10 minutes was put on our front lines. During the day at intervals TILLOY WOOD and front line in vicinity were shelled. Enemy also shelled Right Brigade and Left Battalion H.Qrs. Right Bde. were shelled with 5.9" & 4.2's. Our counter battery fire appeared effective. Div. O.O. No. 171 issued for relief of 167th Infantry Brigade by 169th Infantry Brigade in Right Section.	APP. II
	28th		Hostile artillery much quieter during the day. At 10.30 p.m. the enemy placed a barrage along our front line culminating in intense fire on the extreme left. No infantry action followed. At 11 p.m. a Company of 7th Middlesex Regt. and 2 platoons of 1st London Regiment raided the enemy trenches in N.2.c. & N.8.a. Many Germans were killed and an identification obtained (Normal). See Intelligence Summary No. 52.	APP. III.
	29th		Situation quiet. Weather fine visibility good. Enemy shelled the Brickfield N. of BEAURAINS very persistently during the morning.	
	30th		Quiet day. Hostile artillery shelled our left Front heavily about 9.30 a.m. otherwise normal. 169th Infantry Brigade relieved 167th Infantry Brigade in the right Section. A patrol of 13th London Regiment rushed an enemy sentry post and secured 2 prisoners during the night. Identification normal.	App. I.
	31st		Situation quiet. Our artillery active with counter battery fire. Visibility very good. Very little enemy movement seen.	

Major-General,
Commanding 56th Division.

56th DIVISION. LOCATION TABLE at 6 p.m. MAY 1918. APPENDIX I.

appx. I.

	1	2	3	4	5	6	7	8	9	10	11	12	13	14	15	16
Div. H.Q.	WARLUS															
167th Inf.Bde.H.Q.	(G29d.05.70.)				BERNEVILLE								G34b28(R)			
1st London Regt.	H25b.25.25(L)	G30c.10.2.(S)			DAINVILLE RONVILLE ARRAS CAVES								M5b.16.(S)			
7th Middx. Regt.	G30c.10.25(S)	H31b38(R)			DAINVILLE		ARRAS						N7a.28(R)			
8th "	H31b38(R)				ST SAUVEUR CAVES		DAINVILLE						N1a 65(L)			
168th Inf.Bde.H.Q.	G27b83(R)							G34b28(R)					BERNEVILLE			
4th London Regt.	N1a 65(L)		M5b16(S)			M5b16(S)							ARRAS		DAINVILLE ARRAS	
13th " "	N7a 28(R)		N7a 28(R)			N1a 65(L)							DAINVILLE			
14th " "	M5b16(S)												DAINVILLE			
169th Inf.Bde.H.Q.	BERNEVILLE				G29d.05.70(L)											
2nd London Regt.	DAINVILLE				H31b 38(R)											
5th " "	DAINVILLE				H25b.25.25(L)											
18th " "	BERNEVILLE				G30c.10.25(S)											
Div. Arty. H.Q.	WARLUS															
280th Bde.	M8b.75.40			G27b 91.35.												
281st "	G34b.29.															
Pioneers.	RONVILLE CAVES							ARRAS (G27b77)								
M.G.Battn.H.Q.	WARLUS															

IN THE LINE ——— (red)
IN SUPPORT ——— (blue light)
IN RESERVE ——— (blue dark)

56th DIVISION.   LOCATION TABLE at 6 p.m.   MAY 1918.   APPENDIX I

Appx. I.

	17	18	19	20	21	22	23	24	25	26	27	28	29	30	31
Div. H.Q.	WARLUS														
167th Inf.Bde.H.Q.	G27b.82														BERNEVILLE
1st London Regt.	M5b16(S)		N7a.28(R)						N1a.63(L)						DAINVILLE
7th Middl. Regt.	N7a.28(R)		M5b.16(S)												ARRAS
8th "	N1a.63(L)								M5b.26(S)						DAINVILLE
168th Inf.Bde.H.Q.	BERNEVILLE				G28.b.07										
4th London Regt.	DAINVILLE				H25b.25.25(L)										
13th "	ARRAS		DAINVILLE		M31b.58(R)										
14th "	DAINVILLE		ARRAS		G30c.10.25(S)										
169th Inf.Bde.H.Q.	G28.b.07											G27b.82			
2nd London Regt.	H31b.58(R)											M5b.26(S)			
5th "	H25b.25.25(L)											H31c.50(L)			
18th "	G30c.10.25(S)											N7a.28(R)			
Div. Arty. H.Q.	WARLUS														
280th Bde.	M8b.75.40.														
281st "	G27b.99.35.														
Pioneers.	G27b.77.														
M.G.Battn.H.Q.	WARLUS														

IN THE LINE ────── (red)
IN SUPPORT ────── (blue)
IN RESERVE ────── (dark blue)

SECRET *War Diary Copies* Copy No. 26

56th DIVISION ORDER No. 167.

Appendix II

1st May, 1918.

1. 169th Infantry Brigade will relieve 167th Infantry Brigade on its present front on the night 4th/5th May. All details of relief will be arranged between B.Gs.C. concerned.

2. On relief 167th Infantry Brigade will become Divisional Reserve, and will proceed to BERNEVILLE - DAIEVILLE Area.

3. Maps, air photos, defence schemes, trench stores and dumps will be handed over on relief.

4. Command will pass on completion of relief.

5. Completion of relief will be wired to Div. H.Q. by the Code Word "APPLE".

6. ACKNOWLEDGE.

F. B. Hunsull, Major
for
Lieut-Colonel,
General Staff.

Issued at 8 p.m.

Copy No. 1. 167th Infantry Brigade.
2. 168th Infantry Brigade.
3. 169th Infantry Brigade.
4. 1/5th Cheshire Regt.
5. C.R.A.
6. Right H.A. Group.
7. C.R.E.
8. 56th Div. M.G.Bn.
9. 56th Div. Signal Coy.
10. 56th Div. Gas Officer.
11. A.D.M.S.
12. "Q"
13. A.P.M.
14. D.A.D.O.S.
15. D.A.D.V.S.
16. 56th Div. Train.
17. 56th Div. M.T. Coy.
18. A.D.C.
19. Camp Commandant.
20. 56th Div. Employ. Coy.
21. French Mission.
22. XVII Corps.
23.   "   "
24. 2nd Canadian Divn.
25. 1st Canadian Divn.
26. } War Diary.
27. }
28. File.

SECRET

War Diary Appendix II

Copy No. 17

56th DIVISION ORDER No. 168.

2nd May, 1918.

1. 167th Infantry Brigade will on the night 3rd/4th May take over the front of the 2nd Canadian Infantry Brigade (1st Canadian Division) as far North as the ARRAS - DOUAI (Railway exclusive).

2. On completion of relief the Northern Divisional Boundary will be the ARRAS - DOUAI Railway at H.21.d.3.1. thence along Railway (Railway exclusive to 56th Division) to G.23.d.25.20 - thence along original boundary.

3. 168th Infantry Brigade will on the night 3rd/4th May take over the front of the 167th Infantry Brigade as far North as the ARRAS - CAMBRAI Road (Road inclusive to 168th Infantry Brigade).

4. On completion of relief the inter-brigade boundary will be the ARRAS - CAMBRAI Road at H.32.d.3.2. - thence along the road to ESTAMINET CORNER H.31.d.3.0. (Road inclusive to 168th Infantry Brigade) - thence due West along the Grid line running west through G.36. central to M.32.b.95.10. - M.32.b.10.75. - L.30.c.5.5. - L.28.c.4.5. thence due West.

5. All details of relief to be arranged between B.Gs.C. concerned.

6. Command will pass on completion of relief.

7. On 4th/5th May D.M.G.C. will relieve such M.Gs. in the area to be taken over from 1st Canadian Division as are necessary for the defence of the increased front.

8. Completion of reliefs to be wired to Divisional H.Qrs. by the code word "ORANGE".

9. ACKNOWLEDGE.

F B Hurndall Major
for
Lieut-Colonel,
General Staff.

Issued at :- 9 PM

Copy No. 1. 167th Infantry Brigade.
2. 168th Infantry Brigade.
3. 169th Infantry Brigade.
4. 1/5th Cheshire Regt.
5. C.R.A.
6. C.R.E.
7. 56th Bn. M.G.Corps.
8. 56th Div. Signal Coy.
9. A.D.M.S.
10. A/Q.
11. A.P.M.

No. 12. A.D.C.
13. 2nd Canadian Divn.
14. 1st Canadian Divn.
15. XVII Corps.
16. " "
17. } War Diary.
18. }
19. File.
20. Right H.A.Group.

SECRET. 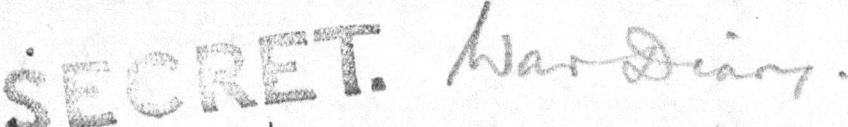 Copy No. 26

56th DIVISION ORDER No. 169.

8th May, 1918.

1. 167th Infantry Brigade will relieve 168th Infantry Brigade on its present front on the night 12th/13th May. All details of relief to be arranged between B.Gs.C. concerned.

2. On relief 168th Infantry Brigade will become Divisional Reserve and will keep 2 battalions in DAINVILLE and 1 Battn. in ARRAS, unless otherwise ordered.

3. Maps, Air photos, Defence Schemes, trench stores and dumps will be handed over on relief.

4. Command will pass on completion of relief.

5. Completion of relief will be wired to Div. H.Q. by the code word "VIMIERA".

6. ACKNOWLEDGE.

F. B. Hurndall
for Major

Lieut-Colonel,
General Staff.

Issued at 8 p.m.

Copy	No.			No.	
	1.	167th Infantry Bde.		16.	56th Div. Train.
	2.	168th Infantry Bde.		17.	56th Div. M.T. Coy.
	3.	169th Infantry Bde.		18.	A.D.C.
	4.	1/5th Cheshire Regt.		19.	Camp Comdt.
	5.	C.R.A.		20.	56th Div. Employ.Co.
	6.	Right H.A. Group.		21.	French Mission.
	7.	C.R.E.		22.	XVII Corps.
	8.	56th Div. M.G. Bn.		23.	" "
	9.	56th Div. Signal Coy.		24.	2nd Can. Div.
	10.	56th Div. Gas Officer.		25.	15th Div.
	11.	A.D.M.S.		26.)	War Diary.
	12.	"Q".		27.)	
	13.	A.P.M.		28.	File.
	14.	D.A.D.O.S.			
	15.	D.A.D.V.S.			

SECRET *War Diary Copies.* Copy No. 26 *Appendix II*

56th DIVISION ORDER No. 170.

18th May, 1918.

1. 168th Infantry Brigade will relieve 169th Infantry Brigade on its present front on the night 21/22nd May. All details of relief to be arranged between B.Gs.C. concerned.

2. On relief 169th Infantry Brigade will become Divisional Reserve and will keep 2 battalions in DAINVILLE and 1 Battn. in ARRAS.

3. Maps, Air photos, Defence Schemes, trench stores and dumps will be handed over on relief.

4. Command will pass on completion of relief.

5. Completion of relief will be wired to Div. H.Q. by the code word "RAMILLIES".

6. ACKNOWLEDGE.

F. B. Hunsdall Major
for
Lieut-Colonel,
General Staff.

Issued at 8 a.m.

Copy No.		No.	
1.	167th Infantry Bde.	16.	56th Div. Train.
2.	168th Infantry Bde.	17.	56th Div. M.T.Coy.
3.	169th Infantry Bde.	18.	A.D.C.
4.	1/5th Cheshire Regt.	19.	Camp Commandant.
5.	C.R.A.	20.	56th Div. Employment Co.
6.	Right H.A.Group.	21.	French Mission.
7.	C.R.E.	22.	XVII Corps.
8.	56th Div. M.G.Battn.	23.	" "
9.	56th Div. Signal Coy.	24.	2nd Can. Div.
10.	56th Div. Gas Officer.	25.	15th Division.
11.	A.D.M.S.	26.)	War Diary.
12.	A/Q.	27.)	
13.	A.P.M.	28.	File.
14.	D.A.D.O.S.		
15.	D.A.D.V.S.		

SECRET.   Copy No. 27

56th DIVISION ORDER No. 171.

27th May, 1918.

1. 169th Infantry Brigade will relieve 167th Infantry Brigade on its present front on the night 30th/31st May. All details of relief to be arranged between B.Gs.C. concerned.

2. On relief 167th Infantry Brigade will become Divisional Reserve and will keep 2 battalions in DAINVILLE and 1 Battalion in ARRAS.

3. Maps, Air photos, Defence Schemes, trench stores and dumps will be handed over on relief.

4. Command will pass on completion of relief.

5. Completion of relief will be wired to Div. H.Q. by the code word "JUTLAND".

6. ACKNOWLEDGE.

F. B. Hurrell
Major
for Lieut-Colonel,
General Staff.

Issued at 8 p.m.

Copy No.		No.	
1.	167th Infantry Brigade.	16.	56th Div. Train.
2.	168th Infantry Brigade.	17.	56th Div. M.T.Coy.
3.	169th Infantry Brigade.	18.	A.D.C.
4.	1/5th Cheshire Regt.	19.	Camp Commandant.
5.	C.R.A.	20.	56th Div. Employ.Coy.
6.	Right H.A.Group.	21.	French Mission.
7.	C.R.E.	22.	XVII Corps.
8.	56th Div.M.G.Bn.	23.	" "
9.	56th Div.Signal Coy.	24.	2nd Can. Division.
10.	56th Div. Gas Officer.	25.	15th Division.
11.	A.D.M.S.	26.)	War Diary.
12.	A/Q.	27.)	
13.	A.P.M.	28.	File.
14.	D.A.D.O.S.		
15.	D.A.D.V.S.		

SECRET   *appx.* III

56th DIVISION TACTICAL PROGRESS REPORT No. 52.
From 6 a.m. 28th May to 6 a.m. 29th May, 1918.

Not to be taken further forward than Bn. H.Qrs.
Previous copy to be burnt.

OPERATIONS.

A raid was carried out at 11 p.m. last night on the enemy's trenches in N.2.c. & d. and N.8.a. & c. Stubborn resistance on the part of the enemy was encountered and many casualties inflicted. One wounded Sergeant Major was captured and two light Machine Guns. The prisoner belonged to the 12th Coy. 3rd Bn. 50 I.R., 214th Division.

ARTILLERY. Our Activity.

Field Artillery. Wire cutting operations on N.2.c. in connection with the raid by right Brigade were completed during the afternoon.

Movement was engaged in N.4.b. and AIRY CORNER.

An NF. call on N.4.c.4.0. was answered at 9.20 p.m. resulting in MOK correction from 'plane.

Instructional shoots were carried out by 4.5" Hows and 18-pdrs.
During the afternoon batteries registered and checked lines.
At 11.0 p.m. all batteries fired in support of raid by 167th Inf.Bde.
During the night harassing fire was carried out, special attention being paid to H.33.d.2.4., roads and tracks N.3.b. and N.4.a., CAMBRAI ROAD, trenches N.4.a. & c. areas H.28.c., N.15.a. and roads and tracks N.9.

Heavy Artillery. Working parties were engaged and dispersed at I.31.b., N.12.b.99. and N.29.a.95.70. 6" Hows. engaged hostile T.M. at N.9.a.31. scoring an O.K.; men were seen to run away; several appeared to be wounded. Dugout at N.21.a.61. was fired on with satisfactory results.

Enemy Activity. Hostile artillery has been normal during the last 24 hours. BLANGY G.24.a., G.18., H.31 central, G.29.a. & c., BRICKWORKS and G.36.a. received considerable attention.

Gas shell were fired during the period on C.T.M.6.a. & c. and N.7.c., G.29.b., G.30.a., G.28.b. and a few on M.10.a. & b.

A 15 cm. How. was active on Grid 91° 30' from M.16.a.99.47.

During the night a T.M. was active on FEUCHY SWITCH from H.34.a.86.61.

During the afternoon and evening TELEGRAPH HILL, ARRAS, BEAUMETZ and TILLOY were shelled intermittently.

Time. From.	To.	No. & nature of rounds.		Locality shelled.	Direction.
11 a.m.	12 noon	200	4.2"	BLANGY, G.24.a.	
11.30 a.m.	1 p.m.	100	4.2"	CAMBRAI RD.G.36.a.9.9.	GUEMAPPE.
	1.35 p.m.	80	5.9"	H.20.a.	91° grid by sound from H.23.a.81.70.
2.0	4.30 p.m.	100	4.2"	CAMBRAI RD. G.36.a.9.9.	GUEMAPPE.
3.20	6.0 p.m.	250	4.2" & 5.9"	BRICKWORKS.	WANCOURT.
4.0	4.45 p.m.	100	4.2"	G.36.a.	-----
	4.18 p.m.	100	4.2"	G.18. area.	-----
5.0	5.30 p.m.	100	4.2"	H.31 central.	-----
During night.		(?)	77 mm.	TILLOY Front and Support trenches.	From G.B. 40°.30' taken from shell scoop at H.25.b.25.25.
1.10	2.0 a.m.	60	(?)	G.29.a. & c.	Four bursts of fire of 15 rds.

TRENCH MORTARS. Ours. 713 rounds were fired in connection with the raid. 12 rounds were fired on target at N.8.a.47.90. at 4.30 a.m. with good effect.

Enemy's. From 2.25 a.m. to 2.35 a.m. 4 rounds fired on NOISY WORK by M.T.M. at N.8.b.8.0. 5 rounds were fired by same T.M. on NOISY WORK between 3.10 a.m. and 3.35 a.m. A L.T.M. was observed firing from vicinity of N.3.a.1.1.

H.T.M. at N.3.d.2.7. and another at approx. N.3.c.85.30 fired on the vicinity of TILLOY WOOD. T.M. at H.28.a.5.5. fired few rounds on BROKEN LANE.

- 2 -

MACHINE GUNS.   Ours. In conjunction with raid carried out by
Right Brigade,   a machine gun barrage was put down from
10.55 p.m. to 11.32 p.m., 24 guns firing a total of 46,250 rds. at
rate of from 50 to 125 rounds per minute.
   Enemy's.   Active during the raid. Engaged our aircraft during
the day.
INTELLIGENCE.   Individual movement was normal.
7.55 a.m. 18 men in parties of threes moved from N.10.a.85.20.
      carrying what appeared to be small boxes dumping them at
      N.10.c.9.9. afterwards returning by same route.
8.20 a.m. 3 linesmen at work on wires from pill box at N.5.a.1.4.
      and S.E. to CARLISLE TRENCH.
4.5 p.m. 7 men got out of trench at N.4.c.65.50 and examined wire.
      Afterwards entered NOVA SCOTIA TRENCH.
   The usual individual movement round KILT TRENCH, CROMARTY TRENCH
and NOVA SCOTIA TRENCH was observed.
1.25 p.m. N.4.c.50.45. 2 men apparently on sentry duty.
6.20 p.m. 2 men carrying sandbags along track through H.34.b. in
      S.E. direction, disappearing at H.34.d.85.90.
   There was slight individual movement during the day on ARRAS -
CAMBRAI Road in N.4.
Information from patrols.
   H.27.d.05.85. A number of men in single file hurried back to post
        at H.27.d.50.80 on sighting our patrol.
   H.27.d.50.80. Much individual movement.
   H.32.b.9.1.   (Gun pits) A thin belt of wire running S. 100 yds.
        W. of WHITE MOUND.
   H.32.d.50.15   Very light fired.
   H.33.a.9.3.   Post unoccupied. There were signs of recent
        occupation, viz. tins and refuse.
LOCATIONS.
   T.Ms.   N.9.a.3.1.   engaged by 6" Hows.
        H.34.a.86.61
        H.3.d.2.7.
        N.3.c.85.30 approx.
        H.28.a.5.5.

   M.Gs.   H.28.a.1.3.
        H.33.c.00.25. (patrol).

H.Q. 56th Divn.
29.5.18.
                                Lieut-Colonel,
                                General Staff.

Further details of Raid.
   The raiding parties penetrated enemy's positions to a depth of over
300 yards on a front of 1000 yds. The Right raiding party crossed
BILL TR. N.8.a. blew up PILL BOX N.8.a.7.7. and reached ELGIN TR.
where they met and killed the enemy garrison. BILL TR. was much
knocked about by our artillery and contained many dead Germans.
   The left raiding party reached all objectives including N.2.a.7.2.
and bombed up towards dug-outs at N.2.d.15.85 where the garrison put
up a strong resistance.
   ORKNEY TR. was found strongly manned and much damaged by our arty.
The surviving garrison hid in small shelters in the trench and were
promptly bayonetted by the raiders.
   A great deal of execution was done at the point of the bayonet and
most of the raiders returned with bloody weapons.
   The enemy's casualties were very heavy and are estimated at over 200.
It was thought a large working party was engaged repairing the damage
caused by the previous day's bombardment.

CONFIDENTIAL.

WAR DIARY

OF

GENERAL STAFF.

56th DIVISION.

From 1st JUNE, 1918.
To   30th JUNE, 1918.

****

Army Form C. 2118.

WAR DIARY
or
INTELLIGENCE SUMMARY.
(Erase heading not required.)

Instructions regarding War Diaries and Intelligence Summaries are contained in F. S. Regs., Part II. and the Staff Manual respectively. Title pages will be prepared in manuscript.

Place	Date	Hour	Summary of Events and Information	Remarks and references to Appendices
WARLUS	June 1.		Quiet day. Enemy shelled our extreme right during the morning with 77 mms. At 9 p.m. the 13th London Regt. raided the enemy's trenches on the CAMBRAI Road about 1,000 yds. East of our front line. 27 prisoners were captured and 1 M.G. Many enemy killed. Our casualties about 20 (1 killed). Identifications normal. Enemy shelled RONVILLE and area fairly heavily with gas during the night.	APP. III
	2.		Congratulatory wire received from Corps Commander on result of raid. Weather fine, visibility good. 168th Inf. Bde. carried out an inter-battalion relief.	APPX. I
	3.		Situation quiet. Our artillery fired on enemy movement. Visibility good. Hostile artillery shelled BLANGY and TILLOY.	
	4.		Quiet day. Nothing to report.	
	5.		Quiet day. O.O. No. 172 issued for the relief of 168th Inf. Bde. by 167th Inf. Bde. on night 8th/9th June. Slight hostile gas shelling of our tracks during night.	APPX. II
	6.		Situation quiet. Weather fine and visibility good. Enemy shelled ARRAS obtaining direct hit on Left Bde. H.Q's. No damage.	
	7.		Enemy shelled vicinity of Right Battn. H.Q., Left Bde., with gas shell from 4 to 6 a.m. His artillery was active during the day on TELEGRAPH HILL. Weather sultry, visibility poor. Situation normal. Quiet day. Heavy shelling on our Right Flank at 9.30 p.m. The enemy subsequently attempted to raid the 2nd Canadian Divn. on our right.	
	8.		The Army Commander visited the G.O.C. in the Left Section; relief reported complete at 2 a.m. 167th Inf. Bde. relieved 168th Inf. Bde. In the Left Section; relief reported complete at 2 a.m. Enemy shelled BLANGY and ST. SAUVEUR, but quiet on forward areas. Considerable enemy movement seen near CAMBRAI Road at dusk. Harassing fire carried out on centres of movement during the night.	APPX. I
	9.		The G.O.C. received verbal orders from Corps Commander to carry out a large scale raid. G.O.C. visited B.G.C. 168th Inf. Bde. and gave him verbal instructions to raid with his Brigade just south of the SCARPE River.	
	10.		Quiet day. 167th Inf. Bde. raided an enemy post and obtained two prisoners; identifications normal. Our casualties two slightly wounded.	APPX. II
	11.		Hostile artillery active in TILLOY region during the morning. Quiet for remainder of day. Operation Order No. 173 issued with instructions for the raid by 168th Inf. Bde.	
	12.		Quiet day. At 3 p.m. the L.R.B. raided the enemy outposts and killed 24 and captured 1 T.M. and destroyed 2 others. Identifications obtained - normal.	APPX. II
	13.		Amendment to O.O. No. 173 issued. Situation normal.	

Army Form C. 2118.

WAR DIARY
or
INTELLIGENCE SUMMARY.
(Erase heading not required.)

Instructions regarding War Diaries and Intelligence Summaries are contained in F. S. Regs., Part II. and the Staff Manual respectively. Title pages will be prepared in manuscript.

Place	Date	Hour	Summary of Events and Information	Remarks and references to Appendices
WARLUS	June 13		Enemy artillery very quiet. 56th Div. Instructions No. 1 issued in connection with forthcoming big raid. O.O. No. 174 issued for co-operation by 167th Inf. Bde. with 168th Inf. Bde. in the large scale raid.	APPX. II
	14		Quiet day. Visibility good. Orders received from XVII Corps to cancel the large scale raid.	APPX. II
	15		Quiet day. O.O. No. 175 issued for relief of 169th Inf. Bde. by 168th Inf. Bde. in Right Section.	APPX. II
	16		Quiet day. Enemy dropped some bombs on ARRAS during the evening. One hostile aeroplane brought down by our A.A. Lewis Guns. Another was shot down by one of our fighting machines and fell just outside our wire.	
	17		Quiet day. Hostile 'planes dropped 6 bombs on ARRAS during the night. 168th Inf. Bde. relieved 169th Inf. Bde. in the Right Section.	APPX. I
	18		Quiet day. Hostile artillery quiet except for a few gas shells on Right Brigade front. Visibility good.	
	19		Quiet day. At 9 a.m. the enemy put down a heavy barrage on our Right Brigade front with 4.2" and 77 mms. lasting 4 minutes.	
	20		O.O. No. 176 issued for readjustment of boundary between Brigade Sections. Very quiet day. Nothing to report. During the night 4 deserters, 358 I.R. (normal) came into our lines. No indications of hostile offensive seen.	APPX. II
	21		Quiet day. Hostile artillery shelled Right Battn. H.Q's, Left Brigade, during the morning. 167th Inf. Bde. carried out an inter-battalion relief.	
	22		G.O.C. and G.S.O. I attended Corps Conference. Quiet day.	APPX. I
	23		Very quiet day. Nothing to report.	
	24.		O.O. No. 177 issued for relief of 167th Inf. Bde. by 169th Inf. Bde. on night 26th/27th June. Quiet day. Abnormal movement of German officers seen during the day inspecting their own lines and apparently examining ours.	APPX. II
	25		At 12.45 a.m. the 1st London Regt. on the right and the 8th Middlesex on the left raided the enemy's outposts in H.33 central and H.27.d. 2 Germans killed, 6 believed wounded; no identifications secured. At 11 a.m. our artillery carried out successful concentrated shoot on gunpits occupied by the enemy in H.27.d. and H.33.b. The enemy did not retaliate. Remainder of the day was quiet.	

Army Form C. 2118.

WAR DIARY
or
INTELLIGENCE SUMMARY.

(Erase heading not required.)

Instructions regarding War Diaries and Intelligence Summaries are contained in F.S. Regs., Part II. and the Staff Manual respectively. Title pages will be prepared in manuscript.

Place	Date	Hour	Summary of Events and Information	Remarks and references to Appendices
WARLUS	June 26		Quiet day. 169th Inf. Bde. relieved 167th Inf. Bde. in the Left Brigade section during night 26th/27th.	
	27		Quiet day. O.O. No. 178 issued referring to readjustment of boundary between 56th Division and 2nd Canadian Division, to be carried out by 6 a.m. June 28th.	APPX. II
	28		Quiet day. Hostile artillery slightly more active.	APPX. I
	29		Weather warm. Visibility good. 168th Inf. Bde. carried out an inter-battn. relief. Situation quiet.	
	30		Hostile artillery more active. Some shelling of TILLOY and area during morning. Also enemy reported to be registering 4.2s. in Right Brigade area.	

2nd July, 1918.

Major-General,
Commanding 56th Division.

56th DIVISION.   LOCATION TABLE at 6 p.m.   June 1918.   APPENDIX 1

	1	2	3	4	5	6	7	8	9	10	11	12	13	14	15	16
Div. H.Q.	WARLUS															
167th Inf.Bde.H.Q.	BERNEVILLE															
1st London Regt.	DAINVILLE					ARRAS			G28b07.ARRAS							H31b38(R)
7th Middx. Regt.	ARRAS								G30c10.25(S)							
8th "	DAINVILLE					DAINVILLE			H25b25.25 (L)							G30c10.25(S)
									H31b3.8 (R)							
168th Inf.Bde.H.Q.	G28b07 ARRAS								BERNEVILLE							
4th London Regt.	G30c10.25(S)		H31b38(R)						DAINVILLE							
13th "	H31b38(R)		G30c10.25(S)						ARRAS	BERNEVILLE						
14th "	H25b25.25(L)								DAINVILLE							
169th Inf.Bde.H.Q.	G27b82 ARRAS															
2nd London Regt.	M6b26(S)															
5th "	H31c50(L)															
18th "	N7a28(R)															
Div. Arty. H.Q.	WARLUS															
280th Bde.	M867540															
281st	G27b99.33															
Pioneers.	G27b77 ARRAS															
M.G.Battn. H.Q.	WARLUS															

KEY
FRONT LINE Bn   RED
SUPPORT "   GREEN
RESERVE "   VIOLET

56th DIVISION.　　LOCATION TABLE at 8 p.m.　　June 1918.　　APPENDIX

	17	18	19	20	21	22	23	24	25	26	27	28	29	30
Div. H.Q.	WARLUS													
167th Inf.Bde.H.Q.	G28 b07 ARRAS													
1st London Regt.	H31 b38(R)													
7th Middx. Regt.	H25 b25.25(L)				G30c10.25(S)						DAINVILLE			ARRAS
8th "	G30c10.25(S)				H25 b25.25(L)						ARRAS			DAINVILLE
168th Inf.Bde.H.Q.	BERNEVILLE	G27 b82 ARRAS												
4th London Regt.	DAINVILLE	M6 b26(S)										G28 b07 ARRAS		
13th "	BERNEVILLE	N7a 28(R)						H31c 50(L)				H31 b38(R)		M6 b26(S)
14th "	DAINVILLE	H31c 50(L)						M6 b24(S)				G30c10.25(S)		N7a 28(R)
169th Inf.Bde.H.Q.	G27 b82	BERNEVILLE										H25 b25.25(L)		
2nd London Regt.	M6 b26(S)	DAINVILLE												
5th "	H31c 50	BERNEVILLE												
18th "	N7a 28	DAINVILLE												
Div. Arty. H.Q.	WARLUS													
280th Bde.	M8 b76.40													
281st "	G27 b99.33													
Pioneers.	ARRAS													
M.G.Battn. H.Q.	WARLUS													

KEY.　FRONT LINE BN.　RED
　　　SUPPORT　"　GREEN
　　　RESERVE　"　VIOLET

SECRET   Copy No. 26

56th DIVISION ORDER No. 172.

5th June, 1918.

1. 167th Infantry Brigade will relieve 168th Infantry Brigade on its present front on the night 8th/9th June. All details of relief to be arranged between B.Gs.C. concerned.

2. On relief 168th Infantry Brigade will become Divisional Reserve and will keep 2 battalions in DAINVILLE and 1 Battalion in ARRAS.

3. Maps, Air photos, Defence Schemes, Trench Stores and Dumps will be handed over on relief.

4. Command will pass on completion of relief.

5. Completion of relief will be wired to Div. H.Q. by the code word "KITCHENER".

6. ACKNOWLEDGE.

F. B. Hurndall Major
for
Lieut-Colonel,
General Staff

Issued at 8 a.m.

Copy No. 1. 167th Infantry Brigade.
2. 168th Infantry Brigade.
3. 169th Infantry Brigade.
4. 1/5th Cheshire Regt.
5. C.R.A.
6. Right H.A.Group.
7. C.R.E.
8. 56th Bn. M.G.Corps.
9. 56th Div. Signal Coy.
10. 56th Div. Gas Officer.
11. A.D.M.S.
12. A/Q.
13. A.P.M.
14. D.A.D.O.S.
No. 15. D.A.D.V.S.
16. 56th Div. Train.
17. 56th Div. M.T.Coy.
18. A.D.C.
19. Camp Commandant.
20. 56th Div. Employ. Coy.
21. French Mission.
22. XVII Corps.
23.   "   "
24. 2nd Canadian Division.
25. 15th Division.
26.) War Diary.
27.)
28. File.

SECRET   Copy No. 18

56th DIVISION ORDER No. 173

11th June, 1918.

1. On a date to be notified later 168th Infantry Brigade will carry out a raid with the object of causing loss to the enemy, destroying his defences and capturing prisoners and material.

2. The boundaries of the area to be raided will be :-

    On the North - The marshy valley of the SCARPE, as far as LANCER LANE, H.23.b.20.45.
    On the East - LANCER LANE to its junction with PELVES LANE at H.29.d.15.80.
    On the South - PELVES LANE from H.29.d.15.80 to our front line in H.32.a. (This southern boundary will be extended into HALIFAX - CALIFORNIA Trench, as far South as H.34.central approx.)

3. The objectives will be :-

    The enemy's outpost positions in H.27.d.
    ICELAND TRENCH.
    IONIAN TRENCH.
    MORAY TRENCH.
    INDIAN TRENCH.
    ITALIAN TRENCH.
    Defences and dugouts in the vicinity of the Railway Cutting in H.28.a, H.22.d. and H.23.c.

4. The troops of 168th Infantry Brigade will move into position on the night proceeding the day of the raid.

5. The B.G.C. 167th Infantry Brigade will arrange with the B.G.C. 168th Infantry Brigade -

(a). For the relief of troops of 167th Inf. Bde. in the FEUCHY Trench system, BROKEN LANE and BATTERY VALLEY (including all Coy. H.Qrs.) and for the temporary accommodation of one Company 168th Inf. Bde. in TILLOY FRONT LINE in H.26.a., if desired by B.G.C. 168th Inf. Bde.

(b). To reoccupy the trenches and area specified in (a), with the exception of the Coy. H.Qrs., as soon as the troops of 168th Inf. Bde. move forward at Zero hour. The Coy. H.Qrs. can be reoccupied as vacated by the Battalion H.Qrs. of 168th Inf. Bde. moving forward.

(c). To vacate such portions of trenches in rear of the TILLOY Systems and North of the CAMBRAI Road, as may be required by the B.G.C. 168th Inf. Bde. for purposes of reassembly.

(d). To reoccupy positions vacated as in (c) above, on the final withdrawal of 168th Inf. Bde. to billets.

(e). To place the Left Battalion H.Q. at the disposal of B.G.C. 168th Inf. Bde. for such time previous to and after the raid as may be considered necessary by B.G.C. 168th Inf. Bde.

(f). To prepare gaps through the wire of BROKEN LANE, the trenches of the FEUCHY System and TILLOY Trench as may be required by B.G.C. 168th Inf. Bde. and to close them after the conclusion of the operation.

/6.

- 2 -

6. Details of Artillery support will be arranged direct by the B.G.C. 168th Inf. Bde. with the C.R.A. and O.C. Right Group H.A.

7. The D.M.G.C. will arrange to place 1 section at the disposal of 168th Inf. Bde. to accompany the raiding troops for the protection of the right flank from attack from ORANGE HILL.

   He will also arrange further details of M.G. co-operation with B.G.C. 168th Inf. Bde. and will arrange direct with the D.M.G.C. 15th Division, for an enfilade creeping barrage from North of the SCARPE and for such other co-operation as is desired and can be afforded.

8. The C.R.E. will arrange to supply Sappers and mobile charges, and to place trench ladders and bridges, as required by B.G.C. 168th Inf. Bde.

9. The A.D.M.S. will arrange for the evacuation of wounded.

10. Prisoners will be handed over to the A.P.M. at ARRAS CITADEL.

11. Zero hour will be communicated later.

12. ACKNOWLEDGE.

B. Pakenham

Lieut-Colonel,
General Staff.

Issued at 1.30 p.m.

Copy No. 1. 167th Infantry Brigade.　　No. 11. "Q"
     2. 168th Infantry Brigade.   12. A.P.M.
     3. 169th Infantry Brigade.   13. A.D.C.
     4. 1/5th Cheshire Regt.   14. XVII Corps
     5. C.R.A.   15. "   "
     6. Right H.A. Group.   16. 2nd Canadian Divn.
     7. C.R.E.   17. 15th Division.
     8. 56th Bn. M.G. Corps.   18.)
     9. 56th Div. Signal Coy.   19.) War Diary.
    10. A.D.M.S.   20. File.

SECRET.   *War Diary Copies*   56th Division G.3/720.

AMENDMENT to 56th DIVISION ORDER No. 173.

Erase para. 10, and substitute :-

10. Prisoners will be handed over to the A.P.M. at the Support Battalion H.Q. at G.30.c.20.30.
     167th Infantry Brigade will detail an escort of 2 N.C.Os. and 15 men to report to the A.P.M. at above H.Q. at Zero plus 120.

H.Q. 56th Divn.   F. B. Hurndall
12th June, 1918.   Major
                                          for   Lieut-Colonel,
                                                   General Staff.

To all recipients of Order No. 173.

167th Infantry Brigade. }
168th Infantry Brigade. }   To ACKNOWLEDGE.
A.P.M.   }

SECRET. *War Diary Copies*
Appx II

56th Division G.3/725.

Copy No. 9

56th DIVISION INSTRUCTIONS No. 1.

For forthcoming Operation by 168th Infantry Brigade.

SYNCHRONISATION OF WATCHES.

1. Watches will be synchronised at the Headquarters of the Left Brigade on Y/Z day at 6 p.m., and on Z day at 10 a.m. and 2 p.m.

2. A Divisional Staff Officer will be at the Left Brigade H.Q. at the above stated times.
   Representatives from the following will be ordered to meet him there.

   168th Infantry Brigade.
   167th Infantry Brigade.
   C.R.A.
   Right H.A. Group.
   56th Bn. M.G. Corps.

3. Synchronisation down to Battalions, Batteries and M.G. Companies will be arranged by Commanders concerned.
   The telephone will not be used for this purpose in advance of Brigade H.Q.

4. ACKNOWLEDGE.

Y. B. Hunnell
Major
for Lieut-Colonel,
General Staff, 56th Division.

13th June, 1918.

Copy No. 1. 167th Infantry Brigade.
      2. 168th Infantry Brigade.
      3. 169th Infantry Brigade.
      4. C.R.A.
      5. Right H.A. Group.
      6. C.R.E.
      7. 56th Bn. M.G. Corps.
      8. O.C. 56th Div. Signal Coy.
      9.) War Diary.
     10.)
     11. File.

SECRET.   *War Diary*   Copy No. _____

56th DIVISION ORDER No. 174.

13th June, 1918.

    In continuation of 56th Div. Order No. 173 of 11th June, 167th Infantry Brigade will co-operate with 168th Infantry Brigade by carrying out a raid on the enemy outpost position in the vicinity of H.33 central.

    B.G.C., 167th Infantry Brigade will communicate all details to B.G.C., 168th Infantry Brigade, C.R.A. and D.M.G.C. so that barrages can be regulated.

    ACKNOWLEDGE.

F. B. Hurndall, Major
for
Lieut-Colonel,
General Staff.

Issued at 1.30 p.m.

Copy No.		No.	
1.	167th Infantry Brigade.	11.	"Q"
2.	168th Infantry Brigade.	12.	A.P.M.
3.	169th Infantry Brigade.	13.	A.D.C.
4.	1/5th Cheshire Regt.	14.	XVII Corps.
5.	C.R.A.	15.	" "
6.	Right H.A.Group.	16.	2nd Canad. Divn.
7.	C.R.E.	17.	15th Division.
8.	56th Bn. M.G.Corps.	18.)	War Diary.
9.	56th Div. Signal Coy.	19.)	
10.	A.D.M.S.	20.	File.

War Diary.

Appx II

SECRET.   Copy No. 26

56th DIVISION ORDER No. 175.

15th June 1918.

1. 168th Infantry Brigade will relieve 169th Infantry Brigade on its present front on the night 17th/18th June. All details of relief to be arranged between B.Gs.C. concerned.

2. On relief 169th Infantry Brigade will become Divisional Reserve and will keep 2 Battalions in DAINVILLE. The location of the third battalion will be notified later.

3. Maps, Air photos, Defence Schemes, Trench Stores and Dumps will be handed over on relief.

4. Command will pass on completion of relief.

5. Completion of relief will be wired to Div. H.Q. by the code word "WELLINGTON".

6. ACKNOWLEDGE.

B Pakenham

Issued at 8 p.m.   Lieut-Colonel,
                                                    General Staff.

Copy No. 1. 167th Infantry Brigade.   No. 15. D.A.D.V.S.
        2. 168th Infantry Brigade.   16. 56th Div. Train.
        3. 169th Infantry Brigade.   17. 56th Div. M.T.Coy.
        4. 1/5th Cheshire Regt.   18. A.D.C.
        5. C.R.A.   19. Camp Commandant.
        6. Right H.A.Group.   20. 56th Div.Emply. Coy.
        7. C.R.E.   21. French Mission.
        8. 56th Bn. M.G.Corps.   22. XVII Corps.
        9. 56th Div.Signal Coy.   23.   "   "
       10. 56th Div. Gas Officer.   24. 2nd Canadian Division.
       11. A.D.M.S.   25. 15th Division.
       12. A/Q.   26.) War Diary.
       13. A.P.M.   27.)
       14. D.A.D.O.S.   28. File.

SECRET   Copy No. 19

56th DIVISION ORDER No. 176.

19th June, 1918.

1. 167th Infantry Brigade will take over the Front of the 168th Infantry Brigade, as far South as the grid line between H.32 and N.2.
   Details of relief to be arranged between B.Gs.C. concerned. Relief to be completed by 6 a.m. 22nd June.

2. On completion of relief the Inter-Brigade Boundary will be the grid line between H.32 and N.2 as far west as H.31.c.15.00 - H.31.c.00.20 - G.36.d.70.00. Thence West along the grid line to G.35.c.00.00 - G.32.b.95.10, L.30.c.50.50, L.28.c.40.50.

3. The Headquarters of the Left Battalion, Right Brigade, will be retained as such by the Right Brigade until completion of the new Battalion Headquarters.

4. Completion of relief to be reported to Div. H.Q. by Code Word "LEMBERG".

5. ACKNOWLEDGE.

J. B. Hurndall
Major
for
Lieut-Colonel,
General Staff.

Issued at 8 p.m.

Copy No. 1. 167th Infantry Brigade.   No. 11. A.D.M.S.
         2. 168th Infantry Brigade.   12. "Q"
         3. 169th Infantry Brigade.   13. A.P.M.
         4. 1/5th Cheshire Regt.   14. A.D.C.
         5. C.R.A.   15. XVII Corps.
         6. Right H.A.Group.   16.   "   "
         7. C.R.E.   17. 2nd Canadian Division.
         8. 56th Bn. M.G.Corps.   18. 15th Division.
         9. 56th Div. Signal Coy.   19.) War Diary.
        10. 56th Div. Gas Officer.   20.)
                                               21. File.

War Diary.   App II

SECRET.   Copy No. 26

56th DIVISION ORDER No. 177.

23rd June 1918.

1.   169th Infantry Brigade will relieve 167th Infantry Brigade on its present front on the night 26th/27th June. All details of relief to be arranged between B.Gs.C. concerned.

2.   On relief 167th Infantry Brigade will become Divisional Reserve and will move, less one battalion, to the DAINVILLE - BERNEVILLE Area.
       One battalion will be accommodated in ARRAS and will be available for work under C.R.E. on and after night 28th/29th. This battalion may be relieved under Brigade arrangements provided work is not interfered with.

3.   Maps, Air photos, Defence Schemes, Trench Stores and Dumps will be handed over on relief.

4.   Command will pass on completion of relief.

5.   Completion of relief will be wired to Div. H.Q. by the code word "CARSO".

6.   ACKNOWLEDGE.

                                                                  Lieut-Colonel,
Issued at 8 a.m.   General Staff.

Copy No. 1. 167th Infantry Brigade.   No. 15. D.A.D.V.S.
        2. 168th Infantry Brigade.   16. 56th Div. Train.
        3. 169th Infantry Brigade.   17. 56th Div. M.T.Coy.
        4. 1/5th Cheshire Regt.   18. A.D.C.
        5. C.R.A.   19. Camp Commandant.
        6. Right H.A.Group.   20. 56th Div.Employ.Coy.
        7. C.R.E.   21. French Mission.
        8. 56th Bn.M.G.Corps.   22. XVII Corps.
        9. 56th Div. Signal Coy.   23.   "   "
      10. 56th Div. Gas Officer.   24. 2nd Canadian Division.
      11. A.D.M.S.   25. 15th Division.
      12. A/Q.   26.) War Diary.
      13. A.P.M.   27.)
      14. D.A.D.O.S.   28. File.

E/J.

War Diary   Appx II

SECRET.   Copy No. 19

56th DIVISION ORDER No. 178.

27th June, 1918.

1. 168th Infantry Brigade will hand over to 6th Canadian Infantry Brigade parts of the TELEGRAPH HILL SWITCH and Support, and part of BLANGY TRENCH and Support.
Details of relief to be arranged between B.Gs.C. concerned.
Relief to be completed by 6 a.m. 28th June.

2. On completion of relief the Boundary between 56th Division and 2nd Canadian Division will be as follows :-
The grid line between N.7 and N.13 produced West as far as M.12.d.2.0. - Junction of SOUTH ALLEY and TELEGRAPH HILL SWITCH M.12.c.95.28. - Junction of SOUTH ALLEY and TELEGRAPH HILL SUPPORT M.12.c.85.55. (SOUTH ALLEY inclusive to 56th Division) - Junction of C.T. & BLANGY Trench at M.11.d.12. (inclusive to 56th Division). - thence to original boundary at M.11.c.2.0.

3. Completion of relief to be wired to Div. H.Q. by code word "CAWNPORE".

4. ACKNOWLEDGE.

                                          F. B. Hurndall
                                               Major
                                            Lieut-Colonel,
                                            General Staff.

Issued at 1.30 p.m.

Copy No.				
1.	167th Infantry Brigade.	11.	A.D.M.S.
2.	168th Infantry Brigade.	12.	"Q"
3.	169th Infantry Brigade.	13.	A.P.M.
4.	1/5th Cheshire Regt.	14.	A.D.C.
5.	C.R.A.	15.	XVII Corps.
6.	Right H.A.Group.	16.	"
7.	C.R.E.	17.	2nd Canadian Division.
8.	56th Bn. M.G.Corps.	18.	15th Division.
9.	56th Div. Signal Coy.	19.)	War Diary.
10.	56th Div. Gas Officer.	20.)	
		21.	File.

"A" Form.
MESSAGES AND SIGNALS.

Army Form C. 2121. (In pads of 100.)

TO:
- 17 Corps
- 2 Can Divn
- 15 Division

Sender's Number.	Day of Month.	In reply to Number.	
G. 701	2		AAA

Details of raid last night aaa one Coy. and one platoon assembled night 31st/1st in old trench H.32.d. and gunpits H.32.b.90 600 yds in front of our front line and lay up till 9 pm evening of 1st aaa Objectives area around Water Tanks and stone dump on CAMBRAI Road 1000 yds east of our front line aaa Captures 24 unwounded and 3 wounded of 50th I.R. normal and 1 M.G. aaa Many enemy claimed killed and many seen running away on the south of CAMBRAI Road aaa Several shelters and dugouts bombed and 1 T.M. blown up aaa Our casualties 1 O.R. killed 18 O.Rs wounded and 1 O.R. wounded and missing aaa Prisoners state their whole company practically wiped out aaa Addsd 17 Corps reptd Flank Divns.

From: 56th Divn.

Place:

Time: 9.50 am

(Z) (sd) F.B. HURNDALL, Major, General Staff

CONFIDENTIAL.

WAR DIARY

OF

GENERAL STAFF

56th DIVISION.

FROM   JULY 1st 1918.
TO   JULY 31st 1918.

------------oOo------------

Army Form C. 2118.

WAR DIARY
or
INTELLIGENCE SUMMARY.

(Erase heading not required.)

Instructions regarding War Diaries and Intelligence Summaries are contained in F.S. Regs., Part II. and the Staff Manual respectively. Title pages will be prepared in manuscript.

Place	Date	Hour	Summary of Events and Information	Remarks and references to Appendices
WARLUS	JULY 1st		At 5.30 a.m. the enemy put a barrage on our front line commencing on the left and extending along the whole front. This lasted 20 minutes. No infantry action. This was repeated at 6 p.m. Otherwise quiet day. Operation Order No. 179 issued for relief of 168th Inf. Bde. by 167th Inf. Bde. on night 5th/6th July.	APPX. II
	2nd		Weather warm. Visibility indifferent. Enemy very quiet. Our artillery carried out most successful shoot on enemy post in old gunpits. Fires were caused and T.M. ammunition exploded. Considerable movement seen at dusk opposite right Bde. front. Local relief suspected.	
	3rd		169th Inf. Bde. carried out an inter-battn. relief.	APPX. I
	4th		Quiet day. Visibility good. A man of 50 I.R. was shot and brought in by 5th London Regt. Identification normal.	
	5th		Quiet day. Some hostile shelling of BLANGY and DAINVILLE. No damage. Our artillery carried out increased harassing fire at night owing to suspected relief of 214th Division. Hostile aeroplanes dropped 6 bombs on ARRAS during the night.	
	6th		Quiet day. 167th Inf. Bde. relieved 168th Inf. Bde. in the Right Section. Situation normal. Our heavy artillery carried out a successful shoot on enemy positions and trench mortars in AIRY WORK.	APPX. I
	7th		Quiet day. Weather warm. Visibility poor. Major HURNDALL, G.S.O. III, left the Division for duty with XVII Corps as G.S.O. II, Training. Orders received from XVII Corps for relief of 56th Division by 2nd Canadian Division and part of 1st Canadian Division. To be complete by 9 a.m. 15th instant. 56th Div. Warning Order No. 180 on above issued.	APPX. II
	8th		Situation quiet. The Q.W.R. (169th Inf. Bde.) raided the enemy trenches on our extreme left front, capturing 3 prisoners and a M.G. Our casualties 11 of whom 10 very slightly wounded. Identifications normal. No knowledge of offensive.	
	9th		Quiet day. Hostile artillery carried out a destructive shoot on one of our 6" batteries. Considerable movement seen in enemy areas. Relief of 214th Division strongly suspected to be in progress.	
	10th		O.O. 181 issued for relief of 56th Division by 1st Canadian Division and 2nd Canadian Division. Quiet day. Thunderstorms. Hostile artillery shelled DAINVILLE, and a few H.V. shells over WARLUS during the morning.	APPX. II

Army Form C. 2118.

WAR DIARY
or
INTELLIGENCE SUMMARY.
(Erase heading not required.)

Instructions regarding War Diaries and Intelligence Summaries are contained in F. S. Regs., Part II. and the Staff Manual respectively. Title pages will be prepared in manuscript.

Place	Date	Hour	Summary of Events and Information	Remarks and references to Appendices
WARLUS	JULY 11th		Situation normal. Nothing to report.	
	12th		Quiet day. 14th London Regt. moved from ARRAS to BERNEVILLE. Orders received from XVII Corps for postponement of Div. Artillery relief for 4 days. Amendment to O.O. 181 issued accordingly.	APPX. I APPX.II
	13th		Quiet day. 168th Inf. Bde. moved from Div. Reserve to AVESNES LES COMTE area on relief by 4th Canadian Inf. Bde., 2nd Canadian Division. 2nd Canadian Inf. Bde. (1st Canadian Division) relieved portion of 169th Inf. Bde. in Left Section, 169th Inf. Bde. moving into Support in ARRAS. Orders received from XVII Corps that the Division was to move into the MONCHY BRETON Area and not the BRETENCOURT Area. O.O. No. 182 issued accordingly.	APPX. I APPX. I APPX.II
	14th		Command of Left Section of Div. front handed over to 1st Canadian Division at 10 a.m. Situation quiet on remainder of front. 168th Inf. Bde. marched from AVESNES LES COMTE Area to LIGNEREUIL Area. 167th Inf. Bde. were relieved by 4th Canadian Inf. Bde., 2nd Canadian Division, in the Right Section and moved into Support in DAINVILLE Area.	APPX. I APPX. I
ROELLECOURT	15th		Command of Right Sector handed over to 2nd Canadian Division at 10 a.m. Div. H.Q. moved to ROELLECOURT into G.H.Q. Reserve. 167th Inf. Bde. moved by train to MONCHY BRETON Area. 168th " " " " march route to CHELERS 169th " " " " train to DIEVAL Area. Scheme for move "A" by bus, "B" by Strategical train, "C" by Tactical Train, issued.	APPX. I APPX.II
	16th		Weather warm and thundery. All troops engaged in reorganising and bathing. Orders received from XVII Corps to move into CHATEAU DE LA HAIE, VILLERS BRULIN, DIEVAL Area, with Div. H.Q. at VILLERS CHATEL. 56th Div. Warning Order No. 183 issued accordingly.	APPX.II APPX.II
	17th		56th Div. Operation Order No. 184 issued for move. G.O.C. went on short leave to ENGLAND. B.G.C. 167th Inf. Bde. assumed temporary command. 133rd A. Bdes G.S.O.I + D.A.C. Battn. Accomodated in bivouacs nr Chateau de la Haie	
	18th		56th Division moved by march route into new area. Div. H.Q. opened at VILLERS CHATEL at 10 a.m. For location of units see Appx. I.	APPX. I
VILLERS CHATEL	19th		Weather fine. All units engaged in training. G.S.O. I, B.Gs.C. Inf. Bdes.and Os.C. Battns.	

Army Form C. 2118.

WAR DIARY
or
INTELLIGENCE SUMMARY.

(Erase heading not required.)

Instructions regarding War Diaries and Intelligence Summaries are contained in F.S. Regs., Part II. and the Staff Manual respectively. Title pages will be prepared in manuscript.

Place	Date	Hour	Summary of Events and Information	Remarks and references to Appendices
VILLERS CHATEL.	JULY 19th		reconnoitred assembly areas for counter-attack on VIII Corps front. O.O. No. 185 issued for relief of 56th Div. Artillery by 2 Army Fld. Arty. Bdes. To be complete by 22nd.	APPX. II
	20th		Thunderstorms. Nothing to report.	APPX. I
	21st.		Divisional Artillery relieved from the line and moved to FREVIN CAPELLE Area.	
	22nd		All units engaged in training.	
	23rd		Nothing to report. Very wet day.	
	24th		Training as usual.	
	25th		Hostile aeroplanes bombed area CHATEAU DE LA HAIE, causing casualties to 168th Inf. Bde.	
	26th		do.	
	27th		do.	
	28th		All units training.	
	29th		Orders received from XVII Corps for 56th Division to relieve the 1st Canadian Division in the line, relief to be complete by morning of August 2nd. O.O. No. 186 issued.	APPX. II
	30th		167th Inf. Bde. moved to BERNEVILLE - DAINVILLE Area by march route.	APPX. I
			169th " " " to CAUCOURT Area by march route.	APPX. II
	31st		O.O. No. 187 issued.	APPX. I
			167th Inf. Bde. and 168th Inf. Bde. took over the Left (TILLOY) and Right (VITASSE) Sections respectively relieving portions of 1st Canadian Division in the line.	

H.Q., 56th Divn.
4th August, 1918.

Major-General,
Commanding 56th Division.

APPENDIX 1

56th DIVISION. LOCATION TABLE at 8 p.m. JULY 1918.

	1	2	3	4	5	6	7	8	9	10	11	12	13	14	15	16
Div. H.Q.	Warlus														Roelcourt	
167th Inf. Bde. H.Q.	Bernéville														Orlencourt	
1st London Regt.	Arras					Arras (Right Section)									Monchy Breton	
7th Middl. Regt.	Dainville					Line (R)									Previllers	
8th "	Dainville			Arras		Support Line (L)									Ostreville	
168th Inf. Bde. H.Q.	Arras (Rt. Sect)					Bernéville							Avesnes le Comte	Lignereuil Chelers		
4th London Regt.	Line (L)					Dainville							Lattre Grand St Quentin Rullecourt	Tinques		
13th "	Support					Arras							" " " "	Bailleul		
14th "	Line (R)					Dainville						Bernéville Fosseux Lignereuil		Aux Grenailles Chelers		
169th Inf. Bde. H.Q.	Arras (left Sect)													Diéval		
2nd London Regt.	Line (R)								Support					Arras	Diéval	
5th "	Support			Line (L)										Arras	La Thieuloye	
16th "	Line (L)			Support					Line (R)					Arras	La Comté	
Div. Arty. H.Q.	Warlus															
280th Bde.	M.8.b.75.40															
281st	G.27.b.99.35															
Attached A.F.A. Bdes. 277. Bde.	G.28.b.15.81															
311 "	G.22.d.05.15															
Pioneers	Arras												Hautville	Gouy en Ternois	Averdoingt	
M.G.Battn. H.Q.	Warlus													Warlus	Magnicourt en Comte	

In the line — RED
In Support — GREEN
In Reserve — BLUE
At Rest — BLACK

56th DIVISION. LOCATION TABLE at 6 p.m. JULY 1918. APPENDIX.

	17	18	19	20	21	22	23	24	25	26	27	28	29	30	31	Aug. 1
Div. H.Q.	Rebecourt Villers Chatel															
167th Inf.Bde. H.Q.	Orlencourt Villers Brulins														Berneville M.14.a.70.95 Reserve	
1st London Regt.	Monchy Breton														Berville	
7th Middlx. Regt.	Frevillers Cambligneul														Dainville M.2.d.0.2 Support	
8th " "	Ostreville Villers Brulin Guestreville														Dainville	
168th Inf.Bde. H.Q.	Chelers Villers au Chateau Bois de la Haie (x.13.b.36)*														G.28.a.98. Sector Support	
4th London Regt.	Tinques Marqueffles Frn.														H.25.d.27 "	
13th " "	Bailleul aux Chateau de Ranailles														H.31.c.5.9. "	
14th c.s.d. "	Chelers " "															
169th Inf.Bde. H.Q.	Diéval														Villers	
2nd London Regt.	Diéval														Bruin	
5th " "	La Thieuvré Beugin														Bethonsart	
18th " "	La Comté														Cambligneul Caucourt	
Div. Arty. H.Q.	Warlus				Aubigny										Warlus	
280th Bde.	M.8.b.74.				Acq. & Frenn Capelle										M.8.b.74	
281st "	G.27.b.95.5.				Acq.										G.27.b.93.35	
Pioneers.	Averdoingt Estree- Cauchie														Arras.	
M.G.Batn. H.Q.	Magnicourt Gauchin en Conté Legal				Hermin										Line (Centre Sector) 2 Coys to Warlus Line (L&R Sectors)	

* Ref. Sheet 44 B.
* On Relief from line 20th/26th G.21st/22nd

IN THE LINE — RED
IN SUPPORT — GREEN
IN RESERVE — BLUE
AT REST — BLACK.

War Diary Apdx II

SECRET Copy No. 27

56th DIVISION ORDER No. 179.

1st July, 1918.

1. 167th Infantry Brigade will relieve 168th Infantry Brigade on its present front on the night 5th/6th July. All details of relief to be arranged between B.Gs.C. concerned.

2. On relief 168th Infantry Brigade will become Divisional Reserve and will move, less one battalion, to the DAINVILLE - BERNEVILLE Area.
One battalion will be accommodated in ARRAS and will be available for work under C.R.E. on and after night 6th/7th July. This battalion may be relieved under Brigade arrangements provided work is not interfered with.

3. Maps, Air photos, Defence Schemes, Trench Stores and Dumps will be handed over on relief.

4. Command will pass on completion of relief.

5. Completion of relief will be wired to Div. H.Q. by the code word "SADOWA".

6. ACKNOWLEDGE.

F. B. Hurndall Major
for Lieut-Colonel,
General Staff.

Issued at 8 p.m.

Copy No. 1. 167th Infantry Brigade.
2. 168th Infantry Brigade.
3. 169th Infantry Brigade.
4. 1/5th Cheshire Regt.
5. C.R.A.
6. Right H.A.Group.
7. C.R.E.
8. 56th Bn. M.G.Corps.
9. 56th Div. Signal Coy.
10. 56th Div. Gas Officer.
11. A.D.M.S.
12. A/Q.
13. A.P.M.
14. D.A.D.O.S.

No. 15. D.A.D.V.S.
16. 56th Div. Train.
17. 56th Div. M.T.Coy.
18. A.D.C.
19. Camp Commandant.
20. 56th Div. Employ. Coy.
21. French Mission.
22. XVII Corps.
23. "   "
24. 3rd Canadian Division.
25. 15th Division.
26.) War Diary.
27.)
28. File.

J/JE.

SECRET. Copy No. 31

56th DIVISION WARNING ORDER No. 180.

Ref. LENS Sheet 11 1/100,000 7th July 1918.
& Trench Maps 1/20,000.

1. 56th Division is to be relieved from the line, commencing on 13th inst., by 2nd Canadian Division and portion of 1st Canadian Division.
   Relief to be complete before daylight on 15th July.

2. 56th Division on relief will be in the BERLENCOURT Area (H.Q. at LE CAUROY) and will be in G.H.Q. Reserve at 24 hours notice.
   It will remain in XVII Corps (H.Q. Chateau, BRYAS from 10 a.m. 15th inst.).

3. Infantry and Artillery reliefs will take place as shown in attached Table 'A'.

4. Machine Gun reliefs will take place 24 hours after infantry reliefs in each section of the line relieved.

5. All troops at the Divisional Reception Camp will join their units or transport lines on the morning of 9th July.

6. Field Artillery guns and equipment will be retained by their units on relief.

7. Moves of Divisional Troops, not mentioned in Table 'A', will be notified later.

8. Command of the Section of the line relieved by 1st Canadian Division will pass at 9 a.m. 14th July.
   Command of the Section of the line relieved by 2nd Canadian Division will pass at 9 a.m. 15th July.

9. The S. boundary of 1st Canadian Division after relief on night 13/14th inst., will be approximately a line E.& W. through H.32.a.8.7

10. Div. H.Q. will close at WARLUS at 9 a.m. 15th July and open at the Chateau, LE CAUROY, at the same hour.

11. ACKNOWLEDGE.

B Pakenham

Issued at 11.30 p.m. Lieut-Colonel,
General Staff.

Copy No. 1. 167th Infantry Brigade.   No. 16. 56th Div. Train.
       2. 168th Infantry Brigade.   17. 56th Div. M.T.Coy.
       3. 169th Infantry Brigade.   18. A.D.C.
       4. 1/5th Cheshire Regiment.   19. Camp Commandant.
       5. C.R.A.   20. 56th Div.Employ.Coy.
       6. Right H.A.Group.   21. French Mission.
       7. C.R.E.   22. XVII Corps.
       8. 56th Bn. M.G.Corps.   23.   "   "
       9. 56th Div. Signal Coy.   24. 3rd Canadian Division.
      10. 56th Div. Gas Officer.   25. 15th Division.
      11. A.D.M.S.   26. 1st Canadian Division.
      12. A/Q.   27. 56th Div. Reception Camp.
      13. A.P.M.   28. 2nd Canadian Division.
      14. D.A.D.O.S.   29. Canadian Corps.
      15. D.A.D.V.S.   30.) War Diary.
                                              31.)
                                              32. File.

TABLE 'A'

MARCH TABLE TO ACCOMPANY 56th DIVISION WARNING ORDER No. 180.

Serial No.	Date. JULY.	Unit.	From.	To.	Remarks.
1.	13th.	168th Inf.Bde. Group & 1/5th Cheshire Pioneers.	DAINVILLE - BERNEVILLE Area.	AVESNES LE COMTE Area.	To march at 2 p.m. Relieved by a Brigade of 2nd Can.Divn.
2.	13/14th.	Portion of 189th Inf.Bde.	Line, left.	ARRAS.	Relieved by portion of 2nd Can.Inf.Bde., 1st Can.Divn. from VICTORY CAMP Area.
3.	14th.	168th Inf.Bde.	AVESNES LE COMTE.	BERLENCOURT (Area A).	
4.	14/15th.	189th Inf.Bde. (Remainder)	Line, left.	ARRAS.	Relieved by a portion of Bde. of 2nd Can.Divn. from DAINVILLE Area.
5.	14/15th.	167th Inf.Bde.	Line, right.	DAINVILLE Area.	- do -
6.	15th.	169th Inf.Bde.Group.	ARRAS.	BERLENCOURT (B Area).	By bus - Transport by road. Route WANQUETIN - AVESNES LE COMTE.
7.	15th.	167th Inf.Bde. Group.	DAINVILLE.	BERLENCOURT (C Area).	- do -
8.	15/16th.	½ 56th Div.Arty.	Line.	Wagon Lines.	On relief by ½ 2nd Can. Div.Arty.
9.	16/17th.	- do -	Line.	- do -	- do -
10.	17th.	56th Div.Arty.	Wagon Lines.	HOUVIN - HOUVIGNEUL Area.	Route - AVESNES LE COMTE - LE CAUROY.

SECRET. Copy No. 30

56th DIVISION ORDER NO. 181.

Ref. LENS Sheet 11, 1/100,000
and Trench Maps 1/20,000.   9th July 1918.

1. 56th Division will be relieved from the line commencing on 13th July by 2nd Canadian Division and portion of 1st Canadian Division. Relief to be complete before daylight on 15th July.

2. 56th Division will on relief be in the BERLENCOURT area (H.Q. at LE CAUROY) and will be in G.H.Q. Reserve at 24 hours notice. It will remain in XVII Corps.

3. (a) On night 13/14th July, 2nd Canadian Infantry Bde. will relieve that portion of 169th Infantry Bde. North of the line PELVES ALLEY (inclusive) in H.32.a - WILDERNESS Avenue (inc.) to G.30.d.91 - G.30.c.80 - due West to G.29.c.50 - thence to G.28.c.95.40.

(b) On night 13/14th July, 167th Infantry Bde. with one company will take over the outposts (South of the grid line running East and West through H.32.central) and forward dispositions of 169th Infantry Brigade South of the line given in para. (a).

(c) On night 14/15th July, 167th Infantry Brigade will be relieved by 4th Canadian Infantry Brigade.

(d) Details of relief in accordance with attached March Table to be arranged between Brigadiers concerned.

(e) Command will pass in each case on completion of relief, which will be reported by wire.

4. Machine Gun reliefs will be carried out 24 hours after Infantry reliefs in each section of the line relieved. Details to be arranged between D.M.G.C's. concerned.

5. Details of Artillery reliefs in accordance with attached March Table will be arranged between C.R.A's. concerned
56th Divisional Artillery will be relieved with guns and equipment.
Progress and completion of relief will be wired to Div. H.Q.

6. Details of R.E. and Pioneer reliefs will be arranged between C.R.E. and O's.C. 1st Bde. C.E. and 2nd Bde. C.E. Reliefs to allow R.E. Field Coys. to move with affiliated Brigade Groups.

7. Relief of Medical Units will be arranged by A.D's.M.S. concerned. Reliefs to allow of Field Ambulances moving with their affiliated Brigade Groups.

8. The command of the front taken over by 1st Canadian Division will pass at 10 a.m., 14th July.
The command of the front taken over by 2nd Canadian Division will pass at 10 a.m., 15th July.

9. Troops of 1st Canadian Division on arrival in 56th Divisional area will come under the tactical control of G.O.C. 56th Division until 10 a.m. on 14th July.
Troops of 2nd Canadian Division on arrival in 56th Divisional area will come under the tactical control of the G.O.C. 56th Divn. until 10 a.m., 15th July.
Similarly, troops of 56th Division on arrival in 2nd Canadian Divisional area will come under the tactical control of G.O.C. 2nd Canadian Division until 10 a.m., 15th July.

10. During progress of relief, no men except those on duty will be allowed outside their billets or in the streets in ARRAS by day.

P.T.O. /11.

- 2 -

11.   Div. H.Q. will close at WARLUS at 10 a.m. 15th July and open at the Chateau, LE CAUROY, at the same hour.

12.   ACKNOWLEDGE.

                                             F. B. Hurndall Major

Issued at 8 p.m.

                                              for Lieut-Colonel,
                                              General Staff.

Copy No.			No.	
1.	167th Infantry Brigade.		16.	56th Div. Train.
2.	168th Infantry Brigade.		17.	56th Div. M.T.Coy.
3.	169th Infantry Brigade.		18.	A.D.C.
4.	1/5th Cheshire Regiment.		19.	Camp Commandant.
5.	C.R.A.		20.	56th Div.Employ.Coy.
6.	Right H.A.Group.		21.	French Mission.
7.	C.R.E.		22.	XVII Corps.
8.	56th Bn. M.G.Corps.		23.	" "
9.	56th Div. Signal Coy.		24.	3rd Canadian Division.
10.	56th Div. Gas Officer.		25.	15th Division.
11.	A.D.M.S.		26.	1st Canadian Division.
12.	A/Q.		27.	2nd Canadian Division.
13.	A.P.M.		28.	Canadian Corps.
14.	D.A.D.O.S.		29.) 30.)	War Diary.
15.	D.A.D.V.S.		31.	File.

MARCH TABLE TO ACCOMPANY 56th DIVISION ORDER No. 181.

Serial No.	Date. JULY	Unit.	From.	To.	Remarks.
1.	12th.	One Bn. 168th Inf.Bde.	ARRAS.	BERNEVILLE.	
2.	13th.	168th Inf.Bde.Group and 1/5th Cheshire Pioneers.	DAINVILLE - BERNEVILLE Area.	AVESNES LE COMTE Area.	To march at 2 p.m. relieved by 4th Can.Inf.Bde.
3.	13/14th.	169th Inf.Bde.	Line.	ARRAS.	On relief by 2nd Can. Inf.Bde. and 1 Coy. 167th Inf.Bde.
4.	14th.	168th Inf.Bde. Group and 1/5th Cheshires.	AVESNES LE COMTE.	LIGNEREUIL LIENCOURT DENIER GRAND RULLECOURT } Area.	1/5th Cheshires to MAIZIERES.
5.	14/15th.	167th Inf.Bde.	Line.	DAINVILLE BERNEVILLE Area.	On relief by 4th Can. Inf.Bde.
6.	15th.	169th Inf.Bde. Group.	ARRAS.	IZEL les HAMEAU PENIN VILLERS Sire SIMON } Area.	By bus. Transport by Road. Route TANQUETIN - AVESNES le COMTE.
7.	15th.	167th Inf.Bde.	DAINVILLE BERNEVILLE Area.	MANIN - GIVENCHY le NOBLE. AMBRINES. BLAVINCOURT. BEAUFORT. } Area.	- ditto -
8.	15th.	Div. H.Q.	WARLUS.	LE CAUROY.	
9.	15/16th.	½ 56th Div.Artillery.	Line.	Wagon Lines.	On relief by ½ 2nd Can. Div. Artillery.
10.	16th.	56th Div.M.G.Bn.	WARLUS.	LIENCOURT.	By bus. Transport by road.

P.T.O.

- 2 -

Serial No.	Date.	Unit.	From.	To.	Remarks.
11.	16/17th.	½ 56th Div.Artillery.	Line.	Wagon Lines.	On relief by ½ 2nd Can. Div. Artillery.
12.	17th.	56th Div. Artillery.	Wagon Lines.	MAGNICOURT. BERLENCOURT. ETREE.-WAMIN. WAMIN. } Area.	Route AVESNES le COMTE - LE CAUROY.

Transport will move by Brigade Groups.
Following distances will be maintained during the March :-

```
Between Batteries of Artillery        ...  ...  ...  500 yards.
   "    Sections of D.A.C.    ...     ...  ...  ...  500   "
   "    Battalions.           ...     ...  ...  ...  500   "
   "    Companies.            ...     ...  ...  ...  100   "
   "    Units and their transport.    ...  ...  ...  100   "
When transport is brigaded, between each Battalion Transport ...  100   "
```

War Diary

SECRET.　　　　　　　　　　　　　　　　　　　56th Division No. G.12/774

AMENDMENT No. 3 to 56th DIVISION ORDER No. 181.

1. Amend March Table Serials 9, 11 and 12, column 2 as follows :-

   For 15/16th, 16/17th and 17th road :-

   19/20th, 20/21st and 21st respectively.

   This relief has been postponed 4 days.

2. 2nd Canadian Divisional Artillery (personnel only) have been ordered to be prepared to relieve the personnel of 56th Div. Artillery at 24 hours notice should the 56th Division be ordered away by G.H.Q. before July 21st.
   　The necessary reconnaissances will be arranged between C.R.A's 56th Division and 2nd Canadian Division.

   　　　　　　　　　　　　　　　　　　　B Pakenham
   　　　　　　　　　　　　　　　　　　　　Lieut-Colonel,
12th July, 1918.　　　　　　　　　　　　　　General Staff.

　　　To all recipients of 56th Div. Order No. 181.

"A" Form.
MESSAGES AND SIGNALS.

Army Form C. 2121.
(In pads of 100.)

War Diary

TO: 56th Div. Artillery.
"Q"

Sender's Number.	Day of Month.	In reply to Number.	
G.468	15		AAA

Ref. 56th Div. Order 181 March Table Serial 15 Column 5 for ANVIN read SAVY sub-area AAA Remarks Column No Road or time restrictions.

From 56th Div.
Place
Time 10.27 p.m.

(Sgd) T.O.M. BUCHAN, Major,
G.S.

"A" Form.
MESSAGES AND SIGNALS.

Army Form C. 2121
(In pads of 100.)

TO	War Diary	To all recipients of O. No 181

Sender's Number.	Day of Month.	In reply to Number.	AAA
G 377	11		

Amendment to 56 Div. Order 181 viz

March Table Sheet No 4 Column 6

Should read 1/5 Cheshires to

GOUY-en-TERNOIS

From: G. Stw.
Place:
Time: 6.30 am

War Diary

SECRET. 56th Division No. G.3/902.

AMENDMENT No. 4 to 56th DIVISION ORDER No. 181 of 9th July, 1918.

Consequent on 56th Division Order No. 182 of 13th instant, the following Amendments will be made in 56th Division Order No. 181 of 9th July :-

Para. 2.   For "BERLENCOURT Area (H.Q. LE CAUROY)"
           Substitute :-
           "MONCHY BRETON Area (H.Q. ROELLECOURT)."

Para. 8.   Add :-
           "except that 416th Field Coy. R.E. will be moved by rail on 15th instant to the Corps School at MARESQUEL."

Para. 11. For "Chateau LE CAUROY", substitute - "ROELLECOURT."

March Table. Cancel March Table attached to 56th Divn. Order No. 181 and substitute the attached.

Para. 12. Cancel and substitute new para. 12 -
           "When in the new area, 169th Inf. Bde. Group will be held ready to move at 4 hours notice to support 1st Corps."

Please ACKNOWLEDGE.

B Pakenham

14th July, 1918.

Lieut-Colonel,
General Staff.

Copies to :-

167th Infantry Brigade.	56th Div. Train.
168th Infantry Brigade.	56th Div. M.T.Coy.
169th Infantry Brigade.	A.D.C.
1/5th Cheshire Regt.	Camp Commandant.
C.R.A.	56th Div. Employ. Coy.
Right H.A.Group.	French Mission.
C.R.E.	XVII Corps. (2)
56th Bn. M.G.Corps.	3rd Canadian Division.
56th Div. Signal Coy.	15th Division.
56th Div. Gas Officer.	1st Canadian Division.
A.D.M.S.	2nd Canadian Division.
A/Q.	Canadian Corps.
A.P.M.	War Diary.
D.A.D.O.S.	File.
D.A.D.V.S.	

J/JE.

AMENDED MARCH TABLE TO ACCOMPANY 56th DIVISION ORDER NO. 181.

Serial No.	Date	Unit	From	To	Remarks
1	JULY 12th	One Bn. 168 Inf. Bde.	ARRAS.	BERNEVILLE.	
2	15th	168 Inf. Bde. Group & 1/5th Cheshire Rgt. (Pioneers).	DAINVILLE - BERNEVILLE Area.	AVESNES-LE-COMTE Area.	To march at 2 P.M. Relieved by 4th Cdn. Inf. Bde.
3	13/14th	169 Inf. Bde. (less portion not relieved).	Line	ARRAS.	On relief by 2nd Cdn. Inf. Bde. & 1 Coy. 167 Inf. Bde.
4	14th	168 Inf. Bde. Group & 1/5th Cheshire Regt. (Pioneers).	AVESNES-LE-COMTE.	LIGNEREUIL Area.	Billets vide AQS.375 of 14th inst. No restrictions as to hour or route.
5	14/15th	167 Inf. Bde.	Line.	DAINVILLE - BERNEVILLE Area.	On relief by 4th Can. Inf. Bde.
6	14/15th	Portion of 169 Inf. Bde.	Line.	No. 1 Camp, WARLUS.	After relief by portions of 2nd & 4th Can. Inf. Bdes.
7	15th	168 Inf. Bde. Group & 1/5th Cheshire Regt. (Pioneers).	LIGNEREUIL Area.	CHELERS Area.	Billets vide AQS.675. No restrictions as to hour or route.
8	15th	169 Inf. Bde. Group.	ARRAS etc.	DIEVAL Area.	By Light Rly. & Bus. Billets vide AQS.675 of 14th inst. Transport by road.
9	15th	167 Inf. Bde. (less 416 Fd. Coy. R.E.).	DAINVILLE - BERNEVILLE Area.	MONCHY - BRETON Area.	By Light Rly. & Bus. Billets vide AQS.675 of 14th inst. Transport by road.

(2)

AMENDED MARCH TABLE TO ACCOMPANY 56th DIVISION ORDER No. 181 (Cont.).

Serial No.	Date.	Unit.	From.	To.	Remarks.
10.	15th.	416th Field Co. R.E.	ARRAS.	Corps School, MARESQUEL.	By train. Arrangements will be notified later.
11.	15th.	Div. H.Q.	WARLUS.	ROELLECOURT.	
12.	15th & 16th	56th Div. M.G.Bn.	WARLUS	MAGNICOURT EN COMTE.	By Light Rly. Transport by road. See APP. 'E' AQS 675 as amended by Admins. Instrs. No. 4.
13.	19th/20th	½ 56th Div. Arty.	Lines.	Wagon Lines.	On relief by ½ 2nd Can. Div. Arty.
14.	20th/21st	do.	do.	do.	do.
15.	21st.	56th Div. Arty.	Wagon Lines.	ANVIN Area.	

(1) Transport will move by Brigade Groups.
Following distances will be maintained during the March :-

```
           Between Batteries of Artillery      ....   ....   300 yards.
              "    Sections of D.A.C.          ....   ....   300   "
              "    Battalions                  ....   ....   300   "
              "    Companies                   ....   ....   100   "
              "    Units and their transport   ....   ....   100   "
           When transport is brigaded, between each Battalion Transport 100   "
```

(2) All units on the march will give precedence to units of 51st Division.

SECRET.   Copy No. 31.

56th DIVISION ORDER No. 182.

13th July, 1918.

1. (a). The move of the Division to the BERLENCOURT Area is cancelled.

   (b). The Division will move instead to the MONCHY BRETON Area.

2.   168th Infantry Brigade Group will remain in the AVESNES Le COMTE area on the 14th inst. and will move to the CHELERS area on the 15th inst.

3.   Dates of all other moves will be as given in Order No. 181

4.   Details of move and billeting areas will be notified later.

5.   ACKNOWLEDGE.

                                                      Tom Buchanmayor

Issued at 10.45 p.m.
                                                      Lieut-Colonel,
                                                      General Staff.

Copy No. 1. 167th Infantry Brigade.   No. 17. 56th Div. M.T.Coy.
        2.   168th Infantry Brigade.   18. A.D.C.
        3.   169th Infantry Brigade.   19. Camp Commandant.
        4.   1/5th Cheshire Regiment.   20. 56th Div. Employ. Coy.
        5.   C.R.A.   21. French Mission.
        6.   Right H.A. Group.   22. XVII Corps.
        7.   C.R.E.   23.   "   "
        8.   56th Bn. M.G. Corps.   24. 3rd Canadian Division.
        9.   56th Div. Signal Coy.   25. 15th Division.
       10.   56th Div. Gas Officer.   26. 1st Canadian Division.
       11.   A.D.M.S.   27. 2nd Canadian Division.
       12.   A/Q.   28. Canadian Corps.
       13.   A.P.M.   29.) War Diary.
       14.   D.A.D.O.S.   30.)
       15.   D.A.D.V.S.   31. File.
       16.   56th Div. Train.

SECRET.   56th Division No. G.3/594.

56th DIVISION.

15th July 1918.

Scheme for Moves whilst in G.H.Q. Reserve.

1. Whilst in G.H.Q. Reserve, the 56th Division will be ready to move at 24 hours' notice.

2. The Division may be called upon to move :-

   'A' By 'Bus.
   'B' By Strategical Train.
   'C' By Tactical Train.

3. Appendix 'A' - "Move by 'Bus" is attached.

   Appendix 'B' - "Move by Strategical Train" - and
   Appendix 'C' - "Move by Tactical Train"
   will be issued later.

4. In the event of any of the above moves being ordered, wires will be sent to all concerned -

   (a) 'BUS MOVE.
   (b) STRATEGICAL TRAIN MOVE.
   (c) TACTICAL TRAIN MOVE.

   as the case may be. At the same time, Zero hour will be notified. On receipt of this wire, units will forward at once to Div. H.Q. the information required in the attached appendices.

5. If ordered to move by 'Bus or Tactical Train, March Tables for the move of transport would be issued at the time.

6. If ordered to move by 'Bus or Tactical Train, troops will take with them, all Lewis Guns, Stokes Mortars and Vickers Guns, and at least 20 filled drums per Lewis gun and 10 filled belts per Vickers gun: also one day's supply of rations on the man.

                                          T. M. Buchan Maj
                                          for
                                          Lieut-Colonel.
                                          General Staff.

Copies to :-
167th Infantry Brigade.
168th Infantry Brigade.   1/5th Cheshire Regt.
169th Infantry Brigade.   D.A.D.V.S.
C.R.A.   56th Div. Train.
C.R.E.   56th Div. M.T. Coy.
56th Bn. M.G. Corps.   A.D.C.
56th Div. Signal Coy.   Camp Commandant.
A.D.M.S.   56th Div. Reception Camp.
A/Q.   56th Div. Employment Coy.
A.P.M.   O.C. 1st Army Bus Coy.
XVII Corps.

E M B U S S I N G   T A B L E.   Reference 1/40000 Map, Sheet 36.B.

Serial No.	Bus Group Commander.	Troops.	Embussing Point.	Head of Convoy.	Routes to Embussing Point.
1.	Brig-General Commanding 168th Infantry Brigade.	168th Inf. Brigade. 56th Bn.M.G.C.(less 2 Coys) Div. Hd.Qrs. H.Q. & No.1.Sec.Div. Signal Coy. H.Q.Div. R.E., 512th Fld.Coy. R.E., 2/2nd Lan.Fld. Amb. Div.Reception Camp.	MONCHY BRETON - CHELERS Road.	CHELERS Cross Roads: (U.16.d.5.2.) facing East.	No restrictions.
2.	Brig-General Commanding 167th Infantry Brigade.	1/5th Cheshire Rgt. 1 Coy.M.G.Bn- 167th Inf. Bde, 416th Fld. Coy.R.E.(if available) 2/1st Lan.Fld.Ambce. Div.Employment Coy. (including Traffic Control Police).	MONCHY BRETON - CHELERS Road.	Tail at MONCHY BRETON. Road Junction, U.1.a.9.9.	No restrictions.
3.	Brig-General Commanding 169th Infantry Brigade.	169th Inf. Brigade. 1 Coy. M.G.Battn. 513th Fld.Coy. R.E. Lan.Fld.Ambce. 2/3rd	DIEVAL - OURTON Road between Road Junction, I.34.c.38. and Road Junction. O.8.central.	May face in either direction.	Field Ambulance not to pass through either BAILLEUL or MONCHY BRETON.

Units will embuss from the head of the convoy in the order given above.

EMBUSSING TABLE.   Reference 1/40000 Map, Sheet 51.C.

Serial No.	Bus Group Commander.	Troops.	Embussing Point.	Head of Convoy.	Routes to Embussing Point.
1.	Brig-General Commanding 168th Infantry Brigade.	168th Inf. Brigade. 56th Bn.M.G.Corps.(less 2 Coys.) Divl. Hd.Qtrs. Hd.Qtrs & No.1.Sect.Div. Signal Coy. Div. R.E. Hd.Qtrs. 512th Fld.Coy. R.E., 2/2nd Ld.Fld.Ambce.	LIENCOURT STATION - BEAUFORT HALT Road.	Either at LIENCOURT STATION or at BEAUFORT HALT.	No restrictions.
2.	Brig-General Commanding 167th Infantry Brigade.	167th Inf. Brigade. 1 Coy. 56th Bn.M.G.C. 416th Fld.Coy.R.E. 2/1st Ldn.Fld.Ambce. Div.Reception Camp. Div.Employment Coy. (including Traffic Control Police).	MAGNICOURT-SUR-CANCHE - AMBRINES Road.	AMBRINES (Rd. junction I.8.b.7.8) facing East.	Troops in BEAUFORT to move via MANIN. M.G.Coy. to move via DENIER. Employment Coy. to move via BERLENCOURT. Otherwise no restrictions.
3.	Brig-General Commanding 169th Infantry Brigade.	169th Inf. Brigade. 1 Coy. 56th Bn.M.G.C. 1/5th Cheshire Rgt. 513th Fld.Coy.R.E. 2/3rd Ldn.Fld.Ambce.	MAIZIERES - PENIN Road.	PENIN. (Road junction G.22.c.7.4.) facing East.	M.G.Coy. to move via SARS-LES-BOIS and MAIZIERES. No Units to pass through AMBRINES. Otherwise no restrictions.

Units will embuss from the head of the convoy in the order given above.

SECRET.

56th Division G.S/834.

AMENDMENT No. 1 to 56th DIVISION ORDER No. 181.

Para. 3. - Erase sub-para. (a) and (b).

and substitute :-

3. (a). On night 13/14th July, 2nd Canadian Infantry Brigade will relieve that portion of 169th Infantry Brigade North of the Line H.32.a.80.95. - H.26.c.5.0. - G.30.d.9.2. - G.30.c.8.0. - due West to G.29.c.5.0. - thence to G.28.c.95.40.

(b). On completion of the relief mentioned in (a) E.G.U., 167th Infantry Brigade will assume command of troops of 169th Infantry Brigade South of the line mentioned in para. (a).

Please ACKNOWLEDGE.

10.7.18.

F. B. Hunsall Mayer
Lieut-Colonel,
General Staff.

AMENDMENT to MARCH TABLE to ACCOMPANY 56th DIV.ORDER No. 181.

ADD new Serial. -

Serial No.	Date. JULY.	Unit.	From.	To.	Line.	Remarks.
5a.	14/15th.	Portion of 169th Inf.Bde.		ARRAS.		After relief.
		Serial 3 Column 3. - after 169th Infantry Brigade ADD:' less portion NOT relieved.'				

To all recipients of 56th Division Order No. 181.

SECRET.   Copy No. 22

56th DIVISION WARNING ORDER No. 183.

16th July 1918.

1. On 18th inst. the following moves will probably take place.

    (a) 168th Infantry Brigade from CHELERS Area to CHATEAU DE LA HAIE Area.

    (b) 167th Infantry Brigade from MONCHY BRETON Area to CAUCOURT Area.

    (c) There will be some adjustment in 169th Infantry Brigade Area, the battalion at LA THIEULOYE and R.E.Cos. at BEUGIN will probably have to move.

    (d) 1/5th Cheshire Regiment (Pioneers) will change billets on 18th inst.

    (e) 56th Div. M.G.Bn. will change billets on 18th inst.

2. Train Companies and Field Ambulances which change billets will march independently under the orders of A.A. & Q.M.G.; they will be allotted to Brigade Groups for billeting purposes.

3. Details will be communicated later.

4. Div. H.Q. will move to VILLERS-CHATEL on 18th inst.

5. ACKNOWLEDGE.

                                                    B. Pakenham
                                                    Lieut-Colonel,
                                                    General Staff.

Issued at 11 p.m.

Copy No. 1. 167th Infantry Brigade.   No. 14. 56th Div. M.T.Coy.
        2. 168th Infantry Brigade.   15. A.D.C.
        3. 169th Infantry Brigade.   16. Camp Commandant.
        4. 1/5th Cheshire Regiment.   17. 56th Div. Receptn. Camp.
        5. C.R.A.   18. 56th Div. Employ.Coy.
        6. C.R.E.   19.) XVII Corps.
        7. 56th Bn. M.G.Corps.   20.)
        8. 56th Div. Signal Coy.   21.) War Diary.
        9. A.D.M.S.   22.)
       10. "Q"   23. File.
       11. A.P.M.
       12. D.A.D.O.S.
       13. 56th Div. Train.

SECRET.   Copy No. 24

56th DIVISION ORDER No. 184.

Ref. Map 1/100,000   17th July 1918.
LENS 11.

1. The 56th Division will move from the ST. POL area and MAGNICOURT and CHELERS sub-areas on the 18th July in accordance with the attached March Table.

2. The above areas will be vacated by 12 noon on 18th July.

3. (a) Allotment of billeting areas to Brigade Groups is shown in 56th Div. AQS. 678 dated 17/7/18.

   (b) 169th Infantry Brigade will readjust their area in accordance with above quoted letter. Move to be complete by 12 noon, 18th inst. No troops to use the MONCHY-BRETON - MAGNICOURT road.

4. On arrival in the CHATEAU de la HAIE area, the 168th Inf. Brigade Group will be at 4 hours' notice to move with a view to reinforcing VIII Corps.

5. Field Ambulances and Companies of the Divisional Train will move under orders to be issued by "Q" Branch.

6. Completion of moves to be reported to Divnl. H.Q.

7. Divisional Headquarters will close at ROELLECOURT at 10:0 a.m., and open at VILLERS CHATEL at the same hour.

8. ACKNOWLEDGE.

                                    Tom Buchan Major
                                    for Lieut-Colonel.
                                    General Staff.

Issued at 11 a.m.

Copy No. 1   167th Infantry Brigade.
        2   168th Infantry Brigade.
        3   169th Infantry Brigade.
        4   1/5th Cheshire Regt.
        5   C.R.A.
        6   C.R.E.
        7   56th Bn. M.G. Corps.
        8   Gas Officer.
        9   A.D.M.S.
        10   "Q".
        11   A.P.M.
        12   D.A.D.O.S.
        13   D.A.D.V.S.
        14   56th Div. Train.
        15   56th Div. M.T. Coy.
        16   A.D.C.
        17   Camp Commandant.
        18   56th Div. Reception Camp.
        19   56th Div. Employment Coy.
        20   French Mission.
        21 } XVII Corps.
        22 }
        23 } War Diary.
        24 }
        25   File.
        26   56th Div. Signal Coy.

                                                P.T.O.

MARCH TABLE TO ACCOMPANY 56th DIVISION ORDER No. 184.

Serial No.	Date.	Unit.	From.	To.	Remarks.
1.	July 18th	168th Inf. Bde.	CHELERS Area.	CHATEAU DE LA HAIE Area.	No road restrictions. To clear the FREVILLERS - VILLERS BRULIN road by 10 a.m.
2.	"	167th Inf. Bde.	MONCHY BRETON Area.	CAUCOURT Area.	Head of column to cross FREVILLERS - VILLERS BRULIN Road at 10.15 a.m.
3.	"	56th Bn.M.G.Corps.	MAGNICOURT.	GAUCHIN L'EGAL.	March under orders of B.G.C. 167th Inf. Bde.
4.	"	1/5th Cheshire Rgt.	AVERDOIGNT.	ESTREE-CAUCHIE or CAMBLAIN L'ABBEE, as allotted by B.G.C. 167th Inf. Bde.	To pass Church at VILLERS-BRULIN at 10.15 a.m.
5.	"	Div. H.Qrs. H.Qrs. & No. 1 Sec. Div. Signal Coy.	ROELLECOURT	VILLERS - CHATEL MINGOVAL.	To move off at 9.0 a.m. Route via AUBIGNY.
6.	"	Div. R.E.	BEUGIN.	As allotted by B.G.C. 169th Inf. Bde.	

NOTE. The following distances will be maintained between units on the march :-

Between Battalions ... ... 500 yards.
" Companies ... ... 100 "
" Unit and its Transport ... 100 "
When Transport is Brigaded, between each Battalion Transport 100 "

SECRET　　　　　　　　　　　　　　　　　　　　　　　　　　　Copy No. 18

56th DIVISION ORDER No. 185.

19th July, 1918.

1.　　The 277th and 311th Army F.A. Brigades will relieve the 56th Div. Artillery in the line on the nights 20th/21st and 21st/22nd July.

2.　　On relief 56th Div. Artillery will rejoin the 56th Divn. in G.H.Q. Reserve and will be accommodated in the FREVIN CAPELLE Area.

3.　　Progress of reliefs and completion of move to be reported to Div. H.Q.

4.　　ACKNOWLEDGE.

T.O.M. Buchan
Major
for
Lieut-Colonel,
General Staff.

Issued at 6 p.m.

Copy No. 1. 167th Infantry Brigade.　　Copy No. 12. 56th Div. Train.
       2. 168th Infantry Brigade.　　　　　　　　　　13. A.D.C.
       3. 169th Infantry Brigade.　　　　　　　　　　14. XVII Corps.
       4. 1/5th Cheshire Regt.　　　　　　　　　　　　15.　　"　　"
       5. C.R.A.　　　　　　　　　　　　　　　　　　　16. 2nd Canadian Divn.
       　　　　　　　　　　　　　　　　　　　　　　　17.) War Diary.
       6. 56th Div. Signal Coy.　　　　　　　　　　　18.)
       7. A.D.M.S.　　　　　　　　　　　　　　　　　　19. File.
       8. "Q"
       9. A.P.M.
     10. D.A.D.O.S.
     11. D.A.D.V.S.

SECRET   Copy No. 26

56th DIVISION ORDER No. 186.

                                                    29th July, 1918.

1.   XVII Corps is relieving the Canadian Corps in the line.

2. (a).   The 56th Division will relieve the 1st Canadian Division.

   (b).   Infantry reliefs will probably commence on night 31st July/
          1st August.

3. (a).   The 56th Division will hold the line with three Brigades in
          the Line.

   (b).   The Divl. Southern Boundary will be M.30.c.8.8.; the Northern
          Boundary will be notified later.

4.   Preliminary moves will take place on July 30th, in accordance with
     attached Table 'A'.

5.   Moves of Field Ambulances will be arranged by the A.D.M.S.

6.   Intervals as below will be observed throughout the move :-

         Between Batteries of Artillery   ...   500 yards.
            "   Sections of D.A.C. or B.A.C. ...   500   "
            "   Battalions   500   "
            "   Companies   100   "
            "   Unit and its Transport   ...   100   "
         When Transport is Brigaded, between
            each Battalion Transport   ...   100   "

7.   Completion of moves will be reported to Div. H.Q.

8.   ACKNOWLEDGE.

                                           T.O.M. Buchan
                                              Major
                                              /fr
                                           Lieut-Colonel,
                                           General Staff.

Issued at 11:30 a.m.

Copy No. 1. 167th Infantry Brigade.   Copy No.16. 56th Div. M.T.Coy.
        2. 168th Infantry Brigade.   17. A.D.C.
        3. 169th Infantry Brigade.   18. Camp Commandant.
        4. 1/5th Cheshire Regt.   19. 56th Div. Reception Camp.
        5. C.R.A.   20. 56th Div. Employ. Coy.
        6. C.R.E.   21. XVII Corps.
        7. 56th Bn. M.G.Corps.   22.   "   "
        8. 56th Div. Signal Coy.   23. 1st Canadian Division.
        9. 56th Div. Gas Officer.   24. 59th Division.
       10. A.D.M.S.   25.)
       11. "Q"   26.) War Diary.
       12. A.P.M.   27. File.
       13. D.A.D.O.S.
       14. D.A.D.V.S.
       15. 56th Div. Train.

TABLE 'A' TO ACCOMPANY 58th DIVISION ORDER No. 186.

Serial No.	Date.	Unit.	From.	To.	Route	Remarks.
1.	JULY 30th.	167th Inf. Bde. Group Composed of :- (167th Inf. Bde. (418th Fld. Coy. R.E. (1 Coy. 58th Bn.M.G.C. (No. 2 Coy. Div. Train.	CAUCOURT Area. (2 Secs.CAMBLIGNEUL (2 Secs.BAJUS. HERMIN. CAUCOURT.	DAINVILLE - BERNEVILLE Area.	AUBIGNY - HERMAVILLE - HABARCQ.	Time will be notified later.
2.	JULY 30th	139th Inf. Bde. Group Composed of :- (139th Inf. Bde. (513th Fld.Coy.R.E. (No. 4 Coy.Div.Train.	DIEVAL Area. BAJUS. DIEVAL.	CAUCOURT Area.	No restrictions.	do.

56th Division No. G.3/985.

SECRET.

Copy No. 14.

In continuation of 56th Division Order No. 186 of 29th inst.:

1. (a) Infantry reliefs will be carried out as follows :-

    Right Section ... 167th Inf. Bde. Night 31st July/1st Aug.
    Centre Section ... 169th " " " 1st/2nd August.
    Left Section ... 168th " " " 31st July/1st Aug.

  (b) Machine Gun reliefs will be carried out in -

    Centre Section ... Night 31st July/1st August.
    Right & Left Sections " 1st/2nd August.

  (c) 56th Div. Artillery will relieve 1st Canadian Div. Artillery on the nights 31st July/1st August and 1st/2nd August.

2. All details of relief will be settled between Brigadiers, D.M.G.O's. and C.R.A's. concerned.

3. (a) Divisional and inter-Brigade boundaries are provisionally as follows :-

  <u>Right Divnl. Boundary.</u>
    M.30.c.70.80 - M.30.a.00.70 - M.23.d.60.15 -
    M.21.c.65.25 - M.20.c.00.10.

  <u>Left Divnl. Boundary.</u>
    H.26.c.95.32 - H.25.d.20.85 - G.30.d.95.43 - G.29.d.00.35 -
    G.35.a.00.60 - G.34.b.30.20 - G.26.b.00.70.

  <u>Centre Brigade Right Boundary.</u>
    N.13.c.95.10 - M.18.a.00.40 - M.12.c.00.00 - thence along grid line to M.9.c.00.00.

  <u>Centre Brigade Northern Boundary.</u>
    N.1.d.40.75 - N.1.c.70.95 - M.5.b.50.00 - M.5.a.60.80 -
    M.5.a.00.00 - M.3.a.60.00.

  (b) Maps are forwarded herewith to B.G's.C. Infantry Brigades, C.R.A., D.M.G.O. and O.C. 56th Div. Signal Coy. showing :-
    (a) Present boundaries.
    (b) Revised boundaries.
    (c) H.Q's.
    (d) Present dispositions (to Inf. Bdes. only).

4. Detailed orders follow.

5. ACKNOWLEDGE.

T.Ohm.Buchan

Lieut-Colonel.
General Staff.

H.Q., 56th Divn.,
29th July 1918.
  Issued to :-
  Copy No. 1 167th Inf. Bde.   Copy No. 6 56th Div. Sig. Coy.
        2 168th Inf. Bde.   7 A/Q.
        3 169th Inf. Bde.   8 56th Div. Train.
        4 56th Bn. M.G.Corps.   9 A.D.M.S.
        5 C.R.E.   10 1st Canadian Divn.
                                    11 C.R.A.

SECRET   Copy No. 27

56th DIVISION ORDER No. 187.

Ref. Sheets 51 B. N.W. 1/20,000   30th July, 1918.
      51 B. S.W. "

     In continuation of 56th Div. Order No. 186 of 29th instant.

1. (a).   Reliefs of the 1st Canadian Division will take place in accordance with attached Table 'A'.
   (b).   Infantry, Artillery and M.G. reliefs to be complete by 6 a.m. 2nd August.
   (c).   Moves of Transport are shown in Table 'B'.

2. (a).   All details of relief will be settled between Brigadiers, D.M.G.Cs. and C.R.As. concerned.
   (b).   Brigades will take over the same system of defence in their sections as at present held by Brigades of 1st Canadian Division.
   (c).   Artillery equipment and guns will not be exchanged.

3.   The C.R.E. will arrange with C.R.E. 1st Canadian Division for the relief of R.E. and pioneers and to take over all current and proposed work.

4.   The A.D.M.S. will arrange with A.D.M.S. 1st Canadian Division for the relief of Field Ambulances.

5.   Moves of units not included in the attached march Table will take place under the orders of the A.A. & Q.M.G.

6.   All maps, defence schemes, programmes of work, air-photos, amps and trench stores will be taken over on relief.

7.   On completion of reliefs the Divisional and Inter-Brigade Boundaries will be as under :-

   Right Divnl. Boundary.
    M.30.c.70.80 - M.30.a.00.70. - M.23.d.60.15 -
    M.21.c.65.25 - M.20.c.00.10 - thence due W.

   Left Divnl. Boundary.
    H.26.c.95.32 - H.25.d.20.85 - G.30.d.95.43 - G.29.d.00.35 -
    G.35.a.00.60 - G.34.b.30.20 - G.26.b.00.70 - thence due W.

   Centre Brigade Right Boundary.
    N.13.c.95.10 - M.18.a.00.40 - M.12.c.00.00 - thence along grid line to M.9.c.00.00 - thence due W.

   Centre Brigade Left Boundary.
    N.1.d.40.75 - N.1.c.70.95 - M.5.b.50.00 - M.5.a.60.80 -
    M.5.a.00.00 - M.3.a.60.00 - thence due W.

8.   Troops of 56th Division on arrival in 1st Canadian Division area will come tactically under the orders of G.O.C. 1st Canadian Division and will report their arrival and location of their H.Qs. to 1st Canadian and 56th Divisions.

9.   Completion of reliefs will be reported to Div. H.Qs.

10.   Command of Brigade Sections will pass on completion of relief in each case.

- 2 -

11. Command of the Divisional front will pass to G.O.C. 56th Division at 10.0 a.m. August 2nd at which hour Div. H.Q. will open at WARLUS.

12. ACKNOWLEDGE.

T. On. Buchan

Lieut-Colonel,
General Staff.

Issued at 2 pm

Copy No. 1. 167th Infantry Brigade.
2. 168th Infantry Brigade.
3. 169th Infantry Brigade.
4. 1/5th Cheshire Regt.
5. C.R.A.
6. C.R.E.
7. 56th Bn. M.G.Corps.
8. 56th Div. Signal Coy.
9. 56th Div. Gas Officer.
10. A.D.M.S.
11. "Q"
12. A.P.M.
13. D.A.D.O.S.
14. D.A.D.V.S.
15. 56th Div. Train.

Copy No.16. 56th Div. M.T.Coy.
17. A.D.C.
18. Camp Commandant.
19. 56th Div. Reception Camp.
20. 56th Div. Employ. Coy.
21. XVII Corps.
22. " "
23. 1st Canadian Division.
24. 50th Division.
25. 3rd Canadian Division.
26. 57th Division.
27.) War Diary.
28.)
29. File.

J/C.

TABLE B. to accompany 56th DIVISION ORDER No. 127.

	Date.				
1.	31st July.	Transport 168 Inf. Bde. & No.3 Co. Train.	CHATEAU DE LA HAIE.	VILLERS AU BOIS - ACQ - HAUTE AVESNES.	To clear HAUTE AVESNES by 1.0 pm.
2.	"	½ 56th D.A.	FREVIN CAPELLE.	BERNEVILLE.	Not to move before 1:30 p.m.
				Line & Wagon Lines.	No restrictions.
3.	1st Aug.	1/5th Cheshire Rgt.	ESTREE-CAUCHIE.	Personnel ARRAS direct Transport - WANQUETIN.	Personnel ARRAS Transport, via HERMAVILLE. Transport to be clear of AUBIGNY by 9 a.m.
4.	do.	Transport 169 Inf. Bde. & No.4 Co. Train.	CAUCOURT Area.	BERNEVILLE.	HERMAVILLE - HABARCQ.	Not to pass through AUBIGNY before 9.15 am & to be clear by 11 am.
5.	do.	Transport 1 Coy. 56th Bn.M.G.C.	CHATEAU DE LA HAIE.	do.	As for Serial 1.	To be clear of main ST.POL - ARRAS Rd. by 11 a.m.
6.	do.	Transport 56th Bn. M.G.Corps less 3 Cos.	LERMIN	do.	AUBIGNY - HERMAVILLE - HABARCQ.	Not to enter AUBIGNY before 11.15 am & to be clear by 12 noon
7.	do.	½ 56th Div. Arty.	FREVIN - CAPELLE	Line & Wagon Lines.	No restrictions.	Not to move before 3 pm. No.1 Co.Div. Train moves under orders of C.R.A.
8.	do.	Transport H.Q. R.E. and two Coys.	BAJUS and CAMBLIGNEUL.	WARLUS BERNEVILLE & WAGNONLIEU.	SAVY - HABARCQ.	To pass through SAVY at 12.15 pm.
9.	2nd Aug.	Div.H.Qrs.	VILLERS CHATEL	WARLUS	No restrictions.	

NOTE: Transport required for special purposes, e.g. Cookers, L.G. Limbers need not conform to above orders.

TABLE A. TO ACCOMPANY 56th DIVISION ORDER No. 187.

Serial No.	Date	Unit	From.	To.	Relieving.	Remarks.
1	July 31st/Aug. 1st.	167th Inf Bde.	DAINVILLE Area	Line. Right Bde. Section.	Portion of 1st Can. Inf. Bde.	
2	do.	168th Inf. Bde.	CHATEAU DE LA HAIE.	Line. Left Bde. Section.	Portion of 2nd & 3rd C.M.Inf.Bdes.	Moves by Rail.
3	do.	Portion of 56th Bn. M.G.Corps.	DAINVILLE Area.	Line. Centre Bde. Section.	Portion of 1st Can. Div. M.G.Bn.	
4	do.	Leading Sections 56th Div. Arty.	HERVEL CAPELLE Area.	Line.	½ 1st Can. D.A.	
5	August 1st	1/5th Cheshire Regt.	ESTREE CAUCHIE.	ARRAS	" "	By march route. See Table B.
6	August 1st	H.Qrs. R.E. 512th Fd.Coy.R.E. 513th Fd.Coy.R.E.	BAJUS and CAMBLIGNEUL.	H.Qrs. WARLUS 2 Coys. ARRAS		By Rail.
7	Aug. 1/2nd.	169th Inf. Bde.	GAUCOURT Area.	Line. Centre Bde. Section.	Portion of 3rd Can. Inf. Bde.	Moves by Rail.
8	do.	56th Bn. M.G.C. less Two Coys.	HERMIN & CHATEAU DE LA HAIE.	Line. Right & Left Bde.Sects.	Portion of 1st Can. Div. M.G.Bn.	Moves by Rail. H.Qrs. by road to WARLUS.
9	do.	Remaining Secs. 56th Div. Arty.	PREVIN CAPELLE Area.	Line.	½ 1st Can. D.A.	

WO95/2935

Army Form W.3091.

Cover for Documents.

(ORIGINAL)

Nature of Enclosures.

WAR DIARY

GENERAL STAFF

56th DIVISION

AUGUST - 1918.

Notes, or Letters written.

56th DIVISION.

AUGUST, 1918.

Army Form C. 2118.

WAR DIARY
or
INTELLIGENCE SUMMARY
(Erase heading not required.)

Instructions regarding War Diaries and Intelligence Summaries are contained in F. S. Regs., Part II. and the Staff Manual respectively. Title pages will be prepared in manuscript.

Place	Date	Hour	Summary of Events and Information	Remarks and references to Appendices
VILLERS-CHATEL.	Aug. 1st.		169th Infantry Brigade relieved the remaining portions of 1st Canadian Division in the Centre Section (TELEGRAPH HILL) of the front line. Quiet day.	APP.I. (14)
WARLUS.	2nd		Div. H.Qrs. moved to WARLUS. G.O.C., 56th Division took over Command of the Right Sector XVII Corps from G.O.C., 1st Can. Divn. at 10 a.m. Situation quiet. Weather wet.	APP.I. (14)
	3rd.		Situation quiet. 168th Infantry Brigade carried out a readjustment of battalion dispositions so as to hold their section with one battalion in the front line, one in support and one in reserve.	APP.I. (14)
	4th.		Quiet day. Hostile artillery fired a few shells on to TELEGRAPH HILL during morning. 137th Infantry Brigade captured 4 prisoners of 39th Minnenwerfer Company, 59th Division about 11 pm. Fresh identification - the 185 Division had been relieved on night 2/3rd Aug.	(14)
	5th.		Situation quiet except for hostile shelling of our battery positions near AGNY.	(14)
	6th.		Quiet day in forward areas. Hostile artillery very active in counter-battery work on our battery positions between AGNY, ACHICOURT and BEAURAINS. 167th Infantry Brigade carried out an inter-battalion relief.	APP.I. (14)
	7th.		Situation normal. Hostile artillery again active on back areas. Operation Order No. 188 issued for the Projection of gas into NEUVILLE VITASSE. 168th Infantry Brigade carried out an inter-battalion relief.	APP.II. (14) APP.I. (14)
	8th.		Quiet day. About 2 a.m. the enemy put down a barrage on our left front line in conjunction with a raid on the Division on our left. Gas was projected into NEUVILLE VITASSE during the night. No hostile retaliation.	(14)
	9th.		Quiet day. Hostile artillery active on our battery areas.	(14)

AUGUST, 1918. Army Form C. 2118.

WAR DIARY
or
INTELLIGENCE SUMMARY.
(Erase heading not required.)

56th DIVISION.

Place	Date	Hour	Summary of Events and Information	Remarks and references to Appendices
WARLUS.	Aug. 10th.		Situation normal. Hostile aeroplanes active. Enemy appeared to be registering over our back areas with air bursts. Visibility fair. Orders received from XVII Corps for the attachment of portions of 78th American Division to this Division in the line for training.	JWW
	11th.		Situation quiet. Enemy attempted to raid one of our outposts (HONEY LANE), Centre Brigade just before dawn but driven off. Weather hot, visibility poor.	JWW
	12th.		Quiet day. Early morning mist. Visibility bad. Hostile artillery active in Right Section.	JWW
	13th.		Situation normal. Visibility poor owing to heat.	JWW
	14th.		Enemy shelled BLANGY TRENCH in Left Section with gas shell of 5.9" calibre. Otherwise quiet. Prisoner of 39th Division captured by 167th Infantry Brigade. Normal identification. Orders received from XVII Corps for relief of 56th Division by 15th Division, relief to be complete by 10 a.m. 18th inst. 56th Div.Warning Order No. 189 issued. Enemy shelled WARLUS with H.V.gun about 11 p.m. At 11.30 p.m. enemy attempted to raid our advanced posts near BOIS DES BOEUFS. Repulsed. None of our men missing.	APP.II. JWW
	15th.		Situation quiet. About 3 a.m. enemy attempted to raid our forward post just South of NEUVILLE VITASSE but repulsed before he reached our wire. 56th Div. O.O.No.190 issued in confirmation of O.O.No. 189. 167th Infantry Brigade relieved by 44th Infantry Brigade, 15th Division. 167th Inf.Bde. moved by rail to IZEL-lez-HAMEAU area. G.O.C. attended Conference at XVII Corps.	APP.II. APP.I.
	16th.		Situation normal. G.S.O.I attended Conference at XVII Corps H.Qrs. 169th Infantry Brigade relieved by 45th Infantry Brigade and moved by rail to GRAND RULLECOURT Area.	APP.I. JWW
	17th.		Quiet day. Slight hostile shelling of TILLOY with 5.9s. Preliminary orders received from XVII Corps to effect that XVII Corps would attack and capture ORANGE and CHAPEL HILLS. The 52nd and 56th and 57th Divisions attacking on the left, centre and right respectively, date to be fixed later. Tanks to co-operate.	JWW

Army Form C. 2118.

WAR DIARY
or
INTELLIGENCE SUMMARY.

56th DIVISION. **AUGUST, 1918.**

(Erase heading not required.)

Instructions regarding War Diaries and Intelligence Summaries are contained in F.S. Regs., Part II. and the Staff Manual respectively. Title pages will be prepared in manuscript.

Place	Date	Hour	Summary of Events and Information	Remarks and references to Appendices
WARLUS.	Aug. 17th.	(Contd).	At Conference held at Div. H.Qrs. attended by B.Gs.C. Infantry Brigades, the G.O.C. explained the above Scheme.	714.1
	18th.		168th Infantry Brigade relieved by 46th Infantry Brigade and moved to MAZIERES Area.	APP.I.
			Relief completed and G.O.C. handed over command of the Divisional Sector to G.O.C., 15th Divn. at 10 a.m. Div. H.Qrs. moved to LE CAUROY	APP.I.
			Orders received from XVII Corps for 169th Infantry Brigade to move to ARRAS on 19th inst. to carry out work in connection with proposed attack. Orders issued accordingly.	714
LE CAUROY.	19th.		169th Infantry Brigade moved to ARRAS and DAINVILLE with H.Qrs. in ARRAS.	APP.I.
			O.O.No.191 issued embodying orders for the attack - date to be notified later	APP.II.
			Orders received from XVII Corps that no dumps to be formed or Artillery to go into the line until receipt of further orders. Orders issued accordingly. The Division was placed back at 8 hours notice to move.	714
	20th.		The Commander-in-Chief visited Div. H.Qrs. and saw the G.O.C.	714
			Orders received from XVII Corps for 169th Infantry Brigade to move to AVESNES-LE-COMTE area and for 168th Infantry Brigade to move to LIGNEREUIL area. before 7 p.m. Orders issued and these Brigades moved accordingly.	APP.I.
	21st.		Orders received from XVII Corps for transfer of 56th Division to VI Corps from 12 noon, 21st inst. Orders received from VI Corps for move of Division to BAVINCOURT area this evening.	714
			O.O.No.192 issued accordingly.	APP.II.
			The Division moved to new area, with exception of Div. H.Qrs.	APP.I.
			For Diary of Events and Operations carried out between 22nd August and 31st August inclusive, see APP.III, for Locations during same period APP.I, and for Orders issued APP.II.	714

6th Sept. 1918.

C. Hull
Major-General,
Commanding 56th Division.

SECRET

Appendix III

REPORT ON OPERATIONS IN VI and XVII CORPS.

From 23rd to 31st August 1918.

Operations in VI Corps Area.

The Division was relieved in the line on the ARRAS front on 15th, 16th and 17th August, the command being handed over in the morning of 18th August.

On 19th August, 169th Infantry Brigade was sent back to ARRAS to carry out preparations for an attack on ORANGE and CHAPEL HILLS, in which the Division had been warned to take part.

This Brigade, however, was sent back to AVESNES-LE-COMTE area on 21st August and 168th Infantry Brigade also marched from the MAIZIERES area to the LIGNEREUIL area.

On this date the G.O.C. was informed of the transfer of the Division to VI Corps for forthcoming operations and at once visited Corps H.Q., but was unable to obtain exact information as to the rule of the Division.

The Division, less Div. H.Q., marched the same night to the area BARLY - ST.AMAND - SAULTY - BAVINCOURT. At 8 a.m. on 22nd the G.O.C. attended a Conference at VI Corps H.Q. when the operations for 23rd August were decided on; on his return to BAVINCOURT at 10.30 a.m. he held a Conference to explain the operations to all concerned.

Officers of all Brigades were despatched forthwith to reconnoitre, the 168th Infantry Brigade was set in motion at 3 p.m. to the preliminary assembly area about BLAIREVILLE (about 7½ miles march) and 167th Infantry Brigade was moved up into the ST.AMAND area to replace it.

At about 3 p.m. 56th Div. Order No. 193 was issued for the operations of 23rd August, based on VI Corps Instructions issued at the morning's Conference, the VI Corps Operation Order not having been received at that hour.

Owing to the short notice and the lateness of the hour at which it was possible to send out reconnaissance parties, they were only able to gain a slight knowledge of the rear assembly areas and to arrange for guides; they had little opportunity of seeing the forward assembly areas or the objectives.

168th Infantry Brigade (with 1st London Regiment of 167th Infantry Brigade attached) moved forward about 9 p.m. to the forward assembly areas (4½ miles) and was drawn up so as to attack through 59th Division, except on the southern portion of the front, where it relieved some of the Guards Division.

This Brigade had marched on the 21st, on the night 21/22nd and again on the 22/23rd had to cover about 13 miles to reach the line from which it was to attack, and as it was by no means fresh, the greatest credit is due to it for the operations on the 23rd August.

The Divisional Artillery also moved into action on the night 22/23rd from BERNEVILLE, which it could not leave on account of traffic restrictions until 8 p.m.

At the same time it had to dump the amount of ammunition required for the operations as this had not been completed.

The remainder of 167th Infantry Brigade was ordered to move to BLAIREVILLE by 9 a.m. 23rd August in Support.

Operations of 23rd August.

The attack started at 4.55 a.m. being supported by 2 Cos. 11th Bn. Tanks Corps, totalling 21 Tanks.

The front was covered by 6 Brigades of Field Artillery forming a creeping barrage.

The objectives for the 168th Infantry Brigade are shewn on the attached Map. They included the Villages of BOIRY-BECQUERELLE and BOYELLES. After the capture of the BLUE Line, the Brigade was to push out and establish posts in BOIRY RESERVE, BOIRY WORKS, BOYELLES RESERVE, the Southern portion of BOYELLES Trench and to approximately T.19.c.6.4.

/The

The 168th Infantry Brigade attacked with 3 Battalions in the line, 13th London Regiment (Kensingtons) on the right, 4th London Regiment in the centre and 14th London Regiment (London Scottish) on the left. The 1st London Regiment detached from 167th Infantry Brigade, were in support. The Guards Division were attacking on the right and the 52nd Division on the left.

Reports received by 6 a.m. indicated that the attack had progressed well, that casualties were slight and the enemy's barrage weak. By 7.30 a.m. it was known that all objectives had been reached and that patrols of the 14th London Regiment were pushing forward. The enemy did not put up a strong resistance excepting in MARC Trench where the 4th London Regiment had met with considerable opposition.

At 8.30 a.m. orders were received from the Corps to keep in touch with the enemy and to occupy the line of BOIRY RESERVE and BOYELLES RESERVE. Instructions were accordingly issued to the 168th Infantry Brigade and the advance recommenced at 11.30 a.m. By 4.30 p.m. the Left and Centre Battalions were reported to have reached the above line, though the position with regard to the Right Battalion was somewhat obscure.

At 4.45 p.m. the Guards Division reported their Left Brigade T.20.central - T.26.central and to be advancing on ST.LEGER MILL. Orders were, therefore, issued to 168th Infantry Brigade to push out strong patrols and feel SUMMIT Trench.

In the meantime the situation on our Right Flank remained uncertain, the Guards Division reporting that we were out of touch with them. Although there appeared to be little doubt that the 13th London Regiment had reached BOYELLES RESERVE, yet their definite position was not established until 9.30 p.m. when they were reported to be in T.20.c. and in touch with the Guards Division.

In the meantime 169th Infantry Brigade and two Coys. M.G.Bn. had been ordered to move up into the BASSEUX Area, and later further orders were issued to 169th Infantry Brigade to move up to the PURPLE Line on the 24th instant.

At 8.40 p.m. orders were issued for the relief of the 168th Infantry Brigade by the 167th Infantry Brigade, the 1st London Regt. rejoining the 167th Infantry Brigade and one Battalion 168th Infantry Brigade being put under the orders of the 167th Infantry Brigade.

At 11.40 p.m. Div. Order No. 194 was issued for the 167th Infantry Brigade to continue the attack next day in accordance with orders received from VI Corps. The first objective was SUMMIT Trench from T.22.b.3.3. to T.16.b.3.8. and thence along the road in T.10.c. refusing the flank northwards so as to join up with 52nd Division on the Northern Boundary. The second objective was FOOLEY RESERVE - HILL SWITCH and CROSS SWITCH, with the object of enveloping CROISILLES from the North, while the Guards Division carried out a similar operation from the South, including CROISILLES SWITCH in their objective.

Operation of August 24th

The attack was entrusted to the 167th Infantry Brigade with 14th London Regiment from the 168th Infantry Brigade in support. 12 tanks and 1 Company 56th Bn. M.G.Corps were put at the disposal of the Brigade for the attack. The infantry advance was covered by six Brigades of Artillery, one battery of each Brigade moving up to forward positions at Zero hour. The Brigade attacked with three Battalions in the line, 8th Middlesex Regt. being on the right, 7th Middlesex Regt. in the Centre and 1st London Regt. on the left.

The attack commenced at 7 a.m. under cover of a creeping barrage which opened on protective barrage lines for 10 minutes, then moving forward at the rate of 100 yards in 4 minutes to beyond the first objective, where it paused for 30 minutes, then moving forward again.

Reports up to 8.35 a.m. showed that the infantry had gone over well and were making progress, tanks and small parties of men

/being

being observed in and about the first objective. By 10.50 a.m. the first objectives were reported captured and patrols pushing out to FOOLEY and CROSS Trenches. 8th Middlesex Regiment also reported that they had troops in the western outskirts of CROISILLES.

At 9 a.m. orders were received from VI Corps that owing to a prisoner's statement that 3 fresh divisions had come into the BULLECOURT - HENDECOURT area, the Division would make preparations to meet a counter attack.

The 169th Infantry Brigade were ordered forward into the neighbourhood of S.17 and one Battalion put at the disposal of 167th Infantry Brigade with orders not to involve it in fighting if possible.

167th Infantry Brigade were at the same time ordered to occupy CROISILLES by peaceful penetration and hold CROISILLES RESERVE and HILL SWITCH. Meanwhile the right Brigade of 52nd Division which was attacking HENIN HILL was compelled to withdraw and take up a position on the forward slopes echelonned to our left rear.

At 1.38 p.m. 167th Infantry Brigade reported their dispositions as follows :- Right Battalion, one Coy. on W. outskirts of CROISILLES with patrols in the Village and 2 Coys in LEGER and SUMMIT Trenches, and 1 Coy. in BOYELLES RESERVE. Centre Battalion, 2 Coys. in SUMMIT TRENCH with patrols in front, Support and Reserve Coys. in depth in rear, and Left Battalion, 2 Coys. in SUMMIT Trench in touch with 52nd Division on left, with Support and Reserve Coys. in rear.

Reports tended to show that CROISILLES had been evacuated and after consultation with B.G.C., 167th Infantry Brigade, Orders were issued at 3.45 p.m. for 167th Infantry Brigade to attack and establish itself in the HINDENBURG SUPPORT LINE between HUMP LANE U.14.a.6.2. and RIVER Road U.1.c.7.2. The attack to be covered by a creeping barrage and the co-operation of 6 Tanks. The 52nd Division were also attacking on the left, Zero hour to be 7.50 p.m.

At 4.7 p.m. B.G.C., 167th Infantry Brigade reported he had not cleared CROISILLES. G.O.C. ordered him to make a certainty of capturing CROISILLES and to send tanks and infantry through the village if it was not in our possession by Zero hour. The Guards Division on our right would co-operate by occupying CROISILLES Tr. E. of the Village.

At 4.40 p.m. the 169th Infantry Brigade was ordered to move up to region E. of BOIRY and BOYELLES and 168th Infantry Brigade to area vacated by them.

The 52nd Division on our left and Guards Divn. on our right both reported being held up by M.G. fire.

At 8.45 p.m. B.G.C., 167th Infantry Brigade reported that the attack had failed. Only one tank came into action, and his troops had met very heavy M.G. fire and gas. He was organising SUMMIT TRENCH as the line of resistance. CROISILLES TRENCH was reported to be only about 2 ft. deep and untenable.

Orders were received from VI Corps about 8.30 p.m. to attack the HINDENBURG LINE the following day, no tanks being available. On G.O.C. pointing out that this line was very strongly wired and held, those orders were modified and the Division was instructed to capture CROISILLES and obtain a footing in SENSEE AVENUE to the N.E. so as to conform to 52nd Division who were attacking on our left. Orders were issued to 167th Infantry Brigade to endeavour to penetrate into CROISILLES and work into outlying trenches of HINDENBURG System, but not to become involved in heavy fighting to obtain the latter.

The Division remained for the night on the line LEGER TR. where touch was obtained with the Guards on the right - SUMMIT Tr. to T.10.d. where touch was maintained with 52nd Division on left.

SECRET

OPERATIONS IN XVII CORPS.

Operations on 25th August 1918.

The situation during the night remained unchanged.

At 8 a.m. the 56th Division and 52nd Division were transferred to XVII Corps which took over their portions of the front from VI Corps. The 52nd Division on left reported that the HINDENBURG Line was very strongly held. The Guards Division on our right reported that CROISILLES was full of M.Gs. which were holding them up. A bombardment of this Village was accordingly arranged. Our front line battalions were shelled severely with gas during the night, in some cases having to wear their gas masks for 6 hours.

169th Infantry Brigade was ordered to reconnoitre the front with the object of attacking and enveloping CROISILLES from the North and secondly of capturing the HINDENBURG Line.

The day was spent in endeavouring to penetrate CROISILLES by pushing patrols forward into the Village. Posts were established at T.22.b.8.6., T.16.b.9.5., T.11.c.0.4, and T.11.a.0.3., but patrols could not make further progress owing to M.Gs. in CROISILLES.

The enemy artillery continued very active all along the front and against our battery areas. Touch was maintained with the Guards Division in LEGER RESERVE and with the 52nd Division at T.10.b.60.60. Both Divisions reported that they were faced with considerable opposition, the 52nd Division deciding later in the evening to withdraw their line to the CROISILLES ST.MARTIN-Sur-COJEUL Road and to vacate the post at the junction of FAT and SUMMIT Trenches, which 167th Infantry Brigade took over.

At 5.30 p.m. 167th Infantry Brigade issued orders for the Brigade to attack next morning and establish itself on the line T.22.d.5.0. - T.23.a.5.2. - T.17.c.9.2. - T.17.b.5.1. and thence along CROISILLES RESERVE and FOOLEY Trench. The attack was to be carried out in conjunction with 52nd Division, who were to endeavour to establish themselves on the line N.27.central - N.22. central, and, if the attack of the Canadian Corps on their left was successful, to continue to push down the HINDENBURG Line in a S.E. direction. At the same time the Corps notified that the Corps Northern Boundary was a line from S. corner of NEUVILLE VITASSE to HENDECOURT CHATEAU.

Zero hour was fixed for 3 a.m.

Operations of 26th August 1918.

The attack proved unsuccessful in reaching the objectives laid down, but some progress was made and posts were established on the line T.22.d.5.0. - T.22.d.8.9. - T.23.a.0.2. - T.23.a.2.9. - T.17.a.5.1. - T.11.c.0.4. with a two platoon post in CROSS SWITCH. The lack of success was mainly due to intense M.G. fire opened from the neighbourhood of CROISILLES immediately after Zero.

Touch was maintained with the Guards Division in LEGER RES. In the meantime the attack of the 52nd Division and of the Canadian Corps further to the left had proved successful. The objectives had been gained, and one battalion of the 52nd Division was pushing on down the HINDENBURG Line on to HENIN HILL.

Orders were issued for the 169th Infantry Brigade to relieve the 167th Infantry Brigade at dusk, the latter withdrawing into the area vacated by the 139th Infantry Brigade. At the same time G.O.C. warned 169th Infantry Brigade, that if the operations on our left proved very successful, it might be necessary to put the Brigade through the 167th Brigade that evening.

About 4 p.m. the 52nd Division reported the HINDENBURG Line between the COJEUL RIVER and HENIN HILL clear of the enemy, and the G.O.C. ordered 169th Infantry Brigade to commence relieving about 6 p.m. In the meanwhile orders were received from the Corps to press the attack vigorously next day. The 52nd Division was to continue to advance down the HINDENBURG Line and the 56th Division

/to

to maintain pressure on CROISILLES, and at the same time be prepared to take advantage of any opportunity to advance afforded by the attacks on our left.   Orders in accordance with the above were issued to 167th Infantry Brigade followed later by orders for 169th Infantry Brigade to push one Bn. on as advanced guard to the HINDENBURG LINE, if 167th Inf. Bde. reported CROISILLES clear of Germans.   However, reports shewed that CROISILLES was still strongly held by M.Gs. and a reconnaissance by O.C., 1st London Regiment, showed that the enemy were still in FOOLEY TRENCH. As a result G.O.C., 169th In. Bde. was ordered to clear up the position in FOOLEY TRENCH, FAT TRENCH and SUMMIT TRENCH immediately on relief.   This he attempted to do with 2nd London Regt. but heavy M.G. fire held this unit up.

Operations of 27th August.

At 3 a.m. orders were issued for 169th Infantry Brigade to continue the advance on the left of the Divisional front, keeping touch with the 52nd Division on the left, the Northern boundary of the Division being the line T.10.b.6.7. - T.12.b.1.3. - U.7.cent. - U.8.c.0.8.   The final objective was given as the line U.8.c.0.8. - U.14 central, the intermediate objective being the Sunken Road running S.W. through T.17.c. central.

CROISILLES VILLAGE and CROISILLES RESERVE were to be kept under a heavy bombardment during the advance.

The barrage opened at 9.36 a.m. and commenced moving forward at 10 a.m. at the rate of 100 yards in 4 minutes.   The attack was carried out by the 2nd London Regiment, the 5th London Regiment (L.R.B.) and 16th London Regiment (Q.W.R.) on their right being prepared to take advantage of any successes.

The attack was successful in reaching FARMER'S AVENUE and SENSEE AVENUE, but the 2nd London Regiment were unable to progress further owing to heavy enfilade M.G. fire from the South.   169th Infantry Brigade now found itself considerably extended on the left. 2 Bns. 168th Infantry Brigade were consequently put at its disposal and it was then enabled to move up the 5th London Regiment, (L.R.B.) to support the 2nd London Regiment.

The attack of the 52nd Division had proved successful and it reported that it was immediately East of FONTAINE-LES-CROISILLES, but the Guards Division on our right, who had attained an initial success, had been heavily counter attacked and had fallen back to LEGER RESERVE, and in some cases to LEGER TRENCH.   Their casualties were reported to have been very heavy and as a result two platoons of the Q.W.R. were sent to hold LEGER RESERVE in their area.

At 12.50 p.m. the 52nd Division reported that its troops were approaching the SENSEE RIVER, and that they would endeavour to assist the 169th Infantry Brigade held up in T.12.a. by coming down the HINDENBURG LINE in T.6 and by clearing SENSEE AVENUE in T.12.b.   52nd Division also said that the 57th Division would pass through them about 4 p.m.   In conjunction with the Guards Division a concentrated heavy bombardment of CROISILLES was arranged to take place from 4 p.m. to 5 p.m.   At the same time orders were issued to 168th Infantry Brigade to take over the right and centre Battalions' frontage from 169th Infantry Brigade, thus releasing that Brigade, so that the advance on the morning's objective could be continued.   168th Infantry Brigade was to be prepared to advance subsequently on BULLECOURT.   One M.G.Coy. was put at the disposal of each of these Brigades.   By 5 p.m. two battalions of the 169th Infantry Brigade were reported to be moving down the HINDENBURG Line from T.5.a. to assemble at the junction of HINDENBURG Line and CROISILLES - FONTAINE Road, in order to clear the trenches in U.13.a., b and d, U.19.b. and U.20.a.   By 6 p.m. progress had been made and the 2nd London Regt. was reported to be in NELLY AVENUE in touch with 52nd Division.

At 5.30 p.m. Advanced Div. H.Qrs. moved to S.11.a.5.6.

/At

At 6.30 p.m. orders were issued for the advance to be continued on the 28th instant, into the BULLECOURT Area.

The 167th Infantry Brigade was ordered to relieve the 168th Infantry Brigade, as a preliminary measure, taking over that evening from the Southern Div. Boundary to HILL SWITCH in T.10.d. On relief 168th Infantry Brigade was to concentrate in rear of 169th Infantry Brigade and to follow up its advance closely next day.

The first objective for the 169th Infantry Brigade was given as QUEENS LANE - JOVE LANE and the trench system in U.13.a. and c. The second objective was BULLECOURT and the trenches in U.28.b. and d. and U.22.d. The 168th Infantry Brigade was allotted the task of mopping up in rear of 169th Infantry Brigade and of protecting its right flank if CROISILLES remained in the enemy's hands. The 167th Infantry Brigade was instructed to keep patrolling towards CROISILLES and, if the Village was evacuated, to occupy the ridge in T.30.a. and NELLY AVENUE. One Company 56th Bn. M.G.Corps was allotted to each Brigade and one Company moved up into close reserve. The jumping off line for the 169th Infantry Brigade was fixed as NELLY AVENUE - MOLE LANE. Zero hour was fixed at 12.30 p.m. in consultation with the 57th Division.

Operations of 28th August.

Night patrols from the 167th Infantry Brigade reported that CROISILLES was still occupied by the enemy and that they had been fired on by M.Gs. At 8.0 a.m. a contact 'plane reported CROISILLES empty and at 8.30 a.m. this was confirmed by patrols of the 167th Infantry Brigade, though Germans were still reported to be holding out at T.24 central. Instructions were consequently issued to 167th Infantry Brigade to push on and secure the high ground in T.24.c.

At 12.30 p.m. the attack of the 169th Infantry Brigade commenced under cover of a barrage creeping at the rate of 100 yards in 4 minutes up to the first objective and thence at the rate of 100 yards in 5 minutes.

The attack progressed successfully and troops were reported at 1.10 p.m. to have crossed FAG ALLEY (U.14.b.), the enemy retiring in front. The enemy still held out in T.24. central and GUARDIAN RESERVE. Orders were issued to 168th Infantry Brigade, who were mopping up behind 169th Infantry Brigade, and to 167th Infantry Brigade to get touch in LEG LANE (U.25.a.). Orders were also issued to 168th Infantry Brigade to mop up the pocket in U.13. (GUARDIAN RESERVE), as this was seriously interfering with the communications of 169th Infantry Brigade in front.

At 4.25 p.m. 169th Infantry Brigade reported its two leading Companies either in or just N. of BULLECOURT with the Reserve Coy. in PELICAN LANE.

Parties of 2nd London Regt., 4th London Regt., and 5th London Regt. (L.R.B.) were close up behind, but there were pockets of Germans all down the HINDENBURG LINE who were still holding out.

At 4.15 p.m. 167th Infantry Brigade reported its troops had reached LEG LANE (U.25.c. & b.) and CRATER TRENCH. The Guards Division meanwhile swung round their left to conform.

The 57th Division, which had relieved the 52nd Division, and was now attacking on our left, reported that it was held up S.W. of RIENCOURT.

At 5.30 p.m. 168th Infantry Brigade reported that the 4th London Regiment were hung up by a pocket of the enemy in U.14.c., but instructions had been issued for this to be dealt with by the 4th London Regiment, working down the HINDENBURG Front and Support Lines, and by the 13th London Regiment in the trenches to the S.E.

At 6.15 p.m. 169th Infantry Brigade reported that portions of its battalions had actually got into BULLECOURT before 4 p.m. but had withdrawn to PELICAN LANE as the M.G. fire was too heavy.

By 6.15 p.m. the pocket of Germans at the HUMP (U.14.c.) had been cleared.

Orders were received from 17th Corps to continue the attack

/on

on 29th August towards QUEANT in co-operation with the Corps on either flank. The objectives allotted to 56th Division were from the SPUR in C.5.c. & d. to the cross roads U.23.d.9.3. (inclusive) and for patrols to push out in front to reconnoitre the DROCOURT - QUEANT LINE. Zero hour was fixed at 1 p.m. owing to the difficulty of reorganising the units who had been engaged in clearing up pockets.

At 7 p.m. orders were issued to 168th Infantry Brigade to complete the mopping up of the HINDENBURG LINE, and to 167th Infantry Brigade to work to the S.E. and obtain touch with 168th and 169th Infantry Brigades in LEG LANE and PELICAN AVENUE.

When this had been effected 168th Infantry Brigade was to take over the front from the Railway at U.26.c.3.6. to U.21.c.2.0. and 169th Infantry Brigade from U.21.c.2.0. along PELICAN LANE to the northern boundary in readiness for the attack on the objectives mentioned above.

The 57th Division reported at 7.45 p.m. that it had been unable to capture RIENCOURT or HENDECOURT. At 7.45 p.m. detailed orders were issued to 168th and 169th Infantry Brigades to attack the objectives given above, Zero hour being at 1 p.m. on 29th inst., and to 167th Infantry Brigade to withdraw into Divnl. Reserve, 1 battalion being placed at the disposal of 168th Infantry Brigade. This battalion was not to be involved in fighting if possible.

At 10.35 p.m. the pocket of Germans in GUARDIAN Trench was still holding out, so 167th Infantry Brigade was ordered to envelope it from the South, it being most important for the artillery to take up positions there for the attack the following day.

At 12 midnight 168th Infantry Brigade reported that their units were very much mixed up in the Sunken Road W. of BULLECOURT and it would be very difficult to reorganise them for the attack.

Operations of 29th August.

By 6.45 a.m. all pockets of Germans were reported to be clear of the enemy and approximately 30 M.Gs. and 100 prisoners were captured in them. The situation on our left, however, was not clear, and B.G.C. 167th Infantry Brigade reported he had been unable to obtain touch with 168th Infantry Brigade in PELICAN AVENUE as it was not a trench but only a track.

At 10.25 p.m. a heavy bombardment was opened by us on BULLECOURT. By 12.30 p.m. all troops were reported to be in their assembly areas.

The attack commenced at 1 p.m. and first reports shewed that the troops started well up to the barrage and that the enemy's fire was not heavy. The attack progressed well on the left but our right and centre were held up by STATION REDOUBT and M.G. fire from BULLECOURT. The 14th London Regt. however, worked round BULLECOURT to the South and by 2.40 p.m. were reported to be through the Village but STATION REDOUBT was still in enemy hands and there were a few enemy M.Gs. still holding out in the Village. The 169th Infantry Brigade on the left advanced as far as the Sunken Road in U.22.c. Meanwhile the 57th Division reported they had entered RIENCOURT and were through HENDECOURT, but there was a nest of German M.Gs. at U.22.b. firing on their right flank. The 13th London Regiment attempted to capture STATION REDOUBT from the North but unsuccessfully, RAILWAY RESERVE Trench being strongly held by the enemy.

Orders were issued to 167th Infantry Brigade to take over the whole Divnl. front from 168th and 169th Infantry Brigades and for these two Brigades to concentrate in and reorganise in stated areas in rear.

The line held by the Division on the night 29/30th was as follows :- PELICAN AVENUE (in touch with 3rd Division) in U.26 - TOWER RESERVE - GORDON RESERVE - line of posts at U.22.d.2.6. - U.22.c.5.9. - U.22.a.1.3. The right of 57th Division was obscure.

Following orders received from XVII Corps, 167th Infantry Brigade was instructed to consolidate and improve this line and to take advantage of an attack by VI Corps on our right to push outposts well in front so as to gain depth East of BULLECOURT.

/Operations

Operations of 30th August.

The relief of 168th and 169th Infantry Brigades by 167th Infantry Brigade was reported completed by 7.30 a.m.

At about 5 a.m. the enemy counter-attacked the line HENDECOURT - BULLECOURT and ECOUST in strength and made progress driving us out of BULLECOURT on to the line PELICAN AVENUE - PELICAN LANE, but our posts to the North were maintained intact.

The 57th Division was driven in to the line of the BULLECOURT HENDECOURT Road and the enemy captured the FACTORY at U.22.b.1.6.

The 3rd Division on our right were driven out of ECOUST. The 167th Infantry Brigade attempted to regain BULLECOURT by bombing operations but without result owing to enemy M.G. fire which was very heavy from STATION REDOUBT and BULLECOURT.

Orders were received from XVII Corps to capture BULLECOURT and STATION REDOUBT on the 31st inst. in conjunction with an attack by VI Corps on LONGATTE. A bombardment by heavy artillery was therefore at once commenced on STATION REDOUBT.

Orders were issued to 168th Infantry Brigade to take over the front on the night 30/31st and capture BULLECOURT and STATION REDOUBT. The battalion of 167th Infantry Brigade on the left flank was to be placed under the orders of 168th Infantry Brigade and were to be entrusted with the capture of the FACTORY in U.22.b.1.8. The Brigade was then to push on and capture the line TANK AVENUE - U.28.b.7.4. - FOX SUPPORT - Junction with JOY RIDE in U.22.d.2.2. - SADDLER LANE - U.22.c.5.4. thence Sunken Road to FACTORY (inclusive). Two tanks operating from 3rd Divn. area were to co-operate in the capture of STATION REDOUBT. The line held by this Division on night 30/31st ran as follows :- In touch with 3rd Division at U.26.c.2.3. - along PELICAN AVENUE - BORDERER LANE - Sunken Road U.21.d. - U.22.a. - U.22.c.0.5. - BEEF ALLEY.

Operations of 31st August.

The 168th Infantry Brigade with one battalion of 167th Infantry Brigade on the left attacked at 5.15 a.m. under a creeping barrage and captured the FACTORY in U.22.b.1.5. and STATION REDCUBT on the right but were held up by M.G. fire from BULLECOURT. The 14th London Regt. reached and captured BULLECOURT AVENUE and RAILWAY RESERVE in U.27.c. and d and T.3. The 3rd Division captured ECOUST on our right.

Bombing attacks were then initiated on BULLECOURT from three sides and by 5 p.m. most of it was in our hands. The enemy still held out in GORDON RESERVE on the Eastern outskirts of the Village.

Orders were received from XVII Corps for the 52nd Division to relieve the 56th Division in the line on the night 31/1st Sept. The 155th Bde. 52nd Division, moved up to HENIN HILL about 1 p.m. relieving 169th Infantry Brigade which marched back to rest at BOILEUX ST. MARC.

During the afternoon the enemy counter-attacked the 3rd Division in ECOUST on our right and drove them out, but a fresh attack by the 3rd Division restored the situation on our immediate right.

The line handed over by 56th Division to 52nd Division ran as follows :- BULLECOURT AVENUE - TOWER RESERVE - Post at U.27.b.9.9. - SADDLER LANE - Sunken Road U.22.a. & c. with FACTORY inclusive. In touch on both flanks.

During the evening 167th and 168th Infantry Brigades on relief by Brigades of 52nd Division marched out of the line to rest in areas round BOYELLES.

Total prisoners captured during these operations :-

/29 Officers

PRISONERS.-

29 Officers - 1,047 O.Rs.

Guns - 2 77 mm. and 1 8" How.

M.Gs. - Over 200.

T.Ms. - Over 50.

Total in VI Corps - 23 Officers   674 O.Rs.
"   " XVII Corps -   6   "   373   "
                      ‗‗   ‗‗‗‗
                      29   1047

CASUALTIES.-

UNIT.	Killed. O.	O.R.	Wounded. O.	O.R.	Missing. O.	O.R.	Injured. O.	O.R.	TOTAL. O.	O.R.
1/7th Middlesex Regt.	2	49	5	210	1	29	-	-	8	288
1/8th Middlesex Regt.	4	38	4	165	-	13	-	-	8	216
1/1st London Regt.	3	39	8	159	2	135	-	-	13	333
1/4th London Regt.	4	34	8	149	1	10	-	-	13	193
1/13th London Regt.	5	43	10	206	-	9	-	-	15	258
1/14th London Regt.	1	56	11	240	1	8	-	1	13	305
1/2nd London Regt.	1	39	11	225	-	14	-	1	12	279
1/5th London Regt.	2	35	11	226	-	28	-	-	13	289
1/16th London Regt.	4	50	9	263	-	30	-	-	13	343
56th Bn.M.G.Corps.	3	13	5	71	-	3	-	-	8	87
1/5th Cheshire Regt.	-	-	-	4	-	-	-	3	-	7
280th Brigade R.F.A.	-	4	3	22	-	-	-	-	3	26
281st Brigade R.F.A.	1	1	1	38	-	-	-	-	2	39
416th (Edinboro')Fld. Coy.R.E.	-	-	-	1	-	-	-	1	-	2
56th Div.Signal Coy.	-	-	-	1	-	-	-	-	-	1
247th Employ.Coy.	-	-	-	1	-	-	-	-	-	1
2/1st Ldn.Field Amb.	-	1	-	3	-	-	-	-	-	4
2/2nd Ldn.Field Amb.	-	1	-	2	-	-	-	-	-	3
2/3rd Ldn.Field Amb.	-	1	-	3	-	-	-	-	-	4
X/56th T.M.Battery.	-	-	-	1	-	-	-	-	-	1
169th T.M.Battery.	-	-	2	2	-	-	-	-	2	2
TOTALS.	30	404	88	1992	5	279	-	6	123	2681

		Offrs.	O.Rs.
Total excluding casualties from gas.	Killed.	30	404
	Wounded.	88	1992
	Missing.	5	279
	Injured.	-	6
	TOTAL.	123	2681

5th Sept. 1918.

Major-General,
Commanding 56th Division.

SECRET   56th DIVISION.   LOCATION TABLE at 6 a.m.   AUGUST 1918.   APPENDIX 1

	17	18	19	20	21	22	23	24	25	26	27	28	29	30	31
Div. H.Q.	Le Cauroy					Bavincourt	Blaireville				S11a55				
167th Inf.Bde.H.Q.	Izel-les-Hameau					Barly	Blaireville		T19c55				U7d09		
1st London Regt.	Izel-les-Hameau					Gouy en Artois	} Offensive								
7th Middx. Regt.	Penin					Barly				Operations					
8th Middx. Regt.	Izel-les-Hameau					Barly									
168th Inf.Bde.H.Q.	Maizières				Lignereuil	St Amand	Blaireville		39d62 S11d81 T8; T14c91 T4b88 U7d74						
4th London Regt.	Houvin-Houvigneul			Magnicourt sur Canche	Gd. Rullecourt	Berles au Bois	} Offensive Operations								
13th " "	Gouy-en-Terrois				Liencourt St Amand										
14th " "	Maisières				Lignereuil	La Cauchie									
169th Inf.Bde.H.Q.	Lignereuil		Arras		Avesnes le Comte	Saulty	{ Basseux Area	{ Purple Line	- Offensive Operations	T4b45 U7d09		T4b45 U7d04	T4b45		
2nd London Regt.	Grand Rullecourt Dainville				Avesnes la Comte	Bavincourt									
5th " "	Lignereuil Arras				Hauteville	Saulty Area									
18th " "	Lignereuil Arras				Noyelle Vion										
Div. Arty. H.Q.	Berneville				Bavincourt	Blaireville					S11a55				
280th Bde.	Berneville					Boisleux-au-Mont									
281st	Simencourt					Boisleux-au-Mont									
Pioneers.	Beaufort				La Bazeque	Blaireville									
M.G. Battn. H.Q.	Le Cauroy			(Berlencourt)	La Bazeque	Blaireville					S11a55				

✻ The Div. marched to new area during night 21/22 Aug.

SECRET 56th DIVISION. LOCATION TABLE at 6 p.m. AUGUST 1918. APPENDIX 1

Ref. Sheets 51B & 51C

	1	2	3	4	5	6	7	8	9	10	11	12	13	14	15	16
Div. H.Q.		WARLUS														
167th Inf. Bde. H.Q.	M14.a.69.															IZEL LES HAMEAU
1st London Regt.	M8.c.91.						SUPPORT						LINE			" PERN
7th Middx. Regt.	M22.d.02.						RESERVE						SUPPORT			" PERN
8th Middx. Regt.	M16.d.95.						LINE						RESERVE			IZEL LES HAMEAU
168th Inf. Bde. H.Q.	8 Rue Pasteur ARRAS															
4th London Regt.	G35.d.18			G36.b.77			RESERVE						LINE			
13th " "	H25.d.27 (L)			G36.b.77 G35.d.13			LINE						SUPPORT			
14th " "	H31.c.50 (R)			ARRAS			LINE									
169th Inf. Bde. H.Q.	33 Rue Jeanne d'Arc. ARRAS															
2nd London Regt.	N7.a.29 (L)						LINE (R)						SUPPORT			
5th " "	M5.a.66						SUPPORT						LINE (L)			
18th " "	M5.a.63 (R)															
Div. Arty. H.Q.	WARLUS															
280th Bde.	M3.d.22.															
281st "	G27.b.99.33															
282nd " A.F.A	M14.a.58.															
180th " "	G28.b.15.67															
Pioneers.	ARRAS															
M.G. Battn. H.Q.	WARLUS															

LINE ———— (red)
SUPPORT ———— (yellow)
RESERVE ———— (black)
DIV. AT REST

SECRET.   Copy No. 19

56th DIVISION ORDER NO. 188.

7th August 1918.

Ref. 1/20,000 Sheet 51 B. S.W. &
    attached tracing.

1.   Gas will be projected on to NEUVILLE VITASSE on the night of August 8th/9th, or the first subsequent favourable night.

2.   <u>TARGETS</u> etc.

    1. The SUGAR FACTORY   at N.19.c.4.4. 47 Drums C.G.
    2. Eastern edge of Village at N.19.b.6.6. 85 Drums C.G.

All projectors are installed at M.24.a.4.3.

3.   O.C. "J" Special Coy. R.E. will inform Division at 6:30 p.m. on the night of the operation as to whether conditions are favourable or not, and a preliminary decision will be made at that time.

If operation is to take place, an officer of "J" Special Coy. R.E. will report at 167th Inf. Brigade H.Q. two hours before Zero, and remain there until the completion of the operation.

2nd Lieut. F. HODKINSON, M.C., R.E., will be in charge of the projector positions.

4.   All projectors will be discharged at Zero, or within 30 minutes after Zero.

5.   The Wind Limits for the operation are S.S.W. to N. by E. (thro' W.).

6.   The following code will be used for this operation :-

"OPERATION WILL TAKE PLACE TONIGHT"   ...   KEN.

"OPERATION WILL <u>NOT</u> TAKE PLACE TONIGHT"   ...   NO KEN.

7.   Reference hour for Zero will be 11 p.m., and will be referred to as "CHARLES".

Zero hour will be notified as "CHARLES" plus or minus so many hours.

8.   The following precautions will be taken :-

(a)   The area marked <u>green</u> on the attached tracing will be cleared of troops by Zero minus 5 minutes, and will not be re-occupied until reported clear of gas by anti-gas personnel.

(b)   In the area marked <u>red</u> on the attached tracing, troops will wear box respirators from Zero minus 2 minutes to Zero plus 40 minutes, or until such time as the area is reported free from gas by anti-gas personnel.

(NOTE: Tracings attached for 59th Divn., 167th and 169th Inf. Bdes. only.)

9.   ACKNOWLEDGE.

Issued at 1 p.m.

                                        Lieut-Colonel.
                                        General Staff.

P.T.O.

Copy No.

1. 167th Infantry Brigade.
2. 168th Infantry Brigade.
3. 169th Infantry Brigade.
4. 1/5th Cheshire Regt.
5. C.R.A.
6. Right H.A. Group.
7. C.R.E.
8. 56th Bn. M.G. Corps.
9. 56th Div. Gas Officer.
10. A.D.M.S.
11. "Q".
12. A.D.C.
13. XVII Corps.
14. "
15. 59th Division.
16. 57th Division.
17. "J" Special Coy. R.E.
18. War Diary.
19. "   "
20. File.

SECRET Copy No. 30

56th DIVISION WARNING ORDER No. 189.

14th August 1918.

1. The 56th Division (including Artillery) is to be relieved from the line by 15th Division, the relief to be completed by 6.0 a.m. 18th instant.

2. On relief, 56th Division will be located in the LE CAUROY Area.

3. Moves to the LE CAUROY Area will be carried out by Light Railway and busses: details will be communicated later by "Q" 56th Division.

4. The outline arrangements for relief are shown in Appendix "A" attached.

5. As far as possible, Artillery and Machine Guns will not be relieved on the same nights as the Infantry they are supporting.

6. While the relief is in progress, units of 15th Division arriving in 56th Divisional Area will come tactically under the command of G.O.C. 56th Division.
Similarly units of 56th Division arriving in 15th Divisional area will come under the orders of G.O.C. 15th Division and will report their arrival and location.

7. It is important that every precaution should be taken to guard against the relief being seen by hostile aircraft.
Should it be considered necessary to carry out reliefs in daylight, the matter will be referred to Div. H.Q. for decision.

8. All the arrangements which have been made for the training of 78th American Division will be handed over by Infantry Brigades and other units on relief. It is possible that the attachment may be postponed until after the conclusion of the relief.

9. Defence Schemes, Air-photos, Trench Maps and Trench Stores will be handed over on relief and receipts taken.

10. Command of Brigade Sections will be handed over to incoming Brigadiers on completion of relief.

11. The hour at which the G.O.C. will hand over command and at which Div. H.Q. will open in the LE CAUROY Area will be communicated later.

12. ACKNOWLEDGE.

B Pakenham
Lieut-Colonel,
General Staff.

Issued at :- 5.30 p/-

Copy No.		No.	
1.	167th Infantry Brigade.	16.	56th Div. Train.
2.	168th Infantry Brigade.	17.	56th Div. M.T.Coy.
3.	169th Infantry Brigade.	18.	A.D.C.
4.	1/5th Cheshire Regt.	19.	Camp Commandant.
5.	C.R.A.	20.	56th Div. Employment Coy.
6.	Right H.A. Group.	21.	French Mission.
7.	C.R.E.	22.	56th Div. Reception Cmp.
8.	56th Bn. M.G.Corps.	23.	XVII Corps.
9.	56th Div. Signal Coy.	24.	" "
10.	56th Div. Gas Officer.	25.	15th Division.
11.	A.D.M.S.	26.	57th Division.
12.	A/Q.	27.	59th Division.
13.	A.P.M.	28.	78th American Division.
14.	D.A.D.O.S.	29-30.	War Diary.
15.	D.A.D.V.S.	31.	File.

P.T.O.

APPENDIX 'A'.

Serial No.	Date. AUGUST.	Unit.	From.	To	In relief of.	Moving to
1.	Night 15/16th.	44th Inf.Bde. Group. (15th Divn.)	Le CAUROY Area. (H.Qrs.IZEL LE HAMEAU).	LINE, Right Section.	167th Inf.Bde. Group.	IZEL LE HAMEAU Area.
2.	do.	2 M.G.Coys. 15th Division.	AMBRINES.	LINE.	M.Gs. covering Centre Section.	AMBRINES.
3.	16th	9th Gordons (Pioneers).	BEAUFORT.	ARRAS.	1/5th Cheshire Rt.	BEAUFORT.
4.	Night 16/17th.	45th Inf.Bde. Group.	LE CAUROY Area (H.Qrs.LIGNEREUIL)	LINE.	169th Inf.Bde.	GRAND RULLECOURT Area.
5.	do.	1 M.G.Coy.	AMBRINES.	LINE.	M.Gs. covering Left Section.	AMBRINES.
6.	Night 17/18th.	46th Inf.Bde. Group.	LE CAUROY Area (H.Qrs.MAZIERES).	LINE.	168th Inf.Bde.	MAZIERES Area.
7.	do.	1 M.G.Coy.	AMBRINES.	LINE.	M.Gs. covering Right Section.	AMBRINES.

SECRET   Copy No. 30

56th DIVISION ORDER No. 190.

                                                    August 15th, 1918.

1.   56th Division Warning Order No. 189 of 14th instant is confirmed with the exception of para. 8 (see para. 8 below).

2.   56th Divisional Artillery will move as under on relief by Brigades of 15th Divisional Artillery :-

   15th/16th and 16th/17th - 281 Bde. R.F.A. from line to wagon lines.
   16th/17th and 17th/18th - 280 Bde. R.F.A.   "   "   "   "   "
   17th/18th - 56th Div. Artillery to MAGNICOURT - ETREE WAMIN Area.

3.   All details of Infantry reliefs will be arranged between Infantry Brigadiers concerned.

4.   Details of relief of R.E. Coys., Field Ambulances, and M.G. Battalion will be arranged direct between C.R.Es., A.D.M.S' and Os.C. M.G.Battalions.

5.   Infantry Brigades and C.R.E. will arrange to hand over a list of all work in progress and contemplated.

6.   Units of 15th Division will come up by Light Railway.
   44th Brigade Group will detrain at WAILLY, R.22.b.7.4. at 9.0 p.m. on 15th instant.
   Times and places of detraining of other units will be notified later.
   137th Inf. Bde. will arrange for guides to meet units of 44th Inf. Bde. at detraining station.   Guides for other units will be arranged between Commanders concerned.

7.   There will be no restrictions for move of transport with the following exceptions :-

   167th Inf. Bde. Transport will move via. BAILLEULVAL and GOUY and 169th Inf. Bde Transport via SOMBRIN.
   The usual intervals will be observed on the march.

8.   56th Div. No. G.10/32 dated 11th Aug. is cancelled and no further moves of American Troops will take place.

9.   Command of Brigade sections will pass on completion of reliefs in that section.

10.   Completion of reliefs will be reported by wiring the name of the Commander of the unit concerned.

11.   Arrival in new areas will be reported to Div. H.Qrs.

12.   ACKNOWLEDGE.

                                            for Lieut-Colonel,
Issued at 7.0 a.m.   General Staff.

Distribution as for Warning Order No. 189, with exception of
        Nos. 20, 21 and 22.

SECRET

56th Division No. G.3/95.

Reference 56th Div. Order No. 190.

On completion of relief 56th Division will remain in XVII Corps and will be in G.H.Q. Reserve prepared to move at 24 hours notice.

H.Q., 56th Divn.
16th Aug. 1918.

T.OM.Buchan Major
for Lieut-Colonel,
General Staff.

To all Recipients of Warning Order No. 189.

J/L.

War Diary

SECRET. COPY No. 19

56th DIVISION ORDER NO. 191.

19th August 1918.

1. On a date and at an hour which will be notified later the XVII Corps will attack with a view to capturing NEUVILLE VITASSE and the CHAPEL HILL, ORANGE HILL locality. The operation will be known as "THISTLE".

2. (a) The attack will be carried out with the 57th Division on the Right, the 56th Division in the Centre, and the 52nd Division on the Left.
    (b) The 15th Division and one Brigade of the 57th Division will be in Corps Reserve.

3. The attached tracing 'A' shews the following information :-

   (a) RED & BLUE Line. - Opening line of Shrapnel barrage mixed with smoke in a proportion of 4 shrapnel to 1 smoke.

   (b) YELLOW Line. - Outpost Line of resistance.

   (c) BLUE Line. - Outpost Support line.

   (d) GREEN Line. - Limit of General Advance and Outpost Line.

   (e) Area enclosed in YELLOW Area of Exploitation.

   (f) BLACK dashes. - Divnl. Boundaries and boundaries between Brigades.

4. After securing the GREEN Line the Division is to be prepared to continue the advance to the line WANCOURT - GUEMAPPE - MONCHY (all inclusive), within the Divnl. boundaries, in co-operation with an advance by VI Corps.

5. The 56th Division will attack with the 167th Infantry Brigade on the Right, the 168th Infantry Brigade on the Left and the 169th Infantry Brigade in Divnl. Reserve.
    The third Battalion of each attacking Brigade will be in Brigade Reserve.

6. The leading Companies of each attacking Battalion will go straight through to the furthest objective.
    Separate parties will be detailed to clear up the intermediate area and to carry out the exploitation.

7. The Barrage will open on the line shewn in RED and BLUE on the attached map. It will creep forward at the rate of 100 yards in 3 minutes for the first 1200 yards. Thence at 100 yards in 4 minutes up to the GREEN Line, and thence to a general line N. & S. through FOSSE FARM at the rate of 100 yards in 3 minutes.
    On reaching the last mentioned line, the Barrage will lift altogether to admit of exploitation.

8. (a). 3 Cos. (27 Mark V Star Tanks) 11th Tank Battn. will co-operate with 56th Division - 1 Company operating with each Brigade. The Tanks operating with the Support Brigades will assist in any "mopping up" operations necessary.

   (b) Attacking Coys. of Tanks will push right through to the final objective. They will then endeavour to exploit the success gained by pushing forward to the enemy Artillery areas marked in YELLOW on the attached Tracing "A", thus enabling the attacking Infantry to capture or destroy enemy guns.

/(c).

- 2 -

    (c). Should opportunity offer 6th (Light) Tank Bn. (24 Whippets) will move along the ARRAS - CAMBRAI Road and assist the Heavy Tanks in exploiting any success.

    (d). Other Tanks will be in Army Reserve.

9.   The Division will be covered by 6 Field Artillery Brigades as follows :-

    Commanding - Brigadier-General R.J.E.ELKINGTON, C.M.G., D.S.O.

        56th Div. Arty.
        71st Bde. R.F.A. (15th D.A.).
        52nd Army Bde. R.F.A.
        126th   - do -
        232nd   - do -

    The 3 Army F.A.Bdes. will come tactically under the Command of C.R.A., 56th Division on arrival in XVII Corps Area.

10.   H.Qrs. will be situated as follows :-

    (a) During the Operations.-

        Adv.Div.H.Q.   AUCKLAND CAVE (RONVILLE CAVES).
        Rear   "   "   ARRAS, CITADEL.
        Adv.Right Bde.H.Q.   Dugouts near junction of NORTH
                                        ALLEY & N.ALLEY SWITCH.
        Adv.Left Bde.H.Q.   N.1.a.5.9.
        Reserve Bde.H.Q.   M.5.a.6.6.

11.   ACKNOWLEDGE.

T.Om-Buchan
Lieut-Colonel,
General Staff.

Issued at 7 a.m.

Distribution :-

Copy No. 1.*167th Infantry Brigade.
        2.*168th Infantry Brigade.
        3.*169th Infantry Brigade.
        4.*1/5th Cheshire Regt.
        5.*C.R.A.
        6.*C.R.E.
        7.*56th Bn. M.G.Corps.
        8.*56th Div. Signal Coy.
        9.*A.D.M.S.
       10.*"Q"
       11. A.P.M.
       12. A.D.C.
  21 & 13.*XVII Corps.
       14. 57th Division.
       15. 52nd Division.
       16.*15th Division.
       17.*3rd Tank Bde.
       18.*   - do -
       19.*War Diary.
       20.*File.

* = Recipients of Maps.

War Diary.

<u>56th Division No. G.A. 13.</u>

AMENDMENT NO. 1 to 56th DIVISION ORDER No. 191.

<u>Para. 5</u> — Line 1, for "167th Infantry Brigade" read — "168th Infantry Brigade."

Line 2, for "168th Infantry Brigade" read — "167th Infantry Brigade".

H.Q., 56th Divn.
19th Aug. 1918.

J/T.

TCHeald Capt
for Lieut-Colonel,
General Staff.

<u>Issued to all Recipients of Order No. 191.</u>

MARCH TABLE TO ACCOMPANY 56th DIV. ORDER No. 192.

Serial No.	Unit.	To.	Route.	Starting Point.	Time.	Remarks.
1.	167th Inf.Bde.Group. 167th Inf. Bde. 416th Fld.Coy. R.E. No. 2 Coy.Div.Train. 2/2nd Fld.Ambulance. Div.Reception Camp.	BARLY - GOUY - EN-ARTOIS.	No restrictions.	MANIN.	10.15 p.m.	
2.	168th Inf.Bde.Group. 168th Inf. Bde. 512th Fld.Coy.R.E. No. 3 Coy.Div.Train. 2/1st Fld.Ambulance.	LA CAUCHIE - BIENVILLERS - GAUDIEMPRE - ST.AMAND - BERLES AU BOIS.	SOMBRIN - SAULTY.	GRAND RULLECOURT.	~~8.0~~ p.m. 9.10	
3&4.	169th Inf.Bde.Group. 513th Fld.Coy.R.E. 169th Inf. Bde. No. 4 Coy.Div.Train. 2/3rd Fld.Ambulance.	BAVINCOURT - SAULTY.	Via. BARLY.	BARLY CHURCH.	10.0 p.m.	
4.	1/5th Cheshire Rgt.	LA BAZEQUE FM.	GRAND RULLECOURT - SOMBRIN - SAULTY.	GRAND RULLECOURT.	~~9.30~~ pm. 10.30	
5.	56th Bn.M.G.Corps.	LA BAZEQUE FM.	GRAND RULLECOURT - SOMBRIN - SAULTY.	ditto.	~~10.0~~ p.m. 10.45	
6.	Mobile Vet.Section.	SAULTY.	MANIN - AVESNES - BARLY.	Start at 10 pm.		Billets allotted by 169 Inf. Bde.

SECRET   Copy No. 27

56th DIVISION ORDER No. 192.

21st Aug. 1918.

Ref. Sheet 51c
1/40,000 &
LENS 11 1/100000

1. The 56th Division was transferred to VI Corps at 12 noon today.

2. The Division, less Artillery, will march on night of August 21st/22nd to the BAVINCOURT Area in accordance with attached Table.

3. Billeting areas and the composition of Brigade Groups are shown on the attached Table.

4. The usual distances between Companies, Battalions, etc. will be observed on the march.

5. Divisional H.Qrs. will remain at LE CAUROY until further orders.

6. Completion of moves will be reported to Div. H.Qrs.

7. ACKNOWLEDGE.

T.O.M. Bucklaw Mayr
Lieut-Colonel,
General Staff.

Issued at 6.0 p.m.

Distribution :-

Copy No. 1. 167th Infantry Brigade.
     2. 168th Infantry Brigade.
     3. 169th Infantry Brigade.
     4. 1/5th Cheshire Regt.
     5. C.R.A.
     6. C.R.E.
     7. 56th Bn. M.G.Corps.
     8. 56th Div. Signal Coy.
     9. 56th Div. Gas Officer.
     10. A.D.M.S.
     11. A/Q.
     12. A.P.M.
     13. D.A.D.O.S.
     14. D.A.D.V.S.

Copy No. 15. 56th Div. Train.
     16. 56th Div. M.T. Coy.
     17. A.D.C.
     18. Camp Commandant.
     19. 56th Div. Employ. Coy.
     20. 56th Div. Recep. Camp.
     21. Mobile Vet. Section.
     22. XVII Corps.
     23.   "   "
     24. VI Corps.
     25.   "   "
     26.} War Diary.
     27.}
     28. File.

SECRET.   Copy No. 23.

56th DIVISION ORDER No. 193.

Ref. Sheets :
51B.S.W. 1/20,000
51C 1/40,000.
                                                                              22nd August 1918.

1. (a). The VI Corps will attack on August 23rd with a view to capturing and consolidating the BLUE LINE shewn on the attached map.

   (b). The Order of attacking Divisions from South to North will be 3rd, Guards, 56th, 52nd Divisions.

2. The attack will be carried out by the 168th Infantry Brigade (H.Qrs. S.9.d.6.2.) with 1 Battalion attached to it from 167th Infantry Brigade.
   512nd Field Coy. R.E., 2 Companies 1/5th Cheshire Regt. and 1 Company and 1 Section 56th Bn. M.G.Corps are placed at the disposal of B.G.C. 168th Infantry Brigade under whose orders they will act.

3. (a). The objective and Divisional Boundaries are shewn on the attached map.

   (b). After the BLUE LINE objective has been captured, 168th Infantry Brigade will push out in co-operation with Tanks and establish Posts in BOIRY RESERVE, BOIRY WORKS, BOYELLES RESERVE, Southern portion of BOYELLES TRENCH, thence to approximately T.19.c.6.4. The protective barrage will creep to beyond the above line and remain there for 1 hour.

   (c). Arrangements will be made by B.G.C. 168th Infantry Brigade for the Posts mentioned in sub-para. (b) to get touch with the Posts of the Brigades on the flanks.

4. Map shewing the creeping barrage is attached. The Divnl. front will be covered by 6 Brigades Field Artillery.

5. The 168th Infantry Brigade, with 1 Battalion 167th Infantry Brigade, the 512nd Field Coy. R.E., 2 Companies 1/5th Cheshire Regiment, 1 Company and 1 Section 56th Bn. M.G.Corps; will move to assembly areas in the neighbourhood of BLAIREVILLE this afternoon under orders of 168th Infantry Brigade. Assembly areas have been communicated verbally to B.G.C. 168th Infantry Brigade.

6. Attacking troops will move forward from the Assembly Areas to forming up places under cover of darkness and not later than 9 p.m.
   The 59th Division will be in occupation of the front from the Div. Northern boundary to S.24.a.2.8. and will be thinned out.
   From S.24.a.2.8. to the Div. Southern Boundary the Line is held by 3rd Guards Brigade who will move out as our troops arrive.

7. (a). 2 Companies, 11th Bn. Tank Corps, will co-operate with 168th Infantry Brigade in the attack. 1 Company (12 Tanks) operating North of the ST.LEGER Railway and 1 Company (9 Tanks) South of the above railway.
   Of the latter Coy. 3 Tanks will be detailed to clear up the Southern portion of BOYELLES.
   (b). Arrangements will be made for 10 Tanks to carry entrenching tools and for the remainder to carry ammunition and water.
   (c). 168th Infantry Brigade will arrange for the necessary personnel (including Observers) to be carried on each Tank.
   (d). Tanks will return to their rendezvous under the orders of B.G.C. 168th Infantry Brigade before the 1 hour's protective barrage ceases.

/3.

- 2 -

8. The following are the positions of neighbouring Divisions and Brigades. -

    Guards Div. H.Q.   RANSART X.13.d.5.5.
    Guards Bde. on
      Right Flank.   BOIRY ST.MARTIN.
    52nd Div. H.Q.   BRETENCOURT.
    156th Bde. H.Q. on
      Left Flank.   BLAIREVILLE.

9. The Division, less troops mentioned in para. 2, will be held at 1 hour's notice from Zero hour.
Horses will not be harnessed or hooked in.

10. The following will be notified later :-

    (i).   S.O.S. Signal.
    (ii).   Medical Arrangements.
    (iii).   Arrangements for co-operation with Contact Aeroplanes.
    (iv).   Synchronization of watches.
    (v).   Signal Communications.

11. The map to be used for the Operations will be 1/20,000 Sheet 51B. S.W. Edition 8d. (Local).

12. Advanced Div. H.Qrs. will open at BLAIREVILLE X.3.d.7.8. at 10 p.m., August 22nd.
Rear H.Qrs. will be at SAULTY CHATEAU.

13. ACKNOWLEDGE.

T.O.M. Birch
Lieut-Colonel,
General Staff.

Issued at 2.30 p.m.

Distribution:-
Copy No. 1. 167th Infantry Brigade.
     8 & 2. 168th Infantry Brigade.
         3. 169th Infantry Brigade.
         4. 1/5th Cheshire Regt.
         5. C.R.A.
         6. C.R.E.
         7. 56th Bn. M.G.Corps.
         9. 56th Div. Signal Coy.
        10. 56th Div. Gas Officer.
        11. A.D.M.S.
        12. "Q".
        13. A.P.M.
        14. 56th Div. Train.

15. A.D.C.
16. Camp Commandant.
17. VI Corps.
18. do.
19. Guards Division.
20. 59th Division.
21. 52nd Division.
22.) War Diary.
23.)
24. File.
25. 11th Bn. Tank Corps.
26. 3rd Bde. Tank Corps.
27. 12 Squadron R.A.F.

SECRET.   Copy No. 23

ADDENDUM No. 1 to 56th DIVISION ORDER No. 193.

Artillery. 1. The C.R.A. will detail one 18-pdr. Battery and one 4.5" How. Battery, and the B.G., H.A. one 6" How. Battery to be at the direct call of the B.G.C., 168th Infantry Brigade, in addition to their other duties, from Zero Hour onwards.
The C.R.A. will arrange for Field and Heavy Artillery Liaison Officers accordingly.

Reliefs. 2. B.G.C., 168th Infantry Brigade will assume command of the portion of the line taken over from the Guards Division on completion of the relief.

S.O.S. 3. The S.O.S. Signal on VI Corps front is GREEN over GREEN over GREEN.
The Signal to denote the assembly of the enemy for counter attack consists of a RED SMOKE BOMB dropped by an aeroplane over the place where the enemy are seen.

Communication with Contact Aeroplanes. 4. A Contact Aeroplane will call for flares to be lit at Zero plus 1 hour & at Zero plus 3 hours. In each case these will be lit by the most advanced troops.

Synchronization of Watches. 5. Watches will be synchronized at 168th Inf. Bde. H.Q. X.3.d.7.8. (BLAIREVILLE) between 5 p.m. and 8 p.m. this evening. C.R.A. & Tank Battalion will synchronize watches at the same place when Div. H.Q. opens.

Zero Hour. 6. Zero hour will be 4.55 a.m. 23rd inst.

Medical Arrangements. 7. The following are the Medical Arrangements :—

   Regimental Aid Post   —   S.17.a.8.3.
   Walking Wounded
      Collecting Post   —   S.2.b.8.0.
   Advanced Dressing
      Station.   —   M.31.b.2.8.

8. ACKNOWLEDGE.

B. Pakenham

Issued at 5.30 p.m.

22nd Aug. 1918.
                                                          Lieut-Colonel,
                                                          General Staff.

To all recipients of 56th Div. Order No. 193.

SECRET 56th Division No. G. 3/121.

SIGNAL INSTRUCTIONS
TO ACCOMPANY 56th DIVISION ORDER No. 193.

Signal communications will be as follows :-

1. **LINES.**
   Buried cable exists from Advanced Div. H.Qrs. to S.9.a.0.8. approximately. From this point cables will be overland or in trenches.
   From Advanced Div. H.Qrs. telephonic communication will be established to :-
   168th Infantry Brigade.
   Both Flank Divisions, Advanced Headquarters.
   VI Corps.
   Rear 56th Division.
   Visual and Wireless Stations.
   Infantry Brigade on the Left.
   In addition, telephonic communication will be established from R.A. Exchange to :-
   Both Flank D.As.
   Rear 56th Divnl. Artillery.
   All Groups.

2. **VISUAL.**
   A Visual Station will be established at X.10.a.1.9., working through a transmitting station at S.1.d.7.0. to the 168th Inf. Bde. Advanced H.Qrs. at S.9.d.6.2.
   The transmitting station at S.1.d.7.0. will be prepared to receive messages from any visual station forward of Brigade H.Qrs. Battalions should be informed of the position of this station as early as possible (See Map "B").

3. **WIRELESS.**
   Wireless Stations will be situated at Advanced Div. H.Qrs. and at Advanced 168th Inf. Bde.
   GROUND WIRELESS.
   A Power Buzzer and Amplifier Station will be established at the Signal Report Centre at S.9.a.0.8. working to a second Power Buzzer and Amplifier Station at Advanced 168th Inf. Bde.
   Each Battalion of the 168th Inf. Bde. in the assault will be accompanied by a Power Buzzer Station working back to the Amplifier Station at Brigade H.Qrs. The Brigade Signal Officer of the 168th Inf. Bde. will have a Loop Wireless Station at his disposal, for communication to a Brigade Report Centre, if one is established (See Map "B").

4. **PIGEONS.**
   24 pigeons, in 12 Infantry Pattern Baskets will be provided for the 168th Infantry Brigade, i.e. 3 pairs per Battalion and 6 pairs in reserve at Brigade H.Qrs. under the orders of the Brigade Signal Officer.

5. **DESPATCH RIDERS.**
   Despatch Riders will run from Advanced Div. H.Q. to a Signal Report Centre at S.9.a.0.8. A runners post will be established at the Signal Report Centre to take despatches on to Advanced Brigade H.Qrs.

6. **AEROPLANES.**
   168th Inf. Bde. and Battalions will put out POPHAM Panels, and positions of Battalion Panels will be reported to Div. Signal Officer as early as possible, for communication to the Squadron R.A.F. concerned.
   A Dropping Station will be established at Advanced Div. H.Q. at X.10.a.1.9.

H.Q., 56th Divn. for Lieut-Colonel,
22nd Aug. 1918. General Staff.

P.T.O.

Distribution :-

    167th Infantry Brigade.
    168th Infantry Brigade. (8).
    169th Infantry Brigade.
    C.R.A. (7).
    56th Bn. M.G.Corps.
    56th Div. Signal Coy.
    A.D.C.
    VI Corps. (2).
    59th Division.
    Guards Division.
    52nd Division.
    11th Bn. Tank Corps.
    3rd Bde. Tank Corps.
    12th Sqd. R.A.F.
    War Diary.
    File.

"A" Form.
Army Form C. 2121.
MESSAGES AND SIGNALS.

Prefix... Code......m	Words.	Charge.	This message is on a/c of:	Recd. at ......m
Office of Origin and Service Instructions. URGENT OPERATIONS PRIORITY B. Pakenham for Lt. Col. G.S.	Sent At......m To...... By...		......Service. (Signature of "Franking Officer.")	Date...... From...... By......

TO {

Sender's Number.	Day of Month.	In reply to Number.	AAA
* G.712	24		

In continuation of 56 Div. Order No. 194 protective barrage will wait ½ hour beyond first objective AAA After reaching first objective RUVU will endeavour to secure FOOLEY Reserve - HILL SWITCH and CROSS SWITCH so as to envelope CROISILLES in conjunction with the Guards Divn on the South AAA RUVU will fix zero hour for this operation and arrange barrage AAA Fresh tanks will be available for this operation AAA To recipients of order No. 194. AAA RUVU, C.R.A. 11 Tank Bn. to ACK.

From YEF
Place
Time 12.10 a.m.

B Pakenham

"A" Form.
MESSAGES AND SIGNALS.

Army Form C. 2121.
(In pads of 100.)

URGENT OPERATIONS PRIORITY

To Lt. Col. G.S.

Sender's Number: G.741
Day of Month: 24

Following moves will take place AAA 169 Bde forthwith to BOIRY & BOYELLES Trenches and Reserve Trenches of same name AAA 168 Bde tomorrow to concentrate by 11 a.m. in squares S.12, S.18, S.23.b. AAA All Infantry Brigades to report their H.Q. early as possible AAA Two Coys. Cheshire Pioneers attached to 167 Bde come under orders of C.R.E. forthwith and will remain in present locations and await orders AAA The battalion 169 Bde now attached to 167 Bde will remain at the call of 167 Bde for the present AAA D.M.G.C. will move forward one M.G.Coy. to DINGO and ELK Trench vicinity and one to BLAIREVILLE AAA Addsd. all recipients of Operation Orders 6 and 17 Corps. AAA ACKNOWLEDGE.

From: YEF

Time: 4.40 p.m.

T.M. Buckle
General Staff.

"A" Form.
MESSAGES AND SIGNALS.

Army Form C. 2121.
(In pads of 100.)

URGENT OPERATIONS
PRIORITY.
for Lt.Col. G.S.

Sender's Number.	Day of Month.	In reply to Number.	
* G.750	24		A A A

Attempt of RUVU on Hindenburg Line met with strong opposition and was not successful AAA RUVU will organise the line LEGER RESERVE and SUMMIT Trench as their main line of resistance from the Southern boundary where touch will be obtained with the Guards Divn to T.10.b.5.0. where touch will be obtained with 52 Divn. AAA 52 Divn. is carrying on line from T.10.b.5.0. along road through T.4.a., T.3.b. AAA RUZU will organise strongly the defence of BOIRY RESERVE and BOYELLES RESERVE between BANK COPSE T.21.c. and T.2.c. 5.0. AAA C.R.A. will arrange protective barrage to cover RUVU main line of resistance AAA Addsd. RUVU RUZU, and C.R.A. reptd. RUJU, D.M.G.C. Grays Group, 52 and Guards Divs: 6 and 17 Corps.

From YEF.
Place
Time 10.35 p.m.

"A" Form.
MESSAGES AND SIGNALS.

Army Form C. 2121.
(In pads of 100.)

NT
PRIORITY
Pakenham
for Lt.Col.G.S.

Sender's Number.	Day of Month.	In reply to Number.	AAA
G.752	24		

In continuation of G.750 of to-night AAA RUVU will endeavour to penetrate CROISILLES to-morrow with strong patrols and establish itself on the line FOOLEY RESERVE CROISILLES RESERVE AAA Having reached this line it will endeavour to obtain footing in SENSEE AVENUE SENSEE RESERVE GUARDIAN RESERVE STRAY RESERVE the intention being to place the Division in a position to attack the Hindenburg Line AAA Progress to be frequently reported AAA Addsd. RUVU C.R.A. Grays Group to ACKNOWLEDGE reptd. RUZU, D.M.G.C. 6 and 17 Corps.

From YEF
Place
Time 10.35 p.m.

Pakenham
General Staff.

"A" Form.
MESSAGES AND SIGNALS.

Army Form C. 2121.
(In pads of 100.)

Sender's Number.	Day of Month.	In reply to Number.	AAA
G.804	26		

Action tonight 26/27 and tomorrow 27 as follows AAA 52 Divn. to continue advance vigorously in conjunction with Canadian Corps towards FONTAINE LES CROISILLES and RIENCOURT LES CAGNICOURT turning HINDENBURG LINE from North AAA 56 Div. will maintain pressure all along line harassing defence of CROISILLES in every way possible and will be ready to take immediate advantage of any opportunity afforded by attack from North to make ground towards FONTAINE LES CROISILLES AAA 6th Corps has similar role but to make ground towards QUEANT AAA RUVU will get touch with 52 Divn. now reported in HINDENBURG LINE by patrols and will also feel CROISILLES AAA If CROISILLES empty RUVU will occupy it and push patrols towards SENSEE AVENUE and SENSEE Reserve AAA RUZU will relieve RUVU early as possible tonight and be prepared to advance tomorrow on HINDENBURG LINE from about U.7.central to U.14.central AAA   Addsd. List 'B'

From: IBF
Time: 4.50 p.m.

(Z)(sd) B.PAKENHAM, Lt-Col.
G.S.

"A" Form.
MESSAGES AND SIGNALS.

Army Form C. 2121.
(In pads of 100.)

TO

Sender's Number.	Day of Month.	In reply to Number.
G.806	26	

In continuation of G.804 if RUVU succeeds AAA in occupying CROISILLES to-day RUZU provided there is sufficient light will push forward one battalion as Advanced Guard this evening to occupy HINDENBURG LINE from approx U.7 central to U.14 central AAA Should this battalion occupy above line it will be supported and advance no further to-night but will send out patrols to keep touch with enemy AAA RUZU will be prepared to advance eastwards tomorrow AAA C.R.A. will arrange artillery support AAA Addsd. List 'B' less Tanks

YEF

From 5.45 p.m.

(Sgd) B.PAKENHAM, Lt.Col.
G.S.

"A" Form.
MESSAGES AND SIGNALS.

Army Form C. 2121.
(In pads of 100.)

URGENT OPERATIONS
PRIORITY

TO 3rd Divn.

Sender's Number: G.887
Day of Month: 28
AAA

17 Corps is to continue attack tomorrow towards QUEANT AAA Canadian Corps will probably co-operate AAA 6 Corps is ordered on ECOUST thence NOREUIL keeping pace with 17 Corps AAA 57 Div is directed on cross-roads U.23.d.9.3. exclusive – RIENCOURT – U.18.a. Spur – CHATEAU HENDECOURT AAA 56 Div will make good the line SPUR in C.5.c. and d. to cross roads U.23.d.9.3. inclusive AAA Attack will be carried out by 168 Bde on right and 169 Bde on left AAA 1 Bn. 167 Bde will be placed at disposal of 168 Bde AAA 168 Bde will be responsible for whole of BULLECOURT and area/South of line joining BULLECOURT and U.29.d.7.8. AAA C.R.A. will inform Bdes. barrage arrangements AAA Zero hour will be notified later and will be approx as for to-day AAA 167 Bde less 1 Bn. will be in Div. Res. and will be assembled about CROISILLES AAA 168 and 169 Bdes will establish Bde H.Qrs. approx on line of the FONTAINE – CROISILLES road AAA Acknowledge AAA Added List B less Tanks and 5 Div. reptd 3 Div.

From: 56 Div
Time: 11.30

MESSAGES AND SIGNALS.

Urgent O/P Priority
(Sd) Blakenham
Ricor?

TO: Inst B (less Tanks)
repeated 3rd Divn

Sender's Number: 5890
Day of Month: 28

AAA

In continuation our 5887 aaa 168 Bde will send out patrols early morning 29th inst to ascertain whether enemy still in occupation of BULLECOURT aaa If no report received by 10am that BULLECOURT has been evacuated by enemy Arty will bombard it commencing 11am by which hour all patrols must be clear of the village aaa Zero hour will be one pm 29th inst at which hour Inf will start and Artillery barrage will open at Zero MINUS 5 mins on the general line of the Sunken Road through U26d –

MESSAGES AND SIGNALS.

27c - 27a - 27b - 21d and 22a aaa At Zero the barrage will commence to move forward and will creep forward at the rate of 100 yds in 6 mins and on reaching final objective will form protective barrage lasting for 30 mins after which it will cease aaa On reaching final objective 168 and 169 Bdes will send out patrols to reconnoitre enemys positions with object of finding if strongly held aaa Contact plane will call for flares at 2pm and 4 pm aaa 76 Bde will be on right of 168 Bde aaa Acknowledge aaa Addsd

From: List B Lts Tanks repd 3 Divn
Place: 56 Div
Time: 9.25

"A" Form.
MESSAGES AND SIGNALS.

Army Form C. 2121.
(In pads of 100.)

URGENT
OPERATIONS
PRIORITY

for Lt. Col. G.

TO: T. M. Buchanan

Sender's Number.	Day of Month.	In reply to Number.	AAA
G.709	23		

Operation Order No. 194 AAA Advance will be continued to-morrow and no respite given to enemy AAA Guards Divn. has been directed on ECOUST and 56 Divn. on CROISILLES so as to take defences of HENIN HILL within their area from the South AAA 52 Divn. is to conform with left of 56 Divn. AAA Zero hour will be 7 a.m. AAA RUVU will carry out the attack AAA First objective will be SUMMIT TR. from T.22.d.3.3. to T.16.b.3.8. thence refusing the flank Northwards so as to join up with 52 Divn on Northern boundary AAA 12 tanks will be at disposal of RUVU for this objective AAA Capture of above objective is to assist Guards Divn to capture ST.LEGER and by gaining a footing on high ground North of CROISILLES to envelope it the Guards Divn conforming on South AAA C.R.A. will put down creeping barrage on present S.O.S. lines first lift at Zero plus 10 minutes AAA Pace of barrage 100 yards in 4 minutes AAA 1 M.G.Coy. is placed at disposal of RUVU AAA ACKNOWLEDGE AAA Addsd.RUVU, C.R.A. 11 Tank Bn. repetd.6 Corps Flank Divs and all concerned.

From: YEF
Place:
Time: 11.40 p.m.

T. M. Buchanan
General Staff

SECRET.   Copy No. 19

56th DIVISION ORDER No. 195.

30th August 1918.

1. 3rd Division is to attack to-morrow morning with the object of capturing ECOUST and LONGATTE and BULLECOURT AVENUE as far North as about C.3.a.5.1.

2. 56th Division will co-operate at the same hour by capturing STATION REDOUBT and by establishing itself on the line TANK AVENUE-trench junction U.28.b.7.4. – FOX SUPPORT – to junction with JOY RIDE U.22.d.2.2. – SADDLER LANE U.22.c.5.4. – thence SUNKEN ROAD to FACTORY (inclusive).

3. Zero hour will be at 5.15 a.m.

4. (a). 168th Infantry Brigade will carry out the operation.

    (b). The 7th Middlesex Regiment will be attached to 168th Infantry Brigade

    (c). The attacking troops will be formed up on the line PELICAN AVENUE – PELICAN LANE – and Sunken Road U.21.d. – U.22.d. & BEEF ALLEY by 3 a.m. 31st inst.

    (d). As soon as the attacking troops are formed up, 167th Inf. Bde. will withdraw all troops East of the forming up line.

    (e). The attack will be carried right through BULLECOURT VILLAGE, and careful arrangements must be made to mop it up.

    (f). 2 Tanks (from 3rd Division) will co-operate by attacking STATION REDOUBT from the S.W., thence they will move along RAILWAY RESERVE to junction with BULLECOURT AVENUE. Thence they will work round the Triangle formed by BULLECOURT AVENUE – RAILWAY RESERVE and ZEPHYR TRENCH. The infantry will NOT wait for the Tanks.

    (g). The Field Artillery Barrage will come down at Zero hour (5.15 a.m.) on the general line U.26.c.7.0. – cross roads U.27.b.1.9. – U.22.c.6.8. – FACTORY.
    It will remain on this line until Zero plus 5 minutes at which hour it will lift and commence to creep at the rate of 100 yards in 6 minutes.
    South of the line U.26. central – U.27. central it will move at the rate of 100 yards in 4 minutes, in order to conform to 3rd Division barrage, until it is 200 yards beyond STATION REDOUBT when the pace will be slowed down to conform to the barrage lines on the N. of U.26.central – U.27 central.

    (h). The Heavy Artillery is bombarding STATION REDOUBT until approximately Zero hour to-morrow.
    The C.R.A. will arrange for it to lift on to further objectives ahead of the creeping barrage.

    (i). A protective Field Artillery Barrage will be formed beyond the objective and will stand for 30 minutes.

5. The main Line of Resistance will be organised along BULLECOURT AVENUE (C.3.a.5.1.) – GORDON RESERVE – CHINA LANE – SADDLER LANE – FACTORY (inclusive).

6. ACKNOWLEDGE.

                                                            B. Pakenham
                                                            Lieut. Colonel,
Issued at 7 p.m.   General Staff.

P.T.O.

SECRET.   Copy No. 23

56th Division Order No. 196.

31st August 1918.

less Artillery

1. The 56th Division will be relieved by the 52nd Division August 31st/Sept 1st.

2. On relief Formations and Units of 56th Division will withdraw into the areas shown on the attached tracing.

3.(a) 169th Infantry Brigade will be relieved by 155th Infantry Brigade on 31st inst., relieving troops arriving about 12 noon.

(b) 167th Infantry Brigade will be relieved by 156th Infantry Brigade on 31st inst, relieving Brigade passing high ground about T.10.b. and d. at 8 p.m.

(c) 168th Infantry Brigade will be relieved by 155th Infantry Brigade night August 31st/Sept. 1st. Relief to be complete by 4 a.m. Sept. 1st.

(d) Details of above reliefs to be arranged between Brigadiers.

4. Relief of Field Coys, Pioneers and Field Ambulances will be arranged between Cs.R.E. and A.D.M.S.

5. Relief of Coys of 56th Bn. M.G. Corps attached to 168th and 167th Infantry Brigades will be arranged by Brigadiers to whom they are attached.
52nd Bn. M.G. Corps less two Coys. is moving into area about T.17.c.

6. Command of Brigade Areas to pass on completion of reliefs which will be wired to this office.

7. Div. H.Qrs. will remain at S.11.a.5.7.

8. Command Right Sector XVII Corps front will pass to G.O.C. 52nd Division on completion of Reliefs.

9. ACKNOWLEDGE.

Issued at 7. a.m.

T. M. Buckton May
Lieut-Colonel,
General Staff.

Distribution:-

Copy No.		Copy No.	
1.	167th Infantry Brigade.	13.	56th. Div. Signal Coy.
2.	168th Infantry Brigade.	14.	56th Div. Train.
3.	169th Infantry Brigade.	15.	Camp Commandant.
4.	C.R.A.	16.	56th Div. Reception Camp
5.	C.R.E.	17.	3rd Division.
6.	1/5th Cheshire Regt.	18.	57th Division.
7.	A.D.M.S.	19.	52nd Division.
8.	"Q"	20.	XVII Corps.
9.	A.P.M.	21.	"
10.	56th Bn. M.G. Corps.	22.	War Diary
11.	Right H.A. Group.	23.	War Diary
12.	13th Squadron R.A.F.	24.	File

Army Form C. 2118.

56th DIVISION. WAR DIARY or INTELLIGENCE SUMMARY.

SEPTEMBER 1918.

(Erase heading not required.)

Instructions regarding War Diaries and Intelligence Summaries are contained in F.S. Regs., Part II. and the Staff Manual respectively. Title pages will be prepared in manuscript.

Place	Date	Hour	Summary of Events and Information	Remarks and references to Appendices
BOILEUX ST. MARC.	Sept 1st.		Relief was reported complete and command passed to G.O.C. 52nd Division at 3.30 a.m. All units engaged in bathing, reorganising and re-equipping. For locations see APP.1.	APP.1.
	2nd.		Units resting.	
	3rd.		The C-in-C. Sir DOUGLAS HAIG, visited Div. H.Q. and congratulated the G.O.C. on the good work of the Division.	
	4th.		Warning Orders received from XVII Corps that 56th Division move up to QUEANT - PRONVILLE area to-morrow, 5th inst., in readiness to relieve the 63rd Division in the line on night 6/7th inst., if the tactical situation permitted. Warning Order No. 197 issued.	APP.II. APP.II.
	5th.		On orders being received from XVII Corps confirming the above, 56th Div.O.O.No. 198 was issued. At 12.10 p.m. Orders received from XVII Corps cancelling above moves. 167th and 169th Infantry Brigades, who had already moved to assembly positions near the new area were accordingly brought back to their original locations. Orders received from XVII Corps that this Division would be transferred to XXII Corps to-morrow, 6th inst., and would relieve the 1st Division in the line. Command of new Sector to pass at 10 a.m. on 9th inst. 56th Div. Warning Order No. 199 issued. 56th Div. Operation Order No. 200 issued.	APP.II. APP.II.
	6th.		168th Infantry Brigade Group moved into new area relieving the 3rd Brigade.	APP.I.
	7th.		168th Infantry Brigade relieved the 2nd Infantry Brigade in Left Section of the 1st Div. Sector. 169th Infantry Brigade moved up to the area vacated by the 168th Infantry Brigade. Weather hot and thundery.	APP.I.
	8th.		167th Infantry Brigade moved to Reserve Brigade Area (BLANGY). 169th Infantry Brigade relieved the 1st Infantry Brigade in the Right Section of the 1st Division Sector.	
LES FOSSES FARM.	9th.		Div. H.Qrs. moved to LES FOSSES FARM and G.O.C. took over Command of the Sector from G.O.C.	APP.I.

Army Form C. 2118.

WAR DIARY
56th DIVISION.   *or*   SEPTEMBER 1918.
INTELLIGENCE SUMMARY.

(Erase heading not required.)

Instructions regarding War Diaries and Intelligence
Summaries are contained in F. S. Regs, Part II.
and the Staff Manual respectively. Title pages
will be prepared in manuscript.

Place	Date	Hour	Summary of Events and Information	Remarks and references to Appendices
LES FOSSES FARM.	9th (Cont'd)		took over Command of the Sector from G.O.C., 1st Division at 10 a.m. The G.O.C. proceeded to England on short leave. Brigadier-General FREETH, C.M.G. assumed command of the Division in his absence. Weather wet.	
	10th.		Situation becoming quieter but hostile artillery still active. Quiet day. Hostile artillery carried out several area shoots. Our heavy artillery bombarded SAILLY EN OSTREVENT, and cut wire in the DROCOURT - QUEANT line North of SAILLY EN OSTREVENT.	
	11th.		Situation normal. Hostile artillery shelled ARRAS - CAMBRAI Road during the evening. ETAING and trenches just South of LECLUSE also lightly shelled. O.O. No. 201 issued for relief of 168th Infantry Brigade by 167th Infantry Brigade on night 13/14th inst. 56th Div. Defence Orders No. 1 issued.	APP.II. APP.III.
	12th.		Situation normal. Enemy rather active with his artillery chiefly on our forward battery areas and the ARRAS - CAMBRAI Road. 169th Infantry Brigade carried out an inter-battalion relief.	APP.I.
	13th.		Quiet day. Scattered hostile shelling all over the area. Our artillery were engaged in cutting wire in front of the Division on our left. 167th Infantry Brigade relieved 168th Infantry Brigade in the left section.	APP.I.
	14th.		Enemy shelled battery positions near ETERPIGNY and also destroyed the CHURCH TOWER in ETAING.	
	15th.		Situation normal. Usual hostile shelling of our battery positions. Hostile aircraft very active. Our artillery continued wire cutting in front of the Division on our left flank. Enemy bombed DURY during the night.	
	16th		XXII Corps Warning Order received with reference to the relief of the 11th Division (our left flank Division) by 4th Division and the extension of Corps front southwards by taking over the Left Divisional Sector of Canadian Corps. At a Conference at 4 p.m. between the B.G.G.S., B.G.C., 56th Divn., and G.S.O.I, arrangements were completed for taking over	

Army Form C. 2118.

WAR DIARY
or
INTELLIGENCE SUMMARY.
(Erase heading not required.)

56th DIVISION. **SEPTEMBER, 1918.**

Place	Date	Hour	Summary of Events and Information	Remarks and references to Appendices
LES FOSSES FARM.	16th	(Contd).	the 3rd Canadian Division front, retaining part of our present front in addition. On this 56th Div. Warning Order No. 202 was issued to all concerned. Later XXII Corps Order No. 71 confirming above, was received, the relief to be complete by 10 a.m. Sept. 20th. Weather bright and sultry. Situation fairly quiet. Hostile aircraft much less active.	
	17th		Details of relief arranged with 3rd Can. Div., 4th Div., and XXII Corps 56th Div. Order No. 203. issued. Situation normal. Weather bright and warm with wind S.W. Heavy thunderstorm during the night, and slight increase of water in the Marshes in front of the sector reported. The 3rd Can. Div. report abnormal enemy movement in their sector. XXII Corps 'Bus' table for the relief received during the afternoon.	APP.II
	18th		Situation quiet. Hostile movement observed has been below normal. The enemy aircraft activity during the last few days has been directed largely against our observation balloons, a large number of which have been destroyed by hostile aircraft. One was brought down in flames this afternoon by hostile aircraft. Hostile artillery quiet in the morning but fairly active in the afternoon. Command of the Right Brigade Sector passed at 8 p.m. from 169th Infantry Brigade to 167th Infantry Brigade prior to relief of 167th Infantry Brigade by 10th Infantry Brigade. Weather warm and bright with good visibility until about 5 p.m. when it became hazy and overcast. 56th Div. Order No. 204 with reference to time at which command of the 3rd Division (Can) would pass to G.O.C., 56th Div. was issued in the evening.	See 56th Div.Order No.203 para.2(b). APP.II.
	19th		The changes in disposition of the Division proceeded according to Div. Order No. 203, the 10th Infantry Brigade taking over from 167th Infantry Brigade and 167th Infantry Brigade relieving 169th Infantry Brigade, which withdrew to reserve Brigade area. See Location Report, Appendix I. Situation during the last 24 hours has been quiet with scattered shelling. Visibility good. E.A. fairly active and succeeded in bringing down another Observation Balloon on the Div. front during the afternoon.	56th Div. Order 203. APP.I.
	20th		56th Div. Order No. 203 completed during the night, and to-day 169th Infantry Brigade has	

Army Form C. 2118.

WAR DIARY
or
INTELLIGENCE SUMMARY.
(Erase heading not required.)

56th DIVISION.

SEPTEMBER, 1918.

Instructions regarding War Diaries and Intelligence Summaries are contained in F.S. Regs., Part II. and the Staff Manual respectively. Title pages will be prepared in manuscript.

Place	Date	Hour	Summary of Events and Information	Remarks and references to Appendices
LES FOSSES FARM.	20th (Contd).		moved into the Support Brigade area allotted replacing the 8th Can. Infantry Brigade. The weather is stormy and cold with heavy showers and bright intervals. During the night the 4th London Regt. reported 3 men who had formed a listening post (Left Bn. of Right Bde. Sector) as missing. The Command of the 10th Infantry Brigade passed to G.O.C. 4th Division at 10 a.m. today and the Division is now complete on its new frontage. Situation fairly quiet except for shelling which has been fairly heavy on RECOURT and SAUDEMONT.	56th Div. Order 203 and 204.
	21st.		Quiet day — notable decrease in hostile artillery particularly in the morning. Weather cold and stormy with wind S.W. and increasing at night. Preliminary orders issued from XXII Corps for continuance of the attack towards CAMBRAI at a date to be notified later.	
	22nd.		Quiet day. Aircraft of both sides fairly active. The Div. Sector appeared to be well patrolled by hostile aircraft over both forward and rear areas. A few H.V. shells fell in the neighbourhood in the late afternoon and evening, after a couple of air bursts earlier in the afternoon. 56th Div. Provisional Defence Scheme dated 22.9.18 was issued in the evening.	APP.III.
	23rd.		Quiet day except for some hostile artillery shelling of region south of SAUDEMONT. Notification received from XXII Corps that we should have 6 extra Brigades of Artillery and 4 extra Companies of M.Gs. for the forthcoming operations.	
	24th.		Hostile artillery active on battery positions near SAUDEMONT and S. of RUMANCOURT. Enemy raided one of our posts near MILL COPSE - 1 N.C.O. and 4 O.R. of 4th London Regt. missing. O.O. No. 205 for continuance of offensive operations towards CAMBRAI issued. O.O. No. 206 amplifying above issued. Hostile aircraft active at night.	APP.II. APP.II.
	25th.		Enemy twice attacked an advanced post of the Right Brigade held by 14th London Regt. during the night but repulsed each time. Hostile artillery less active during day. 5th London Regt. took over a section of the front from our S. boundary to the ARRAS–CAMBRAI road from 2nd Canadian Division. O.O. No.207 and amendment thereto issued.	APP.II.

Army Form C. 2118.

56th DIVISION.   WAR DIARY   SEPTEMBER 1918.
or
INTELLIGENCE SUMMARY.
(Erase heading not required.)

Instructions regarding War Diaries and Intelligence Summaries are contained in F. S. Regs., Part II. and the Staff Manual respectively. Title pages will be prepared in manuscript.

Place	Date	Hour	Summary of Events and Information	Remarks and references to Appendices
VILLERS CAGNICOURT.	26th.		Div. H.Qrs. moved to their Advanced Battle H.Qrs. in a Sunken Road just W. of VILLERS CAGNICOURT. Situation quiet except for scattered harassing fire in the vicinity of our battery positions.	
	27th.		For Diary of the Operations see APPENDIX IV.	APP. IV.
	28th.		168th and 169th Infantry Brigades continued the operations to-day their role being to mop up the CANAL DU NORD as far as PALLUEL. See APPENDIX IV, and for Dispositions APPENDIX I. 167th Infantry Brigade occupied PALLUEL without much opposition and later pushed on into ARLEUX where they established a bridge-head.	
	29th.		Orders received from XXII Corps for relief of the Sector held by 167th Infantry Brigade as far as PALLUEL MARSH by 4th Division, relief to be completed by 6 a.m. 30th inst. O.O. No. 208 issued which also ordered 169th Infantry Brigade to take over 167th Infantry Brigade's positions in PALLUEL. At 3 a.m. the enemy attacked our bridge-head at ARLEUX and recaptured the Village. Subsequently they shelled PALLUEL heavily with mustard gas which compelled us to withdraw our troops, except for small posts guarding the bridges over the SENSEE RIVER.	APP. II.
	30th.		Quiet day. Some hostile shelling of PALLUEL. Orders received from XXII Corps for this Division to extend its front to the East as far as AUBENCHEUL AU BAC. G.591 issued accordingly. (relieving a Bde. of 11th Divn.) 168th Infantry Brigade relieved 34th Infantry Brigade in the above section during the night and 169th Infantry Brigade extended their front as laid down in the above Order.	APP. II. APP. I.

6. October, 1918.

Major-General,
Commanding 56th Division.

SECRET   56th Division No. G.A. 145.

157th Infantry Brigade (4).   D.A.D.V.S.
158th Infantry Brigade (4).   56th Div. Train.
159th Infantry Brigade (4).   56th Div. M.T.Coy.
1/5th Cheshire Regt.   A.D.C.
C.R.A.   Camp Commandant.
50th Bde. R.G.A.   56th Div. Reception Camp.
C.R.E.   56th Div. Employment Coy.
56th Bn. M.G.Corps.   French Mission.
56th Div. Signal Coy.   XXII Corps H.A.
56th Div. Gas Officer.   52nd Squadron R.A.F.
A.D.M.S.
"Q"
A.P.M.
D.A.D.O.S.

    Herewith Report of "Operations carried out by 56th Division during period 27th - 29th September 1918".

6th Oct. 1918.   T.H. Heald Capt
Encl.   for Lieut-Colonel,
J.   General Staff, 56th Division.

OC A Coy
   B "   Forwarded for information
   C "   Please initial and pass quickly
                                   Capt & A/Adjt
7-10-18

SECRET.

OPERATIONS CARRIED OUT BY 56th DIVISION
during period 27th - 29th Sept. inclusive.

Preliminary.

On 21st September, 1918, Provisional Instructions were received from XXII Corps for the 56th Division to take part in operations which First and Third Armies were undertaking in the direction of CAMBRAI. The following was the general plan of operations.

The Canadian Corps was to force the Crossings of the CANAL DU NORD N. of MOEUVRES on a frontage of nearly two miles and to spread out and capture the BLUE LINE (shown on the attached map).

The 11th Division on the left of the Canadian Corps and the 56th Division on the left of 11th Division were to pass over the CANAL DU NORD, under cover of this operation, and to deploy facing North, so as to relieve the Canadians on the BLUE LINE West of W.6.c.5.5. The Division was then to attack North, the final objective being the Road from Q.23.c.7.7. to Q.24.a.10.90.

On 23rd September the above instructions were confirmed by "XXII Corps Instructions for the Offensive No. 1". Six extra Brigades of field artillery, making 8 in all, were placed at the disposal of this Division, but three of these were intended mainly to support the advance of the Left Brigade of the 11th Division.

56th Divisional Operation Orders Nos. 205, 206 & 207 were issued accordingly for the attack. 169th Infantry Brigade was detailed to carry out the attack east of the CANAL and 168th Infantry Brigade to co-operate by clearing the western bank (See Map 'A').

The C.R.E. was detailed to throw bridges across the CANAL (at about W.15.a. and W.9.b.8.7.) as soon as the tactical situation permitted, and to assist 169th Infantry Brigade in crossing the AGACHE RIVER.

2 M.G.Cos. 4th Division, were attached to the Division which, with 2 Cos. 102nd M.G.Bn., made a total of 8 Cos. for the operation. Of these, 4 Cos. were detailed to barrage the ground in front of the infantry as the attack passed northwards across their front and one to barrage the high ground N.E. of ETAING and N. of HAMEL to prevent hostile observation.

One Company was kept in defensive positions on the left of the Divisional front and two Coys. were held in reserve.

Zero hour was fixed for 5.20 a.m. on September 27th.

On the night 25/26th September, 1 Bn. 169th Infantry Brigade took over from 1st Canadian Division a section of the front line from our original Southern boundary to the ARRAS - CAMBRAI road so that, on the day of the attack, it would be close to its crossings and would be ready to mop up the western bank of the CANAL where the enemy had posts established.

Div. H.Qrs. moved to an Advanced Battle H.Qrs. at V.3.a.85.70. on 26th September.

Narrative of Events.

The attack commenced at 5.20 a.m. and the Canadians were reported early to be progressing well. Enemy artillery retaliation on the Divnl. front was light and practically ceased by 5.40 a.m. By 8.15 a.m. reports were received that the Canadians had reached the RED LINE. At 11.50 a.m. it appeared that the enemy were still holding out in W.15.c. central, W.21.c., W.21.a. and that the Canadians were apparently progressing slowly on the left. Our bridging parties, who were timed to reach the Canal bank with their material after the Canadians had cleared it, found themselves opposed by hostile infantry, but the R.E. and Pioneers, pushed on, cleared the western bank and established themselves on their crossings, thus rendering assistance to the Canadians advancing from the South. As soon as the sites were clear bridging operations were put through rapidly and the 169th Infantry Brigade was ordered to cross.

/By

By this time it was evident that there would be a delay in assembling the troops on the BLUE LINE for the Second Phase of the operations and G.O.C. 11th Divn. decided to delay the hour for the attack by 34th Inf.Bde. by 40 mins. This decision was taken at 1.15 p.m. and the G.O.C. 56th Divn. gave orders for the attack by 169th Infantry Brigade to conform.

In the meantime the situation about MARQUION had improved and the latter Village cleared of the enemy. The 5th London Regt. were also reported to have cleared the West Bank of the CANAL in W.9.b. Two bridges had been constructed across the CANAL by the R.E., one in W.15.a. by 512th Field Coy. R.E. and one in W.9.b. by 513th Field Coy. By 12.40 p.m. these bridges were completed and the 2nd London Regt. and 16th London Regt. had commenced crossing. By 2.5 p.m. the crossing of the CANAL had proceeded well and bridges had been constructed by 416th Field Coy. R.E. across the AGACHE RIVER at W.10.a.2.6.

At 3.30 p.m. the attack of the 169th Inf.Bde. east of the CANAL and of the 15th London Regt. west of the CANAL commenced under cover of a heavy artillery, machine gun and mortar barrage. At 3.50 p.m. the troops were reported to have passed through KAMWEZI COPSE and to be advancing close under the barrage. At 4.30 p.m. 168th Inf. Bde. reported that the 15th London Regt. had reached their first objective - the road running E and W through SAUCHY-CAUCHY - capturing 4 M.Gs. and were in touch with 169th Inf.Bde. on the CANAL and that the latter had cleared SAUCHY-CAUCHY and SAUCHY LESTREE.

From 6 p.m. onwards the position became obscure owing to enemy pockets holding out.

The attack had proceeded according to the Time Table as far as Q.29.a. & Q.30.c., SAUCHY-CAUCHY, KAMWEZI COPSE, KIDUNA COPSE and CEMETERY WOOD. These places were taken by the 2nd London Regt. and 16th London Regt. (Q.W.R.) with many prisoners, while the area between the branches of the AGACHE RIVER was cleared by a Company of the 5th London Regt. (L.R.B.) who secured several prisoners.

North of these places, M.G.nests, chiefly along the CANAL banks held up the attack for a time. On the right the 2nd London Regt. were held by M.Gs. in Q.30.c. and in the railway embankment Q.24.c. & d. These nests were attacked by the 2nd London Regt. and 5th London Regt (L.R.B.) four times without success, but a fifth attempt was made and the nests were captured with their garrison by 3.30 a.m.

On the left the Q.W.R. met with considerable opposition from Machine Guns on the CANAL bank in Q.29.a., which completely commanded the swamps in Q.29.a. & c. By working along the AGACHE RIVER to the East of the CANAL in stages as far as Q.23.a.6.0. they eventually surrounded the Machine Guns and inflicted heavy casualties on their teams. 1 Officer and 22 O.Rs. were captured here and 20 O.Rs. were found Dead at their posts.

By 7 p.m. the Q.W.R. were established along the Railway Embankment in Q.23.c. & d. Here another M.G. nest at Q.23.a.70.05. gave trouble,, and held out till dawn, when it was captured with the guns and a few prisoners.

The final objective for the day was, therefore, only reached in its entirety in the early hours of the 28th.

The 13th London Regt. (168th Inf.Bde.) who were advancing on the west bank of the CANAL were also held up by Machine Guns coming from MILL COPSE and both banks of the CANAL, and it was found impracticable to advance in face of them during daylight there being two avenues of approach only through the marsh. Accordingly the Reserve Coy. 13th London Regt. were ordered to clear up the situation as soon as the moon was up. At 2 a.m. this Company advanced from SAUCHY-CAUCHY and reached their final objective without opposition.

At 10.30 p.m. 169th Inf. Bde. having reported that its Right Battn. was on the final objective but Left Battn. still held up, orders were issued for the advance to be continued to the BROWN LINE on the 28th instant, to conform with the Brigade on the Right, and 167th Infantry Brigade was ordered to push out patrols early on the 28th instant into PALLUEL and occupy it if empty.

/At

At 1.30 a.m. 169th Infantry Brigade stated they would reach their final objective by morning, but it would be necessary to arrange an organised attack under a sweeping barrage to clear the enemy out of the ground up to the River SENSEE. This was accordingly arranged and 168th Infantry Brigade were ordered to co-operate by clearing the West bank of the CANAL.

Zero hour was fixed for 10.30 a.m.

Operations on 28th September.

The attack of 168th and 169th Infantry Brigades progressed well and 169th Infantry Brigade reported at 1.30 p.m. that all objectives were captured and posts established North of the BOIS DE QUESNOY and covering the SENSEE River.

The 168th Infantry Brigade was also successful in clearing the west bank of the CANAL. Meanwhile the 167th Infantry Brigade had occupied PALLUEL without serious opposition soon after dawn and at 11.20 a.m. reported that the 8th Middlesex Regiment had established posts on the northern and eastern sides of the Village and were pushing on towards ARLEUX. This they succeeded in entering during the late afternoon and established posts. At 3 a.m. the following morning (29th Sept.) however, the enemy counter-attacked under a heavy artillery barrage and drove them out to their former positions covering PALLUEL which was held and consolidated.

Casualties.		Killed.	Wounded.	Missing.
	Officers.	5	9	—
	O.Rs.	38	269	17

Prisoners.— 12 Officers. 501 O.R.

Material captured.		T.Ms.	M.Gs.
	Light	7	34
	Heavy	3	11

4th Oct. 1918.

T.Om.Buchan Mayor

Major-General,
Commanding 56th Division.

"A" Form
MESSAGES AND SIGNALS.

Army Form C. 2121
(In pads of 100.)

TO URGENT

Sender's Number: G.591
Day of Month: 30.

AAA

168th Bde. will relieve 34th Bde. tonight taking over areas occupied by them AAA 168 Bde. tactical boundaries as follows AAA Right Boundary R.16.d.4.0. - R.21.d.0.0. - R.28 cont. - W.6.a.6.0. thence old Div. Southern Boundary AAA Left Boundary R.7 central Q.24 central AAA M.G.Reliefs take place night of Sept. 30/Oct.1st AAA Artillery arrangements later AAA 169 Bde. will take over tonight up to 168 Bde. Left Boundary AAA Acknowledge AAA Addsd. List 'B'

From Place: 56 Div.

SECRET   56th DIVISION.   LOCATION TABLE at 6 a.m.   September 1918.   APPENDIX I

Ref. Sheet 51ᴮ 1/40000

	1	2	3	4	5	6	7	8	9	10	11	12	13	14	15
Div. H.Q.	S11a55								X Les Fosses Farm N12a07						
167th Inf. Bde. H.Q.	T19c65							G21d90		Bde i/r Res.			P9b85 (L.Bde)		
1st London Regt.	Area S11, S16, S24							H31b59					P9d50 (Line L)		
7th Middx. Regt.	"							H13a12					O17c19 (Support)		
8th Middx. Regt.	"							H20d86					P10b92 (Line R)		
168th Inf. Bde. H.Q.	T14c91							O16a26	P13d63 (Left Bde)				H25a83		
4th London Regt.	Area T7, T8, T13, T14, T20						Area O16,17	P8d18 P11a71 P8d08	(Line L) (Line R) P10b92 (Sup)				H20d77 G18b99 H31b77		
13th "	"														
14th "	"								O17c19						
169th Inf. Bde. H.Q.	S9d61							O16a26	P15b84 (R.Bde)						
2nd London Regt.	Area S11, S16, S17, S23							O17a36 O17c30 O17c19	P15d54 (Sup) P12c55 P15c94				P12c55 P15d54		
5th "	"														
16th "	"														
Div. Arty. H.Q.	S11a55	}Left in line when Div. was relieved					Wancourt Area	N12a07	P21a79 (Line R Group) P19c84 Left Group				P21a82 (Rt Group) P20b5.65 (L Group)		
280th Bde.															
281st "								Wancourt Area							
Pioneers.	S15b64							N11b95							
M.G. Battn. H.Q.	S11a55							N12a07							

X Div. H.Q. opened 9 a.m. 9.9.18.

Line ————
Support ————
Reserve ————
Divn at Rest ————

SECRET 56th DIVISION. LOCATION TABLE at 6 a.m. September 1918. APPENDIX I

	16	17	18	19	20	21	22	23	24	25	26	27	28	29	30
Div. H.Q.	Les Fosses Farm.			N.12.a.o.9.								V.3.b.2.7.			
167th Inf. Bde. H.Q.	P.19.b.8.5. (L. Bde.)										P.15.d.5.4.	N.W.Epinoy			Q.34.b.5.5.
1st London Regt.	P.9.d.5.0. (Line L)			P.15.b.3.2.											Q.35.b.a.2.
7th Middlx. Regt.	O.1.a.1.9.			P.18.c.8.3.							P.15.b.3.2.				Q.30.c.0.9.
8th Middlx. Regt.	P.10.b.9.2. (Line R)			P.15.d.6.4.							Q.30.c.1.0.				Q.30.c.0.2.
168th Inf. Bde. H.Q.	H.25.a.8.3.				P.34.b.2.9. (Rt. Bde.)							Ecowi Chicoin			P.34.a.2.9.
4th London Regt.	H.20.d.77.				Q.20.d.6.5. (Line L)						Q.26.d.6.0.	Q.20.a.6.5.			Q.15.d.6.2.
13th	G.18.d.9.2.				P.18.c.2.2.						Q.35.b.	Q.26.d.6.0.			Q.33.a.4.4.
14th	H.31.b.77.				Q.25.d.6.a (Line R)						Q.31.a.1.7.	Q.33.a.9.4.			P.26.b.9.4.
												Q.20.a.3.3.			
169th Inf. Bde. H.Q.	P.15.b.8.4. (R. Bde.)			Q.21.d.6.5.		O.35.c.Y.3							W.7.c.2.8. N.of S.G.N.		
2nd London Regt.	P.18.c.8.3.			V.2.a.3.6										Q.14.d.88. (Left.)	
5th	P.15.d.3.4. P.15.d.6.2.P			O.13.b.6.5		O.29.b.9.								Q.33.b.a.9 (Right.)	
18th	P.15.c.9.4. P.18.c.8.3			O.13.d.9.8		O.29.c.5.2								Q.34.b.9.2.	
Div. Arty. H.Q.	N.12.a.0.4.				P.21.a.8.2. (Rt. Group)	P.21.a.8.2. (L. Group)									
280th Bde.	P.21.a.8.2. (Rt. Group)				P.34.b.2.8 (Ind. Group)										
281st	P.20.b.05.65. (Left Group)														
Pioneers.	N.11.b.9.6.										P.26.d.6.3.				
M.G. Battn. H.Q.	N.12.a.0.4.											V.3.b.2.7.			

SECRET. *War Diary Copies.* Copy No. 23

56th DIVISION WARNING ORDER No. 197.

4th Sept. 1918.

1. It is probable that 56th Division will relieve 52nd Division to-morrow night.
   The 52nd Division is now distributed in depth about QUEANT and PRONVILLE in support of 63nd Division.

2. It is probable that on the following night 56th Division will relieve 63rd Division in the line, approximately on the front MOEUVRES - INCHY-on-ARTOIS.

3. The present locations of 52nd Division are as follows :-

   157th Inf.Bde. about D.10.c.,D.16.b.,) will probably be relieved by
                    D.17.b.,D.18.a.)   169th Inf.Bde.

   155th Inf.Bde.   "   D.8.d.,D.14.b.   do.   167th " "

   156th Inf.Bde.   "   U.30.b. & U.30.d.   do.   168th " "

   Div. H.Q.   about D.1.c.6.0. (from to-morrow).

   Pioneer Bn.   T.21.d.7.8. (H.Q.).
   410th Fld.Coy.R.E. C.4. central.
   412th   do.   D.2.c. central.
   413th   do.   D.1.c.3.5.

4. ACKNOWLEDGE.

B. Pakenham

Issued at 4.15 p.m.

Lieut-Colonel,
General Staff.

Distribution :

Copy No. 1. 167th Infantry Brigade.   No. 14. D.A.D.O.S.
       2. 168th Infantry Brigade.   15. 56th Div. Train.
       3. 169th Infantry Brigade.   16. Camp Commandant.
       4. C.R.A.   17. 56th Div. Rcoptn.Camp.
       5. 1/5th Cheshire Regt.   18.) XVII Corps.
       6. XVII Corps H.A.   20.)
       7. C.R.E.   21. 52nd Division.
       8. 56th Bn. M.G.Corps.   22. 63rd Division.
       9. 56th Div. Signal Coy.   23.) War Diary.
     10. 56th Div. Gas Officer.   24.)
     11. A.D.M.S.   25. File.
     12. "Q"
     13. A.P.M.

SECRET   *War Diary*   Copy No. 27

56th DIVISION ORDER No. 198.

4th Sept. 1918.

1. 56th Div. Warning Order No. 197, para. 1 is confirmed.
   With reference to para. 2, the relief of the 63rd Division on night 6th/7th September will probably take place but depends upon the Tactical Situation at the time.

2. Details of relief of Brigades of 52nd Division including guides will be arranged direct between B.Gs.C. concerned. Brigadiers of 52nd Division will be at their Headquarters during the evening.

3. Relief of M.G. Battn., R.E., Pioneers and Field Ambulances, will be arranged direct by O.C. M.G.Battn., C.R.E. and A.D.M.S.

4. The Division will move to concentration areas as under where they will halt for 2 hours before moving on to relief :-

Unit.	Concentration Area.	Remarks.
167th Inf. Bde.	Valley in U.23.c. U.29.a.	To clear crossroads T.22.a. 2.8. at 11 a.m. To move on from concentration area at 3 p.m.
169th Inf. Bde.	Valley in U.22.b. U.22.d.	To pass crossroads T.22.a.2.8. at 12 noon. To move on from concentration area at 4.30 pm.
168th Inf. Bde.	Will move straight through.	Not to enter BULLECOURT before 6 p.m.

5. Following intervals will be observed :-

   (a). Up to concentration area - 100 yds. between Coys.
                                            500 yds. between Battns.

   (b). From concentration area forward - 100 yds. between Platoons.

6. Companies of the M.G. Battn. will be attached to Brigades for accommodation and march orders, as under :-

            169th Infantry Brigade   -   'C' Coy.
            167th Infantry Brigade   -   'B' Coy.
            168th Infantry Brigade   -   'A' & 'D' Coys.
   M.G. Battn. H.Qrs. will be with Divnl. H.Qrs.

7. Completion of moves will be reported to 56th Div. H.Qrs. and H.Qrs. 52nd Division at T.23.a.1.7.

8. Div. H.Qrs. will remain at its present location until 10 a.m. September 6th, when command will pass and Div. H.Qrs. open at T.22.a.1.7.

9. No transport is to move beyond the concentration areas before dark.

10. ACKNOWLEDGE.

Issued at 11.45 p.m.

R.C.Heald Capt
for Lieut-Colonel,
General Staff.

P.T.O.

Distribution :-

Copy No. 1.	167th Infantry Brigade.	No. 16. 56th Div. Train.
2.	168th Infantry Brigade.	17. 56th Div. M.T.Coy.
3.	169th Infantry Brigade.	18. Camp Commandant.
4.	C.R.A.	19. A.D.C.
5.	1/5th Cheshire Regt.	20. 56th Div. Recep. Camp.
6.	XVII Corps H.A.	21. 56th Div. Employ. Coy.
7.	C.R.E.	22. French Mission.
8.	56th Bn. M.G.Corps.	23. XVII Corps.
9.	56th Div. Signal Coy.	24. " "
10.	56th Div. Gas Officer.	25. 52nd Division.
11.	A.D.M.S.	26. 63rd Division.
12.	"Q"	27.) War Diary.
13.	A.P.M.	28.)
14.	D.A.D.O.S.	29. File.
15.	D.A.D.V.S.	

SECRET   *War Diary.*   Copy No. 30.

56th DIVISION WARNING ORDER No. 199.

Ref. Sheet 51B 1/40,000   5th Sept. 1918.

1.   56th Division is being transferred to XXII Corps to-morrow and is to relieve 1st Division in the line.

2.   The following will be the probable arrangements for relief :-

     <u>Evening 6th inst</u> - 168th Infantry Brigade moves to 1st Division area.
                             "P" Bde. 56th Div. Arty. moves to 1st Divn. area.

     <u>Night 7th/8th inst.</u> - 168th Inf. Bde. relieves "A" Bde. 1st Divn. in the line.
                              "B" Bde. 56th Div. Arty. relieves Artillery covering "B" Bde. 1st Division.
                              169th Inf. Bde. moves to 1st Divn. area.
                              "A" Bde. 56th Div. Arty. moves to 1st Divn. area.

     <u>Night 8th/9th inst.</u> - 169th Inf. Bde. relieves "B" Bde. 1st Divn. in line.
                              "A" Bde. 56th Div. Arty. relieves Artillery covering "A" Bde. 1st Division.
                              167th Inf. Bde. moves to 1st Divn. area and relieves "C" Bde. 1st Division.

3.   March Tables showing hours of move and grouping of units for the march will be issued later.

4.   Div. H.Q. will probably open at LES FOSSES FARM, N.12.a. at 10 a.m. 9th instant.

5.   ACKNOWLEDGE.

                                                      B Pakenham

                                                      Lieut-Colonel,
Issued at 5.45 p.m.   General Staff.

Distribution :-

Copy No.		No.	
1.	167th Infantry Brigade.	18.	Camp Commandant.
2.	168th Infantry Brigade.	19.	A.D.C.
3.	169th Infantry Brigade.	20.	56th Div. Recep. Camp.
4.	C.R.A.	21.	56th Div. Employ. Coy.
5.	1/5th Cheshire Regt.	22.	French Mission.
6.	XVII Corps H.A.	23.	XVII Corps.
7.	C.R.E.	24.	" "
8.	56th Bn. M.G.Corps.	25.	XXII Corps.
9.	56th Div. Signal Coy.	26.	" "
10.	56th Div. Gas Officer.	27.	1st Division.
11.	A.D.M.S.	28.	52nd Division.
12.	"Q"	29.	63rd Division.
13.	A.P.M.	30.)	War Diary.
14.	D.A.D.O.S.	31.)	
15.	D.A.D.V.S.	32.	File.
16.	56th Div. Train.		
17.	56th Div. M.T.Coy.		

"War Diary"

SECRET   Copy No. 30

56th DIVISION ORDER No. 200.

5th Sept. 1918.

1. 56th Division Warning Order No. 199 is confirmed. Reliefs will take place in accordance with attached Table 'A'.

2. Infantry reliefs will be arranged between B.Gs.C. concerned.

3. Details of relief of Artillery, M.Gs., Field Ambulances, R.E.Coys. and Pioneers will be arranged between Cs.R.A., O.Cs. M.G.Bns., A.Ds.M.S. and Cs.R.E. concerned.

4. The grouping of units of the Division for march orders is shown on the attached Table 'A'.

5. Units of 56th Division on arrival in 1st Division Area will come under orders of G.O.C. 1st Division.

6. Completion of reliefs will be reported to 1st Division H.Q. at LES FOSSES FARM and repeated to 56th Division.

7. 56th Div. H.Qrs. will close at S.11.a.5.5. at 10 a.m. 9th September, and open at LES FOSSES FARM at the same hour, when command of the Sector will pass to G.O.C., 56th Division.

8. ACKNOWLEDGE.

T.O.M. Buchan-Hayn
Lieut-Colonel,
General Staff.

Issued at 11 pm

Distribution.-

Copy No.		No.	
1.	167th Infantry Brigade.	18.	Camp Commandant.
2.	168th Infantry Brigade.	19.	A.D.C.
3.	169th Infantry Brigade.	20.	Div. Recptn. Camp.
4.	C.R.A.	21.	56th Div. Employ.Coy.
5.	1/5th Cheshire Regt.	22.	French Mission.
6.	XVII Corps H.A.	23.	XVII Corps.
7.	C.R.E.	24.	do.
8.	56th Bn. M.G.Corps.	25.	XXII Corps.
9.	56th Div. Signal Coy.	26.	do.
10.	56th Div. Gas Officer.	27.	1st Division.
11.	A.D.M.S.	28.	52nd Division.
12.	"Q"	29.	63rd Division.
13.	A.P.M.	30.)	War Diary.
14.	D.A.D.O.S.	31.)	
15.	D.A.D.V.S.	32.	File.
16.	56th Div. Train.		
17.	56th Div. M.T.Coy.		

TABLE 'A' TO ACCOMPANY 56th DIVISION ORDER No. 200.

Serial No.	Date.	Unit.	Moves to.	Relieving.	Remarks.
1.	Sept. 6th	168th Bde.Group. 168th Bde. A & D Coys. M.G.Bn. 512th Fld.Coy.	Area O.16. Bdo.H.Q. O.16.a.2.6.	3rd Brigade.	(Route:- Via FONTAINE Les CROISILLES. (Clear ARRAS-CAMBRAI Road by 9 a.m.
2.	6th	H.Q.M.G.Bn	O.9.c.3.3.	26th Fld.Coy.	
3.	6th	280 Bde.R.F.A.	1st Div. Area.		Under orders of O.C., 56th Bn. M.G.C.
4.	7/8th	168th Inf.Bde.	Line. Left Bde. Sector. H.Qrs.P.14.c.3.3.	2nd Bde.	Under orders of C.R.A. via FONTAINE LES CROISILLES. Not to enter 1st Div. Area before 7 p.m.
5.	7/8th	280 Bde. R.F.A.	Action covering Right Bde.	59th Bde.R.F.A. H.Q.P.21.a.7.9.	
6.	7/8th	169th Bde.Group. 169th Inf.Bde. B & C Coys. M.G.B. 513th Fld.Coy. 1/5th Ches.Rt.	Res.Bde.Area. O.18.c. N.11.b.95.50.	168th Bde. 23rd Fld.Coy.R.E. 6th Welch Regt.	(Head of column to pass cross road (O.13.b.8.3. at 7 p.m.
7.	7/8th	281 Bde.R.F.A. 56th D.A.C.	1st Divn. Area.	1st D.A.C.	Under orders of C.R.A. Not to enter 1st Div. Area before 8 p.m.
8.	8/9th	169th Bde.	Line Right Bde. Sector. H.Q.P.15.b.8.4.	1st Bde.	

TABLE 'A' (Cont'd).

Serial No.	Date.	Unit.	Moves to.	Relieving.	Remarks.
9.	8/9th	167th Bde.Group. 167th Bde. 416 Fld.Coy.	Res.Bde.Area. O.9.b.9.6.	162nd Bde. 409th Fld.Coy.	(Head of column to pass cross roads (O.13.b.8.8. at 7 p.m.
10.	8/9th	281 Bde.R.F.A.	Action covering Left Bde.	25th Bde.R.F.A. H.Q. P.20.a.1.1.	

NOTE:- Usual intervals will be observed.
Units not shewn above will relieve under orders of A.A.& Q.M.G.

"A" Form
MESSAGES AND SIGNALS.

Army Form C. 2121.
(In pads of 100.)

Priority

Sender's Number.	Day of Month.	In reply to Number.	
G.33	5		A A A

56 Div. Order 198 is cancelled AAA Units will remain in areas occupied by them last night AAA Added all recipients of order.

From: 56 Div.
Place:
Time: 12.20 p.m.

T. John Buchan
Maj.
General Staff.

SECRET. 56th Division G.3/237.

AMENDMENT No. 1 to 56th DIVISION ORDER No. 200.

1. Serial 6, Column 6 - ADD: "Route via HENINEL".

2. Serial 7, Column 6 - ADD: "Route via FONTAINE-LES-CROISILLES". NOT to cross ARRAS - CAMBRAI Road before 6 p.m. and to keep clear of the HENINEL - WANCOURT - GUEMAPPE - O.13.b.8.8. Road between 5 p.m. and 7.30 p.m.

3. Serial 9, Delete all reference to 167th Bde.Group and 167th Inf.Bde.
   416th Field Coy.R.E. will march under orders of C.R.E.

4. ADD new Serial 11 as under :-

Date.	Unit.	Moves to.	Relieving.	Remarks.
Sept.9th.	167th Inf.Bde.	ST.LAURENT - BLANGY FEUCHY Area. Squares H.19, 20, 21, 13, 26.	3rd Bde.	Via NEUVILLE VITASSE. To clear ARRAS - CAMBRAI Rd. by 9 a.m.

5. ACKNOWLEDGE.

B. Pakenham

H.Q., 56th Divn.
6th Sept. 1918.

Lieut-Colonel,
General Staff.

To all recipients of 56th Div.Order No.200.

E.

SECRET.   Copy No. 23

War Diary Copies

56th DIVISION ORDER No. 301.

11th Sept. 1918.

1.   167th Infantry Brigade will relieve the 168th Infantry Brigade in the Left Sector on the night September 13th/14th.

2.   On relief 168th Infantry Brigade will withdraw into the FEUCHY Area and be in Corps Reserve.

3.   All details of relief will be arranged between Brigadiers concerned.

4.   Lorries will be provided for moving troops forward from and back to the FEUCHY Area, under arrangements to be notified by 'Q'.

5.   Completion of reliefs will be reported to Div. H.Q.

6.   ACKNOWLEDGE.

Issued 8 p.m.

                                                    Lieut-Colonel,
                                                    General Staff.

Distribution :-

Copy No. 1. 167th Infantry Brigade.   Copy No. 14. D.A.D.O.S.
        2. 168th Infantry Brigade.   15. 56th Div. Train.
        3. 169th Infantry Brigade.   16. A.D.C.
        4. C.R.A.   17. Camp Commandant.
        5. 50th Bde. R.G.A.   18. 56th Div. Recep. Camp.
        6. 1/5th Cheshire Regt.   19. XXII Corps.
        7. C.R.E.   20. "   "
        8. 56th Bn. M.G.Corps.   21. 3rd Can. Division.
        9. 56th Div. Signal Coy.   22. 11th Division.
       10. 56th Div. Gas Officer.   23.) War Diary.
       11. A.D.M.S.   24.)
       12. "Q"   25. File.
       13. A.P.M.

J/JE

SECRET.   Copy No. 17

56th DIVISION DEFENCE ORDERS No. 1.

1. The 56th Division (less 1 Infantry Brigade) holds the Right Sector of XXII Corps front, with two Brigades in the line.
    The Canadian Corps is on the right.
    The Centre Division, XXII Corps is on the Left.

2. One Infantry Brigade, 56th Division, is in Corps Reserve in the FEUCHY Area.

3. Tactical boundaries are as follows :-

    (a) **Between 56th Division & Canadian Corps.**
    Q.5 central - Q.10 central - Q.13 central - P.24.a.0.7. - cross roads at P.23.d.1.3. - thence along ARRAS - CAMBRAI Road (exclusive).

    (b) **Between 56th Division & Centre Division XXII Corps.**
    J.23.c.0.0. - P.5.a.6.5. - along the SENSEE River to its junction with the COJEUL River at P.9.c.1.4. - thence along the COJEUL River as far West as O.10.d.0.0. road junction O.14.a.0.7. - thence ARRAS - CAMBRAI road (exclusive).

    (c) **Between Right & Left Brigades, 56th Division.**
    K.31.c.central - Q.1.a.5.3. - P.5 central - thence the L'ECLUSE - DURY Road (inclusive to Left Brigade) as far as cross roads P.11.c.7.4. - P.15.a.0.5. - road junction P.19.b.4.7. - thence track via STRIPE COPSE to road junction O.24.c.7.1. (the track inclusive to Right Brigade)

4. The front will be held as a defensive flank organized in depth to protect the left of the Canadian Corps and to link up with the line held by the Centre Division, XXII Corps.

5. The defences of the Canadian Corps on our right are organized approximately as follows :-

    (a) **Outpost line of Resistance.**
    W.25 central - W.2.c.0.0. - Q.27.a.3.5. - Q.14.c.4.6. - Q.14.a.0.0. - with observation posts and patrols in advance.

    (b) **Battle Zone - Main Line of Resistance.**
    BUISSY SWITCH to V.12.a.0.0. - V.5 central, Q.19.c. - P.18.d.0.0.

    (c) **Front Line of Rear Zone of Defense.**
    DROCOURT - QUEANT Line to V.7 central - VIS EN ARTOIS SWITCH to O.23.d.0.0. to CAMBRAI Road O.24.c.2.2.

6. The main line of resistance of the Centre Division on our left is organized approximately as follows :-
    High ground in P.1, I.36., 29 and 23.

- 2 -

7. Tracings showing the dispositions of the Divisions on the right and left have been issued to all concerned.

8. The defences in the Divisional area will be organized as follows :-

(a) <u>The Outpost Zone</u> will extend up to the water in the SENSEE Valley, all the crossings of which will be covered by close direct Machine Gun fire.
   It will not be further advanced for the present unless it is necessary to keep in line with an advance by the Division on our left.

(b) <u>The Outpost Line of Resistance</u> will follow approximately the line of the Sunken Road Q.14.a.1.4. - Q.13.b. - Q.7.d., c. and a - P.6.d.2.4. - P.5.c.40.45 - P.5.d.7.9. - P.5.a.80.05 - P.5.c.0.9. - P.4.d.00.85. - P.4.c.4.7. - P.4.c.2.3. - P.3.d.9.3. - P.3.d.1.1. - P.3.c.3.1. - P.9.a.2.5. - P.8.b.8.4. - P.8.c.8.7.
   (being joined up with 11th Division).
   It is especially necessary to prevent the enemy gaining a footing of any sort on our bank of the SENSEE River, owing to the fact that our Counter-Battery guns have been pushed forward to deal with the enemy artillery enfilading our Salient.
   Consequently the Outpost Line of Resistance must be held to the last and any enemy who got across these rivers must be isolated by fire and counter attacked without delay.

(c) <u>The Main Line of Resistance</u> will follow a line approximately as follows :-

   Q.13.c.4.7. - Q.13.a.4.2. - P.12.d.6.1. - trench along E. face of BOIS DE RECOURT - Sunken Road from P.12.b.3.1. to P.6.d.0.0. - P.6.c.6.3. - thence P.11.b.25.45. - P.5.c.7.2. - P.10.b.75.80. - P.10.a.8.0. - P.10.a.4.4. - P.10.a.0.1. - P.9.d.25.60. - P.9.d.00.45. - P.9.c.5.3. - P.9.c.00.35. - P.8.d.2.2. - P.8.c.80.35.

   (being joined up with 11th Division).

   This will be supported by a series of mutually supporting posts disposed on the reverse slopes.

(d) The B.G.C. Right Brigade will arrange to echelon troops on his right flank so as to -

   (i) Connect his Main Line of Resistance at RECOURT with the Main Line of Resistance of the Canadian Corps.
   (ii) Switch forward to connect his Main Line of Resistance with the left flank of the Outpost Line of Resistance of the Canadian Corps.
   (iii) Be disposed in such depth that the Battle Zone of the Canadian Corps can be flanked by a switch securing the high ground from RECOURT to DURY and P.9.central.

/ 9.

- 3 -

9. The following systems would be fought in turn, in the event of the enemy driving us back :-

   (i). DROCOURT - QUEANT LINE.
   (ii). Trenches in P.8, P.14, P.20 and P.26.
   (iii) Trenches in O.24, O.17, O.11.d. which would be prolonged on the Right by the Rear Zone of the Canadian Corps and on the left by the Centre Division towards BOIRY-NOTRE-DAME.

10. The front is covered by two Groups of Field Artillery, at present each consisting of 1 Brigade R.F.A.
    The 50th Brigade R.G.A. is affiliated to the Division.

11. Defence works for the present will consist chiefly of shell-hole positions and adapted old trenches.
    As much rest and training as possible will be given to the men rather than employing them on elaborate semi-permanent work.

12. 2 Sections of R.E. will be attached to each Brigade in the line.
    These will be employed chiefly on improving Brigade and Battalion Battle H.Qs. and such other work as may be considered necessary by Brigadiers.

13. Brigades in the line will arrange to patrol actively the SENSEE Valley, with a view to noting the nature of the crossings, the depth of the water and whether it rises or falls, whether there are any obstructions in the stream on the Divisional front, the removal of which would lessen the floods in the valley.
    The C.R.E. will arrange to assist in the above reconnaissances, which will be constantly carried out.

Tom Buchan Major

for Lieut-Colonel,
General Staff, 56th Division.

11th Sept. 1918.

Distribution :-

Copy No. 1. 167th Infantry Brigade.
       2. 168th Infantry Brigade.
       3. 169th Infantry Brigade.
       4. 1/5th Cheshire Regt.
       5. C.R.A.
       6. C.R.E.
       7. 50th Bde. H.A.
       8. 56th Bn. M.G.Corps.
       9. 56th Div. Signal Coy.
      10. A.D.M.S.
      11. "Q"
      12. A.D.C.
      13.) XXII Corps.
      14.)
      15. 3rd Canadian Division.
      16. 11th Division.
      17.) War Diary.
      18.)
      19. File.

In the case of a hostile attack being foreseen, the order "Man Battle Stations" will be sent out from Divisional H.Q., on receipt of which -

(a) The troops manning the outpost observation line in the Right Section may be withdrawn to the outpost main line of resistance but leaving behind one or two selected posts to fire the S.O.S.

In the Left Section they may only be withdrawn to points where they can cover the crossings of the river with fire.

All outpost troops must, however, be ready to counter attack to reoccupy their forward posts should the enemy have obtained a small footing only in our Outpost Zone.

(b) The Reserve Battalion in each Brigade will man their counter-attack position for reinforcing or recapturing the Front Line of the Main Line of Resistance.

(c) The Reserve Brigade, less one Battalion placed under the control of the Right Brigade, will move up to assembly positions as follows :-
One Battn. to vicinity of MONT DURY in P.27,
& one Battn. to the DROCOURT - QUEANT LINE
P.21.a. & c.
Adv. Bde. H.Qrs. to join the Right Bde.H.Qrs.

8. ARTILLERY.

8. The front is covered by 4 Brigades of Artillery. Their disposition will be such that the line of the CANAL DU NORD and the crossings of the SENSEE RIVER can be effectively engaged by the bulk of the Supporting Artillery, while the maximum support shall be available on the Main Line of Resistance.

Forward Section should be used for harassing fire and for engaging targets of opportunity.

9. Machine Guns.

Map showing Machine Gun Defence is being circulated to all concerned.

10. ACKNOWLEDGE.

B. Pakenham

Lieut-Colonel,
General Staff, 56th Division.

Distribution :-
Copy No. 1. 167th Infantry Brigade.
2. 168th Infantry Brigade.
3. 169th Infantry Brigade.
4. 1/5th Cheshire Regt.
5. C.R.A.
6. C.R.E.
7. 50th Bde. H.A.
8. 56th Bn. M.G.Corps.
9. 56th Div. Signal Coy.
10. A.D.M.S.
11. "Q"
12. A.D.C.
13.)
14.) XXII Corps.
15. 2nd Canadian Division.
16. 4th British Division.
17.)
18.) War Diary.
19. File.

SECRET   Copy No. 17

56th DIVISION PROVISIONAL DEFENCE SCHEME.

22.9.18.

1. The 56th Division holds the right Sector of XXII Corps front extending from W.4.c.2.6. (N. of MARQUION) to Q.1.c. central S.E. of L'ECLUSE.

   The 2nd Canadian Division, Canadian Corps, is on the right. The Centre Division, XXII Corps, is on the left.

2. The front, which is divided into two Sections called the OISY Section on the Right and the RECOURT Section on the left, is held by two Infantry Brigades, the third being held in Divisional Reserve with the exception that the B.G.C. Right Brigade has a call on one battalion located in V.1.b. in case of necessity.

3. Tactical boundaries are as follows :-

   (a). Between 56th Division and Canadian Corps.
   W.6.central - W.4.c.2.6. - W.2.central - V.6.central - P.26.d.1.3. thence along CAMBRAI ROAD.

   (b). Between 56th Division and Centre Division, XXII Corps.
   K.27 central - P.12 central - P.11.c.8.4. - P.15 central - thence due West to the CAMBRAI ROAD.

   (c). Between Right & Left Brigades, 56th Division.
   Q.12 central - Q.16.d.6.9. - thence following the HIRONDELLE RIVER to Q.19.c.4.0 - SAUDEMONT VILLAGE (inclusive to Left Brigade) - P.24.c.5.0. - thence due West to the CAMBRAI ROAD.

4. The general Scheme of Defence of the Divisional Sector will be as below and as shown on the attached Map 'A' :-

I. Outpost Zone.
   (1). The Outpost Observation Line consists of a series of posts and is shewn in blue on the attached Map 'A'. This has been sited as regards the portion in the Right Brigade Section on forward slopes a short distance West of the CANAL DU NORD to obtain observation over the enemy's forward positions and to enable effective artillery fire to be brought on the crossings and bed of the CANAL where dry. The area between this line and the CANAL must be vigorously patrolled with strong patrols and the enemy must not be allowed to establish himself on the West side of the CANAL further than he is at present. The communications thereto must be continuously harassed with all available weapons.
   In the Left Brigade Section the Outpost Observation Line runs along the edge of the water of the SENSEE RIVER. It is especially necessary to prevent the enemy gaining a footing of any sort on our bank of the SENSEE RIVER, owing to the fact that our counter-battery guns have been pushed forward to deal with the enemy artillery enfilading our Salient. Consequently any enemy who get across in this section will be isolated by fire and counter attacked without delay.

/ (2).

(2). The Outpost Line of Resistance - shewn in Green on attached Map 'A'.

This line will be defended to the last but counter attacks will not be made to regain it if the enemy has crossed the river or Canal in such force that the defence of the main line of resistance would be endangered in case of failure.

II. **The Battle Zone.**

(1). Front Line (Main Line of Resistance)

Shewn in Red on the attached Map 'A'. It is at present not continuous, but in the event of no further advance taking place it will eventually be dug and wired as a continuous defensive line. It has been sited as far as possible on reverse slopes and covers the bulk of our Artillery.

No retirement will be permitted from this line and troops will hold on without reference to the fact that their flank may be exposed owing to the enemy having penetrated some portion of these defences.

Brigades will so dispose troops in depth that counter attacks can be made to regain any portion that has been captured by the enemy or so that they can isolate that portion and prevent further penetration by the enemy.

(2). Support Lines shown dotted Red on attached Map. These have been sited to give depth to the Battle Zone and to give observation on the Front Line of Resistance.

Counter-attacks will be made from these trenches to recapture the Front Line of the Battle Zone.

(3). BUISSY SWITCH Line shown in Brown on attached Map 'A'.

III. **Rear Zone.**

Shown on attached Map in Yellow.
The continuation of these lines of defence in the areas of flank Divisions are as shown on attached Map 'A'.

5. **Responsibilities for Work.**
Brigades in the line are responsible for the defences as far back as the Main Line of Resistance (inclusive).
Lines in rear will be constructed and maintained by the Division.

6. Dispositions are shewn on Map 'B'.

7. **Action in Case of Attack.**

Each Brigade will be responsible for the defence of the Outpost Zone and the Main Line of Resistance. In this task not less than two battalions should be allotted from each Brigade.

The remaining battalion of each Brigade, (in the case of the Right Brigade, one battalion of the Brigade in Divnl. Reserve, in addition), will be at the disposal of the Commanders of the Brigades in the line for reinforcing or for counter attack.

/In

War Diary

SECRET.   Copy No. 98

56th DIVISION ORDER NO. 204.

Ref. 51.B. 1/40,000.   18th Sept. 1918.

1.   With reference to para. 12 of 56th Division Order No. 203 of 17th inst., the Command of the Front taken over from 3rd. Canadian Division will pass to G.O.C., 56th Division on conclusion of the Infantry Relief instead of at 10 a.m. 20th inst.

2.   On 20th inst., 169th Infantry Brigade will readjust its dispositions so as to have :-

        Bde H.Q.   -   O.35.c.7.3.
        1 Battn.   -   V.1.b. (no change).
        1 Battn.   -   O.29.b.
        1. Battn.   -   O.36.a.

replacing 8th Canadian Infantry Brigade in the Support Brigade area.

Details to be arranged by B.G.C. 169th Infantry Brigade with B.G.C. 8th. Canadian Infantry Brigade.

3.   ACKNOWLEDGE.

                                            B. Pakenham
                                            Lieut-Colonel,
Issued at 6 p.m.   General Staff.

Distribution :-

Copy No.		No.	
1.	167th Inf. Bde.	16.	56th Div. Train
2.	168th Inf. Bde.	17.	56th Div. M.T. Coy.
3.	169th Inf. Bde.	18.	Camp Commandant.
4.	C.R.A.	19.	A.D.C.
5.	1/5th Ches. Regt.	20.	56th Div. Recep. Camp.
6.	50th Bde R.G.A.	21.	56th Div. Employ. Coy.
7.	C.R.E.	22.	French Mission.
8.	56th Bn. M.G.C.	23.)	XXII Corps.
9.	56th Div. Signal Coy.	24.)	
10.	56th Div. Gas Officer.	25.	4th British Division.
11.	A.D.M.S.	26.	11th Division.
12.	"Q"	27.	3rd. Canadian Division.
13.	A.P.M.	28.)	War Diary.
14.	D.A.D.O.S.	29.)	
15.	D.A.D.V.S.	30.	File.

SECRET.

56th DIVISION WARNING ORDER No.202.

Copy No. 28

16th Sept. 1918.

1. 56th Division is to take over the front of the 3rd Canadian Division on the right as far South as W.4.c.2.6. and to hand over a portion on its left to the 4th (British) Division which is to relieve 11th Division.
   The reliefs to be completed by 20th inst.

2. The reliefs will probably be carried out as follows :-

   (a). On the night 18/19th Sept. "A" Brigade, 4th Division, will take over the present frontage of 167th Infantry Brigade plus that portion of 139th Infantry Brigade frontage lying North of the New Northern Boundary (see para.3(a)).

   (b). On the night 18/19th September, 167th Infantry Brigade will relieve 169th Infantry Brigade on the remaining portion of its present front.
   On relief, 169th Infantry Brigade will proceed to an area in the vicinity of VIS-EN-ARTOIS, where it will be in Div. Reserve.

   (c). On the night 19/20th September, the frontage of the 3rd Canadian Division as described in para. 1, will be relieved as follows:-
   167th Inf. Bde. will extend its right and take over that portion of the frontage North of the New Inter-Brigade Boundary described in para. 3 (c).
   168th Inf.Bde. will take over the remainder of the frontage down to the New Southern Divisional Boundary.

3. The new Boundaries will probably be as follows, but are subject to alteration :-

   (a). <u>Northern Divisional Boundary.</u>
   K.27 central - Q.12 central - Q.11.c.8.4. - P.15 central (leaving present Right Brigade H.Qrs. to 56th Divn.) - thence due West to the CAMBRAI Road (leaving present Left Brigade H.Qrs. to 4th Division).

   (b). <u>Southern Divisional Boundary.</u>
   W.6 central - W.4.c.2.6. - W.2 central - V.6 central - P.26.d.1.3. thence along CAMBRAI ROAD.

   (c). <u>Final Inter-Brigade Boundary.</u>
   Q.12 central - Q.16.d.6.9. - thence following the HIRONDELLE RIVER to Q.19.c.4.0. - SAUDEMONT Village (inclusive to Left Brigade) - Q.24.c.5.0. - thence due West to the CAMBRAI Road.

4. Details of Artillery reliefs etc. will be issued later.

5. Div. H.Q. will probably remain unchanged.

6. ACKNOWLEDGE.

B. Pakenham
Lieut-Colonel,
General Staff.

Issued at 8.15 p.m.

Distribution :-

Copy No.					
1.	167th Inf.Bde.	11.	A.D.M.S.	21.	56th Div.Emp.C.
2.	168th Inf.Bde.	12.	"Q".	22.	French Mission.
3.	169th Inf.Bde.	13.	A.P.M.	23.)	XXII Corps.
4.	C.R.A.	14.	D.A.D.O.S.	24.)	
5.	1/5th Ches.Regt.	15.	D.A.D.V.S.	25.	4th Brit.Divn.
6.	50th Bde.R.G.A.	16.	56th Div. Train.	26.	11th Divn.
7.	C.R.E.	17.	56th Div.M.T.Coy.	27.	3rd Can.Divn.
8.	56th Bn.M.G.C.	18.	Camp Commdt.	28.)	War Diary.
9.	56th Div.Signal Coy.	19.	A.D.C.	29.)	
10.	56th Div. Gas Officer.	20.	56th Div.R.Camp.	30.	File.

"A" Form.
MESSAGES AND SIGNALS.

Army Form C. 2121.
(In pads of 100.)

PRIORITY

for Lt.Col.G.S.

TO: War Diary

Sender's Number.	Day of Month.	In reply to Number.	
G.209	16		AAA

Amendment No. 1 to Div. Warning Order 202 AAA Para. 3 (a) for Q.12 central and Q.11.c.8.4. read P.12 central and P.11.c.8.4. AAA Para. 3 (c) line 4 for Q.24.c.5.0. read P.24.c.5.0. AAA Addsd all recipients of Order.

From 56 Divn.

General Staff

SECRET.   Copy No. 28

56th DIVISION ORDER No. 203.

Ref. 51B. 1/40,000.   17th Sept. 1918.

With reference to 56th Div. Warning Order No. 202 of 16th inst.

1. Para. 1 is confirmed.

2. The relief will be carried out as follows :-

    (a) On the night 18/19th inst. 10th Infantry Brigade, 4th Division, will relieve 167th Infantry Brigade on its present frontage. Command to pass on conclusion of relief.

    (b) On the night 18/19th inst., 167th Infantry Brigade will relieve 169th Infantry Brigade on its present frontage. Command to pass at 6 p.m. 18th instant.

    (c) On the night 19/20th September, 10th Infantry Brigade, 4th Division, will take over from 167th Infantry Brigade the portion as far South as the new Northern Divisional Boundary. Command to pass on conclusion of the relief.

    (d) On the night 19/20th September, 167th Infantry Brigade will take over from 8th Canadian Infantry Brigade the frontage held by its Left Battalion. Command to pass on conclusion of the relief.

    (e) On the night 19/20th September, 168th Infantry Brigade will take over from 8th Canadian Infantry Brigade the frontage held by its Right Battalion down to the New Southern Divisional Boundary. Command to pass on conclusion of the relief.

    (f) On the night 20/21st September, 167th and 168th Infantry Brigades will readjust their dispositions to conform to the new Inter-Brigade Boundary. Command to pass on conclusion of the relief.

3. Para. 3 regarding boundaries is confirmed, with the exception that present Right Brigade H.Qrs. 56th Division will pass to the 4th Division, and present Left Brigade H.Qrs. will be retained by Left Brigade, 56th Division.

4. 169th Infantry Brigade on relief will be disposed as follows:

    (a) 1 Battn. to V.1.b.8.8. (Bn.H.Q.) and trenches N. & S. of it, in relief of the P.P.C.L.I. of 7th Canadian Infantry Brigade. This Battalion will be tactically at the call of 8th Canadian Infantry Brigade prior to the conclusion of the relief, and at the call of 168th Infantry Brigade after the Divnl. relief is complete.

    (b) 1 Battn. to O.13.b. (H.Q. O.13.b.65.50.)

    (c) 1   "   "   N.24.d. (H.Q. N.24.d.1.0.)

    (d) Bde. H.Qrs. O.21.d.6.5.

5. Machine Gun reliefs will be arranged by the D.M.G.C. with the D.M.G.Cs. of 4th Division and 3rd Canadian Division. He will arrange to relieve 1 Coy. of 3rd Canadian Division on the night 18/19th September and the remainder on the night 20/21st September. None of the M.G. reliefs are to take place on the same night as the Infantry they cover.

/6.

6. 168th Infantry Brigade will be moved up within relieving distance on 19th inst., by bus, under arrangements to be made by 'Q' 56th Division.

7. The Canadian Corps has agreed to place bivouac accommodation for one Brigade at the disposal of 56th Division in the following area S. of the CAMBRAI Road from the afternoon of 20th September onwards :- P.35.c.7.0 - O.36.d.0.0. - O.20 cent. O.14.b.0.3.

8. Artillery reliefs will be arranged between Os.R.A. concerned. Details of Artillery Support will be communicated later.

9. The C.R.E. & A.D.M.S. will arrange details of reliefs of R.E., Pioneers and Field Ambulances with the C.R.E. and A.Ds.M.S. of the 4th Division and 3rd Canadian Division respectively.

10. During the reliefs regulation distances must be strictly maintained by all units on the march and great care must be taken to obviate the possibility of the enemy observing any unusual movement.

11. The 102nd M.G.Bn. (less 2 Coys.) will remain under the orders of 56th Division.

12. Command of Divisional Sectors will pass as follows :-

Left Bde. Sector, 56th Divn. to G.O.C. 4th Div. at 10 a.m. on September 20th.

From Present Corps Southern Boundary to New Southern Division Boundary. From G.O.C. 3rd Canadian Division to G.O.C. 56th Division at 10 a.m. Sept. 20th.

13. Progress and completion of reliefs will be reported by wire.

14. Div. H.Q. will remain as at present located.

15. ACKNOWLEDGE.

Blakenham
Lieut-Colonel,
General Staff.

Issued at 6 p.m.

Distribution :-

Copy No.		No.	
1.	167th Inf. Bde.	16.	56th Div. Train.
2.	168th Inf. Bde.	17.	56th Div. M.T.Coy.
3.	169th Inf. Bde.	18.	Camp Commandant.
4.	C.R.A.	19.	A.D.C.
5.	1/5th Chos. Regt.	20.	56th Div. Recep. Camp.
6.	50th Bde. R.G.A.	21.	56th Div. Employ. Coy.
7.	C.R.E.	22.	French Mission.
8.	56th Bn. M.G.C.	23.)	
9.	56th Div. Signal Co.	24.)	XXII Corps.
10.	56th Div. Gas Offr.	25.	4th British Division.
11.	A.D.M.S.	26.	11th Division.
12.	"Q"	27.	3rd Canadian Division.
13.	A.P.M.	28)	
14.	D.A.D.O.S.	29)	War Diary.
15.	D.A.D.V.S.	30.	File.

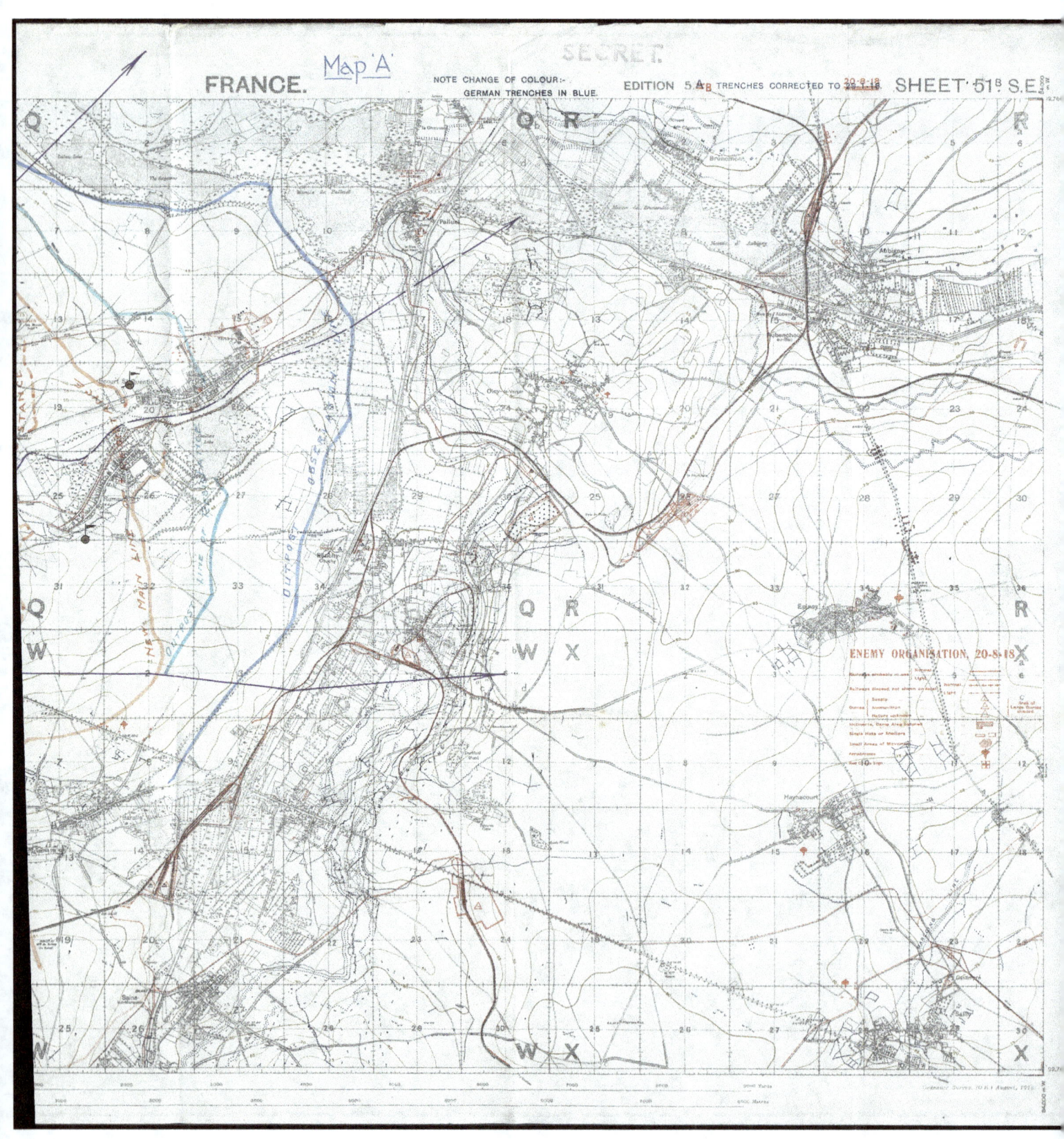

VERY SECRET.   Copy No......

56th DIVISION ORDER No. 205.

24th September 1918.

1.   Offensive operations towards CAMBRAI will be continued on a date which will be notified later

2.   The general plan will be as follows :-

(a).   On X/Y night 169th Infantry Brigade will take over from the Canadian Division in line the frontage from 56th Divn. Southern Boundary to the ARRAS - CAMBRAI Road (exclusive). The 32nd Brigade, 11th Division will similarly be relieving Canadians on the South of this road.

(b).   The main assault will be made on the front W.4.c. - W.26.c. by the Canadian Corps, who will force the passage of the CANAL DU NORD and spread outwards through the opening made and secure the general line (BLUE LINE) FONTAINE NOTRE DAME (excl.) - LA MAISON NEUVE (X.20.c.) - SAUCHICOURT FARM (W.12.a.) - Railway line in W.5.d., b & a, W.4.b. to CANAL DU NORD.

(c).   When the crossings over the CANAL in W.26 & W.21 are thus opened, 11th Division will cross about Zero plus 255 minutes and deploy in a position to advance N. & N.E. to secure the high ground on the S. bank of the SENSEE.
        The hour at which 11th Division will attack from the BLUE LINE will be at Zero plus 9 hours.

(d).   The left flank of 11th Division will advance on a line about 500 yds. East of a line from SAUCHICOURT FARM, thence along the trench from that Farm to Q.36 central, the objective of the left Brigade (34th) being OISY LE VERGER.

(e).   169th Infantry Brigade is to cross the CANAL North of the ARRAS - CAMBRAI Road (exclusive), deploy facing North and, relieving all troops of 1st Canadian Division, will attack from the general line of the Railway in W.4.a. and b. - W.5.a. and c. - W.6.c. and clear the enemy from the ground between the CANAL and the MARQUION Line (inclusive). The Northern limit of this attack is shown on the attached Map.

3.   Crossings over the CANAL will probably be allotted as follows :-

    169th Inf.Bde. - from W.4.c.2.6. to ARRAS - CAMBRAI Road
                                                            (exclusive).
    11th Division - Crossings South of above.

4.   Assembly areas will be communicated later.

5.   168th Infantry Brigade is to co-operate with 169th Inf. Bde. by clearing the enemy from the West of the CANAL DU NORD from about W.4.c.0.5. to MILL COPSE (inclusive), advancing from South to North and keeping pace with the left of 169th Infantry Brigade.

6.   167th Infantry Brigade is to have a Company about Q.10.c. or Q.16.a., with a L.T.M. and 2 Vickers Guns, ready to push patrols out towards PALLUEL and the CANAL if ordered, with the object of securing the CAUSEWAY in Q.10.d. and of joining hands with 169th Infantry Brigade in Q.17.c.

/7.

- 2 -

7. Details of Artillery Support will be communicated later.

(a). 8 R.F.A. Bdes. will be at the disposal of 56th Division of which one will be reserved to deal with enemy North of the SENSEE and three will provide barrage for the 11th Division.
The remainder will be employed in the following phases. -

    (i). To prolong the initial barrage of the main assault (para. 2 (b)), concentrating on crossings from about the Corps Southern Boundary to Q.23 central.

    (ii). To assist the main attack by dealing with selected targets on a time-table programme.

    (iii). To provide a barrage to cover the advance of 169th Brigade and a standing barrage to protect the left of 11th Division.
Both these barrages will roll forward as 169th Inf. Bde. advances.

(b). Barrage Maps will be issued direct by C.R.A.

8. (a). 56th Division will have at its disposal :-

    2 Cos. 4th Div. M.G.Bn.
    2 Cos. 102nd M.G.Bn.
    4 Cos. 56th Div. M.G.Bn.

Of these at least 64 guns will be sited to bring barrage fire E. of the CANAL and 16 guns on the high ground N. & N.E. of L'ECLUSE.
16 guns will be kept in defensive positions and the remainder (less 2 guns with 167th Inf. Bde. (para. 3) will be kept mobile.

(b). Barrage Maps will be issued by D.M.G.C.

9. C.R.A. will emplace, if possible, 2 Batteries of 6" M.T.Ms. and 168th Inf. Bde. will find emplacements for 168th and 169th L.T.M. Batteries.
The objectives in each case will be the CANAL DU NORD and vicinity from about W.4.c.0.5. - Q.23.a.7.0.

10. The closest liaison possible will be maintained by :-

    56th Div. H.Q. with 11th Division.
    169th Inf. Bde. with Left Brigade 11th Division (34th).
    168th Inf. Bde. with 169th Infantry Brigade.

Alternative means of communication will be organized in each case and liaison officers provided so as to ensure synchronization of action according to plan.

11. Instructions as to aeroplane contact patrols will be issued later.
A dropping station will be established at 56th Div. Adv. H.Q.

12. The C.R.E. will reconnoitre the crossings over the CANAL DU NORD in the area allotted to 169th Infantry Brigade, as far as possible.
He will arrange to assist 169th Infantry Brigade infantry to cross the CANAL DU NORD and AGACHE River and, subsequent to the attack, to improve the crossings of the CANAL DU NORD and

/approaches

approaches to them on the Corps front for horse traffic, as early as possible, for the use of 11th Division, in order to relieve congestion at the crossing on the main ARRAS - CAMBRAI Road.

13. The position of 169th Infantry Brigade Adv. H.Q. will be W.7.c.4.6., which it will share with 34th Infantry Brigade.

14. Adv. Div. H.Q. will be at V.3.b.2.6. Rear H.Q. remaining at FOSSE FARM.

15. ACKNOWLEDGE.

B. Pakenham
Lieut-Colonel,
General Staff.

Issued at 8 a.m.

Distribution :-
Copy No. 1. 167th Infantry Brigade.
2. 168th Infantry Brigade.
3. 169th Infantry Brigade.
4. 1/5th Cheshire Regt.
5. C.R.A.
6. 50th Bde. R.G.A.
7. C.R.E.
8. 56th Bn. M.G.Corps.
9. 56th Div. Signal Coy.
10. A.D.M.S.
11. "Q".
12. A.D.C.
13.) XXII Corps.
14.)
15. 11th Division.
16. 4th British Division
17. 1st Can. Division.
18. 2nd Can. Division.
19. Canadian Corps.
20.) War Diary.
21.)
22. File.

War Diary

SECRET   Copy No. 20

56th DIVISION ORDER No. 206.

24th Sept. 1918.

In continuation of 56th Div. Order No. 205 of today :-

1. Re Para. 2 (a) - The 1/5th London Regt. (L.R.B.) of 169th Inf. Bde. will be relieving troops of 18th Canadian Battn. (H.Q., V.6.d.8.8. belonging to 4th Canadian Inf. Bde. (H.Q., V.3.b.2.6.).
   B.G.C. 168th Inf. Bde. will take command of the L.R.B. on conclusion of the relief until such time as B.G.C. 169th Inf. Bdo. arrives at his own Bde. H.Q. on Y. day.
   B.G.C. 169th Inf. Bde. will arrange for the necessary wiring of L.R.B. H.Q. to H.Q. of 168th Inf. Bde.

2. Re Para. 2 (d) - This will be amended to read as follows :-

   11th Division will advance with their left flank 300 yds. East of the following line, viz:- SAUCHICOURT FARM - along trench from that FARM to Q.36.central, the objective of the Left (34th) Bde. being OISY LE VERGER.

3. Re Para. 2 (c) - This para. will be amended to read as follows :-

   169th Inf. Bde. is to cross the CANAL astride of the ARRAS - CAMBRAI Road, deploy facing North and, relieving all troops of 3rd Canadian Inf. Bde. West of W.6.c.5.5. will attack from the general line of the Railways in W.4.a. & b. - W.5.a, b. & d. - W.6.c. and clear the enemy from the ground between the CANAL and the MARQUION Line (inclusive). It will keep one platoon on the West of the CANAL in liaison with 168th Inf. Bde. The Northern limit of this attack will be the line of the Sunken Road in Q.23.b. and Q.24.a, where touch will be obtained with the 34th Inf. Bde., and posts will be pushed out in advance of this.
   In the event of the 34th Inf. Bde. not capturing OISY LE VERGER on Z. day, B.G.C. 169th Inf. Bde. will consolidate a line in touch with the left of 34th Inf. Bde.

4. Re Para. 3.

   Crossings over the CANAL are allotted to 169th Inf. Bde. as far S. as W.15.a.8.5.
   As the 1st Canadian Division moves North from the RED Line, troops of the 32nd Inf. Bde. will move along parallel to the advance on the West bank of the CANAL, mopping up as far as the ARRAS - CAMBRAI Road.
   169th Inf. Bde. should similarly arrange to clear their crossing places North of that road. 11th Division will be throwing a bridge about W.15.a.9.7. and near the main road which will be available for the use of 169th Inf. Bde. if completed in time.

5. Re Para. 4.

   Assembly areas are available for 169th Inf. Bde. in the valley V.6.c. & d, V.12.a, also in V.5.a. & c, V.4.b. & d. (BUISSY SWITCH exclusive).

6. Re Para. 6. In line 1 and 2 erase the words "Q.10.c. or" and insert after "Q.16.a." the words "or c".
   In line 3 erase the words "PALLUEL and".
   In line 4 erase the words "securing the causeway in Q.10.d. and of"

/7.

7. The following are the times at which the 1st Canadian Division are due to arrive at and leave the various lines on the Map.

       RED LINE - Arrive Zero plus 111 minutes.
                     Leave Zero plus 208 "

       GREEN LINE - Arrive Zero plus 298 minutes.
                       Leave Zero plus 324 "

       BLUE LINE. - Arrive Zero plus 400 minutes.

169th Inf. Bde. and 11th Division will attack from the BLUE Line at Zero plus 540 minutes.

8. **Re Para. 8.**

The two Companies of 4th Div. M.G. Battn. will move into action on Y/Z night, under arrangements to be made between O.Cs. 56th and 4th Div. M.G. Battalions.

9. O.C. 56th Div. Signal Coy. will arrange for a cable wagon to be at Adv. H.Q. of 169th Inf. Bde. at Zero hour on Z. day, so as to maintain communication in the event of 169th Inf. Bde. moving forward.

10. 169th Inf. Bde. will establish its advanced H.Q. on the morning of Y. day.
168th Inf. Bde. is establishing Adv. H.Q. at about Q.20.a.7.4.

11. Adv. Div. H.Q. will open at V.3.b.2.6. at 3.0 p.m. on 26th inst.

12. ACKNOWLEDGE.

                                          Lieut-Colonel,
                                          General Staff.

Issued at 8.0 p.m.

Distribution.

Copy No.		No.	
1.	167th Infantry Brigade.	12.	A.D.C.
2.	168th Infantry Brigade.	14-13.	XXII Corps.
3.	169th Infantry Brigade.	15.	11th Division.
4.	1/5th Cheshire Regt.	16.	4th British Division.
5.	C.R.A.	17.	1st Canadian Division.
6.	50th Bde. R.G.A.	18.	2nd Canadian Division.
7.	C.R.E.	19.	Canadian Corps.
8.	56th Bn. M.G.Corps.	20.)	
9.	56th Div. Signal Coy.	21.)	War Diary.
10.	A.D.M.S.	22.	File.
11.	"Q"		

SECRET   Copy No. 24

56th DIVISION ORDER No. 207.

25th Sept. 1918.

In continuation of 56th Division Orders Nos. 205 and 206.

1. Re Para. 2 (c) of Order No. 205, line 2, for "255" substitute "348" minutes.

2. Instructions for the action of Machine Guns are attached as Appendix "A" (issued to Infantry Brigades only).

3. (a). The S.O.S. signal will be a rifle grenade bursting into RED over RED over RED.

   (b). The signals in use by the Canadian Corps are :-

   (i). S.O.S. or "We are held up here". — Rifle Grenade rocket RED over RED over RED, or three RED Very Lights.

   (ii). "We are here". — Three White Very Lights.

   (iii). "O.K. Stop your fire". — Three GREEN Very Lights, or Rifle Grenade Rocket GREEN over GREEN over GREEN.

   Note - Written copies of the above must not be taken into the attack.

4. Hours at which Contact 'Planes will call for flares will be notified later. Troops of 169th Infantry Brigade will have white linen strips and small tin discs attached to the inside of the flap of their Box Respirators. When the aeroplane calls for troops to show their position these flaps will be opened and waved to and fro towards the aeroplane. Red Ground Flares will also be lit.
   Dropping Stations will be located as follows :-

56th Division H.Qrs.	V.3.a.85.70.
169th Inf. Bde. H.Qrs.	V.12.b.2.0.
168th Inf. Bde. H.Qrs.	Q.20.a.6.4.
167th Inf. Bde. H.Qrs.	P.20.a.15.80.

5. One Troop Corps Cavalry Regiment will be attached to the Division and will be located in the neighbourhood of Advanced Div. H.Qrs. O.C. Troop will detail four Troopers to be attached to 169th Brigade and to report at their Headquarters at UPTON QUARRY, O.35.c.7.3. at 5.0 p.m. September 26th.

6. Z. day will be September 27th. Zero hour will be notified later.

7. Arrangements for synchronizing watches will be notified later.

8. ACKNOWLEDGE.

T.M.Buchanan
for Lieut-Colonel,
General Staff.

Issued at 2.0 p.m.

P.T.O.

Distribution :-

Copy No. 1. 167th Infantry Brigade.
       2. 168th Infantry Brigade.
       3. 169th Infantry Brigade.
       4. 1/5th Cheshire Regt.
       5. C.R.A.
       6. 50th Bde. R.G.A.
       7. C.R.E.
       8. 56th Bn. M.G. Corps.
       9. 56th Div. Signal Coy.
     10. A.D.M.S.
     11. "Q"
     12. A.D.C.
     13.)
     14.) XXII Corps.
     15.)

No. 16. XXII Corps H.A.
    17. 11th Division.
    18. 4th British Division.
    19. 1st Canadian Division.
    20. 2nd Canadian Division.
    21. Canadian Corps.
    22. 52nd Sqd. R.A.F.
    23. O.C. Troop, XXII Corps Cav. Regt.
    24.) War Diary.
    25.)
    26. File.

War Diary

SECRET.   56th Division G.A.38.

ADDENDUM to 56th DIVISION ORDER No. 207.

1.   Contact 'planes will call for flares at :-

        ZERO plus 525 minutes.
        ZERO plus 660 minutes.

2.   Watches will be synchronised at Adv/Div. H.Qrs. between 3 and 4 p.m., 26th inst.

    Representatives of the following will attend :-

        167th Infantry Brigade.
        168th Infantry Brigade.
        169th Infantry Brigade.
        C.R.A. with such H.A. as C.R.A. considers necessary.
        56th Bn. M.G.Corps.
        Div. Signal Coy.

3.   ACKNOWLEDGE.

B Pakenham

H.Q., 56th Divn.
25.9.18.

Lieut-Colonel,
General Staff.

E/J.

To all recipients of 56th Div. Order No. 207.

SECRET.

INSTRUCTIONS No. 1 to ACCOMPANY 56th DIVISION ORDERS Nos. 205, 206, 207.

The following is the projected Time Table in the forthcoming operations :-

1. A. Canadian Divn.   ZERO   Canadians Attack.
                          Z plus 111   "   capture RED LINE.
                          Z plus 298   "   "   GREEN LINE.
                          Z plus 400   "   "   BLUE LINE.

    B. 11th Division.
       34th Brigade. Z plus 223   Leave assembly area (BUISSY SWITCH)
                      Z plus 293   Arrive at crossings.
                      Z plus 333   Commence crossing CANAL between
                                     W.26.b.0.0. & W.21.a.0.6.
                      Z plus 348   Leading troops are across CANAL.
                      Z plus 444   Reach assembly area, W.11.c. &
                                     W.17.a.
                      Z plus 504   Advance from above assembly
                                     position.
                      Z plus 540   Reach BLUE LINE.
                      Z plus 568   Commence advancing at rate of
                                     100 yds. in 4 minutes.
                      Z plus 648   Reach Line of Railway from R.26.a.
                                     80.00 to R.25.c.60.65.
                      Z plus 678   Assault on L'OISY LE VERGER.

    C. 11th Division.
       32nd Brigade. Z plus 208   Companies in Line moving North
                                     mop up hostile posts West of
                                     CANAL.
                      Z plus 311   Advance to CANAL.
                      Z plus 351   Arrive at CANAL.
                      Z plus 371   Commence crossing between
                                     W.20.d.0.4. & W.15.c.3.3.
                      Z plus 386   Leading troops across CANAL.
                      Z plus 470   Arrive assembly area W.17.c. &
                                     d. and W.23.a. & b.

2. Special Signals shewing the capture of various lines will be fired from 11th Div. H.Qrs. W.7.c.2.7. as under and runners will be despatched to G.O.C., 34th Infantry Brigade :-

    RED LINE   A series of RED Rockets bursting into two REDS.

    GREEN LINE   A series of GREEN Rockets.

    BLUE LINE   A series of WHITE Rockets.

3. The 34th Infantry Brigade is not moving from its position of Assembly East of the CANAL unless it is known that the BLUE LINE is captured, information as to this being obtained by pushing patrols forward and by observation of signal rockets.

4. In the event of considerable hostile opposition, the attack of the 11th Division will be

    (i). Delayed.
    (ii). Postponed.

    Case 1. G.Os.C. 34th and 32nd Brigades will notify 11th Div. H.Qrs. the hour at which they decide the advance from the BLUE LINE can start. A new ZERO hour will then be fixed and the infantry and artillery programme will be carried out, timing the advances and lifts as if from ZERO plus 500 as detailed in the Schedule above.

/Case 2.

Case 2. The hostile opposition may be such as to prevent any further advance from the BLUE LINE; in which case the 32nd & 34th Infantry Brigades will relieve the 1st Canadian Division in the line within the limits of 11th Division Zone under orders to be issued by Canadian Corps.

5. Reference Case 1 above, B.G.C. 169th Infantry Brigade, acting in close Liaison with B.G.C. 34th Infantry Brigade, will take similar action, informing Div. H.Qrs.

6. Reference Case 2, B.G.C., 169th Infantry Brigade will be prepared to relieve troops of the 1st Canadian Division within his Zone, under orders to be issued by Div. H.Qrs.

7. Should there be a delay in the capture of the RED LINE of more than 1 hour, the Brigades of the 11th Division are not to move from their positions at ZERO without reference to 11th Divn. H.Qrs. In this eventuality 169th Infantry Brigade will take similar action.

8. ACKNOWLEDGE.

Tom Buchanan
Lieut-Colonel,
General Staff.

25.9.18.

Copies to :- 167th Infantry Brigade.
168th Infantry Brigade.
169th Infantry Brigade.
C.R.A.
56th Bn. M.G.Corps.
XXII Corps.
XXII Corps H.A.
52nd Squadron R.A.F.
11th Division.
1st Canadian Division.
Canadian Corps.
C.R.E.
50th Bde. R.G.A.
File.
War Diary.

SECRET.

Duplicate   Affx. IV

OPERATIONS CARRIED OUT BY 56th DIVISION
during period 27th - 29th Sept. inclusive.

Preliminary.
On 21st September, 1918, Provisional Instructions were received from XXII Corps for the 56th Division to take part in operations which First and Third Armies were undertaking in the direction of CAMBRAI. The following was the general plan of operations.

The Canadian Corps was to force the Crossings of the CANAL DU NORD N. of MOEUVRES on a frontage of nearly two miles and to spread out and capture the BLUE LINE (shown on the attached map).

The 11th Division on the left of the Canadian Corps and the 56th Division on the left of 11th Division were to pass over the CANAL DU NORD, under cover of this operation, and to deploy facing North, so as to relieve the Canadians on the BLUE LINE West of W.6.c.5.5. The Division was then to attack North, the final objective being the Road from Q.23.c.7.7. to Q.24.a.10.90.

On 23rd September the above instructions were confirmed by "XXII Corps Instructions for the Offensive No. 1". Six extra Brigades of field artillery, making 8 in all, were placed at the disposal of this Division, but three of these were intended mainly to support the advance of the Left Brigade of the 11th Division.

56th Divisional Operation Orders Nos. 205, 206 & 207 were issued accordingly for the attack. 169th Infantry Brigade was detailed to carry out the attack east of the CANAL and 168th Infantry Brigade to co-operate by clearing the western bank (See Map 'A').

The C.R.E. was detailed to throw bridges across the CANAL (at about W.15.a. and W.9.b.8.7.) as soon as the tactical situation permitted, and to assist 169th Infantry Brigade in crossing the AGACHE RIVER.

2 M.G.Cos. 4th Division, were attached to the Division which, with 2 Cos. 102nd M.G.Bn., made a total of 8 Cos. for the operation. Of these, 4 Cos. were detailed to barrage the ground in front of the infantry as the attack passed northwards across their front and one to barrage the high ground N.E. of ETAING and N. of HAMEL to prevent hostile observation.

One Company was kept in defensive positions on the left of the Divisional front and two Coys. were held in reserve.

Zero hour was fixed for 5.20 a.m. on September 27th.

On the night 25/26th September, 1 Bn. 169th Infantry Brigade took over from 1st Canadian Division a section of the front line from our original Southern boundary to the ARRAS - CAMBRAI road so that, on the day of the attack, it would be close to its crossings and would be ready to mop up the western bank of the CANAL where the enemy had posts established.

Div. H.Qrs. moved to an Advanced Battle H.Qrs. at V.3.a.85.70. on 26th September.

Narrative of Events.
The attack commenced at 5.20 a.m. and the Canadians were reported early to be progressing well. Enemy artillery retaliation on the Divnl. front was light and practically ceased by 5.40 a.m. By 8.15 a.m. reports were received that the Canadians had reached the RED LINE. At 11.50 a.m. it appeared that the enemy were still holding out in W.15.c. central, W.21.c., W.21.a. and that the Canadians were apparently progressing slowly on the left. Our bridging parties, who were timed to reach the Canal bank with their material after the Canadians had cleared it, found themselves opposed by hostile infantry, but the R.E. and Pioneers, pushed on, cleared the western bank and established themselves on their crossings, thus rendering assistance to the Canadians advancing from the South. As soon as the sites were clear bridging operations were put through rapidly and the 169th Infantry Brigade was ordered to cross.

/By

By this time it was evident that there would be a delay in assembling the troops on the BLUE LINE for the Second Phase of the operations and G.O.C. 11th Divn. decided to delay the hour for the attack by 34th Inf.Bde. by 40 mins. This decision was taken at 1.15 p.m. and the G.O.C. 56th Divn. gave orders for the attack by 169th Infantry Brigade to conform.

In the meantime the situation about MARQUION had improved and the latter Village cleared of the enemy. The 5th London Regt. were also reported to have cleared the West Bank of the CANAL in W.9.b. Two bridges had been constructed across the CANAL by the R.E., one in W.15.a. by 512th Field Coy. R.E. and one in W.9.b. by 513th Field Coy. By 12.40 p.m. these bridges were completed and the 2nd London Regt. and 16th London Regt. had commenced crossing. By 2.5 p.m. the crossing of the CANAL had proceeded well and bridges had been constructed by 416th Field Coy. R.E. across the AGACHE RIVER at W.10.a.2.6.

At 3.30 p.m. the attack of the 169th Inf.Bde. east of the CANAL and of the 13th London Regt. west of the CANAL commenced under cover of a heavy artillery, machine gun and mortar barrage. At 3.50 p.m. the troops were reported to have passed through KAMWEZI COPSE and to be advancing close under the barrage. At 4.30 p.m. 168th Inf. Bde. reported that the 13th London Regt. had reached their first objective - the road running E and W through SAUCHY-CAUCHY - capturing 4 M.Gs. and were in touch with 169th Inf.Bde. on the CANAL and that the latter had cleared SAUCHY-CAUCHY and SAUCHY LESTREE.

From 6 p.m. onwards the position became obscure owing to enemy pockets holding out.

The attack had proceeded according to the Time Table as far as Q.29.a. & Q.30.c., SAUCHY-CAUCHY, KAMWEZI COPSE, KIDUNA COPSE and CEMETERY WOOD. These places were taken by the 2nd London Regt. and 16th London Regt. (Q.W.R.) with many prisoners, while the area between the branches of the AGACHE RIVER was cleared by a Company of the 5th London Regt. (L.R.B.) who secured several prisoners.

North of these places, M.G.nests, chiefly along the CANAL banks held up the attack for a time. On the right the 2nd London Regt. were held by M.Gs. in Q.30.c. and in the railway embankment Q.24.c. & d. These nests were attacked by the 2nd London Regt. and 5th London Regt (L.R.B.) four times without success, but a fifth attempt was made and the nests were captured with their garrison by 3.30 a.m.

On the left the Q.W.R. met with considerable opposition from Machine Guns on the CANAL bank in Q.29.a., which completely commanded the swamps in Q.29.a. & c. By working along the AGACHE RIVER to the East of the CANAL in stages as far as Q.23.a.6.0, they eventually surrounded the Machine Guns and inflicted heavy casualties on their teams. 1 Officer and 22 O.Rs. were captured here and 20 O.Rs. were found dead at their posts.

By 7 p.m. the Q.W.R. were established along the Railway Embankment in Q.23.c. & d. Here another M.G. nest at Q.23.a.70.05. gave trouble,, and held out till dawn, when it was captured with the guns and a few prisoners.

The final objective for the day was, therefore, only reached in its entirety in the early hours of the 28th.

The 13th London Regt. (168th Inf.Bde.) who were advancing on the west bank of the CANAL were also held up by Machine Guns coming from MILL COPSE and both banks of the CANAL, and it was found impracticable to advance in face of them during daylight there being two avenues of approach only through the marsh. Accordingly the Reserve Coy. 13th London Regt. were ordered to clear up the situation as soon as the moon was up. At 2 a.m. this Company advanced from SAUCHY-CAUCHY and reached their final objective without opposition.

At 10.30 p.m. 169th Inf. Bde. having reported that its Right Battn. was on the final objective but Left Battn. still held up, orders were issued for the advance to be continued to the BROWN LINE on the 28th instant, to conform with the Brigade on the Right, and 167th Infantry Brigade was ordered to push out patrols early on the 28th instant into PALLUEL and occupy it if empty.

/At

At 1.30 a.m. 169th Infantry Brigade stated they would reach their final objective by morning, but it would be necessary to arrange an organised attack under a sweeping barrage to clear the enemy out of the ground up to the River SENSEE. This was accordingly arranged and 168th Infantry Brigade were ordered to co-operate by clearing the West bank of the CANAL.

Zero hour was fixed for 10.30 a.m.

Operations on 28th September.

The attack of 168th and 169th Infantry Brigades progressed well and 169th Infantry Brigade reported at 1.30 p.m. that all objectives were captured and posts established North of the BOIS DE QUESNOY and covering the SENSEE River.

The 168th Infantry Brigade was also successful in clearing the west bank of the CANAL. Meanwhile the 167th Infantry Brigade had occupied PALLUEL without serious opposition soon after dawn and at 11.20 a.m. reported that the 8th Middlesex Regiment had established posts on the northern and eastern sides of the Village and were pushing on towards ARLEUX. This they succeeded in entering during the late afternoon and established posts. At 3 a.m. the following morning (29th Sept.) however, the enemy counter-attacked under a heavy artillery barrage and drove them out to their former positions covering PALLUEL which was held and consolidated.

Casualties.		Killed.	Wounded.	Missing.
	Officers.	8	9	—
	O.Rs.	38	269	17

Prisoners.— 12 Officers. 501 O.R.

Material captured.		T.Ms.	M.Gs.
	Light	7	34
	Heavy	3	11

T. Oh. Buchan Major
for.
Major-General,
Commanding 56th Division.

4th Oct. 1918.

War Diary

SECRET   56th Division G.A. 67.

AMENDMENT No. 1 to 56th DIVISION ORDER No. 206.

Amend para. 7, last two lines to read :-

169th Infantry Brigade and 11th Division will attack from the BLUE LINE at ZERO plus 540 minutes, at which hour they will close up under the Barrage. The first lift of the Barrage on the 56th Division front will be at ZERO plus 570 and on 11th Division front at ZERO plus 568.

ACKNOWLEDGE.

H.Q., 56th Divn.
26.9.18.

T. John Buckinhay
Lieut-Colonel,
General Staff.

J.   To all recipients of 56th Div. Order No. 206.

War Diary.

SECRET.   Copy No. 25

Ref. Sheet 51B.   56th DIVISION ORDER NO. 208.
1/40,000   29th September 1918

1.   167th Infantry Brigade will be relieved to-night September 29/30th by one Bn. of 11th Brigade 4th Division, under the orders of 10th Brigade, and by 169th Infantry Brigade.

2.   Boundary between 56th Division and 4th Division will be Q.4.d.00.00. thence South to Q.16.d.00.80, thence along HIRONDELLE RIVER to SAUDEMONT (exclusive to 56th Division). Right Division boundary will remain unaltered.

3.   Command of respective sectors will pass on completion of reliefs.

4.   Machine Guns in Sector to be taken over by 4th Division will be relieved 30/31st September.

5.   O.C., 56th Bn. M.G.Corps will detail one Company to act with 169th Infantry Brigade.

6.   Guides of 167th Infantry Brigade will meet incoming Bn. 4th Division, at ST.SERVINS FARM O.24.d.2.8. at 5.45 p.m.

7.   Details of relief will be arranged between Brigadiers and D.H.G.Os. concerned.

8.   Area to which 167th Infantry Brigade will withdraw will be notified by 'Q'.

9.   Progress of reliefs will be reported to Div. H.Qrs.

10. ACKNOWLEDGE.

                                                    T. OM Buchan Huy
Issued at 12 noon.
                                                    Lieut-Colonel,
                                                    General Staff.

Distribution :-
   Copy No. 1. 167th Infantry Brigade.
           2. 168th Infantry Brigade.
           3. 169th Infantry Brigade.
           4. 1/5th Cheshire Regt.
           5. C.R.A.
           6. 50th Bde. R.G.A.
           7. C.R.E.
           8. 56th Bn. M.G.Corps.
           9. 56th Div. Signal Coy.
          10. 56th Div. Gas Officer.
          11. A.D.M.S.
          12. "Q"
          13. A.P.M.
          14. D.A.D.O.S.
          15. D.A.D.V.S.
          16. 56th Div. Train.
          17. A.D.C.
          18. Camp Commandant.
          19.) XXII Corps.
          20.)
          21. XXII Corps H.A.
          22. 4th Division.
          23. 11th Division.
          24. 52nd Squadron R.A.F.
          25.) War Diary.
          26.)
          27. File.

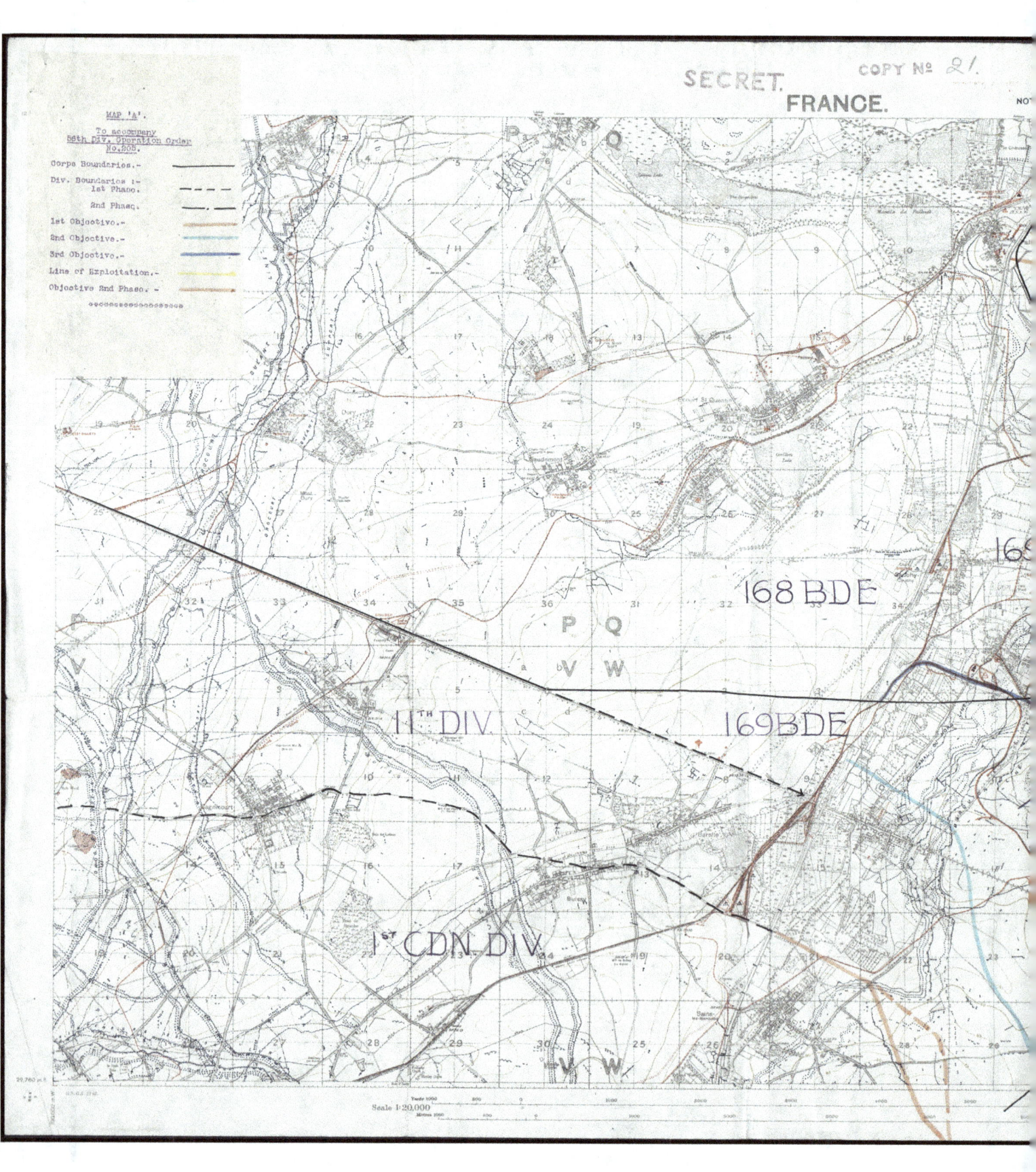

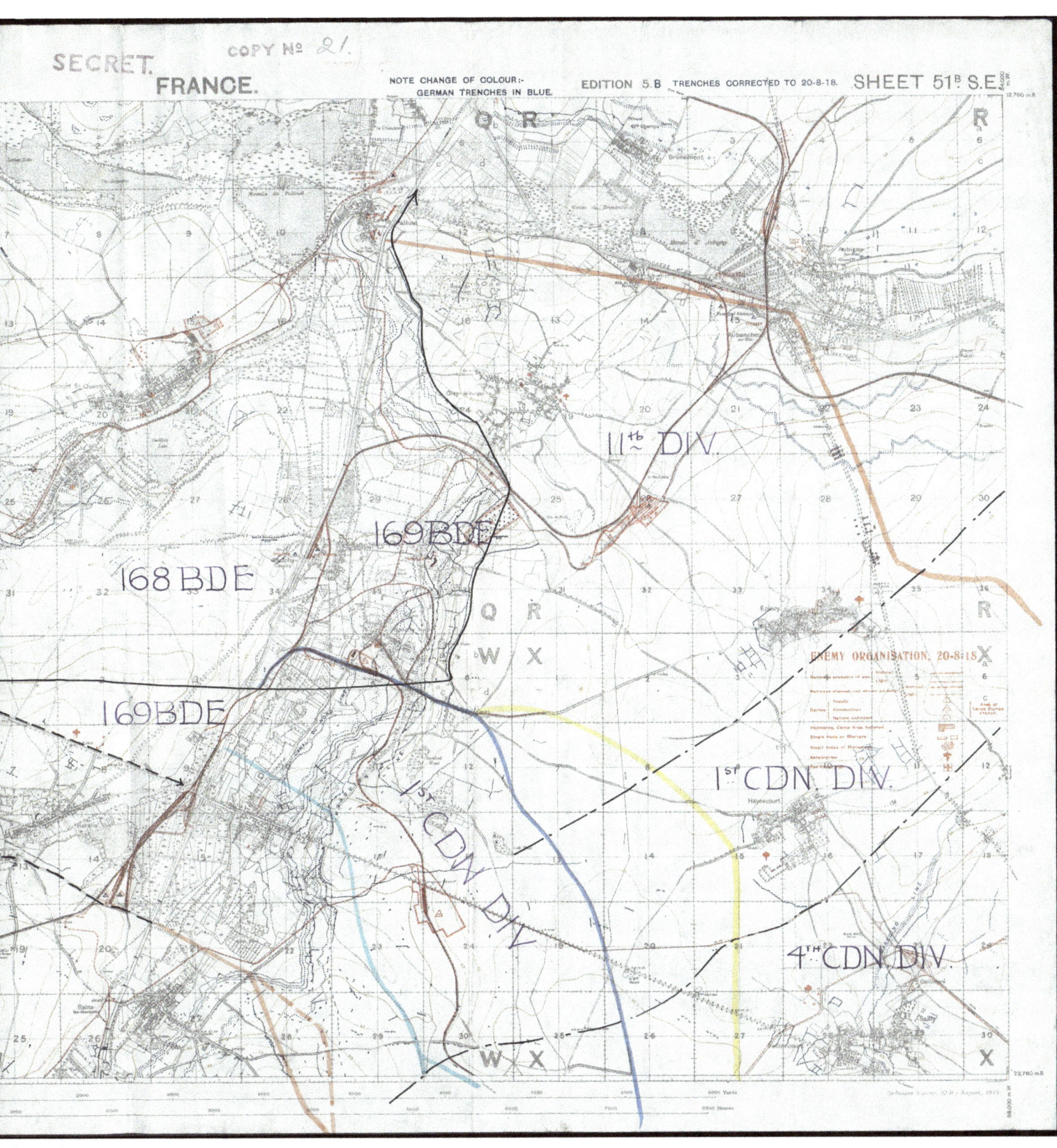

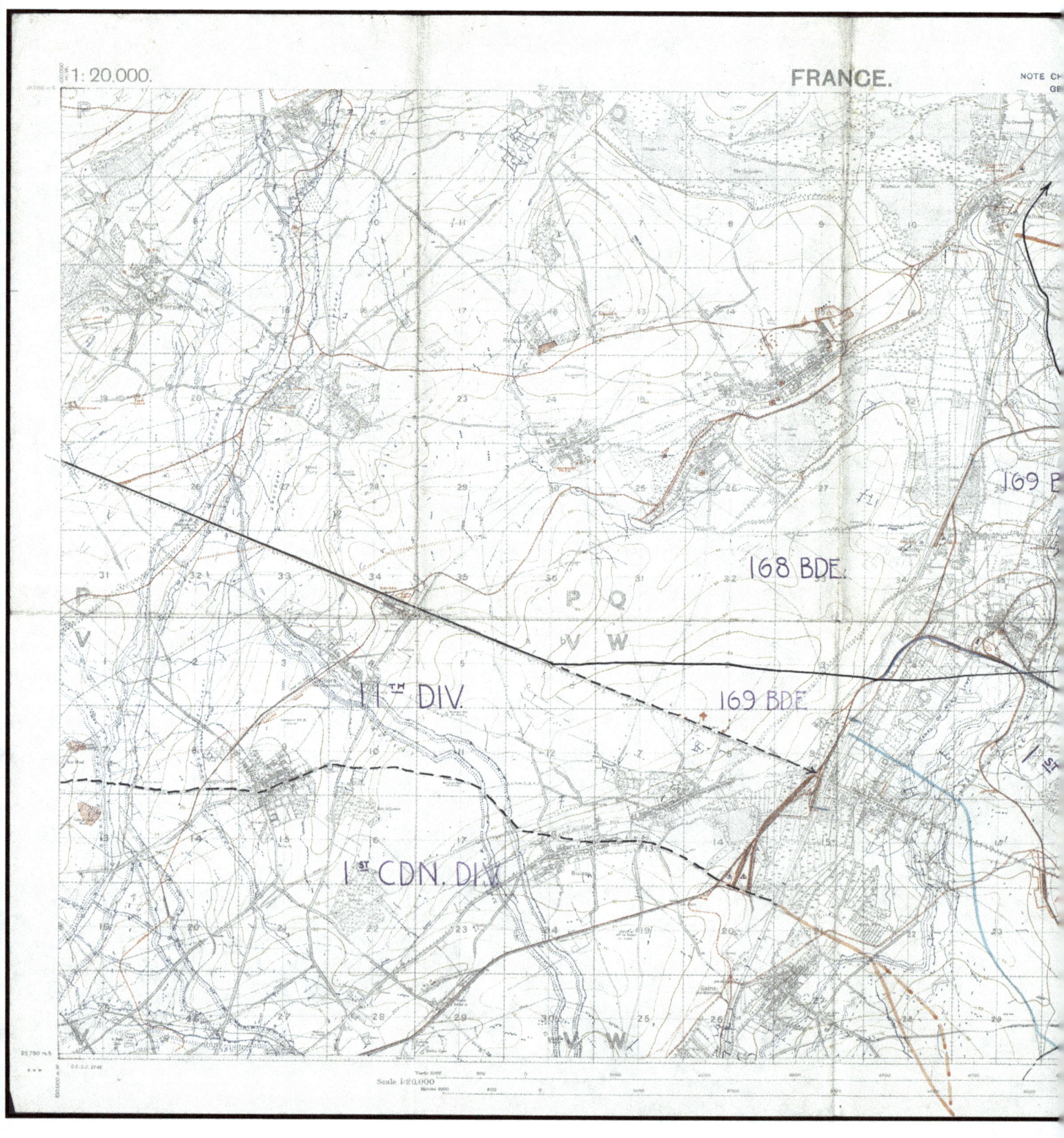

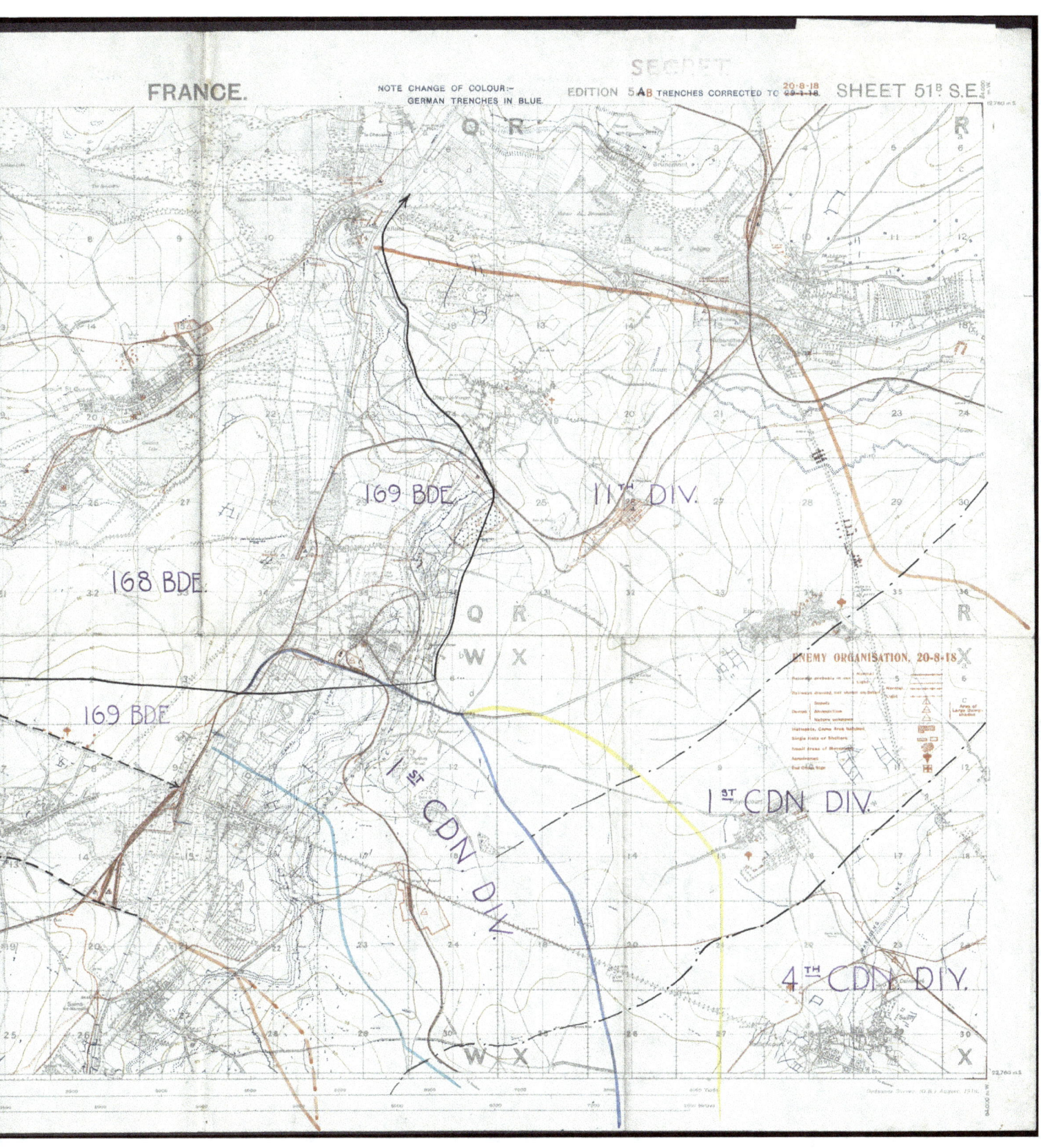

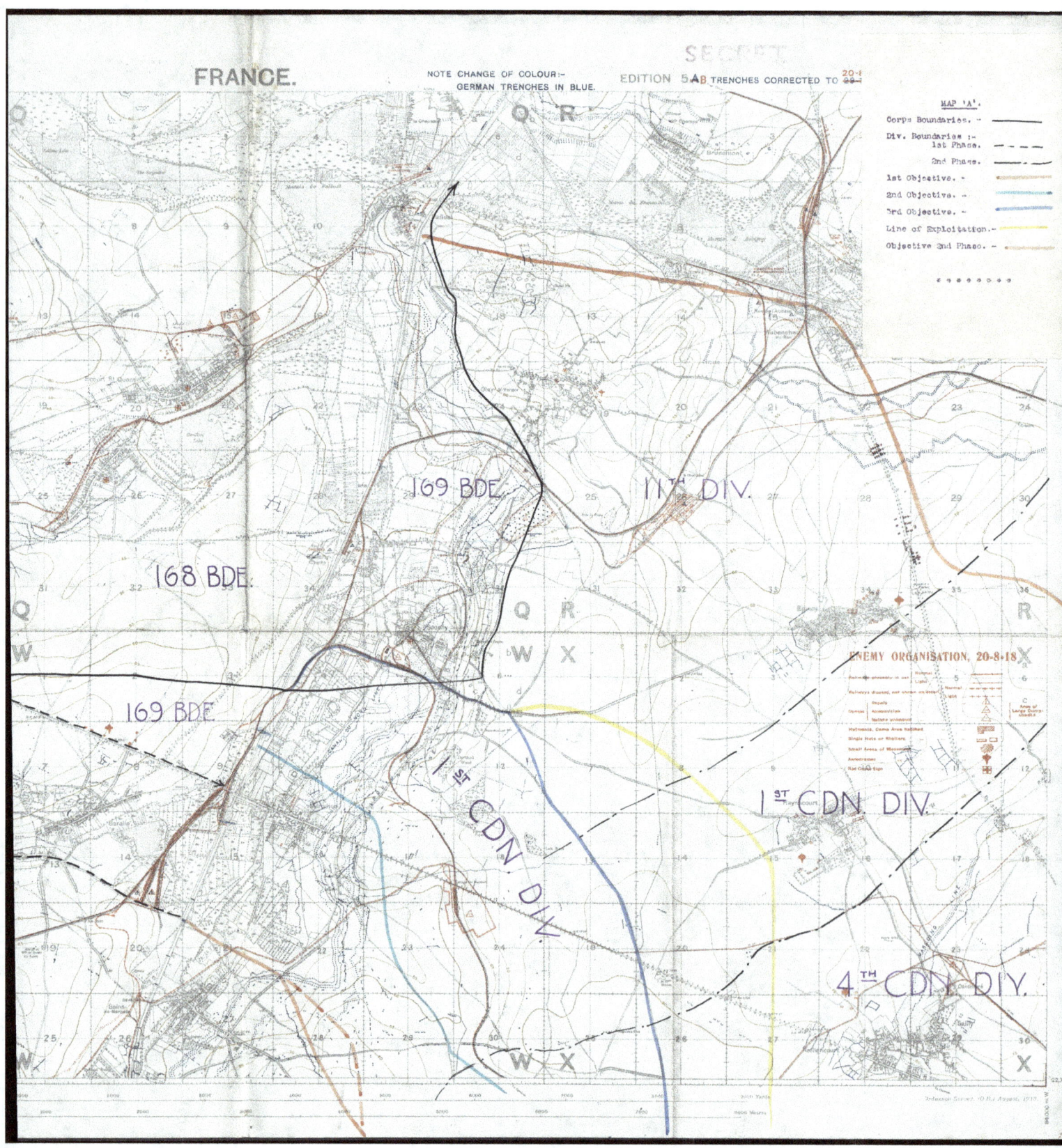

56th DIVISION.

WAR DIARY or INTELLIGENCE SUMMARY.

OCTOBER 1918.

Army Form C. 2118.

Place	Date	Hour	Summary of Events and Information	Remarks and references to Appendices
VILLERS-LES-CAGNICOURT.	Oct. 1st.		Enemy fairly quiet. Some shelling of OISY LE VERGER and Right Brigade area during morning. Enemy attacked one of our posts at PALLEUL, but was repulsed without securing identifications. O.O. No. 209 issued for a Gas Projector attack on AUBENCHEUL.	APP.II.
	2nd.		Enemy shelled OISY LE VERGER and battery positions in Right Brigade area, and at 7 p.m. put down a barrage on the front troops, but no infantry action followed. At 2330 gas was successfully projected into AUBENCHEUL. 167th Infantry Brigade moved up into close reserve and arrived in new area by 0800.	APP.I.
	3rd.		Quiet day. Enemy shelled the ARRAS - CAMBRAI Road during the morning.	
	4th.		Usual hostile harassing fire in the Right Section. O.O. No. 210 issued for relief of 169th Infantry Brigade by 167th Infantry Brigade on night 5/6th inst. G.S.O.I proceeded to England on short leave.	APP.II.
	5th		Hostile Artillery quieter. Enemy very alert and opened heavy M.G. fire on the approach of our patrols during the night. Orders received from XXII Corps that this Division would be transferred to Canadian Corps on 10th inst. but remaining in present position. Also that 102nd M.G. Bn. would be transferred to 49th Division on 7th inst. O.O.211 issued. 167th Infantry Brigade relieved 169th Infantry Brigade in the left section. 169th Infantry Brigade moved into Div. Reserve.	APP.II. APP.I.
	6th.		Quiet day. Slight hostile shelling of OISY le VERGER with 4.2's. Enemy set fire to AUBENCHEUL AU BAC during the day and the Village is burning in several places. 56th Div. O.O. No. 212 issued for attack on AUBENCHEUL AU BAC in conjunction with 11th Div. on our right. During the night our patrols penetrated into AUBENCHEUL AU BAC and found it unoccupied. Posts were, therefore, established through this Village on the CANAL bank in touch with 11th Division on the right flank.	APP.III.
	7th		Quiet day. Hostile artillery inactive. Weather fine and windy.	

Army Form C. 2118.

WAR DIARY
or
INTELLIGENCE SUMMARY.
(Erase heading not required.)

56th DIVISION.   OCTOBER 1918.

Instructions regarding War Diaries and Intelligence Summaries are contained in F. S. Regs., Part II. and the Staff Manual respectively. Title pages will be prepared in manuscript.

Place	Date	Hour	Summary of Events and Information	Remarks and references to Appendices
VILLERS-LES-CAGNICOURT.	Oct. 8th.		At 0530 our artillery bombarded ARLEUX and AUBIGNY AU BAC in conjunction with operation being carried out by the Canadian Corps on our Right. Hostile artillery rather more active. Considerable enemy movement seen, mostly individual. Many fires and explosions were seen behind the enemy's lines, not caused by our shell fire.	
	9th.		Quiet night.	
		1204	Orders received from XXII Corps for this Division to extend its right to FRESSIES in relief of 11th Division. The 11th Division thus being freed to follow up the enemy, who were evacuating the area between the CANAL de l'ESCAUT and the CANAL de la SENSEE in consequence of the capture of CAMBRAI by the Canadian Corps. The relief to be complete by midnight. 168th Infantry Brigade on completion of relief were also ordered to push patrols into and clear FRESSIES.	
		1315	Orders issued by wire and 56th Div. O.O. No. 214 issued.	APP. II.
		1345	On information received from 22nd Corps that the enemy was withdrawing on 11th Division front, 167th and 168th Infantry Brigades were ordered to push patrols across the CANAL de la SENSEE into ARLEUX and AUBIGNY AU BAC and BRUNEMONT to ascertain if occupied but were not to become involved in fighting. Orders received from XXII Corps for transfer of 52nd A.F.A.Bde. from 11th Division to 56th Division.	
		1500		
		1530	167th Infantry Brigade reported their patrols unable to enter ARLEUX owing to hostile M.G. fire but 4 Germans killed in outskirts. Identification normal.	
		1650	168th Infantry Brigade reported one of their patrols had crossed the CANAL at ABBE DU VERGER FARM, and captured a prisoner - normal identification - but held up by hostile M.G.fire.	
		1807	Orders received from XXII Corps for the co-operation of 56th Div. Artillery in an attack which 8th Division and 1st Canadian Division were making on the DROCOURT - QUEANT Line on our left flank. 56th Div. Artillery ordered accordingly. Relief ordered in O.O.214 completed as ordered.	
VILLERS-LES-CAGNICOURT.	10th		Quiet night. 168th Infantry Brigade patrols held up outside FRESSIES by hostile M.G. fire. Hostile artillery rather more active. Our patrols endeavoured to obtain footing across the CANAL DE LA SENSEE and in AELEUX, but on each occasion found the enemy holding the crossings and causeways with M.Gs.	
		1930	Orders were issued for 168th Infantry Brigade to capture FRESSIES under cover of an artillery barrage.	

56th DIVISION.

WAR DIARY
or
INTELLIGENCE SUMMARY.

(Erase heading not required.)

Army Form C. 2118.

OCTOBER 1918.

Place	Date	Hour	Summary of Events and Information	Remarks and references to Appendices
VILLERS-LES-CAGNICOURT.	Oct. 11th		At 0700 this morning 168th Infantry Brigade attacked the Village of FRESNES under a barrage. The operation was completely successful - 2 Officers and 30 O.R. were made prisoners and our line advanced past FRESNES to the CANAL. Our casualties were 1 killed and 9 O.R. wounded. Subsequently 9 further prisoners were brought in.	
		0920	On the 8th Corps on our left capturing VITRY en ARTOIS, and reporting the enemy in retreat towards DOUAI, orders were received from XXII Corps for this Division to keep the crossings of the CANAL de la SENSEE under Artillery fire from ARLEUX northwards. Orders issued to C.R.A. accordingly and 167th Infantry Brigade were instructed to push forward patrols to obtain a footing in ARLEUX if possible. 167th Infantry Brigade made several attempts but were unable to reach ARLEUX owing to hostile M.G. fire.	
		1207.	New left forward boundary received from XXII Corps which made ARLEUX inclusive to this Division. The situation remained quiet during the day.	APP. I.
		1700	The Division passed to the Command of the Canadian Corps. 169th Infantry Brigade relieved the 168th Infantry Brigade in the right Section of the Divnl. front. 168th Infantry Brigade moved into Div.Reserve in region of SAUDEMONT.	
VILLERS CAGNICOURT.	12th	1035.	1st Can. Divn. having reported that they had captured ARLEUX and trench system running North from the Village, but enemy M.Gs. still firing from S.E. edge of the Village. 167th Inf. Bde. were therefore ordered to co-operate in clearing ARLEUX and to relieve all troops of 1st Can. Division up to our northern Div. Boundary. 169th Bde. were ordered to extend their left and take over a portion of the front held by 167th Infantry Brigade.	
		1230	169th Infantry Brigade were ordered to endeavour to cross the CANAL de la SENSEE tonight and capture AUBIGNY AU BAC. The C.R.E. was ordered to construct the necessary bridges. The C.R.E. was also instructed to bridge all gaps in the PALLEUL - ARLEUX Road, and be prepared to throw a pontoon across the CANAL at ABBE DU VERGER FARM. During the afternoon 167th Infantry Brigade succeeded in clearing out the enemy posts in ARLEUX, capturing 19 prisoners, and took over their new section from 1st Can. Divn. By 2250 they had cleared the Triangle formed by the CANAL EAST of ARLEUX and established posts on the banks. Orders received from Canadian Corps for relief by 4th Can. Divn. relief to be complete by 1000, 16th inst. Warning Order No. 215 issued.	APP. II.

Army Form C. 2118.

WAR DIARY
or
INTELLIGENCE SUMMARY.
(Erase heading not required.)

56th DIVISION. OCTOBER 1918.

Instructions regarding War Diaries and Intelligence Summaries are contained in F.S. Regs., Part II. and the Staff Manual respectively. Title pages will be prepared in manuscript.

Place	Date	Hour	Summary of Events and Information	Remarks and references to Appendices
VILLERS CAGNICOURT.	Oct. 13th		During the night a party of Q.W.R. (169th Inf.Bde.) succeeded in establishing a footing on the North bank of the CANAL de LA SENSEE opposite AUBIGNY AU BAC, and the 416th Field Coy. R.E. constructed a floating bridge to the N. bank. A Company of 2nd London Regt. then crossed and formed up on the North bank and another Coy. of the same battalion assembled on the western outskirts of the Village. The total strength of these two Coys. amounted to 6 Officers and 165 O.R.	
			At 0515 the attack on AUBIGNY commenced under a creeping barrage from the S.E. The attack was completely successful, the Village being captured and 4 Officers and 203 O.R. being taken prisoners. During the day Posts were at once established on the Northern and Eastern outskirts and steps taken to construct another bridge alongside the site of the broken bridge carrying the road leading from AUBENCHEUL to AUBIGNY	
		0800	167th Infantry Brigade were ordered to pass a Company over the CANAL at AUBENCHEUL and push westwards along the N. bank of the CANAL. A battalion of 168th Infantry Brigade was put at the disposal of 169th Infantry Brigade in order to release troops to reinforce AUBIGNY.	
		1045	the enemy counter-attacked under a heavy barrage and forced our troops back on to the CANAL where they maintained their original bridgehead.	
		1305	To relieve the situation at AUBIGNY AU BAC, 167th Infantry Brigade were ordered to make an attempt to cross the CANAL de la SENSEE, if not strongly held, East of ARLEUX, thus threatening the enemy's flank.	
			By 1520 it was apparent that the enemy were holding the West bank of the CANAL near ARLEUX, and 167th Infantry Brigade were unable to effect a crossing, also that 169th Infantry Brigade had only about 10 men holding their bridgehead. Permission was therefore given to 169th Infantry Brigade to withdraw to the South bank of the CANAL at dusk. They were to keep the bridge intact however.	
			From information received from prisoners it seemed probable that the enemy intended to make a further retirement tonight. O.O. 216 issued to deal with any such contingency. O.O.No.217 issued in confirmation of Warning Order No. 215. 10th Can. Inf. Bde. arrived in this area preparatory to relieving 169th Infantry Brigade and came under the orders of G.O.C. 56th Divn. The enemy made two attacks on the bridgehead held by 169th Inf. Bde. at AUBIGNY AU BAC but was repulsed on each occasion.	APP.II. APP.II. APP.I.

Army Form C. 2118.

56th DIVISION.   WAR DIARY   OCTOBER 1918.
or
INTELLIGENCE SUMMARY.

(Erase heading not required.)

Place	Date	Hour	Summary of Events and Information	Remarks and references to Appendices
VILLERS CAGNICOURT.	14th		Quiet night. 167th Infantry Brigade made an attempt to cross the CANAL just E. of ARLEUX, but the enemy were alert and opened fire with M.Gs. at short range. 169th Infantry Bde. maintained patrols on the North bank of the CANAL by AUBIGNY AU BAC. Hostile artillery less active during the day. 10th Can. Inf. Bde. relieved 169th Infantry Brigade in the right section, the bridgehead and bridge at AUBIGNY AU BAC being handed over intact. 169th Infantry Brigade moved to SAUCHY CAUCHY area. 11th Can. Inf. Bde. arrived in the area relieving 168th Infantry Brigade who entrained for ARRAS.	APP.I.
	15th		Quiet day. Owing to breakdown on railway 168th Infantry Brigade remained the night at MARQUION arriving at ARRAS about 1200. During the evening the enemy rushed the bridgehead at AUBIGNY AU BAC and destroyed the bridge, but failed to get any identification. 11th Can. Inf. Bde. relieved 167th Infantry Brigade in Left Section of the Divl. Front. 167th Infantry Brigade moved to RUMANCOURT area. 12th Can. Inf. Bde. arrived and billeted at SAUCHY CAUCHY - BARALLE area.	APP.I.
ETRUN.	16th		Quiet night. G.O.C. 4th Can. Division assumed command of Divl. front at 1000. Div.H.Q. moved to ETRUN. 167th Infantry Brigade to 'Y' Huts, ETRUN.	
	17th		Units engaged in cleaning up and refitting. G.Os.C. conference at Div.H.Q.	
	18th		Units engaged in cleaning up and refitting.	
	19th		Units engaged in cleaning up and refitting.	
	20th.		Church Parade. Divisional Artillery withdrawn from line and moved into rest in RAMILLIES - ESWARS Area under XXII Corps.	
	21st.		Units engaged in training. Distribution of medals by G.O.C. to Officers and O.R. of 168th Infantry Brigade at ARRAS.	
	22.		Units engaged in training. G.10/113 issued - Instructions re nature of training to be carried out.	

56th DIVISION.

WAR DIARY
or
INTELLIGENCE SUMMARY.

Army Form C. 2118.

OCTOBER 1918

Place	Date	Hour	Summary of Events and Information	Remarks and references to Appendices
ETRUN.	23rd.		Units engaged in training.	
	24th.		Units engaged in training. Major-General Sir J.F.N.BIRCH, K.C.M.G., C.B., M.G.R.A. G.H.Q. visited Divisional H.Q.	
	25th.		Units training.	
	26th.		Units training.	
	27th.		Church Parades. Canadian Corps issued instructions that organization detailed in G.H.Q. pamphlet O.B./1919 will be brought into force forthwith in British Divisions, where this has not already been done.	
	28th.	1400	Units Training. G.O.C. discussed points on training with Officers and N.C.Os. of 167th Infantry Brigade.	
	29th.		Units Training.	
		1430.	G.O.C. discussed points on training with Officers and N.C.Os. of 169th Infantry Brigade.	
	30th.		Orders received for 56th Division to move into Corps Reserve under 22nd Corps in DOUCHY - LIEU ST.AMAND area on 31st.	App 2 App 11
		1700	56th Div. Order No. 218 issued.	
BASSEVILLE	31st.		56th Division relieved 51st Division in Corps Reserve in XXII Corps with H.Q. at BASSEVILLE. Orders received for 56th Division to be prepared to relieve 49th Division in line on Nov. 3rd.	

Major-General,
Commanding 56th Division.

SECRET   56th DIVISION.   LOCATION TABLE at 6 a.m.   October 1918.   APPENDIX I

	1	2	3	4	5	6	7	8	9	10	11	12	13	14	15	16
Div. H.Q.	V.3.b.2.7.															
167th Inf. Bde. H.Q.	O.34.b.5.5		P.34.a.2.9.			Q.36.a.2.5.(Left Bde)					Q.36.a.2.9			Q.23.b.4.5.		P.34.a.2.8
1st London Regt.	O.35.b.0.2.		O.34.a.4.0.			Q.23.a.5.0.Q.16.c.2.0.(Rt)					Q.16.2.2.0.			Q.22.a.0.0.9.(Left)		Ruyau-
7th Middx. Regt.	O.20.c.0.9.		Q.26.d.6.0.			Q.23.b.3.4.(Left)								Q.11.a.3.3.(Cent)		court
8th Middx. Regt.	Q.20.c.0.1.		P.25.b.9.2.			Q.34.b.4.2.					R.26.d.1.3.(Right)			O.17.d.3.a.(Right)		AREA.
168th Inf. Bde. H.Q.	W.16.b.3.5.	X.1.c.1.5. (R. Bde)									P.34.a.2.8				ARRAS	
4th London Regt.	Q.25.b.6.0.	R.31. cent.				R.25.d.0.3. (Right)				R.31.c.0.0.9.5. X.2.d.2.7.	R.31.c.0.5.0.	Q.26.d.6.				
13th "	Q.33.c.0.9.9.	R.25.c.5.3. (Left)				P.31. cent.				R.25.c.9.	R.25.b.9.1.				ARRAS	
14th "	P.35.b.7.1.R.25.d.0.3.(Right)										Q.31.a.6.9.					
169th Inf. Bde. H.Q.	Q.36.a.4.5. (Left Bde)					P.34.a.2.9.						X.1.c.1.5.			X.1.c.15.	HAUTE
2nd London Regt.	Q.14.d.5.0.(L) Q.23.a.6.0.					Q.31.a.4.0.				Q.25.d.6.6.		R.31.c.0.5.0.				AVESNES
5th "	Q.33.b.3.4.(R)			Q.34.b.2.2.		R.35.b.9.2.						R.28.b.5.0.(R)			SAUCHY LESTREE	AREA.
16th "	Q.30.d.4.2.			Q.25.b.3.4. (R)		Q.25.d.6.0.						R.39.d.9.2.(L)			SAUCHY CAUCHY	
Div. Arty. H.Q.	V.3.b.2.7.			Q.30.d.3.3.												
280th Bde.	V.3.b.8.5			Q.30.c.3.2.												
281st "	O.27.a.6.3.															
Pioneers.	P.26.d.6.3.															Maroeuil.
M.G. Battn. H.Q.	V.3.b.2.7.															

Key.   In Line. ───   " Support ═══   " Res. ═══   Divn. of Rest. ───

SECRET.   56th DIVISION.   LOCATION TABLE at 6 a.m.   OCTOBER 1918.   APPENDIX 1.

	17	18	19	20	21	22	23	24	25	26	27	28	29	30	31
Div. H.Q.	ETRUN														BASSÉVILLE
167th Infe.Bde.H.Q.	V'HUTS.														DOUCHY
1st London Regt.	L.2.c.														THONVILLE
7th Mach. Gun Regt.	(Sheet														DOUCHY
8th Middlx. Regt.	51C.)														MOULIN
168th Infe.Bde.H.Q.	⎱ARRAS														⎱DOUCHY
4th London Regt.	⎰														⎰
13th " "															
14th " "															
169th Infe.Bde.H.Q.	⎱HAUTE														⎱LIEU
2nd London Regt.	⎰AVESNES														⎰ST.
5th " "	AREA.														AMAND.
16th " "															
Div. Arty. H.Q.	MAROEUIL				CAMBRAI										
280th Bde.					RAMILLIES									THIANT.	
281st "					ESWARS									THIANT.	
Pioneers.	MAROEUIL														MEUVILLE
M.G. Battn. H.Q.	ANZIN														BASSÉVILLE

SECRET   Copy No. 17

56th DIVISION ORDER No. 209.

Oct. 1st 1918.

1. On night 1st/2nd October, should wind conditions be favourable, a gas projector operation will be carried out against enemy in AUBENCHEUL-au-BAC.
   Should wind conditions be unfavourable the discharge will take place on the first favourable night.

2. Site of projectors and targets are shewn on the attached map (issued to C.R.A., 11th Division, 168th Inf. Bde., XXII Corps).

3. The operation will take place with any winds between W. through S. to S.S.E. inclusive.
   The above wind limits are liable to alteration in accordance with the situation on our right.

4. Zero will be 3.0 a.m., 2nd October, 1918.

5. All troops within the boundaries of the zone coloured PINK on annexed sketch map should wear their box respirators from zero minus 5 minutes until ordered by an Officer to remove them.
   Should the tactical situation permit it, all troops in the area coloured YELLOW should be withdrawn at least 15 minutes before Zero, and, on resuming occupation, should beware of gas from 'Shorts'.

6. In order to deceive and confuse the enemy, the Artillery will open up a sharp burst of fire on to the targets indicated on annexed map, from Zero minus 3 minutes until Zero plus 2 minutes, and from Zero plus 10 minutes to Zero plus 15 minutes.

7. As communication will be practically impossible from the projector sites to O.C., "G" Special Coy. R.E. (the location of whose H.Q. will be notified later) the Section Officers concerned will be responsible for correctness of wind readings and for the discharge.
   These Officers will as far as possible keep in touch with the Infantry concerned.

8. C.R.A. and O.C. "G" Special Coy. R.E. will arrange to synchronize time at 17.30 at Div. H.Qrs.

9. The following code will be used :-

    SPADE   —   Wind forecast favourable, operation proceeding.

    SHOVEL   —   Wind forecast unfavourable, operation will not take place.

    PICK   —   Previously favourable, now unfavourable, operation postponed.

10. ACKNOWLEDGE.

Lieut-Colonel,
General Staff.

Issued at :- 12.30 p.m.
Distribution
Copy No. 1. 168th Infantry Brigade.
         2. 169th Infantry Brigade.
         3. 1/5th Cheshire Regt.
         4. C.R.A.
         5. 50th Bde. R.G.A.
         6. C.R.E.
         7. 56th Bn. M.G. Corps.
         8. 56th Div. Signal Coy.
         9. 56th Div. Gas Officer.
        10. A.D.M.S.

No. 11. "Q"
    12. XXII Corps.
    13. "
    14. XXII Corps H.A.
    15. 11th Division.
    16. "G" Special Coy. R.E.
    17.) War Diary.
    18.)
    19. File.

"A" Form
MESSAGES AND SIGNALS.

Army Form C. 2121 (In pads of 100.)

D.R.L.S.

TO — War Diary

Sender's Number: G.659
Day of Month: 2nd

Reference O.O. 209 of 1.10.18 Operation will take place at 23.30 to-night.

From: 56 Div.
Time: 1225

General Staff

SECRET.   *War Diary.*   Copy No. 23

56th DIVISION ORDER No. 210.

4th October 1918.

1. 167th Infantry Brigade will relieve 169th Infantry Brigade in the left Brigade Sector on October 5/6th.

2. On relief 169th Infantry Brigade will withdraw to area vacated by 167th Infantry Brigade and will be in Divisional Reserve.

3. Details of relief to be arranged between B.Gs.C. concerned.

4. Completion of relief to be reported by Code word "SALLY".

5. ACKNOWLEDGE.

B Pakenham
Lieut-Colonel,
General Staff.

Issued at 08.00.

Distribution:-
Copy No. 1. 167th Infantry Brigade.
         2. 168th Infantry Brigade.
         3. 169th Infantry Brigade.
         4. 1/5th Cheshire Regt.
         5. C.R.A.
         6. 78th Bde. R.G.A.
         7. C.R.E.
         8. 56th Bn. M.G.Corps.
         9. 56th Div. Signal Coy.
        10. 56th Div. Gas Officer.
        11. A.D.M.S.
        12. "Q".
        13. A.P.M.
        14. D.A.D.O.S.
        15. 56th Div. Train.
        16. 56th Div. Reception Camp.
        17.) XXII Corps.
        18.)
        19. XXII Corps H.A.
        20. 11th Division.
        21. 4th Division.
        22. 52nd Squadron R.A.F.
        23.)
        24.) War Diary.
        25. File.

War Diary

SECRET   56th Division No. G.3/458.

AMENDMENT No. 3 to 56th DIVISION ORDER No. 211.

    The 56th Division will be transferred to Canadian Corps on the evening of 11th October.

    The S.O.S. Signal will remain RED over RED over RED.

H.Q. 56th Divn.
11th Oct. 1918.

                                                 T. M. Buchan Mayr
                                                 Lieut-Colonel,
                                                 General Staff.

To all Recipients of Order No. 211.

SECRET *War Diary* 56th Division No. G.3/441.

AMENDMENT No. 2 to 56th DIVISION ORDER No. 211.

The date of transfer of the 56th Division to Canadian Corps is postponed and will be notified later.

H.Q., 56th Divn.
9th Oct. 1918.

T. M. Buchan, Major
Lieut-Colonel,
General Staff.

To all Recipients of Order No. 211.

SECRET.   56th Division G.3/423.

War Diary Corps

AMENDMENT No. 1 to 56th DIVISION ORDER No. 211.

Para. 3 is cancelled and the following substituted :-

    The 102nd M.G.Battn. (less two Companies attached to the 4th Division) will be transferred to 49th Division at 1000 on 7th inst.

    The Company now in the line will be withdrawn on night 6/7th inst. under the orders of O.C., 56th Bn. M.G.Corps, and will concentrate in O.30.a. The H.Qrs. and remaining Company will remain at ANZIN.

                                                         T.H.Heald Capt
                                                   for   Lieut-Colonel,

H.Q., 56th Divn.   General Staff.
5.10.18.

Distribution:-
       56th Bn. M.G.Corps.
       102nd Bn. M.G.Corps.
       XXII Corps. (2).
       "Q"
       49th Division.

War Diary

SECRET   Copy No. 22

56th DIVISION ORDER No. 211.

Ref.Map 51B.   5th October, 1918.

1. At 1000 on October 10th the 56th Division will be transferred to the Canadian Corps, and will remain in line on its present front.

2. The following are the dates of relief of Brigades on the Right and Left Flank of the Division:-

    6th/7th Oct.   'A' Brigade, 1st Canadian Division relieves
                    Right Brigade, 4th British Division.

    9th/10th Oct.   'A' Brigade, 2nd Canadian Division relieves
                    Left Brigade, 11th Division.

3. The two Coys. 102nd M.G. Battn. attached 56th Division will be withdrawn from the line on 6th/7th October and concentrated in the neighbourhood of P.34.a. under the orders of O.C. 56th Bn. M.G.Corps. At 1000, October 7th, they will be transferred to 49th Division.

4. ACKNOWLEDGE.

                                                T.C.M. Buchanan Major
                                                Lieut-Colonel,
                                                General Staff.

Issued at 2.0 p.m.

Distribution :-

Copy No. 1. 167th Infantry Brigade.   No. 13. A.P.M.
         2. 168th Infantry Brigade.   14. D.A.D.O.S.
         3. 169th Infantry Brigade.   15. 56th Div. Train.
         4. 1/5th Cheshire Regt.   16) XXII Corps.
         5. C.R.A.   17)
         6. 78th Bde. R.G.A.   18) Canadian Corps.
         7. C.R.E.   19)
         8. 56th Bn. M.G.Corps.   20. 49th Division.
         9. 56th Div. Signal Coy.   21. 102nd M.G. Battn.
        10. 56th Div. Gas Officer.   22) War Diary.
        11. A.D.M.S.   23)
        12. "Q"   24 File.

J.

"A" Form.
MESSAGES AND SIGNALS.

Army Form C. 2121.
(In pads of 100.)

TO: All recipients Order 212

Sender's Number.	Day of Month.	In reply to Number.	
G.981	7		A A A

56th Div. Order No. 212 is cancelled
as our troops have now reached the
objectives laid down therein

From 56th Divn.

General Staff

SECRET.   Copy No....22

56th DIVISION ORDER No. 212.

Ref. Sheet 51B.S.E.   8th October 1918.
1/20,000

1. (a). On a date to be notified later the 11th Division will carry out an attack with the object of establishing themselves on the line M.19.d.7.5. – CRUCIFIX – R.23.b.0.4. – thence the line of the CANAL from R.17.c.8.5. to Railway Bridge at R.15.b.7.4. (exclusive).

   (b). The 11th Division will be attacking with two Brigades in line, the 32nd Infantry Brigade being on the left.

   (c). Extracts from 11th Division Instructions No. 4 are attached for 168th Brigade, C.R.A. and D.M.G.C.

2. The 168th Infantry Brigade will attack concurrently with the 11th Division, clearing all ground down to the CANAL west of the Railway R.21.a.4.5. – R.15.b.7.0. – R.15.b.7.4. (Railway inclusive).

3. The attack of 168th Infantry Brigade will be covered by 3 Brigades R.F.A. and a portion of 56th Bn. M.G.C.

4. G.O.C. 168th Infantry Brigade will arrange the artillery and M.G.Barrage direct with O.C. Right Group R.F.A. and O.C. 56th Bn. M.G.C. respectively. He will also arrange to co-ordinate his attack with that of the 32nd Infantry Brigade.

5. C.R.A. in consultation with G.O.C. 168th Infantry Brigade, will allot tasks for the heavy artillery.

6. After the completion of the capture of the Village, G.O.C. 168th Infantry Brigade will relieve all troops of the 11th Divn. up to the Bridge at R.16.a.3.3. (inclusive).

7. ACKNOWLEDGE.

                                                        Lieut-Colonel,
                                                        General Staff.

Issued at 2 p.m.

Distribution :-
   Copy No. 1. 167th Infantry Brigade.
           2. 168th Infantry Brigade.
           3. 169th Infantry Brigade.
           4. 1/5th Cheshire Regt.
           5.) C.R.A.
           6.)
           7. 78th Bde. R.G.A.
           8. C.R.E.
           9. 56th Bn. M.G.Corps.
          10. 56th Div. Signal Coy.
          11. A.D.M.S.
          12. "Q"
          13.) XXII Corps.
          14.)
          15.) Canadian Corps.
          16.)
          17. XXII Corps H.A.
          18. Canadian Corps H.A.
          19. 11th Division.
          20. 4th British Division.
          21. 52nd Squadron R.A.F.
          22. War Diary.
          23. File.
          24. A.P.M.

SECRET   Copy No. 25

56th DIVISION ORDER No. 213.

9th Oct. 1918.

1. The 169th Infantry Brigade will relieve the 168th Infantry Brigade in the Right Section on October 11th/12th.

2. On relief 168th Infantry Brigade will withdraw into Divisional Reserve into positions vacated by 169th Infantry Brigade.

3. All details of relief to be arranged between B.Gs.C. Infantry Brigades concerned.

4. Completion of relief to be reported to Div. H.Qrs.

5. ACKNOWLEDGE.

T.M. Buchan Mayor
Lieut-Colonel,
General Staff.

Issued at 2.0 p.m.

Distribution :-

Copy No. 1. 167th Infantry Brigade.
         2. 168th Infantry Brigade.
         3. 169th Infantry Brigade.
         4. 1/5th Cheshire Regt.
         5. C.R.A.
         6. 78th Bde. R.G.A.
         7. C.R.E.
         8. 56th Bn. M.G.Corps.
         9. 56th Div. Signal Coy.
        10. 56th Div. Gas Officer.
        11. A.D.M.S.
        12. "Q"
        13. A.P.M.
        14. D.A.D.O.S.

No. 15. D.A.D.V.S.
    16. 56th Div. Train.
    17. Camp Commandant.
    18. 56th Div. Receptn. Camp.
    19.) XXII Corps.
    20.)
    21. XXII Corps H.A.
    22. 1st Canadian Division.
    23. 11th Division.
    24. 52nd Squadron R.A.F.
    25.) War Diary.
    26.)
    27. File.

War Diary

SECRET.   Copy No. 25

56th DIVISION ORDER No. 214.

9th October 1918.

1. The following reliefs take place tonight, to be completed by 12 midnight.

    (a) 168th Infantry Brigade will relieve the 11th Division up to the line M.14.central – M.26 central – M.26.c.00 – R.35.c.27 – thence due west to original southern boundary.

    (b) 167th Infantry Brigade will relieve the 168th Infantry Brigade up to RAILWAY BRIDGE R.15.b.75 (inclusive to 168th Infantry Brigade).

2. On completion of reliefs, the inter-Brigade boundary will run as follows :-

    Bridge at R.15.b.75 (inclusive to 168th Infantry Brigade) thence via Railway through R.15.d.89 – R.21.a.34 – R.20.d.55 (all inclusive to 168th Infantry Brigade) thence via road junction R.26.a.19 to inter-Brigade boundary at R.30.a.40.

3. Details of reliefs to be arranged between B.Gs.C. concerned.

4. D.M.G.C. will arrange for the relief of machine guns direct with D.M.G.C., 11th Division, having three Companies in position and the Reserve Company East of the CANAL.

5. On completion of relief, 168th Infantry Brigade will push forward patrols to clear FRESSIES.

6. Redistribution of Artillery will be notified by C.R.A.

7. Completion of reliefs to be reported by wire.

8. ACKNOWLEDGE.

Tom Buckwell hugs
Lieut-Colonel.
General Staff.

Issued at 13.15

Distribution :-

Copy No.		Copy No.	
1	167th Infantry Brigade.	15	D.A.D.V.S.
2	168th Infantry Brigade.	16	56th Div. Train.
3	169th Infantry Brigade.	17	A.D.C.
4	1/5th Cheshire Regt.	18	56th Div. Reception Camp.
5	C.R.A.	19)	XXII Corps.
6	78th Brigade R.G.A.	20)	
7	C.R.E.	21	XXII Corps H.A.
8	56th Bn. M.G.Corps.	22	11th Division.
9	56th Div. Signal Coy.	23	1st Cdn. Division.
10	56th Div. Gas Officer.	24	52nd Sqn. R.A.F.
11	A.D.M.S.	25)	War Diary.
12	"Q".	26)	
13	A.P.M.	27	File.
14	D.A.D.O.S.		

War Diary

SECRET.   Copy No. 30

56th DIVISION WARNING ORDER No. 215.

Ref. Sheet 51B.   12th October 1918.
1/40,000.

1. The 56th Division will be relieved in the line by the 4th Canadian Division. Infantry relief to be complete by 10 a.m. 16th inst.

2. On relief 56th Division will move back probably to MAROEUIL Area and will be held in Army Reserve.

3. Table of reliefs will be issued later.

4. Incoming units will take over the dispositions and boundaries existing on day of relief.

5. Infantry reliefs will be carried out under arrangements to be made between B.Gs.C. concerned.

6. M.G. reliefs will be carried out on 16th inst., and night 16/17th under arrangements between respective D.M.G.Cs.

7. Details of Artillery reliefs will be notified later.

8. Reliefs of R.E. and Pioneers will be arranged between Cs.R.E. concerned and of Field Ambulances between A.Ds.M.S.

9. ACKNOWLEDGE.

                                                        T.M. Buckingham
                                                        Lieut-Colonel,
                                                        General Staff.

Issued at 2000.

Distribution:-
Copy No. 1. 167th Infantry Brigade.   No. 18. Camp Commandant.
         2. 168th Infantry Brigade.   19. A.D.C.
         3. 169th Infantry Brigade.   20. 56th Div.Receptn.Camp.
         4. C.R.A.   21. 56th Div.Employ.Coy.
         5. 1/5th Cheshire Regt.   22. French Mission.
         6. Canadian Corps H.A.   23. Canadian Corps.
         7. C.R.E.   24.   do.
         8. 56th Bn. M.G.Corps.   25. 78th Bde.R.G.A.
         9. 56th Div.Signal Coy.   26. 5th Squadron R.A.F.
        10. 56th Div. Gas Officer.   27. 1st Canadian Division.
        11. A.D.M.S.   28. 2nd Canadian Division.
        12. "Q"   29. 4th Canadian Division.
        13. A.P.M.   30.) War Diary.
        14. D.A.D.O.S.   31.)
        15. D.A.D.V.S.   32. File.
        16. 56th Div. Train.
        17. 56th Div. M.T.Coy.

E.

War Diary

SECRET.   Copy No. 24

56th DIVISION ORDER No. 216.

13th October 1918.

1. From information received from prisoners, it is probable that the enemy intends to carry out a further withdrawal tonight.

2. (a) At dawn tomorrow, 167th Infantry Brigade will push strong patrols across the CANAL in K.36. in the direction of BRUNEMONT and BUGNICOURT. The C.R.E. will arrange crossings over the CANAL for these patrols.

   (b) 169th Infantry Brigade will push patrols forward at dawn through AUBIGNY AU BAC.

   (c) Arrangements will be made beforehand for establishing visual communication with these patrols.

3. The C.R.E. will be prepared to build pontoon bridges at AUBENCHEUL and at about K.36.b.90.10 as soon as the patrols report that the enemy has withdrawn.

4. (a) 167th Infantry Brigade will then be prepared to advance to the line BUGNICOURT - CANTIN (exclusive)

   (b) The 10th Canadian Infantry Brigade will be prepared to cross the CANAL at AUBENCHEUL AU BAC and passing through 169th Infantry Brigade to push forward to FRESSAIN and FECHAIN.

5. C.R.A. will detail one Field Artillery Brigade each to move forward in support of 167th Infantry Brigade and the 10th Canadian Infantry Brigade.

6. D.M.G.C. will detail one M.G. Company to accompany 167th Inf. Brigade. Its affiliated M.G. Company will accompany the 10th Canadian Inf. Brigade.

7. No forward move under para. 4 above will be made without orders from G.O.C. 56th Division.

8. The 10th Canadian Inf. Brigade will be prepared to move at one hour's notice from 5 a.m. October 14th. G.O.C. 169th Inf. Brigade will send 10 men to H.Q., 10th Canadian Inf. Brigade, Q.36.a.2.9 this evening to act as guides.

9. The Engineer Company attached to the 10th Canadian Inf. Bde. will be prepared to bridge the CANAL at FRESSIES at short notice tomorrow under orders of C.R.E. 56th Division.

10. The 1st Canadian Division will be co-operating on the left of the 56th Division.

11. ACKNOWLEDGE.

T.O.M. Buckley
for Lieut-Colonel.
General Staff.

Issued at 1700

Copy No.				
1	167th Inf. Brigade.		No. 14	A.D.C.
2	168th Inf. Brigade.		15/16	Canadian Corps.
3	169th Inf. Brigade.		17	Canadian Corps H.A.
4	1/5th Cheshire Regt.		18	1st Canadian Divn.
5	C.R.A.		19	2nd " "
6	78th Bde. R.G.A.		20	4th " "
7	C.R.E.		21	5th Sqn. R.A.F.
8	56th Bn. M.G. Corps.		22/23	10th Cdn. Inf. Bde.
9	56th Div. Signal Coy.		24/25	War Diary.
10	A.D.M.S.		26	File.
11	A/Q.			
12	D.A.P.M.			
13	56th Div. Train.			

SECRET.   Copy No. 30

56th DIVISION ORDER No. 217.

13th October 1918.

1.   56th Division Warning No. 215 is confirmed.

2.   Infantry reliefs will take place in accordance with attached Table.

3.   Machine Gun reliefs will be carried out 24 hours after Infantry reliefs in each Brigade Sector. Details to be arranged between D.M.G.Cs. concerned.

4.   Instructions as regards moves by rail and /bus and billeting areas will be issued by 56th Division "Q".

5.   Mounted personnel and transport will proceed by road - no restriction as to time or route except that the main ARRAS - CAMBRAI road will not be used.

6.   Instructions for the relief of units not mentioned in the attached March Table will be issued by 'Q'.

7.   On relief, 56th Division will pass into Army Reserve under orders of Canadian Corps.

8.   Command will pass to G.O.C., 4th Canadian Division at 1000, 16th inst.

9.   Div. H.Q. will close at VILLERS LES CAGNICOURT at 1000 on 16th inst. and open at ETRUN at the same hour.

10. ACKNOWLEDGE.

Issued at 2000.

T.O.M. Buchanan
Lieut-Colonel,
General Staff.

Distribution :-

Copy No.		No.	
1.	167th Infantry Brigade.	17.	56th Div. M.T.Coy.
2.	168th Infantry Brigade.	18.	A.D.C.
3.	169th Infantry Brigade.	19.	Camp Commandant.
4.	1/5th Cheshire Regt.	20.	56th Div. Receptn.C.
5.	C.R.A.	21.	56th Div. Employ.Coy.
6.	78th Bde. R.G.A.	22.)	Canadian Corps.
7.	C.R.E.	23.)	
8.	56th Bn. M.G.Corps.	24.	Canadian Corps H.A.
9.	56th Div. Signal Coy.	25.	4th Canadian Divn.
10.	56th Div. Gas Officer.	26.	1st Canadian Divn.
11.	A.D.M.S.	27.	2nd Canadian Divn.
12.	"Q"	28.	5th Squadron R.A.F.
13.	D.A.P.M.	29.	10th Can.Inf.Bde.
14.	D.A.D.O.S.	30.)	War Diary.
15.	D.A.D.V.S.	31.)	
16.	56th Div. Train.	32.	File.

P.T.O.

MARCH TABLE TO ACCOMPANY 56th DIVISION ORDER No. 217.

Serial No.	Date. OCTOBER.	Unit.	From.	To.	Remarks.
1.	13th.	10th Can.Inf.Bde.Group.	ARRAS.	SAUCHY CAUCHY) Area. SAUCHY LESTREE)	Bde. H.Qrs. to Q.36.a.2.5. Move by bus.
2.	14th.	10th Can.Inf.Bde.	SAUCHY CAUCHY Area.	LINE Right.	In relief of 169th Inf.Bde.
3.	14th.	11th Can.Inf.Bde.Group.	MAROEUIL.	RUMANCOURT Area.	In relief of 169th Inf.Bde.
4.	14th	168th Inf. Bde.	RUMANCOURT Area.	ARRAS.	
5.	14th.	169th Inf. Bde.	LINE Right.	SAUCHY CAUCHY Area.	
6.	15th.	12th Can.Inf.Bde.Group.	MAROEUIL.	SAUCHY CAUCHY Area.	In relief of 169th Inf.Bde.
7.	15th.	169th Inf. Bde.	SAUCHY CAUCHY Area.	HAUTE AVESNES.	
8.	15/16th.	11th Can. Inf. Bde.	RUMANCOURT Area.	LINE Left.	In relief of 167th Inf.Bde.
9.	15/16th	167th Inf. Bde.	LINE Left.	RUMANCOURT Area.	
10.	16th	167th Inf. Bde.	RUMANCOURT Area.	'Y' Huts L.2.0.	
11.	....	Field Coys. R.E. 1/5th Cheshire Regt.	....	MAROEUIL.	Under orders to to issued by C.R.E.
12.	....	56th Bn. M.G.Corps.	....	ANZIN.	Under orders of D.M.G.C.

SECRET.   Copy No. 26

56th DIVISION ORDER NO. 213.

30th October 1918.

Ref. Maps 1/100,000 LENS 11 & VALENCIENNES 12
     & 1/40,000 Sheet 51C and 51B.

1. 56th Division is transferred to XXII Corps and will move to-morrow to the area BASSEVILLE – LIEU ST.-AMAND – NOYELLES – DOUCHY – NEUVILLE SUR L'ESCAUT, where it will be in Corps Reserve.

2. Dismounted personnel will move by bus under instructions to be issued by 56th Division 'Q'.

3. Mounted personnel and transport will move by road in accordance with the attached March Table.

4. For the purposes of the move both by bus and by road, units will be grouped as follows :-

    167th Inf. Bde. Group.   167th Inf. Bde.
                                    416th Field Coy. R.E.
                                    2/2nd Field Ambulance.
                                    1/5th Cheshire Regt.
                                    Div. H.Q. (incl. Employment Coy. &
                                                H.Q. Div. R.E.).
                                    No. 2 Coy. Train.

    168th Inf. Bde. Group.   168th Infantry Brigade.
                                    512th Field Coy. R.E.
                                    2/1st Field Ambulance.
                                    56th Div. M.G.Bn.
                                    No. 3 Coy. Train.
                                    S.A.A. Section D.A.C.

    169th Inf. Bde. Group.   169th Infantry Brigade.
                                    513th Field Coy. R.E.
                                    2/3rd Field Ambulance.
                                    Div. Reception Camp.
                                    No. 4 Coy. Train.

5. Units not mentioned in this order will move under instructions to be issued by 56th Div. 'A/Q'.

6. On arrival in the new area units will be located in accordance with a Table to be issued later by 56th Div. 'A'.

7. Intervals will be observed as follows on the march :-

    100x between Sections of Transport.
    500x between each Brigade Group transport column.

8. Cookers of units may if necessary march independently, under orders of Brigadiers, in order to allow of breakfast being given before embussing.

9. Each Infantry Brigade Group Transport column will march under the orders of a Senior Officer detailed by the Infantry Brigade concerned.

10. Div. H.Q. will close at ETRUN at 9 a.m. on 31st inst. and open at LA BASSEVILLE (6 miles N.E. of CAMBRAI) on arrival.

11. ACKNOWLEDGE.

                                                        T.J.M. Buchanan
                                                        Lieut-Colonel,
Issued at 1700   General Staff.

P.T.O.

Distribution :-

Copy No. 1.	167th Infantry Brigade.	17.	A.D.C.
2.	168th Infantry Brigade.	18.	Camp Commandant.
3.	169th Infantry Brigade.	19.	56th Div. Recsptn. Camp
4.	1/5th Cheshire Regt.	20.	French Mission.
5.	C.R.A.	21.)	XXII Corps.
6.	C.R.E.	22.)	
7.	56th Bn. M.G.Corps.	23.)	Canadian Corps.
8.	56th Div. Signal Coy.	24.)	
9.	56th Div. Gas Officer.	25.	51st Division.
10.	A.D.M.S.	26.)	War Diary.
11.	"Q"	27.)	
12.	A.P.M.	28.	File.
13.	D.A.D.O.S.		
14.	D.A.D.V.S.		
15.	56th Div. Train.		
16.	56th Div. M.T.Coy.		

MARCH TABLE FOR MOVE BY ROAD ISSUED WITH 56TH DIVISION ORDER No. 213.

Serial no.	Unit.	From.	To.	Starting Point.	Hour of Start.	Route & Remarks.
1. 31st Oct.	168th Infantry Bde. Group.	ARRAS, etc.	MARQUION Area.	Road junction H.31 central (TILLOY LES MOFFLAINES).	10.15 a.m.	Via main CAMBRAI Road. Transport of this Group is not to use the main road between ARRAS and the starting point. It will be formed up on the FLANGY-TILLOY Road, and will not pass the start- ing point until 169th Bde. Bus column is clear of that point. Billets from Area Commandant, BOURLON.
2. 31st Oct.	167th Infantry Bde. Group.	'Y' Huts, etc.	do.	Road junction L.8.b. 3.8.	9.45 a.m.	Via. ARRAS - not to enter main ST.POL-ARRAS Road before 169th Inf. Bde. Bus column is clear. Billets as in Serial No. 1.
3. 31st Oct.	169th Infantry Bde. Group.	HAUTE AVESNES, etc.	do.	Under Brigade arrangements.		Via. ARRAS. Units from HAUTE AVESNES to move to starting point via cross-roads K.6.c. 2.8. (LABESSET) - No unit to pass road junction L.1.d.7.8. before 10.30 a.m. Billets as in Serial No. 1.
4. Nov. 1st.	168th Infantry Bde. Group.	MARQUION Area.	New area.	SAUCHICOURT FARM cross-roads (Sheet 51B.N.6.d.2.3.)	9 a.m.	Via. EPINOY - ARANCOURT - PAILLENCOURT - ESTRUN - BORDAIN - PAVE DE VALENCIENNES.
5. Nov. 1st.	167th Infantry Bde. Group.	do.	do.	do.	10 a.m.	do.
6. Nov. 1st.	169th Infantry Bde. Group.	do.	do.	do.	9 a.m.	do.

Operations carried out by 56th Division between
October 10th - October 16th whilst under the Command
of the Canadian Corps.

The position on the 10th October, 1918, was as follows :-
The Division was holding a very extended front of about
8000 yards along the line of the CANAL de la SENSEE from PALLUEL
inclusive to a line M.14 central - M.26 central (just S.E. of
FRESSIES, which was still held by the enemy) thus covering the
left flank of the Canadian Corps during their advance on CAMBRAI.

Two Brigades were in the front line, viz:- the 167th Infantry
Brigade on the left, and the 168th Infantry Brigade on the right,
the dividing line between the two Brigades being the Railway
Bridge R.15.b.7.5. (inclusive to the right Brigade). The 169th
Infantry Brigade were in support near SAUDEMONT. The 11th Divn.
was on the right and the 1st Canadian Division on the left.
Divisional Headquarters were at VILLERS CAGNICOURT.

The 168th Infantry Brigade having reported that the enemy were
still holding out in FRESSIES in strength, orders were issued
to the 168th Infantry Brigade to attack and capture the Village
the next day under cover of a barrage.
At 0700 hours on 11th October, the 168th Infantry Brigade
with 2 Companies of 13th London Regiment attacked. The operation
was completely successful - 2 Officers and 39 O.R. were made
prisoners and our line advanced to the Canal thus clearing the
enemy from the south side of the Canal along the entire divisional
front. Our casualties were only 1 O.R. killed and 9 wounded.

On the VIII Corps on our left capturing VITRY-en-ARTOIS and
reporting the enemy in retreat towards DOUAI, orders were issued
to the C.R.A. to keep the crossings of the CANAL de la SENSEE
from ARLEUX northwards under fire and the 167th Infantry Brigade
were instructed to push forward patrols to obtain a footing in
ARLEUX if possible. This Brigade made several attempts but were unable
to do so owing to hostile M.G. fire.

During the day a new left forward boundary was laid down by the
XXII Corps, making ARLEUX inclusive to this Division.

At 1700 hours the Division passed to the Command of the Canadian
Corps.

That night the 169th Infantry Brigade relieved the 168th Infantry
Brigade in the Right Section and the 168th Infantry Brigade moved
into Reserve near SAUDEMONT.
Early on the 12th October the 1st Canadian Division reported
that they had captured ARLEUX and trench system running North from
the Village, but enemy M.Gs. were still firing from S.E. edge of the
Village. 167th Infantry Brigade were ordered to co-operate in
clearing ARLEUX and to relieve all troops of 1st Can. Divn. up to
our northern Div. Boundary. 169th Infantry Brigade were ordered
to extend their left and take over a portion of the front held by
167th Infantry Brigade.
169th Infantry Brigade were further ordered to endeavour to cross
the Canal de la Sensee during the night and capture AUBIGNY-AU-BAC.
The C.R.E. was ordered to construct the necessary bridges. The C.R.E.
was also instructed to bridge all gaps in the PALLEUL - ARLEUX Road,
and be prepared to throw a pontoon across the CANAL at ABBE DU VERGER
FARM.
During the afternoon 167th Infantry Brigade succeeded in clearing
out the enemy posts in ARLEUX, capturing 19 prisoners, and took over
their new section from 1st Can. Divn. By 2250 they had cleared the

Triangle formed by the CANAL East of ARLEUX and established posts on the banks.

Orders were received from the Canadian Corps for the relief of this Division by the 4th Canadian Division, the relief to be complete by 1000 on the 16th inst.

Operations on 13th October - During the preceding night a party of 16th London Regiment (Q.W.R. - 169th Inf.Bde.) succeeded in establishing a footing on the North bank of the Canal de LA SENSEE opposite AUBIGNY-AU-BAC, and the 416th Field Coy. R.E. constructed a floating bridge to the N. bank. A Company of 2nd London Regiment then crossed and formed up on the North bank and another Coy. of the same battalion assembled on the western outskirts of the Village. The total strength of these two Coys. amounted to 6 Officers and 165 O.R.

At 0515 the attack on AUBIGNY commenced under a creeping barrage from the S.E. The attack was completely successful, the Village being captured and 4 Officers and 203 O.R. being taken prisoners. Posts were at once established on the Northern and Eastern outskirts and steps taken to construct another bridge alongside the site of the broken bridge carrying the road leading from AUBENCHEUL to AUBIGNY.

167th Infantry Brigade were ordered to pass a Company over the CANAL at AUBENCHEUL and push westwards along the N. bank of the CANAL. A battalion of 168th Infantry Brigade was put at the disposal of 169th Infantry Brigade in order to release troops to reinforce AUBIGNY. At 1045 the enemy counter-attacked under a heavy barrage and forced our troops back on to the CANAL where they maintained their original bridgehead.

To relieve the situation at AUBIGNY-AU-BAC, 167th Infantry Brigade were ordered to make ~~the~~ an attempt to cross the CANAL de la SENSEE, if not strongly held, East of ARLEUX, thus threatening the enemy's flank.

By 1520 it was apparent that the enemy were holding the West bank of the CANAL near ARLEUX, and 167th Infantry Brigade were unable to effect a crossing, also that 169th Infantry Brigade had only about 10 men holding their bridgehead. Permission was therefore given to 169th Infantry Brigade to withdraw to the South bank of the CANAL at dusk. They were to keep the bridge intact however.

(A detailed account of the Operations against AUBIGNY-AU-BAC is attached hereto).

From information received from prisoners it appeared probable that the enemy intended to make a further retirement, orders were accordingly issued to meet such contingency.

The 10th Canadian Infantry Brigade arrived in this area preparatory to relieving 169th Infantry Brigade and came under the orders of G.O.C. 56th Divn.

The enemy made two attacks on the bridgehead held by 169th Infantry Brigade ~~held by 169th Infantry Brigade~~ at AUBIGNY-AU-BAC but was repulsed on each occasion.

Oct. 14th - Quiet night. 167th Infantry Brigade made an attempt to cross the CANAL just N. of ARLEUX, but the enemy were alert and opened fire with M.Gs. at short range. 169th Infantry Brigade maintained patrols on the North bank of the CANAL by AUBIGNY-AU-BAC.

/Hostile

Hostile Artillery less active during the day.

10th Canadian Infantry Brigade relieved 169th Infantry Brigade in the right section, the bridgehead and bridge at AUBIGNY-AU-BAC being handed over intact.

169th Infantry Brigade moved to SAUCHY CAUCHY area.

11th Can. Infantry Brigade arrived in the area relieving 168th Infantry Brigade who entrained for ARRAS.

October 15th - During the evening the enemy rushed the bridgehead at AUBIGNY-AU-BAC held by the 10th Can. Inf.Bde. but failed to obtain any identifications.

11th Can. Inf. Bde. relieved 167th Infantry Brigade in Left Section of the Divnl. Front.

167th Infantry Brigade moved to RUMANCOURT area.

12th Canadian In. Bde. arrived and billeted at SAUCHY CAUCHY - BARALLE area.

Oct. 16th - Quiet night. G.O.C. 4th Can. Division, assumed command of Divnl. front at 1000. Div. H.Qrs. moved to ETRUN. 167th Infantry Brigade to 'Y' Huts, ETRUN.

Operations carried out by 56th Division between
October 10th - October 16th whilst under the Command
of the Canadian Corps.

The position on the 10th October, 1918, was as follows :-
The Division was holding a very extended front of about
8000 yards along the line of the CANAL de la SENSEE from PALLUEL
inclusive to a line M.14 central - M.26 central (just S.E. of
FRESSIES, which was still held by the enemy) thus covering the
left flank of the Canadian Corps during their advance on CAMBRAI.

Two Brigades were in the front line, viz:- the 167th Infantry
Brigade on the left, and the 168th Infantry Brigade on the right,
the dividing line between the two Brigades being the Railway
Bridge R.15.b.7.5. (inclusive to the right Brigade). The 169th
Infantry Brigade were in support near SAUDEMONT. The 11th Divn.
was on the right and the 1st Canadian Division on the left.
Divisional Headquarters were at VILLERS CAGNICOURT.

The 168th Infantry Brigade having reported that the enemy were
still holding out in FRESSIES in strength, orders were issued
to the 168th Infantry Brigade to attack and capture the Village
the next day under cover of a barrage.
At 0700 hours on 11th October, the 168th Infantry Brigade
with 2 Companies of 13th London Regiment attacked. The operation
was completely successful - 2 Officers and 39 O.R. were made
prisoners and our line advanced to the Canal thus clearing the
enemy from the south side of the Canal along the entire divisional
front. Our casualties were only 1 O.R. killed and 9 wounded.

On the VIII Corps on our left capturing VITRY-en-ARTOIS and
reporting the enemy in retreat towards DOUAI, orders were issued
to the C.R.A. to keep the crossings of the CANAL de la SENSEE
from ARLEUX northwards under fire and the 167th Infantry Brigade
were instructed to push forward patrols to obtain a footing in
ARLEUX if possible. This Brigade made several attemps but were unable
to do so owing to hostile M.G. fire.

During the day a new left forward boundary was laid down by the
XXII Corps, making ARLEUX inclusive to this Division.

At 1700 hours the Division passed to the Command of the Canadian
Corps.

That night the 169th Infantry Brigade relieved the 168th Infantry
Brigade in the Right Section and the 168th Infantry Brigade moved
into Reserve near SAUDEMONT.
Early on the 12th October the 1st Canadian Division reported
that they had captured ARLEUX and trench system running North from
the Village, but enemy M.Gs. were still firing from S.E. edge of the
Village. 167th Infantry Brigade were ordered to co-operate in
clearing ARLEUX and to relieve all troops of 1st Can. Divn. up to
our northern Div. Boundary. 169th Infantry Brigade were ordered
to extend their left and take over a portion of the front held by
167th Infantry Brigade.
169th Infantry Brigade were further ordered to endeavour to cross
the Canal de la Sensee during the night and capture AUBIGNY-AU-BAC.
The C.R.E. was ordered to construct the necessary bridges. The C.R.E.
was also instructed to bridge all gaps in the PALLEUL - ARLEUX Road,
and be prepared to throw a pontoon across the CANAL at ABBE DU VERGER
FARM.
During the afternoon 167th Infantry Brigade succeeded in clearing
out the enemy posts in ARLEUX, capturing 19 prisoners, and took over
their new section from 1st Can. Divn. By 2250 they had cleared the

Triangle formed by the CANAL East of ARLEUX and established posts on the banks.

Orders were received from the Canadian Corps for the relief of this Division by the 4th Canadian Division, the relief to be complete by 1000 on the 16th inst.

Operations on 13th October - During the preceding night a party of 16th London Regiment (Q.W.R. - 169th Inf.Bde.) succeeded in establishing a footing on the North bank of the Canal de LA SENSEE opposite AUBIGNY-AU-BAC, and the 416th Field Coy. R.E. constructed a floating bridge to the N. bank. A Company of 2nd London Regiment then crossed and formed up on the North bank and another Coy. of the same battalion assembled on the western outskirts of the Village. The total strength of these two Coys. amounted to 6 Officers and 165 O.R.

At 0515 the attack on AUBIGNY commenced under a creeping barrage from the S.E. The attack was completely successful, the Village being captured and 4 Officers and 203 O.R. being taken prisoners. Posts were at once established on the Northern and Eastern outskirts and steps taken to construct another bridge alongside the site of the broken bridge carrying the road leading from AUBENCHEUL to AUBIGNY.

167th Infantry Brigade were ordered to pass a Company over the CANAL at AUBENCHEUL and push westwards along the N. bank of the CANAL. A battalion of 168th Infantry Brigade was put at the disposal of 169th Infantry Brigade in order to release troops to reinforce AUBIGNY. At 1045 the enemy counter-attacked under a heavy barrage and forced our troops back on to the CANAL where they maintained their original bridgehead.

To relieve the situation at AUBIGNY-AU-BAC, 167th Infantry Brigade were ordered to make an attempt to cross the CANAL de la SENSEE, if not strongly held, East of ARLEUX, thus threatening the enemy's flank.

By 1520 it was apparent that the enemy were holding the West bank of the CANAL near ARLEUX, and 167th Infantry Brigade were unable to effect a crossing, also that 169th Infantry Brigade had only about 10 men holding their bridgehead. Permission was therefore given to 169th Infantry Brigade to withdraw to the South bank of the CANAL at dusk. They were to keep the bridge intact however.
(A detailed account of the Operations against AUBIGNY-AU-BAC is attached hereto).

From information received from prisoners it appeared probable that the enemy intended to make a further retirement, orders were accordingly issued to meet such contingency.

The 10th Canadian Infantry Brigade arrived in this area preparatory to relieving 169th Infantry Brigade and came under the orders of G.O.C. 56th Divn.
The enemy made two attacks on the bridgehead held by 169th Infantry Brigade AUBIGNY-AU-BAC but was repulsed on each occasion.

Oct. 14th - Quiet night. 167th Infantry Brigade made an attempt to cross the CANAL just N. of ARLEUX, but the enemy were alert and opened fire with M.Gs. at short range. 169th Infantry Brigade maintained patrols on the North bank of the CANAL by AUBIGNY-AU-BAC.

/Hostile

Hostile Artillery less active during the day.

10th Canadian Infantry Brigade relieved 169th Infantry Brigade in the right section, the bridgehead and bridge at AUBIGNY-AU-BAC being handed over intact.

169th Infantry Brigade moved to SAUCHY CAUCHY area.

11th Can. Infantry Brigade arrived in the area relieving 168th Infantry Brigade who entrained for ARRAS.

October 15th - During the evening the enemy rushed the bridgehead at AUBIGNY-AU-BAC held by the 10th Can. Inf. Bde. but failed to obtain any identifications.

11th Can. Inf. Bde. relieved 167th Infantry Brigade in Left Section of the Divnl. Front.

167th Infantry Brigade moved to RUMANCOURT area.

12th Canadian In. Bde. arrived and billeted at SAUCHY CAUCHY - BARALLE area.

Oct. 16th - Quiet night. G.O.C. 4th Can. Division, assumed command of Divnl. front at 1000. Div. H.Qrs. moved to ETRUN. 167th Infantry Brigade to 'Y' Huts, ETRUN.

CONFIDENTIAL.

REPORT ON A SURPRISE ATTACK ON AUBIGNY-au-BAC
13th October 1918.

Although on a small scale, this operation contained several points of interest.

PART 1.   On the 11th October, 169th Infantry Brigade had taken over the Right Sector of the Divisional Front from 168th Infantry Brigade, which that morning had captured FRESSIES, thenceforth included in the Right Sector.

On the 12th October an attack on AUBIGNY was proposed, with the object of ascertaining the enemy's strength and in the hope of hastening or interfering with his retirement.

The L.R.B. and the Q.W.R. being widely extended over a considerable front, it was decided to employ the Reserve battalion the 2nd LONDON Regiment: 1 Company to carry out the attack, with 1 Company in close Support.

Between our lines and those of the enemy lay the CANAL DE LA SENSEE, here about seventy feet wide, all bridges over which had been destroyed.

South of AUBIGNY-AU-BAC were two of these damaged bridges, 1250 yards apart, each guarded by a German Post.

It was decided to attempt a crossing between these 2 bridges. Absolute silence was essential.

416th Field Company R.E. was to construct rafts to carry over an Officers Patrol of the Q.W.R. as soon as possible after dark.

This patrol having effected a landing was to ascertain whether a sufficiently large area, free of the enemy, existed for the assembly of the attacking Company.

The R.E. were then to construct a floating footbridge for the passage of the Company of the 2nd LONDON Regiment.
(I may here say that, in spite of the very short time available for getting up material and making reconnaissances and arrangements, the bridging operations were carried out with the greatest skill and efficiency. Unfortunately Lt. A.E.ARNOLD, R.E. who took a leading part in the work was killed during the day).

In order to get the advantage of most complete surprise, the barrage was arranged to creep in a North Westerly direction, i.e. against the flank of the enemy's position.

PART 2.   Lt. ARNOLD, 416th Field Coy. R.E., taking into consideration the material available, elected to proceed at once with the construction of the footbridge and not to pass the patrol over on rafts.

This task was quietly and successfully completed and at 0300 it was reported that the Q.W.R. Patrol was across the Canal but could not move more than 10 paces in any direction without being challenged by German Posts, of which three appeared to exist in the immediate vicinity of the landing place. As the enemy had not opened fire, I ordered the patrol to make a bold attempt to capture the Posts without raising an alarm, before abandoning the enterprise.

1 Platoon of the 2nd LONDON Regiment was passed over the bridge, two Germans were captured and no alarm was raised.

The passing of the troops over the bridge presented considerable difficulties in itself. The night was very dark and rain was falling. The bridge was, from its nature, unstable and no form of handrail existed.

However, the remaining Platoons crossed soon afterwards and the Company, under the command of Captain D.SLOAN, was ready in position about half an hour before Zero, which had been fixed for 0515.

The assembly area was far from being a good one, being intersected by 2 streams LA NAVIE and LA PETITE NAVIE of which nothing was known. From the nature of the ground it was impossible to follow the barrage in the usual way. Platoons were directed to make their own way to various points as soon as the barrage started; the barrage was to stand for 5 minutes to enable platoons to approach.

In spite of these very considerable difficulties and of the assembly having taken place in great darkness, the attacking Company carried out its instructions to the letter and effected a complete surprise, appearing as it did on the least threatened side of the enemy's position. Two machine gun teams which offered resistance were captured after two or three of the enemy had been killed, but for the most part the enemy appeared to be completely mystified by the appearance of our men from such an unexpected quarter, and about 160 prisoners were mopped up in the village without trouble.

Platoons moved direct to the spots where they had been ordered to establish Posts and by about 0650 all the prearranged Posts had been established.

A few of the enemy who had not so far been directly involved in our attack now approached our Posts and gave themselves up, but others from various positions around the village opened Machine Gun and sniping fire against our Posts, causing several casualties and greatly restricting movement. On our part every advantage was taken of available targets and losses were inflicted upon the enemy.

At 0600 two Platoons from the Supporting Company had reported to Captain SLOAN and were used to reinforce certain Posts.

It was not found possible to establish Posts near the Station (R.9.b.) owing to the enemy being in strength near the dumps and Railway sidings. For the same reason it was found impossible to patrol towards BRUNEMONT. A considerable force from this direction later co-operated in the hostile counter-attack.

About 0700 two hostile Machine guns which were troubling one of our Posts at close range were engaged with rifle grenades and then rushed, 12 prisoners being taken.

The two remaining Platoons of the Support Company reported to Captain SLOAN at about 0930.

Between 0915 and 1015 hostile parties were observed in several places from our Infantry O.P. in the BOIS DE QUESNOY and were engaged by LEFT GROUP R.F.A. whose F.O.O. shared the O.P.. Many casualties were inflicted.
Trench Mortars firing from old trenches in R.10.b. were engaged and their crews put to flight.

About 1000 the enemy put down a heavy barrage on AUBIGNY and also concentrated many machine guns on the village. Half an hour afterwards the enemy's Reserve battalion, assisted by troops from BRUNEMONT, made a most determined attack, suffering heavy losses from their own barrage and from our fire. One by one, however, our small Posts were outflanked - one was entirely destroyed by a heavy trench mortar - and gradually pressed back to the LA PETITE NAVIE stream where a stand was made and the enemy prevented from debouching from the village.

His Machine Gun and sniping fire soon became very troublesome from the enclosed country on the flanks and it became advisable to fall back further to the canal bank if our party was not to be completely sacrificed.

A small bridgehead was maintained for a considerable time, but by 1700 all our troops were back behind the Southern bank of the Canal.

PART 3. Four Stokes mortars were very ably handled throughout the day by C.S.M. BUTCHER, and O.C. 2nd Londons testifies to the importance of the work they performed.

Captain SLOAN's Company, which carried out the attack, had been employed carrying bridging material for 2 hours during steady rain before advancing to their assembly. Owing to the darkness, streams and marsh, every man was thoroughly wet through by dawn. The behaviour of this Company was most praiseworthy.

PART 4.

		Officers	O.R.
Strength of the Company employed in the Attack		3	87
Strongest possible numbers available for defence of village (not allowing for casualties which had occurred)		6	165
Prisoners captured by the above-mentioned.		4	203
Total casualties of 2nd Londons for the day (estimated).	killed:	NIL	20
	Wounded:	2	90
	Wounded & Missing or Missing	1	30
	Total	3	140

Three enemy Machine Guns were brought back, and ten others thrown into streams.

PART 5. The enterprise may be considered to have achieved the following results:-

/(i)

- 4 -

(i) Shewed the enemy that we are alert and that he will not be able to retire untroubled.

(ii) A considerably larger number of prisoners than the total of the force employed by us.

(iii) Very heavy casualties inflicted upon the enemy.

(iv) Possibly useful identifications and a large source of information from prisoners.

* (v) The throwing of a footbridge across the canal and the establishing of a bridgehead.

* Note: The Bridgehead mentioned in the final para. of PART 2 was re-established later on in the same day. The footbridge was destroyed by hostile Artillery on the 14th but was repaired before handing over to the 10th CANADIAN Brigade.

E. S. Coke. Brigadier General,
Commanding 169th Infantry Brigade.

15th October 1918.

G3/499.

Report on Operations

AUBIGNY-AU-BAC

13 Oct 1918.

1918 OCT

Passt education officer
Tony

CANADIAN CORPS.
G.M.77/3.
26th December 1918.

56th Division.
―――――――――

    The Corps Commander has directed the compilation of a report covering the operations of the Canadian Corps from July 25th to Nov.11th 1918.

    To complete this report it is requested that a narrative covering the operations of the 56th Division from Oct.10th/Oct.16th be forwarded to reach this office before Jany.10th 1919.

    If this report cannot be completed by this date, will you please advise the earliest possible date that it may be expected.

                            Lieut-Colonel
                            for B.G.G.S
                            Canadian Corps.

G.C.O.	
G.S.O.1	
G.S.O.2	
G.S.O.3	

CONFIDENTIAL.

REPORT ON A SURPRISE ATTACK ON AUBIGNY-au-BAC.

13th October 1918.

Although on a small scale, this operation contained several points of interest.

PART 1.   On the 11th October, 169th Infantry Brigade had taken over the Right Sector of the Divisional Front from 168th Infantry Brigade, which that morning had captured FRESSIES, thenceforth included in the Right Sector.

On the 12th October an attack on AUBIGNY was proposed, with the object of ascertaining the enemy's strength and in the hope of hastening or interfering with his retirement.

The L.R.B. and the Q.W.R. being widely extended over a considerable front, it was decided to employ the Reserve battalion the 2nd London Regiment: 1 Company to carry out the attack, with 1 Company in close Support.

Between our lines and those of the enemy lay the CANAL DE LA SENSEE, here about seventy feet wide, all bridges over which had been destroyed.

South of AUBIGNY-AU-BAC were two of these damaged bridges, 1250 yards apart, each guarded by a German Post.

It was decided to attempt a crossing between these 2 bridges. Absolute silence was essential.

416th Field Company R.E. was to construct rafts to carry over an Officers Patrol of the Q.W.R. as soon as possible after dark.

This patrol having effected a landing was to ascertain whether a sufficiently large area, free of the enemy, existed for the assembly of the attacking Company.

The R.E. were then to construct a floating footbridge for the passage of the Company of the 2nd London Regiment.
(I may here say that, in spite of the very short time available for getting up material and making reconnaissances and arrangements, the bridging operations were carried out with the greatest skill and efficiency.   Unfortunately Lt. A.E.ARNOLD, R.E. who took a leading part in the work was killed during the day).

In order to get the advantage of most complete surprise, the barrage was arranged to creep in a North Westerly direction, i.e. against the flank of the enemy's position.

PART 2.   Lt. ARNOLD, 416th Field Coy. R.E., taking into consideration the material available, elected to proceed at once with the construction of the footbridge and not to pass the patrol over on rafts.

This task was quietly and successfully completed and at 0300 it was reported that the Q.W.R. Patrol was across the Canal but could not move more than 10 paces in any direction without being challenged by German Posts, of which three appeared to exist in the immediate vicinity of the landing place. As the enemy had not opened fire, I ordered the patrol to make a bold attempt to capture the Posts without raising an alarm, before abandoning the enterprise.

/ 1 Platoon

1 Platoon of the 2nd London Regt. was passed over the bridge, two Germans were captured and no alarm was raised.

The passing of the troops over the bridge presented considerable difficulties in itself. The night was very dark and rain was falling. The bridge was, from its nature, unstable and no form of handrail existed.

However, the remaining Platoons crossed soon afterwards and the Company, under the command of Captain D. SLOAN, was ready in position about half an hour before Zero, which had been fixed for 0515.

The assembly area was far from being a good one, being intersected by 2 streams LA NAVIE and LA PETITE NAVIE of which nothing was known. From the nature of the ground it was impossible to follow the barrage in the usual way. Platoons were directed to make their own way to various points as soon as the barrage started; the barrage was to stand for 5 minutes to enable platoons to approach.

In spite of these very considerable difficulties and of the assembly having taken place in great darkness, the attacking Company carried out its instructions to the letter and effected a complete surprise, appearing as it did on the least threatened side of the enemy's position. Two machine gun teams which offered resistance were captured after two or three of the enemy had been killed, but for the most part the enemy appeared to be completely mystified by the appearance of our men from such an unexpected quarter, and about 160 prisoners were mopped up in the village without trouble.

Platoons moved direct to the spots where they had been ordered to establish Posts and by about 0630 all the prearranged Posts had been established.

A few of the enemy who had not so far been directly involved in our attack now approached our Posts and gave themselves up, but others from various positions around the village opened Machine Gun and sniping fire against our Posts, causing several casualties and greatly restricting movement. On our part every advantage was taken of available targets and losses were inflicted upon the enemy.

At 0600 two Platoons from the Supporting Company had reported to Captain SLOAN and were used to reinforce certain Posts.

It was not found possible to establish Posts near the Station (R.9.b.) owing to the enemy being in strength near the dumps and Railway sidings. For the same reason it was found impossible to patrol towards BRUNEMONT. A considerable force from this direction later co-operated in the hostile counter-attack.

About 0700 two hostile Machine guns which were troubling one of our Posts at close range were engaged with rifle grenades and then rushed, 12 prisoners being taken.

The two remaining Platoons of the Support Company reported to Captain SLOAN at about 0930.

Between 0915 and 1015 hostile parties were observed in several places from our Infantry O.P. in the BOIS DE QUESNOY and were engaged by LEFT GROUP R.F.A. whose F.O.O. shared the O.P. Many casualties were inflicted.

/ Trench

- 3 -

Trench Mortars firing from old trenches in R.10.b. were engaged and their crews put to flight.

About 1000 the enemy put down a heavy barrage on AUBIGNY and also concentrated many machine guns on the village. Half an hour afterwards the enemy's Reserve battalion, assisted by troops from BRUNEMONT, made a most determined attack, suffering heavy losses from their own barrage and from our fire. One by one, however, our small Posts were outflanked - one was entirely destroyed by a heavy trench mortar - and gradually pressed back to the LA PETITE NAVIE stream where a stand was made and the enemy prevented from debouching from the village.

His Machine Gun and sniping fire soon became very troublesome from the enclosed country on the flanks and it became advisable to fall back further to the canal bank if our party was not to be completely sacrificed.

A small bridgehead was maintained for a considerable time, but by 1700 all our troops were back behind the Southern bank of the Canal.

PART 3.   Four Stokes mortars were very ably handled throughout the day by C.S.M. BUTCHER, and O.C. 2nd London Regt. testifies to the importance of the work they performed.

Captain SLOAN's Company, which carried out the attack, had been employed carrying bridging material for 2 hours during steady rain before advancing to their assembly. Owing to the darkness, streams and marsh, every man was thoroughly wet through by dawn. The behaviour of this Company was most praiseworthy.

PART 4.

		Officers.	O.R.
Strength of the Company employed in the Attack		3	87
Strongest possible numbers available for defence of village (not allowing for casualties which had occurred)		6	165
Prisoners captured by the above-mentioned.		4	203
Total casualties of 2nd London Regt. for the day (estimated)	Killed:	NIL	20
	Wounded:	2	90
	Wounded & Missing or Missing	1	30
	Total	3	140.

Three enemy Machine Guns were brought back, and ten others thrown into streams.

PART 5.   The enterprise may be considered to have achieved the following results :-

/ (i)

- 4 -

(i). Shewed the enemy that we are alert and that he will not be able to retire untroubled.

(ii). A considerably larger number of prisoners than the total of the force employed by us.

(iii). Very heavy casualties inflicted upon the enemy.

(iv). Possibly useful identifications and a large source of information from prisoners.

* (v). The throwing of a footbridge across the canal and the establishing of a bridgehead.

* Note: The Bridgehead mentioned in the final para. of PART 2 was re-established later on in the same day. The footbridge was destroyed by hostile Artillery on the 14th but was repaired before handing over to the 10th Canadian Brigade.

(Sd) E.L. COKE,

Brigadier-General,
Commanding 169th Infantry Brigade.

15th Oct. 1918.

CONFIDENTIAL.

REPORT ON A SURPRISE ATTACK ON AUBIGNY-au-BAC.

13th October 1918.

Although on a small scale, this operation contained several points of interest.

PART 1.   On the 11th October, 169th Infantry Brigade had taken over the Right Sector of the Divisional Front from 168th Infantry Brigade, which that morning had captured FRESSIES, thenceforth included in the Right Sector.

On the 12th October an attack on AUBIGNY was proposed, with the object of ascertaining the enemy's strength and in the hope of hastening or interfering with his retirement.

The L.R.B. and the Q.W.R. being widely extended over a considerable front, it was decided to employ the Reserve battalion the 2nd London Regiment: 1 Company to carry out the attack, with 1 Company in close Support.

Between our lines and those of the enemy lay the CANAL DE LA SENSEE, here about seventy feet wide, all bridges over which had been destroyed.

South of AUBIGNY-AU-BAC were two of these damaged bridges, 1250 yards apart, each guarded by a German Post.

It was decided to attempt a crossing between these 2 bridges. Absolute silence was essential.

416th Field Company R.E. was to construct rafts to carry over an Officers Patrol of the Q.W.R. as soon as possible after dark.

This patrol having effected a landing was to ascertain whether a sufficiently large area, free of the enemy, existed for the assembly of the attacking Company.

The R.E. were then to construct a floating footbridge for the passage of the Company of the 2nd London Regiment.
(I may here say that, in spite of the very short time available for getting up material and making reconnaissances and arrangements, the bridging operations were carried out with the greatest skill and efficiency.   Unfortunately Lt. A.E.ARNOLD, R.E. who took a leading part in the work was killed during the day).

In order to get the advantage of most complete surprise, the barrage was arranged to creep in a North Westerly direction, i.e. against the flank of the enemy's position.

PART 2.   Lt. ARNOLD, 416th Field Coy. R.E., taking into consideration the material available, elected to proceed at once with the construction of the footbridge and not to pass the patrol over on rafts.

This task was quietly and successfully completed and at 0300 it was reported that the Q.W.R. Patrol was across the Canal but could not move more than 10 paces in any direction without being challenged by German Posts, of which three appeared to exist in the immediate vicinity of the landing place.   As the enemy had not opened fire, I ordered the patrol to make a bold attempt to capture the Posts without raising an alarm, before abandoning the enterprise.

/ 1 Platoon

1 Platoon of the 2nd London Regt. was passed over the bridge, two Germans were captured and no alarm was raised.

The passing of the troops over the bridge presented considerable difficulties in itself. The night was very dark and rain was falling. The bridge was, from its nature, unstable and no form of handrail existed.

However, the remaining Platoons crossed soon afterwards and the Company, under the command of Captain D. SLOAN, was ready in position about half an hour before Zero, which had been fixed for 0515.

The assembly area was far from being a good one, being intersected by 2 streams LA NAVIE and LA PETITE NAVIE of which nothing was known. From the nature of the ground it was impossible to follow the barrage in the usual way. Platoons were directed to make their own way to various points as soon as the barrage started; the barrage was to stand for 5 minutes to enable platoons to approach.

In spite of these very considerable difficulties and of the assembly having taken place in great darkness, the attacking Company carried out its instructions to the letter and effected a complete surprise, appearing as it did on the least threatened side of the enemy's position. Two machine gun teams which offered resistance were captured after two or three of the enemy had been killed, but for the most part the enemy appeared to be completely mystified by the appearance of our men from such an unexpected quarter, and about 160 prisoners were mopped up in the village without trouble.

Platoons moved direct to the spots where they had been ordered to establish Posts and by about 0630 all the prearranged Posts had been established.

A few of the enemy who had not so far been directly involved in our attack now approached our Posts and gave themselves up, but others from various positions around the village opened Machine Gun and sniping fire against our Posts, causing several casualties and greatly restricting movement. On our part every advantage was taken of available targets and losses were inflicted upon the enemy.

At 0600 two Platoons from the Supporting Company had reported to Captain SLOAN and were used to reinforce certain Posts.

It was not found possible to establish Posts near the Station (R.9.b.) owing to the enemy being in strength near the dumps and Railway sidings. For the same reason it was found impossible to patrol towards BRUNEMONT. A considerable force from this direction later co-operated in the hostile counter-attack.

About 0700 two hostile Machine guns which were troubling one of our Posts at close range were engaged with rifle grenades and then rushed, 12 prisoners being taken.

The two remaining Platoons of the Support Company reported to Captain SLOAN at about 0930.

Between 0915 and 1015 hostile parties were observed in several places from our Infantry O.P. in the BOIS DE QUESNOY and were engaged by LEFT GROUP R.F.A. whose F.O.O. shared the O.P. Many casualties were inflicted.

/ Trench

Trench Mortars firing from old trenches in R.10.b. were engaged and their crews put to flight.

About 1000 the enemy put down a heavy barrage on AUBIGNY and also concentrated many machine guns on the village. Half an hour afterwards the enemy's Reserve battalion, assisted by troops from BRUNEMONT, made a most determined attack, suffering heavy losses from their own barrage and from our fire. One by one, however, our small Posts were outflanked – one was entirely destroyed by a heavy trench mortar – and gradually pressed back to the LA PETITE NAVIE stream where a stand was made and the enemy prevented from debouching from the village.

His Machine Gun and sniping fire soon became very troublesome from the enclosed country on the flanks and it became advisable to fall back further to the canal bank if our party was not to be completely sacrificed.

A small bridgehead was maintained for a considerable time, but by 1700 all our troops were back behind the Southern bank of the Canal.

PART 3.   Four Stokes mortars were very ably handled throughout the day by C.S.M. BUTCHER, and O.C. 2nd London Regt. testifies to the importance of the work they performed.

Captain SLOAN's Company, which carried out the attack, had been employed carrying bridging material for 2 hours during steady rain before advancing to their assembly. Owing to the darkness, streams and marsh, every man was thoroughly wet through by dawn. The behaviour of this Company was most praiseworthy.

PART 4.

		Officers.	O.R.
Strength of the Company employed in the Attack		3	87
Strongest possible numbers available for defence of village (not allowing for casualties which had occurred)		6	165
Prisoners captured by the above-mentioned.		4	203
Total casualties of 2nd London Regt. for the day (estimated)	Killed:	NIL	20
	Wounded:	2	90
	Wounded & Missing or Missing	1	30
	Total	3	140

Three enemy Machine Guns were brought back, and ten others thrown into streams.

PART 5.   The enterprise may be considered to have achieved the following results :-

/ (i)

(i). Shewed the enemy that we are alert and that he will not be able to retire untroubled.

(ii). A considerably larger number of prisoners than the total of the force employed by us.

(iii). Very heavy casualties inflicted upon the enemy.

(iv). Possibly useful identifications and a large source of information from prisoners.

* (v). The throwing of a footbridge across the canal and the establishing of a bridgehead.

---

* Note: The Bridgehead mentioned in the final para. of PART 2 was re-established later on in the same day. The footbridge was destroyed by hostile Artillery on the 14th but was repaired before handing over to the 10th Canadian Brigade.

(Sd) E.L. COKE,

Brigadier-General,
Commanding 169th Infantry Brigade.

15th Oct. 1918.

Appendix NA.   War Diary

CONFIDENTIAL.   A.U.988.

Headquarters,
    56th Division.

    I beg to submit herewith a report on operations carried out by the Brigade under my command during the period 27th - 28th September 1918.

    Prior to the action 169th Infantry Brigade was out of the line, with two Battalions between UPTON WOOD and the CAMBRAI ROAD and one Battalion just East of the HENINCOURT - BURY ROAD.

    On the 24th and 25th September I received orders to take over a small portion of the Line West of the CANAL DU NORD and immediately North of the CAMBRAI ROAD on the night 26th/28th and to cross the CANAL on the morning of the 27th as soon as the CANADIANS had secured MARQUION and the ground immediately North of it. The Brigade was then to deploy Northwards and to attack SAUCHY LESTREE, SAUCHY CAUCHY, and the ground between the CANAL DU NORD and OISY LE VERGER, the final objective being the line of the SENSEE Road from Q.35.a.8.1. through Q.33.b. to Q.34.c.2.8.

    On the night 25th/26th September the L.R.B. took over the portion of the front line mentioned above, the 168th Infantry Brigade being already in line on my left.

    On the night 26th/27th the 2nd London Regt. and Q.W.R. moved to assembly positions in valleys just South of the CAMBRAI ROAD in V.8. and V.2. respectively, Brigade H.Q. being established at the QUARRY W.7.c.0.0.

Operations on 27th September 1918.

    The Time Table for the CANADIAN attack on my right fixed the capture of MARQUION at 10.15 a.m. and the carrying of the ground to the North so far as the railway line running N.W. and S.E. immediately South of SAUCHY LESTREE (the Blue Line) by 12 noon, Zero hour for the CANADIAN attack being fixed for 5.20 a.m., the attack of my Brigade being fixed for 2.40 p.m. from the Blue Line.

    I ordered the L.R.B. to send one Company, as soon as our barrage would permit, to clear the enemy from the vicinity of the CANAL on my front and to establish posts as soon as possible East of the CANAL to cover the R.E. who were detailed to throw a bridge over at W.9.b.2.7. and to protect the crossing.

    I ordered the 2nd London Regt. to proceed from their Assembly area at 9.20 a.m. and the Q.W.R. at 10.20 a.m. (4 hours and 5 hours respectively after ZERO). The 2nd London Regt. were to cross by a bridge which the R.E. were ordered to throw across South of the CAMBRAI ROAD at W.15.a.0.7., the Q.W.R. being ordered to cross by the more Northerly bridge already referred to at W.9.b.2.7. The former bridge was to be ready at 11 a.m. and the latter at 12 noon.

    At 11.45 a.m. however the enemy were still in MARQUION and to the South and North of it and were preventing any work by the R.E. One of our aeroplanes flying low over MARQUION had been heavily fired upon at 11.50 a.m.

- 2 -

It therefore seemed impossible for the Brigade to conform to the Time Table and be in position on the BLUE LINE by 2.40 p.m. G.O.C. 11th Division was similarly of opinion with regard to his 34th Infantry Brigade who were to attack on my right at the same hour. After consultation with Division, it was therefore decided to postpone the attack 40 minutes i.e. to attack at 3.20 p.m.

At 12 noon it was reported that MARCOING was clear and the 2nd Londons started crossing as ordered about that time, and the Q.V.R. at 1 p.m. The L.R.B. followed the Q.V.R. and all were across and in position on the Blue Line by 3 p.m. A considerable amount of opposition was met with after crossing the Canal and before reaching the line of Deployment. The Q.V.R. captured at least 80 prisoners before forming up for the attack.

Dispositions for the Attack.

The dispositions for the attack were as follows :-

<u>2nd Londons</u> on the Right from the Cross Roads W.8.c.8.4. to the East branch of the APACHE River W.8.a.4.5.

<u>Q.V.R.</u> on the Left from the West branch of the APACHE River W.4.b.5.5. to CANAL DU NORD W.4.a.7.8.

<u>L.R.B.</u> One Company between the East and West branches of the APACHE River to clear the ground between the branches of the river to their junction at Q.25.c.4.1. and to prevent any movement between BAUCHY LECTURE and BAUCHY CAMONT.
Two Companies in immediate support to the 2nd Londons.
The Fourth Company was already engaged in covering the crossing of the CANAL at W.9.b.8.7.

The Attack.

The attack proceeded according to the amended Time Table as far as Q.20.a. and Q.20.c., the BANQUERS, SAUCHY COPSE, MIDDLE COPSE and ORCHARD WOOD being taken, with many prisoners. The Company of L.R.B. cleared the area between the branches of the APACHE River without casualties and secured several prisoners.

North of these places Machine Gun nests, chiefly along the Canal Banks, held up the attack for a time. On the Right the 2nd London Regt. were held by Machine Guns in the enemy trench line in Q.20.c. and the railway embankment in Q.24., c & d. These nests were attacked by the 2nd London Regt. and L.R.B. four times without success, but a fifth attempt was made and the enemy were captured with their Machine Guns by 5.30 a.m.

On the Left the Q.V.R. met considerable opposition from Machine Guns on the CANAL BANK in Q.20.a. which held complete command over the swamps in Q.20.a & c. By working along the APACHE River to the East of the CANAL in stages as far as Q.25.a.4.5. they eventually surrounded the Machine Guns and inflicted heavy casualties on the team. 1 Officer and 29 O.R. with their Machine Guns were captured from this nest, 20 O.R. being found dead at their posts the next day.

- 2 -

By 7 p.m. the Q.W.R. were established along the railway embankment running East and West through Q.29.c & d.

Another nest was located on the road embankment leading to the CANAL bridge at Q.29.a.70.05. which completely covered the surrounding country. This was repeatedly attacked with rifle grenades after dusk. Eventually at dawn the Q.W.R. worked round it and the garrison fled Northwards, leaving their Machine Guns and a few prisoners.

The final objective for the day was thus reached in its entirety in the early hours of the 28th.

Operations 28th September 1918.

At 9 p.m. on the 27th I received orders to proceed with the attack the next morning and clear the area up to the number East of PAILLUEL. Zero hour was fixed for 10.30 a.m.

I ordered the 2nd Londons to assemble one Company for the attack on the line Q.29.a.7.8. to Q.24.a.0.2. and the Q.W.R. to supply a Company to mop up.

The attack proceeded with hardly any opposition and posts were established at Q.12.c.8.8., Q.11.d.7.7. and Q.11.d.0.8.

Supplies of Ammunition &c. were carried forward on Pack Convoys which followed closely the attacking Battalions. The entire operation - the assembly, approach march, crossing of the Canal, the deployment, and the advance to the final objective - went without a hitch.

Excellent communication was maintained throughout the day, the forward Report Centre "Point H" being invaluable. By 8 p.m. Brigade H.Q. was established at VAUCOURT FARM.

Casualties sustained by the Brigade were as follows :-

	Officers.	O.R.
Killed	5	24
Wounded	6	132
Missing	-	11
Total	11	167

The number of Prisoners captured by the Brigade exceeds 400, and the following list shows the number of weapons at present returned

| Heavy T.M. | 3 | Heavy M.Gs. | 11 |
| Light " | 6 | Light " | 23 |

Brigadier General,
Commanding 160th Infantry Brigade.

1st October 1918.

56th Division.
General Staff
War Diary
for
November 1918.

56 Ch D W

Army Form C. 2118.

56th DIVISION.

WAR DIARY
or
INTELLIGENCE SUMMARY.

(Erase heading not required.)

NOVEMBER 1918.

Instructions regarding War Diaries and Intelligence Summaries are contained in F.S. Regs., Part II. and the Staff Manual respectively. Title pages will be prepared in manuscript.

Place	Date	Hour	Summary of Events and Information	Remarks and references to Appendices
BASSEVILLE.	NOV. 1st	1000	G.O.C. & G.S.O.I attended Conference at Corps H.Q.	
		1400	G.O.C's Conference to discuss forthcoming operations.	
			O.O. No. 219 issued for relief of 49th Division in line on night of Nov. 2/3rd by 56th Divn.	APP. II.
MONCHAUX.	2nd	1140	Orders received from 22nd Corps for 49th Division to place one fresh Infantry Brigade at our disposal to co-operate on our left flank. Moves completed as laid down in O.O.219. Div. H.Q. opened at MONCHAUX at 15 hours.	APP. I.
			O.O.No.220 issued for the continuance of the attack by 168th and 169th Infantry Brigades on 4th November in conjunction with Divisions on either flank.	APP.II.
			Addendum to O.O.220 issued.	APP.II.
	3rd		Quiet night. Reliefs in the line completed and G.O.C. 56th Division assumed command at 1000.	
		1020	The 4th Can. Divn. on our left having reported that the enemy were withdrawing from their front, and that their troops had entered ESTREUX, G.35 was issued ordering 148th, 168th and 169th Infantry Brigades to push forward strong patrols and make good a line FME du MOULIN to CEMETERY F.27.d. and then the RED LINE as laid down in O.O.220. Boundaries being as laid down in O.O.220.	
		1220	168th Infantry Brigade reported their patrols had entered SAULTAIN and met no opposition. There were from 1100 to 1500 civilians there.	
		1235	G.365 issued laying down new forward boundaries.	
		1320	The two squadrons of cavalry and cyclists attached to this Division were ordered to push on as soon as the line FME du MOULIN - CEMETERY F.27.c. had been gained and seize the crossings of the river AUNELLE at LE PISSOT SEBOURQUIAUX - RUE DE VERTMEZ. 168th and 169th Brigade were ordered to support these troops closely and make good any crossings thus gained.	
		1610	148th Infantry Brigade reported that 168th Infantry Brigade had obtained touch with 4th Canadian Division at a point E. of their front troops thus squeezing them out as laid down in O.O.220. They were, therefore, ordered to withdraw to HAULCHIN preparatory to rejoining the 49th Division.	
		1710	168th Infantry Brigade reported they were on their 1st objective and had captured 7 prisoners, and they were moving to the RED LINE.	

Army Form C. 2118.

56th DIVISION.   WAR DIARY   NOVEMBER 1918.
or
INTELLIGENCE SUMMARY.
(Erase heading not required.)

Instructions regarding War Diaries and Intelligence
Summaries are contained in F.S. Regs., Part II.
and the Staff Manual respectively. Title pages
will be prepared in manuscript.

Place	Date	Hour	Summary of Events and Information	Remarks and references to Appendices
MONCHAUX.	Nov. 3rd.	2100	Mounted troops and Infantry of both Brigades reached the RED LINE and reported they were held up by hostile M.G. fire. The cavalry were unable to reach the AUNELLE River.	APP.II.
		2030	On orders being received from XXII Corps for continuance of advance at dawn each Division operating independently, G390 issued as Warning Order.	
		2200	O.O.No. 221 issued with detailed orders for the advance.	
	4th		The advance was resumed at dawn and by 10 a.m. 169th Infantry Brigade had captured SEBOURG and passed their leading battalion the Q.W.R. over the AUNELLE River. Meanwhile the 168th Infantry Brigade had seized the village of SEBOURQUIAUX and bridgehead at LE PISSOT and obtained touch with 169th Brigade on the E. side of the river. Our troops were then held up by the enemy, who were holding the high ground East of the river in force. One Company of the Q.W.R. obtained a footing on the high ground, but were counter-attacked and compelled to withdraw. The 4th Canadian Division on our left were held up outside the Village of ROMBIES, and the 11th Division on our right who had captured the southern part of SEBOURG had advanced across the river to the high ground beyond, were counter attacked and driven back to the E. outskirts of SEBOURG. It was apparent that no further advance could be made without an organised attack in co-operation with the Divisions on either flank. Orders were issued accordingly. Zero hour being fixed for 0530 on 5th inst. Div. H.Q. moved at 1000 to TAMARS and at 1500 to SAULTAIN. 1 Officer and 49 O.R. were captured during the day and also three British Tanks with German markings. For location of units see App. I.	
SAULTAIN.	5th.		Quiet night. The attack was continued at 0530, the Belgian frontier being crossed shortly afterwards and good progress was made. The 5th London Regt. (L.R.B.) the leading battalion of the right Brigade (169) advanced over the high ground E. of the River AUNELLE and by 0730 reported the capture of ANGREAU meeting little opposition. Troops of 168th Brigade also captured the high ground E. of the river, but were held up by M.G. fire from the Village of ANGRE. The 4th Canadian Division on the left captured the Village of ROMBIES and advanced across the river to the high ground beyond but were held up by hostile M.G. fire. The 11th Division on our right also attacked and captured ROISIN.	

Army Form C. 2118.

56th DIVISION.

WAR DIARY
or
INTELLIGENCE SUMMARY.

(Erase heading not required.)

NOVEMBER 1918.

Instructions regarding War Diaries and Intelligence Summaries are contained in F. S. Regs., Part II. and the Staff Manual respectively. Title pages will be prepared in manuscript.

Place	Date	Hour	Summary of Events and Information	Remarks and references to Appendices
SAULTAIN	NOV. 5th.	0900	Orders were issued to 168th and 169th Infantry Brigades to advance after they had captured the crossings of the GRANDE HONNELLE River, to the high ground beyond. The cavalry would then push through and capture ONNEZIES - MONTIGNIES - AUDREGNIES and infantry would support closely.	
		1525	The hostile opposition appearing very strong in ANGRES an attack by 168th Infantry Brigade was arranged to commence 1815 under cover of an artillery barrage rolling to the outskirts of the Village.	
		1815	The attack progressed satisfactorily and our troops reached the outskirts of ANGRES, but were unable to progress further owing to hostile M.G. fire.	APP.I.
		2015	O.O.No.222 issued for the continuation of the attack on the 6th inst. Zero hour being 0530.	
		1825	Orders received from 22nd Corps that 63rd Division would take over the left section of our front on night 6/7th November or would attack through on morning of 7th November. The 189th Brigade of 63rd Division would move to SEBOURQUIAUX by noon 6th inst. and would be under the orders of 56th Division until 63rd Division took over. Prisoners captured 9 O.R.	
	6th		Quiet night except for some hostile artillery fire on our front line. Towards dawn our front troops were heavily shelled with gas and H.E.	
		0530	The attack commenced but our troops were compelled to wear gas masks. The right Brigade met very heavy opposition, the L.R.B. being driven back to their starting point. The 2nd London Regiment managed to cross LA GRANDE HONNELLE River and obtain a footing on the Eastern bank capturing about 20 prisoners. The Left Brigade captured ANGRES with the 14th London Regiment, who also crossed the river and established themselves on the Eastern bank. The left Battalion, the 13th London Regiment, also crossed the river North of ANGRES capturing about 80 prisoners, but were heavily counter attacked and driven back. They attacked again and succeeded in crossing the river and establishing themselves on the high ground E. of the river, but were again counter attacked and driven West of the River. About 1000 the 2nd London Regt. were also counter attacked and driven back to their starting points. Local fighting took place during the course of the day but the line remained the same, i.e. we held the Villages of ANGREAU and ANGRES, and the Western banks of LA GRANDE HONNELLE River. We maintained a bridgehead across the river at ANGRES.	

Army Form C. 2118.

56th DIVISION.
WAR DIARY or INTELLIGENCE SUMMARY.
NOVEMBER 1918.

(Erase heading not required.)

Instructions regarding War Diaries and Intelligence Summaries are contained in F.S. Regs., Part II. and the Staff Manual respectively. Title pages will be prepared in manuscript.

Place	Date	Hour	Summary of Events and Information	Remarks and references to Appendices
SAULTAIN.	Nov. 6th	1630	Orders issued for relief of 168th and 169th Infantry Brigades by 63rd Division and 167th Infantry Brigade respectively on night 6/7th inst.	
			O.O.225 issued for the continuation of the attack on the 7th inst; by the 167th Infantry Brigade on a one brigade front. The 63rd Division and 11th Division cooperating on either flank. Zero hour was fixed for 0900.	APP.II.
			During the evening the left Brigade crossed the LA GRANDE HONNELLE River and established themselves on the high ground to the East without opposition. Prisoners captured during the day - 4 Officers and 104 O.R. Locations.	App.I.
	7th		Quiet night. The 63rd Division took over the frontage of the left Brigade and 167th Infantry Brigade relieved 169th Infantry Brigade in the right section. The Division now holds a frontage of one Brigade.	
		0900	Patrols who attempted to push on were fired on by the enemy. The attack was therefore commenced at 0900 and made good progress. By 1030 the 7th Middlesex had captured ONNEZIES. The 167th Infantry Brigade reached its first objective at 1330 hours capturing a few prisoners and one gun. The advance was continued during the afternoon, MONTIGNIES was captured and progress made. East of the BAVAI - HENSIES road. Hostile opposition stiffened very considerably after the road was crossed, the artillery and M.G. fire being heavy.	
		1500	Div. H.Q. moved from SAULTAIN and opened at SEBOURG. Orders (G.596) were issued for the advance to be continued on the 8th inst. our line at the end of the day ran along the BAVAI - HERSIES - HERSIES road E. of AUTREPPE - Western outskirts of BOIS de RAMPEMONT - E. of MONTIGNIES. Quiet night.	APP. II
SEBOURG	8th	0800	The attack was resumed by 167th Infantry Brigade. Our troops advanced meeting little opposition, and by 1115 had reached their objectives capturing the villages of ATHIS, FAYTLE FRANC and ERQUENNES and were pushing patrols out towards RINCHON. The enemy in his retreat has destroyed practically all the bridges and blown craters at all road junctions. The Divisions on both flanks also advanced meeting very little opposition. In addition to which the weather has been very wet, almost continuous rain for three days, thus making cross country tracks impassable.	

Army Form C. 2118.

56th DIVISION

WAR DIARY
or
INTELLIGENCE SUMMARY.
(Erase heading not required.)

NOVEMBER 1918.

Instructions regarding War Diaries and Intelligence Summaries are contained in F. S. Regs., Part II. and the Staff Manual respectively. Title pages will be prepared in manuscript.

Place	Date	Hour	Summary of Events and Information	Remarks and references to Appendices
SEBOURG.	Nov. 8th		The advance has been so rapid that it has not been possible to repair the damage to keep pace with the advance. Supply lorries cannot proceed further than LA GRANDE HONNELLE River. The 167th Infantry Brigade held the line PETIT MORON FAIT RINCHON FERLIBRA with outposts in front during the night. Orders issued for the advance to be resumed to the MONS MAUBEUGE Road at 0730. Prisoners captured 6.	
FAY LE FRANC	9th.		The advance was resumed at 0700 and no opposition was met. 167th Infantry Brigade freed the villages of CORON RUEvde BURY, QUEVY and QUEVY le PETIT. The Division held the line of the MONS MAUBEUGE Road for the night.	
		2330	Orders received from XXII Corps for the advance to be resumed on the 10th inst. in a North Easterly direction, objectives being HARVENG and high ground East of River NOUVELLE. Orders issued accordingly and giving new Boundaries. Div. H.Q. moved to FAY LE FRANC, opening there at 1000.	
	10th		The advance was resumed this morning and progress made, the 1st London Regt., who were leading, preceded by cavalry, captured the village of HARVENG. They were, however, held up by hostile M.G. fire from the high ground E. of the River NOUVELLE.	
			Orders received from XXII Corps that the 63rd Division would carry on the advance as advanced Guard to the Corps, the 56th and 11th Divisions being in Support. The 63rd Divn. to take, over the whole front after today's objectives had been gained. Orders issued accordingly. Relief reported complete and command passed to G.O.C. 63rd Division at 2330.	
	11th	0730	Orders received from XXII Corps that an armistice had been signed and hostilities would cease at 1100 hours today. Troops were to stand fast until further orders. Orders issued accordingly.	
		1100	Hostilities ceased. For locations see Appx. I.	
	12th		The Division engaged in cleaning up and reorganising. Working parties also detailed to mend roads and fill in craters blown up by the enemy in his retreat.	

Army Form C. 2118.

56th DIVISION.

WAR DIARY
or
INTELLIGENCE SUMMARY.
(Erase heading not required.)

NOVEMBER 1918.

Instructions regarding War Diaries and Intelligence Summaries are contained in F.S. Regs. Part II. and the Staff Manual respectively. Title pages will be prepared in manuscript.

Place	Date	Hour	Summary of Events and Information	Remarks and references to Appendices
FAY LE FRANC	Nov. 12th		XXII Corps letter G.4519 received giving general outline of plans for advance of British Armies to the Rhine, 56th Division to move forward with the Second Army.	
	13th		Nil.	
	14th		Notification received from XXII Corps that the 282nd Army Brigade R.F.A. would be attached to 56th Division.	
	15th		First Army Commander made official entry into MONS. Representatives of each Infantry Brigade took part in the ceremonial march.	
	16th		56th Division with XXII Corps transferred to Second Army from 1200.	
	17th to 20th		Nothing of interest to report.	
	21st		XXII Corps Nos. G.4703 and 4704 were received notifying XXII Corps transferred from Second Army to First Army at 1200, 22nd November. Orders for the Divn. for the advance to the Rhine cancelled.	
	22nd		Visit to MONS battlefield by motor lorry. Brigadier-General ELKINGTON, C.R.A., explained the situation to the troops.	
	23rd		Nil.	
	24th		Order No. 224 issued relating to the move of the Division to the new HARVENG Area.	Appx. II
	25th		G.O.C. held a conference at 168th Brigade H.Q. on subject of Education. Brigade Commanders, C.Os. and all Unit Education Officers were present.	
	26th		167th and 169th Inf. Bdes. moved into new area.	

Army Form C. 2118.

56th DIVISION.

WAR DIARY
or
INTELLIGENCE SUMMARY.

NOVEMBER 1918.

(Erase heading not required.)

Instructions regarding War Diaries and Intelligence Summaries are contained in F. S. Regs., Part II. and the Staff Manual respectively. Title pages will be prepared in manuscript.

Place	Date	Hour	Summary of Events and Information	Remarks and references to Appendices
FAY LE FRANC	Nov. 27th		King Albert of Belgium visits MONS. The G.O.C. and Brigade Commanders invited to attend. 168th Inf. Bde. moved into new area.	APPX. I
HARVENG	28th		Divisional H.Q. moved to HARVENG.	
	29th 30th		Nothing to report.	

4th Dec. 1918.

R. Hull
Major-General,
Commanding 56th Division.

SECRET 56th DIVISION. LOCATION TABLE at 1800 6 a.m. November 1918. APPENDIX 1
Sheets 51A, 51, 45

	1	2	3	4	5	6	7	8	9	10	11	12	13	14	15	16
Div. H.Q.	BASSE-VILLE	MONCH-AUX		SAULTAIN			SEBOURG		FAYT-LE FRANC							
187th Inf. Bde. H.Q.	DOUCHY	MAING		SAULTAIN	SEBOURG		ONNEZIES	FAYT-LE FRANC	D9c02		W27a10 BOUGNIES			D6d40		
1st London Regt.		I12a J16d18		"	SEBOURG-QUIAUX				HARVENG	QUEVY-GRAND	HARVENG	"				
7th Middx. Regt.		DOUCHY J24a26		"	SEBOURG		D9c02		QUEVY-LE PETIT	LA DESSUS	W20	"				
8th Middx. Regt.		I11a J24a26		"	SEBOURG-QUIAUX		ONNEZIES	FAYT-LE FRANC	QUEVY-LE GRAND	BAREGNIES R2d 85	E3a44			E2b58		
168th Inf. Bde. H.Q.	DOUCHY	K20b90		SAULTAIN	A20a33		A.20.c.05	AUTREPPE	C2d.04	D9c 21			SARS-EN-BRUYÈRE			
4th London Regt.	"	AULNOY	SAULTAIN		A14a91		SEBOURG	"	HARDRET	D1d45						
13th	"	F10d.23	F1gd.55		A8c.91		"	"	ERQUENNES	D8d.88.						
14th	"	MAING	E30a		A15a.cnt.		"	"	FERLIBRAY	D9d40						
169th Inf. Bde. H.Q.	LIEU ST AMAND	K20b90		SAULTAIN	A20a05		A20c05	ANGREAU		ATHIS						
2nd London Regt.	"	K16b62 F27c95			F27c95 A20c05		SEBOURG	"		"						
5th	"	K20b90 L1b 25			A20c05		"	"		ERQUENNES						
16th	"	K16b62 F25d 87			A20c05		"	"		ATHIS						
Div. Arty. H.Q.	BASSE-MONCHAUX VILLE			SAULTAIN			SEBOURG		FAYT-LE FRANC							
280th Bde.	THIANT	K26a.12		"	A9.d91			B14.d.99		BAREGNIES QUEVY-PETIT						
281st	"	L21.b.97		"	A.19.b.12			B12.C.25								
Pioneers.	NOUVILLE	J7.b41.		SAULTAIN			A20a.00		B20b22	ATHIS						
M.G. Battn. H.Q.	BASSE-MONCHAUX VILLE			SAULTAIN			A19d88	FAYT-LE FRANC	D9c02	QUEVY-LE PETIT HARVENG	QUEVY-LE-PETIT					BIAUGIES

IN THE LINE ―――
IN SUPPORT ―――
IN RESERVE ―――
DIV. AT REST ―――

SECRET   56th DIVISION.   LOCATION TABLE at 18:00.   NOVEMBER 1918.   APPENDIX

	17	18	19	20	21	22	23	24	25	26	27	28	29	30
Div. H.Q.	FAYT-LE-FRANC											HARVENGT		
167th Inf. Bde. H.Q.	QUEVY-LE-PETIT									QUEVY-LE-GRAND			
1st London Regt.	BOUGNIES									GOEGNIES-CHAUSSEE			
7th Middx. Rgt.	BOUGNIES									QUEVY-LE-GRAND			
8th Middx. Rgt.	QUEVY-LE-PETIT												
168th Inf. Bde. H.Q.	SARS-LA-BRUYERE									GIVRY			
4th London Regt.	SARS-LA-BRUYERE									VILLERS-SRE-NICOLE			
13th " "	RIEU-DE-BURY									VILLERS-SIRE-NICOLE			
14th " "	BLAREGNIES						EUGIES			GIVRY			
169th Inf. Bde. H.Q.	ATHIS				BLAUGIES					HARVENGT				NOUVELLE
2nd London Regt.	ATHIS									HARMIGNIES			
5th " "	ERQUENNES									HARMIGNIES			
18th " "	ATHIS									BOUGNIES				GENLY
Div. Arty. H.Q.	FAYT-LE-FRANC											HARVENGT		
280th Bde.	BLAREGNIES									GOEGNIES-CHAUSSEE			
281st "	QUEVY-LE-PETIT									VIEUX RENG			
Pioneers.	ATHIS											SPIENNES		
M.G. Battn. H.Q.	BLAUGIES											VILLERS ST GHISLAIN		

AMENDMENT to 56th DIVISION G.A.191.
(Addendum to 56th Div.Order No.220).

In para. 4 for 18th & 26th Bde. R.F.A. substitute 51st Divnl. Artillery.

H.Q. 56th Divn.
2nd Nov. 1918.

Tom Buckarhuey
Lieut-Colonel,
General Staff.

To all recipients of G.A.191.

War Diary

SECRET.　　　　　　　　　　　　　　　　　　　　56th Division G.A.191.

ADDENDUM to 56th DIVISION ORDER No. 220.

2nd November 1918.

1.　　　The left boundary of the Division (including 148th Infantry Brigade attached) will be from E.17.c.0.2. - F.15.d.0.2. - F.11 central;

　　　　The right boundary has been modified so as to include the CEMETERY F.27.c.7.6. entirely to 11th Division.

2.　　　148th Infantry Brigade, (49th Division) with H.Qrs. at J.23.b.8.8. has been placed under the orders of G.O.C. 56th Division for the operations of 4th November.

　　　　It will hold the front from the FAMARS - QUAROUBLE road (exclusive) to the left Corps boundary as given in para. 1 above.

(a).　Its task on 4th inst. will be to mop up under a barrage such part of the area in the triangle E.30.a.0.0. - F.13.c.5.2. - E.18.d.7.0. as has not been already captured before Zero hour.

(b).　It will also be prepared to advance on left of 56th Divn. to capture ESTREUX in the event of this Village not being attacked by 4th Can. Divn.

3. (a).　The following mounted troops will be attached to the Division :-

　　　O.C. Lieut-Colonel HINDHAUGH, Commanding. Two Squadrons Australian Light Horse, One Coy. New Zealand Cyclists quartered at the BOLT FACTORY - THIANT.

(b).　O.C. Mounted Troops will remain in close touch with Div. H.Q. and be prepared to move at 1 hours notice after Zero hour on 4th inst.

4.　　　The 18th & 26th Brigades, R.F.A. are placed at the disposal of 56th Division for forthcoming operations, making 8 Arty.Bdes. in all.

5.　　　The following will be the Brigades on the flanks of the Division :-

　　　On right - 33rd Inf. Bde. 11th Divn. - H.Q. QUERENAING.
　　　On left - 11th Can.Inf.Bde. - 4th Can.Divn. - H.Q. K.3.a.6.0.

6.　　　B.Gs.C. Infantry Brigades will arrange for liaison with neighbouring Brigades as follows :-

　　　169th Inf.Bde. - with 11th Divn. - (1). At cross-roads L.1.b.
　　　　　　　　　　　　　　　　　　　　 (2). At Cemetery F.27.c.
　　　　　　　　　　　　　　　　　　　　 (3). At Cross-roads F.29.b.9.2. (LE TALANDIER), where a joint post will be established.

　　　Liaison points for 168th Inf. Bde. will be communicated later.

7.　　　An Officer of the Divisional Staff will visit H.Q. of 168th and 169th and 148th Infantry Brigades between 1500 and 1600 hours on 3rd November to synchronize watches. B.Gs.C. those Brigades will arrange to synchronize with all troops attached to them except Artillery.

　　　Synchronization will also be carried out at Div. H.Q. at 1700 and 2100 hours on 3rd November. Representatives of the following will attend :-

　　　C.R.A.　for R.F.A. & attached Heavy Arty.
　　　D.M.G.C.
　　　C.R.E.
　　　Corps Mounted Troops attached.

- 2 -

8. The colour of the flares will be RED.

9. (a). The S.O.S. Signal of XXII and of Canadian Corps is RED over GREEN over RED.

   (b). In addition Canadian Corps is using the following light signals :-

   O.K. - Rifle Grenade - GREEN over GREEN over GREEN.

   WE ARE HERE - Three WHITE Very Lights in quick succession.

10. ACKNOWLEDGE.

B Pakenham
Lieut-Colonel,
General Staff.

Issued at 2000.

Distribution :-

167th Infantry Brigade.
168th Infantry Brigade.
169th Infantry Brigade.
1/5th Cheshire Regt.
C.R.A.
C.R.E.
56th Bn. M.G.Corps.
56th Div. Signal Coy.
A.D.M.S.
'Q'
D.A.P.M.
D.A.D.O.S.
56th Div. Train.
A.D.C.
Camp Commandant.
22nd Corps. (2 copies).
49th Division.
4th Division.
11th Division.
4th Canadian Division.
52nd Squadron R.A.F.
War Diary (2 copies).
File.
148th Infantry Brigade.
XXII Corps Mounted Troops attached 56th Divn.

War Diary

SECRET.   Copy No. 23

56th DIVISION ORDER No. 220.

Reference Maps 1/20,000 Sheet 51A N.E.   2nd Nov. 1918.
              1/40,000   "   51.

1. (i). The advance will be continued by XXII Corps on 4th inst., the attack being carried out by 11th Division on the right and by 56th Division on left.
   (ii). The 33rd Bde., 11th Division, will be on the right.
         'A' Bde. 4th Can. Divn. will be on the left.
         H.Q. of above will be communicated when known.
   (iii). Zero hour will be notified separately.

2. (i). The objective of XXII Corps is the general line of the left bank of the AUNELLE River about G.7.b.5.5. - high ground in L.3.d. & b. - F.29.d. - F.23 central - F.16 central.
   (ii). The Canadian Corps is to cover the left of XXII Corps, placing its right flank about F.16 central and capturing ESTREUX.

3. The attack will be carried out by 169th Infantry Brigade on the right and by 168th Infantry Brigade on the left.

4. The objective and Divisional boundaries are shown on the attached map.
   The dividing line between 168th & 169th Infantry Brigades will be - fork-roads K.6.a.7.4. (incl. to 168th Bde.) - cross-roads F.25.b.4.3. (incl. to 168th Bde) - fork roads F.22.c.0.1. (incl. to 168th Bde.) - F.23 central.

5. (i). The attack will be conducted in two stages.
         The 1st objective will be the Spur from CEMETERY (F.27.c.)- F.27.a. - F.21.c. - F.20.b.
         The 2nd objective will be the RED LINE shown on attached map.
   (ii). After reaching the RED LINE, Brigades will push out patrols to exploit towards the line of the Pte. AUNELLE River.
         It is important to get in information rapidly from these patrols, since if there is any sign of enemy retreat, the G.O.C. intends to push on mounted troops to secure the crossings and will order the leading Brigades to support them.

6. (i). The Division will be covered by 6 R.F.A.Bdes.
   (ii). The C.R.A. will issue Artillery Instructions, showing grouping of Field Artillery and also Barrage Maps.
   (iii). The C.R.A. will place 1 Battery R.F.A. at the disposal of each attacking Infantry Brigade as soon as SAULTAIN is captured, with a view to close support and anti-tank defence.
   (iv). 3 Batteries of 6" Hows. and 1 Battery of 60-pdrs. will be directly under the orders of the G.O.C. 56th Division.

7. 168th and 169th Brigade H.Qrs. will, in the first instance, be located not further West than the FAMARS - QUERENAING road.
   After the final objective has been captured they will be established in the vicinity of SAULTAIN.

8. The O.C. 56th Bn. M.G.C. will place 2 Sections (8 guns) at the disposal of each attacking Brigade for use as weapons of opportunity, and to form the advanced line of M.G.Defence to cover consolidation of the line finally reached.
   He will arrange M.G.defence in depth behind this advanced line, and will keep at least 1 Coy. in Div.Reserve.

/9.

- 2 -

9. The C.R.E. will place 1 Section R.E. and 1 Platoon of Pioneers at the disposal of each attacking Brigade for such R.E. work as may be required, the remainder being in readiness to move forward, as necessary.

10. Advanced Dressing Station will be at J.15.c.6.4.
Main Dressing Station will be at I.29.d.9.3.

11. Div. H.Q. will be at MONCHAUX SUR ECAILLON.

12. ACKNOWLEDGE.

T. ᴅᴜ Bickan
Major
Lieut-Colonel,
General Staff.

Issued at 0600.

Distribution :-
Copy No. 1. * 167th Infantry Brigade.
2. * 168th Infantry Brigade.
3. * 169th Infantry Brigade.
4. * 1/5th Cheshire Regt.
5. * C.R.A.
6. * C.R.E.
7. * 56th Bn. M.G.Corps.
8. * 56th Div. Signal Coy.
9. * A.D.M.S.
10. * 'Q'.
11. ˣ D.A.P.M.
12. ˣ D.A.D.O.S.
13. ˣ 56th Div. Train.
14. ˣ A.D.C.
15. ˣ Camp Commandant.
16. ˣ 22nd Corps.
17.)
18. ˣ 49th Division.
19. ˣ 4th Division.
20. ∅ 11th Division.
21. ∅ 4th Canadian Division.
22. ˣ 52nd Squadron R.A.F.
23.)
24.) War Diary.
25. File.

* Maps already issued.
∅ Map herewith.
ˣ No map.

War Diary

SECRET.   Copy No. 24

56th DIVISION ORDER No. 221.

Ref. 1/40,000 Sheets 51A & 51.   3rd November 1918.

1. The advance is to be resumed to-morrow towards the BAVAI - HENSIES road, which is to be the final objective of the present phase.

2. 169th Infantry Brigade will remain on the right of the Divisional front and 168th Infantry Brigade on the left.

3. The infantry advance will commence at 0600 hours.

   1st bound. The high ground on the line A.21 central - A.15 central - A.9 central, securing the crossings of the AUNELLE River.

   2nd bound. To secure the crossings of LA GRANDE HONNELLE river between B.13.c.0.0. and a point about 1500 yards N. of ANGRE.

4. With reference to 56th Div. G.A.222 of this date, the artillery now in position will cover the infantry across the AUNELLE River.
   For the advance beyond this, the following artillery will be placed directly under B.Gs.C. Infantry Brigades :-

   168th Inf. Bde. - 281 R.F.A.Bde.
   169th Inf. Bde. - 280 R.F.A.Bde.

   The remainder of the Arty. will be directly under the C.R.A. and will move forward in support as necessary.

5. 167th Infantry Brigade will remain in Divnl. Reserve and will move to AULNOY at 0800 tomorrow.
   Attention is called to 56th Div. G.A.222 of this date re movement on roads.
   It will be prepared for a further advance during the day.

6. The C.R.E. will place 1 Section R.E. and 1 Platoon of Pioneers at the disposal of each Bde. in the line with a view to assisting the infantry to cross the AUNELLE and GRANDE HONNELLE Rivers.
   He will arrange to throw bridges suitable for artillery over those rivers, and repair roads where damaged.

7. The O.C. 56th Div. M.G.Bn. will keep the 2 Sections now attached to each Brigade in the line under their orders, and, with the remainder of his battalion and attached Companies of 102nd M.G.Bn., will arrange to establish M.G. defence in depth for each bound.

8. The Mounted Troops attached to the Division, if they have not already secured the crossings of the AUNELLE River, will continue the advance at 0530 hours and make them good.
   They will then push forward towards LA GRANDE/HONNELLE River and feel for the enemy, with a view to securing the crossings over that stream.
   They will forward their reports to the joint Bde. H.Q. at SAULTAIN.

9. The Southern Div. Boundary is extended forward from A.17.d.0.0. - A.14.a.0.0. - A.15.a.9.9.
   The inter-brigade boundary will run from F.23 central - A.14.d.0.0. - A.16.b.3.7. - A.11.d.4.5. - A.12 central - B.2.d.2.6.

/10.

- 2 -

10.   The advance will be general, but each Division will act independently.

   Brigades will carry out the advance with vigour and temporary opposition will be promptly brushed aside, so as to deny the enemy the opportunity of settling down in organized positions.

   The principle of exploiting soft spots will be carried out by Brigades.

   The inter-Brigade and Divisional Boundaries will not be taken as restricting tactical movements.

11.   168th and 169th Infantry Brigades will establish their Bde. H.Q. by 0800 hours to-morrow in SAULTAIN.

12.   Div. H.Q. will open at FAMARS at 1000 hours to-morrow and close at MONCHAUX at the same hour.

13.   ACKNOWLEDGE.

T.H.Heald Capt
for Lieut-Colonel,
General Staff.

Issued at

To List 'C' less 148th Inf.Bde., 49th Divn. 102nd M.G.Bn., D.A.D.V.S. and Div. Reception Camp.

SECRET.   *War Diary*   Copy No. 24

56th Division Order No. 222.

5th November 1918.

1. 168th and 169th Infantry Brigades will continue the pursuit of the enemy with vigour tomorrow.

2. The final objective for this phase of the operations is the line MONS - AULNOIS (VALENCIENNES Sheet 2K.).
   The first and second bounds will be those given in 56th Div. No. G.449 of today.
   Subsequent objectives will be communicated later.

3. The Canadian Corps on our left are advancing to-morrow to the line of the high ground overlooking the HONNELLE River in S.29.a. - S.23.c. and a. - S.16.d. - thence line of QUIEVRAIN - CRESION Road. They will also exploit to gain crossings over the river.

4. The advance will commence at 0530 hours.

5. (a). Infantry Brigades will arrange their own artillery support.

   (b). One Arty. Bde. is attached to each of 168th and 169th Infantry Brigades.
   The 5 remaining Brigades R.F.A. will be under the C.R.A. and will be available, with the attached Heavy Arty., to support Brigades as required.

6. The enemy troops opposed to the Division are for the most part scattered rearguards of tired Divisions.
   It will be impressed upon all ranks that they must act with boldness and that it is now no longer necessary for an advance to be made in continuous lines, or for units to be always in close touch with units on their flanks.
   Tactical points should be chosen as objectives and made good, and then, if necessary, the intervening ground mopped up.
   As soon as enemy Machine Gun nests are located the artillery should be informed, and the latter should push forward boldly into action to deal with them, if necessary, by direct fire.

7. Boundaries beyond those at present given out will be communicated later.

8. The O.C. 56th Div. M.G.Bn. will continue to establish M.G. defence in depth as the advance progresses.

9. The O.C. Corps Mounted Troops will move his troops forward in close support of the left of 168th Infantry Brigade and will cross LA GRANDE HONNELLE River at the first opportunity.
   He will then push forward with the object of:-
   (a). Securing the crossings of LA PETITE HONNELLE River in T.19 and T.26.
   (b). Keeping touch with the enemy.
   He will be prepared to cover the left flank of 168th Infantry Brigade with his cyclists if necessary.

10. The next move of Div. H.Q. will be to the CHATEAU DE SEBOURG.

11. ACKNOWLEDGE.

B Pakenham
Lieut-Colonel,
General Staff.

Issued at 2015.

To List 'C' less Serials 19, 23, 24 and 26.

War Diary

SECRET.   Copy No. 25

56th DIVISION ORDER No. 223.

6th November 1918.

1. The attack will be resumed to-morrow - ultimate objectives as before.

2. 63rd Division will be attacking on the left and will be moving along level with 56th Division, which will be attacking on a single Brigade front under a rolling barrage.
    11th Division will be attacking on the right.
    It will not be directly attacking the BOIS D'ANGRES, but will be attacking AUTREPPE Village from the South.

3. 167th Infantry Brigade will carry out the attack.

4. Div. Tactical Boundary will be as follows :-

   (a). Between 56th Divn. and 63rd Divn.
    A.13.d.0.0. - A.15 central - A.12.a.0.0. - T.26.c.0.0. - T.27.d.0.0. - B.4 central - C.1 central - C.2.b.0.2. - C.3.c.1.6. - C.4.d.0.0. - C.6.d.9.7.

   (b). Between 56th Div. and 11th Divn.
    A.19.d.0.0. - A.24.d.0.0. - B.14 central - B.15 central - B.16.d.0.0. - thence due East.

   (c). After 11th and 56th Divisions have reached the line of the BAVAI - MONTIGNIES Road the Southern boundary between them forward of A.24.d.0.0. will run B.20.d.0.0. - B.21.a.0.0. B.16.d.0.0. - thence due East thus giving the BOIS D'ANGRES and AUTREPPE to 56th Division.

5. The objectives of 56th and 63rd Divisions will be -

   First - Road B.14.b.6.4. - B.8.c.6.7. - B.7.b.8.9. - T.26.c.0.0. - thence BAVAI Road to T.13.c.8.7.

   Second - general line B.17.c.2.0. - B.10 central - B.4.a.2.3. - T.27.b. - T.21 central - T.15 central.

6. (a). 4 Bdes R.F.A. will cover 167th Infantry Brigade.

   (b). The barrage will be co-ordinated and communicated by C.R.A. and Barrage Maps will be issued.

   (c). The barrage will be arranged to come down on an arbitrary line. Should this line be found later to be too far back, a certain number of lifts will be omitted.

   (d). The barrage will be brought down at Zero hour and stand for 4 minutes, when it will roll forward at the rate of 100 yards in 4 minutes.

   (e). The C.R.A. will arrange to bombard with Heavy Artillery such points as B.G.C. 167th Infantry Brigade may desire.

   (f). After reaching the first objective, the barrage will roll on and form a protective barrage for 30 minutes.

7. On reaching the first objective, the infantry will halt for 2 hours and then resume the advance under a rolling barrage.

/8.

- 2 -

8. One Squadron of Corps Mounted Troops is placed at the disposal of B.G.C. 167th Infantry Brigade for the purpose of gaining touch with the enemy after the second objective has been gained and if the opposition has not been severe.
   B.G.C. 167th Infantry Brigade will give the O.C. Squadron a definite task to carry out.

9. (a). O.C. 56th M.G.Bn. will place 2 Sections at the disposal of 167th Infantry Brigade and be prepared also to secure the ground in depth as the advance progresses.

   (b). He will arrange to barrage the Western end of the BOIS D'ANGRES between the Southern Divisional Boundary and a point fixed by B.G.C. 167th Infantry Brigade with short bursts of fire until Zero plus 80 minutes.

10. 167th Infantry Brigade will send forward early morning patrols to discover if the enemy has withdrawn or not. If he has withdrawn the barrage will be cancelled, but information must reach Div. H.Q. by 0700.

11. Zero hour will be communicated later, probably 0800 hours.

12. ACKNOWLEDGE.

B. Pakenham
Lieut-Colonel,
General Staff.

Issued at 1630.

To List 'C' less Serials 4/19, 23, 24 and 26, plus 2nd Can. Divn.

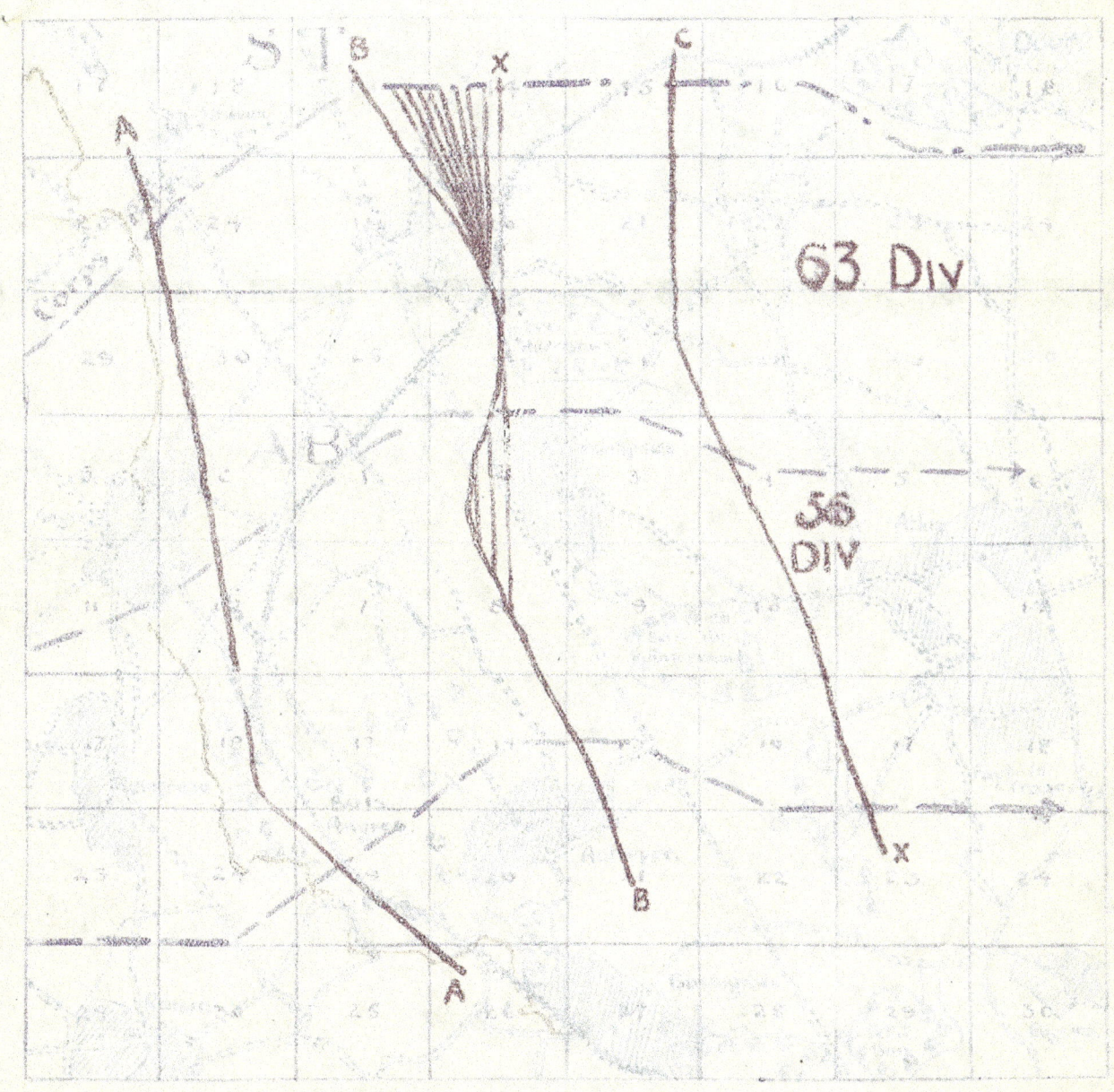

BARRAGE MAP.

Barrage stands for 4 mins on Line 'A'.
Then rolls at 100ˣ in 4 mins until it reaches Line "B"
Barrage stands on B for 2 hours; it then swings at 100ˣ in 4 mins until Line X is reached and thence to Line C where it stands for 15 minutes.

Canadian Corps. *Office Copy* 56th Division G.S/499

     In forwarding this report I desire to state that the plan was initiated and carried out entirely under the orders of the B.G.C., 169th Infantry Brigade, who deserves great credit for a successful exploit.

     The O.C., 2nd Londons, who personally supervised the operation, is worthy of much praise, and the Battalion has added another success to its many achievements.

Major General,
Commanding 56th Division.

16.10.18.

Copy to 169th Infantry Brigade.

To H.Q.
56th Division

GENERAL STAFF,
56th DIVISION.
No. G3/499
Date. 15-10-18

BM 436

Herewith rough Advanced Copy
of Report.
Clean copies follow.

E.S. Coke Brig Gen.
169 Inf Bde.

G.O.C.	
G.S.O.1	✓
G.S.O.2	Tgmb
G.S.O.3	

10 00
15/10/18

Parts of Sheets
45 & 51
Scale 1:40000

Sheet 45
Sheet 51

63 Division

56 Division

"A" Form.
MESSAGES AND SIGNALS.

Army Form C.2
(In pads of 100)

Prefix	Code	m	Words.	Charge.	This message is on a/c of:	Recd. at ....m.
Office of Origin and Service Instructions.			Sent At ....m. To By		...................Service. (Signature of "Franking Officer.")	Date........ From........ By........

Urgent Operation
PRIORITY
(Sd.) T.O.M. Prelap
for [illegible] Maj.

TO { Dist C. Bns 18, 19 & 23 to 26

Sender's Number.	Day of Month.	In reply to Number.	AAA
G416	4		

Warning Order aaa 168 and 169 Bdes will continue attack tomorrow aaa 11th Div and 4th Can Div are cooperating aaa Zero hour 0530 aaa Jumping off line Sunken Road A.20.d.7.5 to Road junction A.14.b.6.7 thence to A.8.d.6.9 aaa Barrage to come down on line A.21.a.4.0 - A.9.a.4.6 aaa To lift at Zero plus 4 mins. and to move at rate 100 yds in 4 mins. aaa Objective highground A.16.c and a. A.10.c and a. and support line about A.9.c.0.0 - A.5.a.0.0 - S.28.d.2.0. which protective barrage will cover for 15 mins. aaa Patrols will

From			
Place			
Time			

The above may be forwarded as now corrected. (Z)

....
Censor.   Signature of Addressor or person authorised to telegraph in his name.

* This line should be erased if not required.

(3796.) Wt. W 492/M1647. 650,000 Pads. 5/17. H.W. & V., Ld. (E. 1187.)

MESSAGES AND SIGNALS.

then push forward to exploit with object securing crossings of the ANGREAU and GRAND HONELLE Rivers aaa Corps mounted troops will follow up advance and exploit with same object aaa Acknowledge aaa Added List "C" less serials 18-19 and 23 to 26.

From 56 DW
Place
Time 1900
(Z) (sd) TvM ...
Lt Col SS

"A" Form.
MESSAGES AND SIGNALS.

Army Form C. 2121.
(In pads of 100.)

TO { List "C" Nos 18, 19 & 23 to 26.

Sender's Number.	Day of Month.	In reply to Number.	AAA
G422	4		

56 Div. G416 is confirmed with following alteration aaa Opening line of barrage will be A21a4.0 - A9a50 aaa Forming up line of left of 168 Bde will be altered accordingly aaa Liaison posts with Canadians will be established at A9a2.7 - A4c1.9 - S28d10 aaa acknowledge aaa addsd all recipients of G416

From: 56 Div
Place:
Time: 2010

MESSAGES AND SIGNALS.

Army Form C. 2121.
(In pads of 100.)

Office of Origin and Service Instructions: Urgent Operation
(sd) T.O.M Burslem
for Mot Gen

This message is on a/c of: War Diary

TO	168 Bde	CRA	11th Div
	169 "	Corps Cav	4th Can Div
	167 "	22nd Corps	

Sender's Number: G501
Day of Month: 5

Advance will be continued with vigour tomorrow aaa Infantry advance to commence 0530 aaa Brigadiers to arrange own arty. support aaa 1st and 2nd objectives as in G449 of today aaa Mounted troops to move forward in close support of left of 168 Bde and be prepared to exploit across PETITE HONELLE with view to securing crossings about AUDRIGNIES aaa Acknowledge aaa Addsd all concerned

From: 56 Div
Time: 1815

(sd) T.O.M Burslem Major

"A" Form
MESSAGES AND SIGNALS.

Army Form C. 2121.
(In pads of 100.)

Prefix	Code	m.	Words	Charge	This message is on a/c of	Recd. at ... m.
Office of Origin and Service Instructions			Sent At ... m. To By		................Service. (Signature of "Franking Officer")	Date. From By

TO	168	'C'	22 Corps	Corps HA
	169	RAGG	11 Div	52 Sqdn RAF
	690	Signals	63 Div	Corps Cavalry
			56 Div Train	

Sender's Number	Day of Month	In reply to Number	AAA
G596	7		

56 Div Order No. 224 aaa 167 Bde. will continue advance tomorrow over Objective line C2 central C8 central C14 central aaa 11 Div objective C15 d OO to HARGIES aaa 63 Div objective approx line T24 T90 aaa 167 Bde will commence advance at 0700 aaa 11 Div attacking at 0600 63rd Div attacking about 0600 aaa 167 Bde will push out patrols beyond objective to locate enemy line of resistance and gain ground if opposition is slight aaa MGns and 2 troop MG Bdn will be at disposal of

From
Place
Time

The above may be forwarded as now corrected. (Z)

Censor. Signature of Addressor or person authorised to telegraph in his name
* This line should be erased if not required.

"A" Form
MESSAGES AND SIGNALS.

Army Form C. 2121
(In pads of 100.)

Prefix......Code......m.	Words	Charge	This message is on a/c of:	Recd. at......m.
Office of Origin and Service Instructions	Sent			Date............
	At ....m.		..................Service.	From ....
	To			
	By		(Signature of "Franking Officer")	By..........

TO { (2)

| Sender's Number. | Day of Month. | In reply to Number. | AAA |

167 Bde also Squadron Corps Mounted Troops aaa 167 Bde will not put artillery fire south of a line running 200 yds north of Southhook Rd boundary inclusive mountaineer reciprocate aaa acknowledge aaa Addsd but B Coy he

From 66 Div
Place
Time

The above may be forwarded as now corrected. (Z)

Censor. Signature of Addressor or person authorised to telegraph in his name.

*This line should be erased if not required.

Order No. 1625. Wt. W3253/ P 511. 27/2 H. & K., Ltd. (E. 2634).

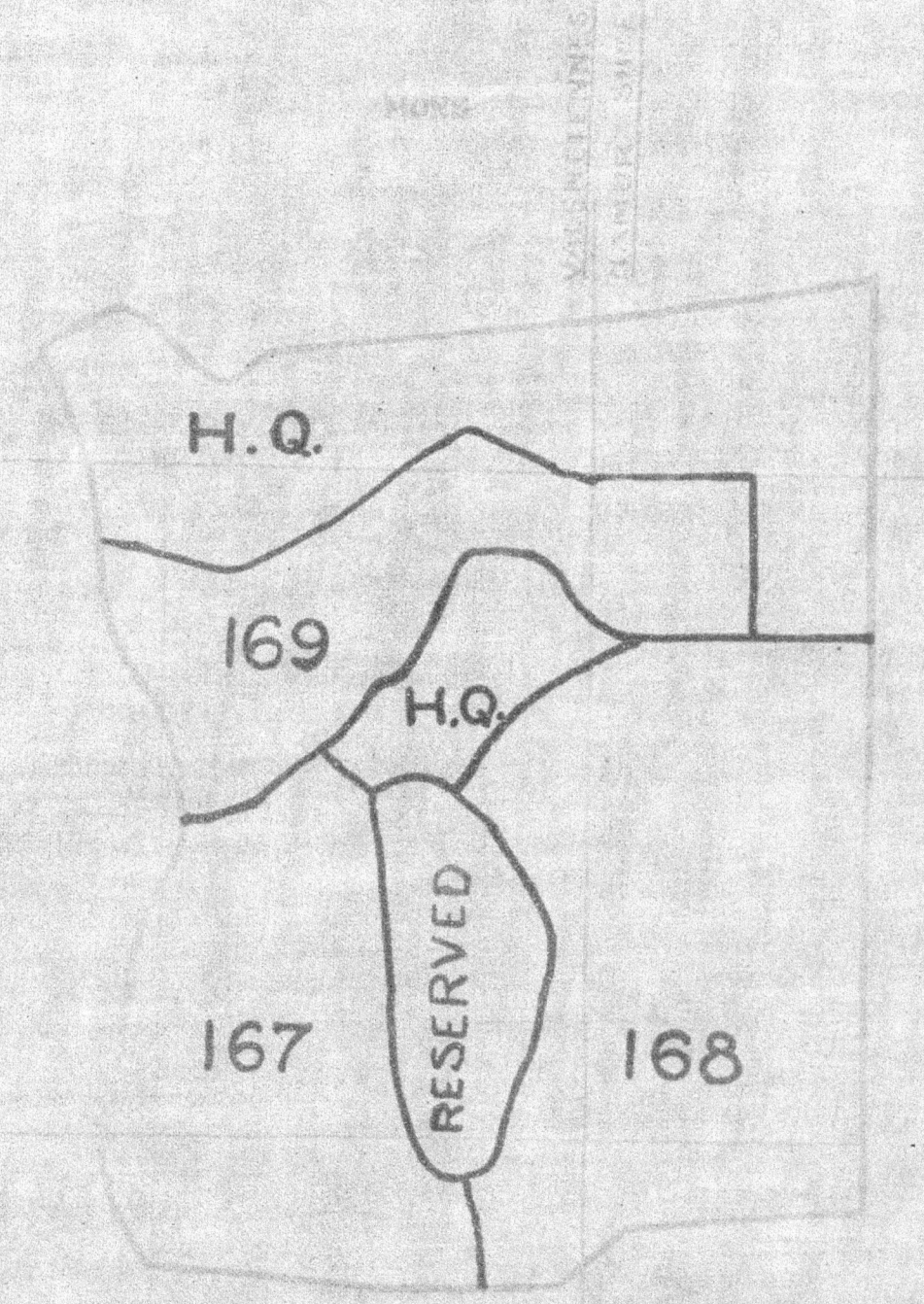

SECRET   Copy No. 22

56th DIVISION ORDER No. 224

24th Nov. 1918.

1. The 56th Division, less Artillery, will move in accordance with the attached March Table into the new area notified in 56th Div. G.A. 309 of 22nd Nov. 1918.

2. The move of the Divisional Artillery will take place later as accommodation becomes available on the departure of the Artillery now located in the new area.

3. Owing to 63rd Division not occupying the same areas as are allotted to units of this Division, and owing to Artillery attached to 63rd Division not moving until a later date, it will not be possible for units to take up their final locations in the first instance; moves of units, however, will be reduced to a minimum and final adjustments made as soon as the accommodation becomes available.

4. Detailed instructions as to billets will be issued by 56th Div. A. & Q. Tracing showing new areas is attached.

5. The following distances will be observed on the march.

    500 yds. between Battalions.
    100 "   "   Companies.
    100 "   "   a unit and its transport.
    100 "   "   transport of units when Brigaded.

6. 56th Div. H.Q. will close at FAYT-LE-FRANC at 1100 on 28th instant and open at HARVENG at the same hour.

B Pakenham
Lieut-Colonel,
General Staff.

Issued at 0630.

To List 'C' less 13 - 16.

Tracing to Nos. 1 - 7, 12, 17 - 20 and 23.

P.T.O.

MARCH TABLE TO ACCOMPANY 56th DIVISION ORDER No. 224.

Serial No.	Date.	Unit.	Moves To	Route.	Remarks.
1.	Nov. 26th	169 Bde. Group. 169 Bde. 513 Fld.Coy.R.E. 2/5 Fld.Amb.Lee. No.4 Coy.Div.Train. S.A.A. Sec.D.A.M.	HARICHIES HARVENG (Bde.HQ.) BOUGNIES, NOUVELLES, Area.	LA FOLIE - CAMP PERDU HARICHIES - QUEVY LE PETIT.	Start at 0900. Replaces 190 Inf.Bde. which moves out via BUGIES and SARS LA BRUYERE.
2.	do.	167 Bde. Group. 167 Bde. 416 Fld.Coy.R.E. 2/1 Fld.Amb.Lee. No.2 Coy. Train.	Readjusts to New Area vide attached Map.		Not to use the FRAMERIES - QUEVY-LE-PETIT BOUGNIES Road after 1200. 11th Div. clear QUEVY-LE-GRAND and BOUGNIES - CHAUSSE by 1200.
3.	27th	168 Bde. Group. 168 Bde. 512 Fld.Coy.R.E. No. 3 Coy.Train.	New Area vide Map.	QUEVY-LE-PETIT Cross Roads E.15.c.	Not to cross GIVRY - EAVAI Rd. before 1300. Replaces portions of 188 and 189 Bdes. 188 Bde. march out via FRAMERIES and occupy area vacated by 188 Bde. 189 Bde. march to AULFOIS via GIVRY - EAVAI Road clearing cross rds. E.15.c. by 1500.
4.	28th	56th Bn. M.G.C.	VILLERS ST. GHISLAIN.	No restrictions.	To start 0900.
5.	do.	1/5 Cheshire Rgt.	SPIENNES.	No restrictions.	Companies concentrate at SPIENNES as ordered by O.C. Bn. starting 0900.
6.	do.	Div. H.Q. H.Q. R.E. R.A. and details.	HARVENG.	No restrictions.	Under orders of Camp Commandant, starting 0900.

56th Division No. G.A.299.

XXII Corps.

With reference to your G.4628 of 17th instant, the following notes have been compiled on the operations since September 26th:-

INFANTRY.

1. To maintain rapid communication 2 mounted Orderlies per Battalion and 4 per Brigade H.Qrs. (this is a minimum) are essential.

   Communication by 'phone between flanking Brigades was found to be impossible.

   A cable cart was of the utmost value and it is recommended that in all future operations one cart should be attached to the Brigade in the line. A reserve of cable should be brought along in a limbered wagon with Brigade H.Qrs.

   The necessity for Brigade and Battalion H.Q. being well forward has been repeatedly emphasized — otherwise C.Os. cannot keep touch with an ever-changing situation — but this obviously increases the difficulties of communication from the rear.

2. The final objective should never be altered and should be made as far distant as practicable.

3. Rapidity of digging and proper concealment of all trenches requires far more practice. The erection of some wire obstacles should be a matter of second nature.

4. Too much dependence is placed on L.G. sections, these frequently being asked to do what should be done by riflemen. This points to a want of faith in the rifle — a matter for training on full sized ranges.

   L.T.M. Battery was used with good effect on several occasions, concentrated shoots in conjunction with Artillery Groups being very useful in clearing the enemy out of centres of resistance. The supply of ammunition still presents great difficulties if additional men are not attached.

   Full use was not made of the section L.T.M. Battery which was attached to each Battalion. Such are the weapons "par excellence" for dealing with hostile M.G. nests and local centres of resistance. The Stokes Mortar is pre-eminently suited to deal with hostile M.Gs. located in buildings.

   In this connection far more training is required in "spotting" these guns, as reports are constantly received to the effect that an advance has been hung up by M.G. fire, impossible to locate. This points to the necessity for highly trained observers with Company and Platoon Commanders, in addition to Battalion Scouts.

5. Liaison with flank Brigades by all possible means was most important and generally was carried out. Much value was derived from the attached Mounted Troops whose reports were generally accurate.

6. A far higher training in reading small scale maps by all Company and Platoon officers is necessary.

/7.

7. Where broad and deep canals have to be crossed some form of light boat is recommended, the collapsible Berthon boat (in 3 sections) being far too heavy for use by patrols.

8. Each man going into action should be given an extra pair of socks.

ARTILLERY.

9. The barrage put down on the 1st November was very intense. Thereafter, the enemy never waited for the full weight of our Artillery to come into action. The problem for the Artillery then became a matter of dealing with machine gun nests, isolated guns and small parties of the enemy who were delaying our advance and enabling the main body of the enemy to retire. The enemy blew up bridges and roads whenever possible to delay the advance of our guns. In these circumstances, the following points were emphasised :-

(a). The benefit of alloting artillery to each Battalion Commander in the front line. The Battery Commander by remaining with the Battalion Commander and keeping good communication with his Battery could bring fire to bear in a very short time on targets as they were encountered. In practice, it was generally found that a full Battery was too large a Unit and four guns or even a section was of more use.

(b). When more than one Artillery Brigade was available for an Infantry Brigade, the necessity of keeping them echeloned in depth, and maintaining all but one Brigade on wheels. If resistance was encountered the Brigade or Brigades remaining on wheels in rear could be moved up to reinforce the Artillery in the line to put down a Barrage for an attack, or, if no resistance was encountered, a Brigade in rear could advance through the Artillery in action, which in turn would get on wheels as the advancing Brigade came into action.

This procedure enabled Brigades to get occasional day's rests and obviated the danger of getting the roads choked with advancing Artillery.

10. COMMUNICATIONS.

For a time, communication by orderly between units became the only feasible plan. Owing to the rapid movement these orderlies had the utmost difficulty in locating units. In this Divisional Artillery, the system of using village churches as Report Centres was successfully tried, but owing to the cessation of hostilities the trial was not as exhaustive as could be wished. Notices shewing change of location were simply stuck on church doors or railings, and orderlies were instructed to at once proceed to the church for information on entering a village.

The necessity of using only picked men of the highest intelligence for orderly work was particularly emphasised.

11. OFFICERS PATROLS.

These were found to be of great value, and not only was accurate information sent back, but also a good deal of moral support given to the Infantry, the Artillery patrols often entering villages with the Infantry patrols.

C.Hull.
Major-General,
Commanding 56th Division.

26th Nov. 1918.

Copies to :- 167th Inf. Bde. (4).   C.R.E. (4).
168th Inf. Bde. (4).   D.A.G.C. (5).
169th Inf. Bde. (4).   A/Q.   (1).
C.R.A.   (4).

To List 'C'. *Order 224* 56th Division G.3/528.

Until further notice 56th Division Lists 'A', 'B' & 'C' will be composed as under :-

1. 167th Infantry Brigade.))
2. 168th Infantry Brigade.))
3. 169th Infantry Brigade.))
4. C.R.A.))
5. C.R.E.))
6. "Q".) List 'A'.)
7. 56th Bn. M.G.Corps.))
8. 56th Div. Signal Coy.)) List 'B'.)
9. XXII Corps.))
10. 11th Division.)
11. 63rd Division.) List 'C'
12. 56th Div. Train.)
13. Corps H.A.)
14. H.A.Group.)
15. 52nd Squadron R.A.F.)
16. Corps Cavalry.)
17. 1/5th Cheshire Regt.)
18. A.D.M.S.)
19. A.P.M.)
20. D.A.D.V.S.)
21. A.D.C.)
22. Camp Commandant.)
23. Div. Reception Camp.)

With Tracing.

H.Q. 56th Divn.
8th Nov. 1918.

E.

R.H.Franklin Lt
for Lieut-Colonel,
General Staff.

WAR DIARY

GENERAL STAFF

56th DIVISION.

DECEMBER 1918.

Army Form C. 2118.

WAR DIARY
56th DIVISION
INTELLIGENCE-SUMMARY.

DECEMBER, 1918.

(Erase heading not required.)

Instructions regarding War Diaries and Intelligence Summaries are contained in F.S. Regs., Part II and the Staff Manual respectively. Title pages will be prepared in manuscript.

Place	Date	Hour	Summary of Events and Information	Remarks and references to Appendices
HARVENGT.	Dec. 1st.		282nd A.F.A.Bde. joined the Division and were billeted at BOUGNIES. For locations see App. I.	APP. I.
	3rd.		The G.O.C. dined with His Majesty the King at SEBOURG.	
	5th.		His Majesty King George passed through the Divisional area.	
	28th.		In consequence of the limited accommodation in 167th Infantry Brigade area, that Brigade plus 416th Field Coy. R.E. and No. 2 Coy. Train A.S.C., were ordered to move to MONS. This Brigade Group accordingly marched to new area. For locations see App. II. The G.O.C. proceeded to England on short leave. Brigadier-General R.J.G. ELKINGTON, C.M.G., D.S.O. assumed command of the Division during his absence.	APP. II.
			During the month the troops have been engaged in Educational Training for the most part. A short period of Military Training has been carried out each day. Labour has been provided for keeping the roads in the area in repair and for clearing the obstructions caused by the enemy having blown up the railway bridges at NOUVELLES and SPIENNES in his retreat, which had caused certain areas to become flooded.	
	3.1.19.			

Bakenham Lieut Col
for Brigadier-General,
Commanding 56th Division.

SECRET   56th DIVISION.   LOCATION TABLE at 6 a.m.   DECEMBER. 1918.   APPENDIX I

	1	2	3	4	5	6	7	8	9	10	11	12	13	14	15	16
Div. H.Q.	Harveng															
167th Inf.Bde.H.Q.	Quevy-le-grand															
1st London Regt.	Goegnies-Chaussee.															
7th Middx. Rgt.	Quevy-le-grand															
8th Middx. Rgt.	Quevy-le-petit															
168th Inf.Bde.H.Q.	Givry															
4th London Regt.	Villers-Sire-Nicole															
13th " "	Villers-Sire-Nicole															
14th " "	Givry.															
169th Inf.Bde.H.Q.	Nouvelles															
2nd London Regt.	Harmignies															
5th " "	Harmignies															
16th " "	Genly.															
Div. Arty. H.Q.	Harveng.															
280th Bde.	Goegnies-Chaussee.															
281st "	Vieux-Reng.															
282nd A.F.A.Bde.	Bougnies															
Pioneers.	Spiennes.															
M.G. Battn. H.Q.	Villers St Ghislain.															

SECRET   56th DIVISION.   LOCATION TABLE at 6 a.m.   December 1918.   APPENDIX II

	17	18	19	20	21	22	23	24	25	26	27	28	29	30	31
Div. H.Q.	Harveng.											Harveng.			
167th Inf. Bde. H.Q.	Quevy-le-Grand											155 Boulevard Dolez, Mons.			
1st London Regt.	Goegnies Chaussee.											27 Rue de Gades, Mons.			
7th Middx. Regt.	Quevy-le-Grand.											42 Rue de Nimy, Mons.			
8th Middx. Regt.	Quevy-le-Petit.											96 Boulevard Dolez, Mons.			
168th Inf. Bde. H.Q.	Gury.											Gury.			
4th London Regt.	Villers-Sre-Nicole.											Villers-Sre-Nicole.			
13th " "	Villers-Sre-Nicole.											Quevy-le-Grand			
14th " "	Gury.											Gury.			
169th Inf. Bde. H.Q.	Nouvelles											Nouvelles.			
2nd London Regt.	Harmignies											Harmignies			
5th " "	Harmignies											Harmignies			
18th " "	Genly.											Genly.			
Div. Arty. H.Q.	Harveng.											Harveng.			
280th Bde.	Goegnies Chaussee.											Goegnies Chaussee.			
281st "	Vieux-Reng.											Rouveroy.			
282nd A.F.A. Bde.	Bougnies.														
Pioneers.	Spiennes											Spiennes			
M.G. Battn. H.Q.	Villers-St-Ghislain											Villers-St-Ghislain			

Original.

Headquarters, 56th Division.

General Staff

War Diary.

January 1919.

Army Form C. 2118.

WAR DIARY
or
INTELLIGENCE SUMMARY.
(Erase heading not required.)

Instructions regarding War Diaries and Intelligence Summaries are contained in F. S. Regs., Part II. and the Staff Manual respectively. Title pages will be prepared in manuscript.

Place	Date	Hour	Summary of Events and Information	Remarks and references to Appendices
HARVENGT	1919 Jan.		During the month the Division remained in the same area. (See Appendix 1.) The troops were engaged in Educational Training and Sports with a short period of military training each day. Owing to demobilisation the Division ceased to be effective as a fighting unit towards the end of the month.	
	Jan. 13th		Orders were received from XXII Corps for the transfer of the 1/14th London Regiment (London Scottish) from this Division to 9th Division in Germany, entraining 16th January.	
	Jan. 16th		The 1/14th London Regiment (London Scottish) entrained at Mons accordingly.	
	Jan. 25th		The G.O.C. Major General Sir. G. P. A. Hull, K.C.B., returned from England and reassumed command of the Division.	

Tom Bracker Tiny
General Staff.

Major-General.

Commanding 56th Division.

Appendix 1.

56th DIVISION
LOCATION TABLE, ~~1st January 1919.~~

Ref. sheet 45 & 51. 1/40,000.

UNIT.	HEADQUARTERS 1st January.	HEADQUARTERS 23rd January.
56th Divisional H.Q.	HARVENGT.	HARVENGT.
167th Inf. Bde. H.Q.	MONS.	MONS.
7th Middlesex Regt.	MONS.	MONS.
8th Middlesex Regt.	MONS.	MONS.
1st London Regt.	MONS.	JEMAPPES.
167th T.M. Battery.	MONS.	MONS.
168th Inf. Bde. H.Q.	GIVRY.	GIVRY.
4th London Regt.	VILLERS-SIRE-NICOLE.	VILLERS-SIRE-NICOLE.
13th London Regt.	QUEVY-LE-GRAND.	GIVRY.
14th London Regt.	GIVRY.	
168th T.M. Battery.	GIVRY.	GIVRY.
169th Inf. Bde. H.Q.	NOUVELLES.	NOUVELLES.
2nd London Regt.	HARMIGNIES.	HARMIGNIES.
5th London Regt.	HARMIGNIES.	HARMIGNIES.
16th London Regt.	GENLY.	GENLY.
169th T.M. Battery.	NOUVELLES.	NOUVELLES.
1/5th Cheshire Regt.	SPIENNES.	SPIENNES.
56th Divnl. Arty. H.Q.	HARVENGT.	HARVENGT.
280th Bde. R.F.A.	GOEGNIES-CHAUSSEE.	GOEGNIES-CHAUSSEE.
281st Bde. R.F.A.	ROUVEROY.	ROUVEROY.
282nd Bde. A.F.A., R.F.A.	NOIRCHAIN.	NOIRCHAIN.
56th D.A.C.	CIPLY.	CIPLY.
C.R.E. Headquarters.	HARVENGT.	HARVENGT.
416th Field Coy. R.E.	MONS.	MONS.
512th Field Coy. R.E.	VILLERS-SIRE-NICOLE.	VILLERS-SIRE-NICOLE.
513th Field Coy. R.E.	ASQUILLIES.	ASQUILLIES.
A.D.M.S.	HARVENGT.	HARVENGT.
2/1st London Fld. Ambce.	QUEVY-LE-PETIT.	QUEVY-LE-PETIT.
2/2nd London Fld. Ambce.	GIVRY.	GIVRY.
2/3rd London Fld. Ambce.	MONS.	MONS.
56th Battn. M.G.C.	VILLERS-ST-GHISLAIN.	VILLERS-ST-GHISLAIN.

ORIGINAL.

GENERAL STAFF,

56th DIVISION.

W A R   D I A R Y

FEBRUARY 1919.

Army Form C. 2118.

56TH DIVISION – GENERAL STAFF
WAR DIARY

INTELLIGENCE SUMMARY

(Erase heading not required.)

Instructions regarding War Diaries and Intelligence Summaries are contained in F.S. Regs., Part II. and the Staff Manual respectively. Title pages will be prepared in manuscript.

Place	Date	Hour	Summary of Events and Information	Remarks and references to Appendices
HARVENGT.	1919. February Feb. 25th		Nothing of importance occurred during the month. The 1/7th Bn. Middlesex Regt. (167th Infantry Brigade) was transferred to 41st Division, Second Army.	

T.S.M. Bresnay
Major-General,
Commanding 56th Division.

ORIGINAL

56th DIVISION.

GENERAL STAFF

WAR DIARY.

MARCH,

1919.

Army Form C. 2118.

WAR DIARY
INTELLIGENCE SUMMARY.

(Erase heading not required.)

Instructions regarding War Diaries and Intelligence Summaries are contained in F.S. Regs., Part II. and the Staff Manual respectively. Title pages will be prepared in manuscript.

Place	Date	Hour	Summary of Events and Information	Remarks and references to Appendices
HARVENGT.	1919. March 1 - 13.		Nothing of importance to record.	
	14		Nos. 2 and 3 Coys., 56th Divnl. Train moved to CIPLY.	
	14/15		281st Brigade, R.F.A., moved to MESVIN.	
	18		2/1st London Field Ambulance (Transport & Stores) moved from QUEVY-LE-PETIT to JEMAPPES.	
	18/19		168th Infantry Brigade moved to CUESMES.	
	19		513th Field Coy. R.E. moved from ASQUILLIES to JEMAPPES.	
	20th		1/5th Bn. Cheshire Regt. moved from SPIENNES to JEMAPPES. 280th Brigade R.F.A. moved to FLENU.	
	23		1/5th Bn. London Regt., 169th Inf. Bde., moved from HARMIGNIES to QUAREGNON. 1/16th " " " " " " " GENLY.	
	24		1/2nd Bn. London Regt., 169th Inf. Bde. moved from HARMIGNIES to QUAREGNON.	
	28th		H.Q., 56th Divnl. Engineers moved from HARVENGT to JEMAPPES.	
JEMAPPES	29		The following further moves to JEMAPPES took place :- 56th Divisional Headquarters. 169th Infantry Brigade H.Q. 247th (Divnl.) Employment Coy. 1/1st London Mobile Veterinary Section. 56th Divisional Train H.Q.	
	30		167th Infantry Brigade H.Q. moved to JEMAPPES	
	31st		Table showing location of units of the Division on this date is attached.	App. I

McCarthy Capt
for Brigadier-General,
Commanding 56th Division.

App. I

56 DIVISION
LOCATION TABLE.

Ref. Sheet .45.   1/40000.

UNIT.	HEADQUARTERS.
1. 56th. Divisional Headquarters.	JEMAPPES (815 Grand Route)
2. 167th. Infantry Bde. H.Q.	JEMAPPES (16 Rue de Representative)
3. 8th. Middlesex Regt.	JEMAPPES (The Convent)
4. 1st. London Regt.	JEMAPPES (The Convent)
5. 168th. Infantry Bde. H.Q.	CUESMES (261 Rue Chaussee)
6. 4th. London Regt.	CUESMES.
7. 13th. London Regt.	CUESMES.
8. 169th. Infantry Bde. H.Q.	JEMAPPES (815, Grand Route)
9. 2nd. London Regt.	QUAREGNON.
10. 5th. London Regt.	QUAREGNON.
11. 16th. London Regt.	QUAREGNON.
12. 1/5th. Cheshire Regt.	JEMAPPES (The Convent)
13. 56th. Divl. Artillery H.Q.	HARVENGT.
14. 280th. Brigade R.F.A.	FLENU.
15. 281st. Brigade R.F.A.	MESVIN.
16. 282nd. A.F.A.Brigade R.F.A.	NOIRCHAIN.
17. 56th. Divl. Ammunition Column.	CIPLY.
18. C.R.E. H.Q.	QUAREGNON (23 Route de Mons)
19. 416th. Field Coy. R.E.	JEMAPPES (78, Rue de la Station)
20. 512th. Field Coy. R.E.	CUESMES.
21. 513th. Field Coy. R.E.	JEMAPPES (36, Rue de Lloyd George)
22. A.D.M.S.	JEMAPPES (857, Grand Route)
23. 2/1st. London Field Ambulance. (Stores JEMAPPES)	MONS (Halte Repas)
24. 2/2nd. London Field Ambulance.	CUESMES.
25. 2/3rd. London Field Ambulance.	MONS (Orphanage, Rue Lainir)
26. 56th. Battn. M.G.Corps.	JEMAPPES (831, Grand Route)
27. 56th. Divisional Train H.Q.	JEMAPPES (56, Grand Rue)
28. 56th.Div.Train Nos.1,2,3&4 Coys.	JEMAPPES (58, Grand Rue)
29. Divl. Baths and Claims Officer.	JEMAPPES (789, Grand Route)
30. Divisional Canteen.	JEMAPPES (68, Grand Rue)
31. Divisional Linen Store.	JEMAPPES (15, Rue de Jericho)
32. D.A.D.O.S.	JEMAPPES (569, Grand Route)
33. D.A.D.V.S.	JEMAPPES (928, Grand Route)
34. Mobile Veterinary Section.	JEMAPPES (928, Grand Route)
35. D.A.P.M.	JEMAPPES (797, Grand Route)
36. 247th. (Div) Employment Coy.	JEMAPPES (789, Grand Route)
37. 56th. M.T. Coy.	MONS (12, Rue de la Prison)
38. Cadre Town Major (Lt. COUCKE)	JEMAPPES (2, Grand Rue)

Army Form C. 2118.

HQ 25 56 VO 39

WAR DIARY
or
INTELLIGENCE SUMMARY.
(Erase heading not required.)

Instructions regarding War Diaries and Intelligence Summaries are contained in F.S. Regs., Part II. and the Staff Manual respectively. Title pages will be prepared in manuscript.

Place	Date	Hour	Summary of Events and Information	Remarks and references to Appendices
JEMAPPES, BELGIUM.	1919. APRIL.			
	Apl. 1st - 30th		Divl. H.Q. still in JEMAPPES.	
	Apl. 1st - 19th		Nothing to report.	
	20th		Brig.-General E.S. D'E. COKE, C.M.G., D.S.O. relinquished Command of Division and proceeded to U.K. on short leave prior to taking up duties with the Lowland Division (Army of Rhine). Lt.-Col. A.F. PRECHTEL, D.S.O., T.D. 282nd Army Bde. R.F.A. assumed Command of Division.	
	Apl. 21st - 30th		Nothing to report.	

[signature]
Lieut.-Colonel,
Commanding 56th Division.

CONFIDENTIAL.

G.O.C.
British Troops in France & Flanders.
(Records Section)

A.A. & Q.M.G.
56th DIVISION.
AQA 541.
Date..........

Herewith War Diaries for the month of May 1919 for the undermentioned :-

   General Staff, 56th. Divsn.

   A.A. & Q.M.G. 56th. Divsn.

The War Diaries for the remainder of Units of this Division will be forwarded to you direct by the Units concerned.

17/5/1919.

        Lieut-Colonel.
       Commanding 56th. Division.

WAR DIARY
or
INTELLIGENCE SUMMARY.

Army Form C. 2118.

HQ G E 6
MAY 1917

56 Division. "G" (Erase heading not required.)

Place	Date	Hour	Summary of Events and Information	Remarks and references to Appendices
			Nothing to fair. Dull 1st, Snow intension 18th	Censor

Wynne Capt
for General S(O)/1 56° Division

www.ingramcontent.com/pod-product-compliance
Lightning Source LLC
Chambersburg PA
CBHW080820010526
44111CB00015B/2584